BUILDINGS OF NEVADA

Buildings of
NEVADA

JULIE NICOLETTA

with Photographs by

BRET MORGAN

OXFORD

UNIVERSITY PRESS

2000

OXFORD
UNIVERSITY PRESS

Oxford   New York
Athens   Auckland   Bangkok   Bogotá   Buenos Aires   Calcutta
Cape Town   Chennai   Dar es Salaam   Delhi   Florence   Hong Kong   Istanbul
Karachi   Kuala Lumpur   Madrid   Melbourne   Mexico City   Mumbai
Nairobi   Paris   São Paulo   Shanghai   Singapore   Taipei   Tokyo   Toronto   Warsaw

and associated companies in

Berlin   Ibadan

Copyright © 2000 by the Society of Architectural Historians
1365 North Astor Street, Chicago, Illinois, 60610-2144

Published by Oxford University Press, Inc.
198 Madison Avenue, New York, New York 10016
www.oup.com

Oxford is a registered trademark of Oxford University Press

LIBRARY OF CONGRESS CATALOGING-IN-PUBLICATION DATA
Nicoletta, Julie
Buildings of Nevada / Julie Nicoletta ; with photographs by Bret Morgan.
p.   cm. — (Buildings of the United States)
Includes bibliographical references and index
ISBN 0-19-514139-3
1. Architecture—Nevada—Guidebooks. 2. Nevada—Guidebooks.
I. Morgan, Bret. II. Title. III. Series.
NA730.N3 N53   2000
720'.9793—dc21   00-044609

1   3   5   7   9   8   6   4   2

Printed in the United States of America
on acid-free paper

To the memory of

Adolf K. Placzek

Founding Editor in Chief of
Buildings of the United States
1913–2000

Buildings of the United States is a series of books on American architecture compiled and written on a state-by-state basis. The primary objective of the series is to identify and celebrate the rich cultural, economic, and geographical diversity of the United States as it is reflected in the architecture of each state. The series has been commissioned by the Society of Architectural Historians, an organization dedicated to the study, interpretation, and preservation of the built environment throughout the world.

Initial and ongoing major support for Buildings of the United States comes from the National Endowment for the Humanities, an independent federal agency; the Graham Foundation for Advanced Studies in the Fine Arts; the Pew Charitable Trusts; the University of Delaware; and the College of Fellows of the American Institute of Architects.

Buildings of Nevada has been supported in part by the National Endowment for the Humanities, the Nevada Humanities Committee, an anonymous foundation, the Las Vegas Chapter of the American Institute of Architects, and individual members of the Society of Architectural Historians.

Foreword

Buildings of Nevada is the sixth of a projected fifty-eight volumes in the series Buildings of the United States, which is sponsored by the Society of Architectural Historians (SAH). This volume is dedicated to the Founding Editor in Chief, Adolf K. Placzek, who served in that capacity from the early 1980s to 1989 and who died during the spring of 2000.

The idea for such a series was in the minds of the founders of the SAH in the early 1940s, but it was not brought to fruition until Nikolaus Pevsner, the eminent British architectural historian who had conceived and carried out Buildings of England, originally published between 1951 and 1974, challenged SAH to do for this country what he had done for his. That was in 1976, and it was another ten years before we were able to organize the effort, commission authors for the initial group of volumes, and secure the first funding, a grant from the National Endowment for the Humanities. Matched by grants from the Pew Charitable Trusts, the Graham Foundation, and the Michigan Bicentennial Commission, this enabled us to produce the first four volumes, *Buildings of Michigan, Buildings of Iowa, Buildings of Alaska,* and *Buildings of the District of Columbia,* all of which were published in 1993. *Buildings of Colorado* followed in 1997. Another fourteen volumes are expected in the next five years, with the others to follow.

Although Buildings of England provided the model, in both method and approach Buildings of the United States was to be as different as American architecture is from English. Pevsner was confronted by a coherent culture on a relatively small island, with an architectural history that spans more than two thousand years. Here we are dealing with a vast land of immense regional, geographic, climatic, and ethnic diversity, with most of its buildings—wide-ranging, exciting, and sometimes dramatic—essentially concentrated into the last four hundred years, although with significant Native American remains stretching back well beyond that. In contrast to the national integrity of English architecture, therefore, American architecture is marked by a dynamic heterogeneity, a heterogeneity woven of a thousand strands of originality, or, actually, a unity woven of a thousand strands of heterogeneity. It is this quality that Buildings of the United States reflects and records.

Unity born of heterogeneity was a condition of American architecture from the first European settlements of the sixteenth and seventeenth centuries. Not only did the buildings of the Russian, Spanish, French, Dutch, Swedish, and English colonies differ according to national origin (to say nothing of their differences from Native American structures); but in the translation to North America they also assumed a special scale and character, qualities that were largely determined by the aspirations and traditions of a people struggling to fashion a new world in an abundant but demanding land. Diversity marked even the English colonies of the Eastern Seaboard, though they shared a common architectural heritage. The brick mutations of English prototypes in the Virginia Colony were very different, for example, from the wooden architecture of the Massachusetts Bay Colony. They were different because Virginia was a farm and plantation society dominated by the Anglican church, whereas Massachusetts was a communal society nurtured entirely by Puritanism. But they were different also because of natural resources and the traditions of the parts of England from which the settlers had come. As the colonies became a nation and developed westward, similar radical contrasts became the way of America's growth. The infinite variety of physical environments, together with the complex origins and motivations of the settlers, made it inevitable that each new state would have a character uniquely its own.

The primary objective of each volume, therefore, is to record, analyze, and evaluate the architecture of the state. The authors are trained architectural historians who are thoroughly informed in the local aspects of their subjects. In each volume, special conditions that shaped the state, together with the building types necessary to meet those conditions, are identified and discussed: barns, silos, mining buildings, factories, warehouses, bridges, and transportation buildings take their places alongside the familiar building types conventional to the nation as a whole—churches, courthouses, city halls, commercial structures, and the infinite variety of domestic architecture. Although the great national and international masters of American architecture receive proper attention, especially in the volumes for the states in which they did their greatest work, outstanding local architects, as well as the buildings of skilled but often anonymous carpenter-builders, are also brought prominently into the picture. Each volume is thus a detailed and precise portrait of the architecture of the state that it represents. At the same time, however, all of these local issues are examined as they relate to architectural developments in the country at large. Volumes will continue to appear state by state until every state is represented. When the overview and inventory are completed, the series will form a comprehensive history of the architecture of the United States.

These volumes deal with more than the highlights and the high points of architecture in this country. They deal with the very fabric of American architecture, with the context in time and in place of each specific building, with the entirety of urban and rural America, with the whole architectural patrimony. This fabric includes modern architecture, as, on the other end of the scale, it includes pre-Columbian and Native American remains. But it must be said, regretfully, that the series cannot cover every building of merit; practical considerations have dictated some difficult choices in the buildings that are represented in this as in other volumes. There are, unavoidably, omissions from the abundance of structures built across the land, the thousands of modest but lovely edifices and the vernacular attempts that merit a second look but which by their very multitude cannot be included in even the thickest volume.

Thus it must be stated in the strongest possible terms that omission of a building from this or any volume of the series does not constitute an invitation to the bulldozers and the wrecking ball. In every community there will be structures not included in Buildings of the United States that are clearly deserving of being preserved. Indeed, it is hoped that the publication of this series will help to stop at least the worst destruction of architecture across the land by fostering a deeper appreciation of its beauty and richness and of its historic and associative importance.

The volumes of Buildings of the United States are meant to be tools of serious research in the study of American architecture. But, they are also intended as guidebooks for everyone interested in the buildings of this country and are designed to facilitate such use; they can and should be used on the spot, indeed, should lead the user to the spot. It is our earnest hope that they will be not only on the shelves of every library from major research centers to neighborhood public libraries but that they will also be in a great many raincoat pockets, glove compartments, and backpacks.

During the long gestation process of the series, we have incurred many debts. We are especially grateful, both for financial support and for confidence in our efforts, to the National Endowment for the Humanities, the Pew Charitable Trusts, the Graham Foundation for Advanced Studies in the Fine Arts, the College of Fellows of the American Institute of Architects, and, for this volume, the Nevada Humanities Commission, an anonymous foundation, the Las Vegas Chapter of the American Institute of Architects, and the University of Delaware, and many individual members of the SAH. We are thankful, too, to the members of our Leadership Development Committee: J. Carter Brown, Madelyn Bell Ewing, Elizabeth Harris, Ada Louise Huxtable, Philip Johnson, Keith Morgan, Victoria Newhouse, and Robert Venturi.

We are very grateful to Dean Larry Clark of the University of Missouri and to Provost Mel Schiavelli and Deans Mary Richards, Margaret Andersen, and Thomas DiLorenzo of the College of Arts and Science at the University of Delaware for providing institutional support for two successive editors in chief of the series.

Our gratitude extends to many other individuals. These include a large number of presidents, executive committees, and boards of directors of the SAH, going back at least to the adoption of the project by the Society in 1979, and a series of executive directors covering that same span. All of these individuals have supported the series in words and deeds, and without them it would not have seen the light of day.

We would also like to express our appreciation to the current members of our editorial board, listed earlier in this volume, and the following former members: Adolf K. Placzek, Richard Betts, Catherine Bishir, J. A. Chewning, S. Allen Chambers, Jr., Alex Cochran, John Freeman, David Gebhard, Alan Gowans, Alison K. Hoagland, William H. Jordy, Robert Kapsch, Henry Magaziner, Tom Martinson, Sally Kress Tompkins, and Robert J. Winter.

We have tried to establish as far as possible a consistent terminology of architectural history, and we are especially appreciative of the efforts of J. A. Chewning in the creation of the series glossary included in every volume. The *Art and Architecture Thesaurus,* a comprehensive publication and database compiled by The Getty Art History Information Program and published by Oxford University Press, has also become an invaluable resource.

In our fund-raising efforts we have benefited enormously from the services of our wonderful directors of development, first Anita Nowery Durel and then Barbara Reed, as well as assistant director of development William Cosper, and of our administrative staff: fiscal coordinator Hillary Stone and then fiscal manager William Tyre.

Editorial work for this volume was overseen by our excellent managing editor for the series, Cynthia Ware. Janet Wilson was the copy editor and proofreader, and the index was compiled by AEIOU. Maps were prepared by Kelley Graphics of Kensington, Maryland. Research assistants at the University of Delaware were Jhennifer Amundson, Anna Andrzewjewski, Heather Campbell, Martha Hagood, Nancy Holst, Amy Johnson, Sarah Killinger, and Louis Nelson.

Finally, there are our loyal colleagues in this enterprise at Oxford University Press in New York and Cary, North Carolina, especially Ed Barry, Claude Conyers, Karen Casey, Stephen Chasteen, Matt Giarratano, Nancy Hoagland, Robert Oppedisano, and Leslie Phillips.

To all of these we are enormously grateful.

Osmund Overby
Damie Stillman
William H. Pierson, Jr.

Acknowledgments

In researching and writing a book of this scope, one incurs a number of debts. This project began when I moved to Nevada to become the architectural historian in the State Historic Preservation Office in Carson City. In my travels around the state I quickly became intrigued by its architecture and the rapidity with which much of the state was changing. My colleagues provided my introduction to Nevada's architecture. Ron James, state historic preservation officer, encouraged me to take on the project of writing the first historic guide to Nevada architecture. Ron provided invaluable information and advice and wrote initial drafts for the sections on the Comstock Lode; county courthouses; the University of Nevada, Reno (UNR), and a number of buildings in the Capitol Complex in Carson City. Alice Baldrica, Gene Hattori, Rebecca Palmer, Susie Kastens, and Barb Prudic all engaged in long conversations about Nevada's history and buildings.

In Reno, Mella Harmon served as a dedicated and thorough researcher and fact checker; without her diligent work, this book would not have been completed. Don Fowler, director of the Historic Preservation Program at UNR, provided student assistance and tips for contacts in other parts of the state. Amy Chatowsky took research photographs. Maurice Nespor discussed the rise of the architectural profession in the state.

Staff at tribal, federal, state, and local agencies and organizations assisted in providing access to sites and in obtaining information and photographs, most notably Earl Briggs, Nevada Department of Public Works; Linda Eissmann, Nevada State Parks; Dennis Freitas, Nevada Department of Transportation; Bob Furlow, Department of Energy, Las Vegas; Ted Howard, Shoshone-Paiute Tribes of Duck Valley; Pansilee Larson, North Central Nevada Historical Society; Keith Myhrer, Nellis Air Force Base; and the staff of the Bureau of Reclamation, Lower Colorado Region.

Libraries and archives provided critical information on Nevada's buildings and builders. In particular, Kathryn Totton and the staff of Special Collections, UNR; Kathy War and the staff of Special Collections, University of Nevada, Las Vegas (UNLV); Jeanne Brown and the staff of the Architecture Studies Library, UNLV; Lee Brumbaugh and the staff of the Nevada Historical Society in Reno; Christopher Driggs of the Nevada State Library and Archives; and the staffs of the Nevada State Museum; the Nevada Northern Railway Museum; the Northern Nevada and Las Vegas chapters of the American Institute of Architects; and the Las Vegas News Bureau provided expert assistance in finding historic photographs, architects' papers and plans, and information on contemporary architects.

Bret Morgan traveled throughout Nevada to take most of the photographs that illustrate this book. His images reflect a keen eye and immense skill in capturing structures in the context of their environments. Others who provided advice and insights into Nevada architecture are Eric Anderson, Tim Bentler-Jungr, Phil Caterino, Tim Davis, Keith Eggener, Pat Hicks, Kim Hoagland, Carolyn Jungr, Jessica Langsam, Ethan Nelson, Elizabeth White, and colleagues at the University of Washington, Tacoma, especially Mike Allen, Linda Desmarteau, and John Peterson.

For financial support, many thanks go to the organizations whose contributions are acknowledged in the front of this volume. I also thank the University of Washington, Tacoma, for granting me a leave of absence for one quarter to complete the first draft.

Many people read drafts of all or parts of the manuscript, greatly improving it in the process. In particular, I appreciate the careful readings by Kathleen Curran, Mella Harmon, Ron James, Carol Herselle Krinsky, Michelle McFadden, Damie Stillman, and Janet Wilson.

For his constant encouragement during this project, I owe my greatest debt to my husband, Michael Kucher.

Julie Nicoletta

Photographing the buildings of Nevada took me to many remote, lonely, and improbable places. Julie Nicoletta's unique knowledge of Nevada and her thorough advance work made my photography of this far-flung project manageable and enjoyable. The owners and stewards of many properties made their sites available for study and photography, including Ryan Crockett, Walter Cuchine, Marshall Hanson, Turkey Stremmel, and the staff of the Clark County Heritage Museum. Gregory Cook of Bechtel was very helpful in arranging access and providing insight at the Nevada Test Site. Marilyn Berry was an enthusiastic tour guide at the Hawthorne Army Ammunition Depot. Film was developed at Hi-Fi Photo Lab in San Francisco, and prints were made at San Francisco's superb Rayko Darkroom Center.

Throughout this project, Roseann Dal Bello provided critical insight and encouragement.

Bret Morgan

Contents

List of Maps

Guide for Users of This Volume

Buildings of Nevada begins with an introduction that provides a historical and environmental context for understanding the state's buildings and landscape. The introduction is followed by five regional sections. Within each of these, cities, towns, and rural vicinities are arranged in one of several sequences: for the northwestern and southern regions, a spiral path beginning with the region's largest city and working outward; for the northern and central regions, a linear arrangement following trails, railroads, and highways; for the south-central region, a large loop through the middle of the state passing through a number of remote mining towns, some of which have become ghost towns.

For each place, numbered guidebook entries for buildings and sites follow walking or driving tour order. Heading information includes the current name (sometimes followed in parentheses by an earlier name) of the building or site; the date of construction; the architect, if known; and the dates of major additions or alterations and their architects, if known.

Entries are keyed by site number to maps of the five regions and of selected cities and towns. Useful complements to this volume are guidebooks containing information on accommodations and hours of operation for museums and historic sites and the highway map produced annually by the Nevada Department of Transportation. Many local historical societies and visitor information centers throughout the state offer additional information on historic buildings and sites in their towns.

Almost all the sites discussed in this book are visible from public roads or public property. Some properties that are not accessible to the public are included, however, because of their importance in understanding Nevada's architectural history. We know that readers will respect the property rights and privacy of others as they view the buildings.

Buildings of Nevada is intended to present an overview of the state's architecture. Buildings and sites included here were chosen as representative of the varieties of architectural styles, building types, and physical settings and their geographic distribution. Although the guidebook entries are intended to include only extant buildings, given the rapid pace of development in Nevada, a number of the structures described here will have been demolished or substantially altered by the time this book is available to readers.

Deciding what to include in a book such as this requires making tough choices. *Buildings of Nevada* is meant to serve as an introduction and as a springboard for further exploration of the state's diverse built environment.

BUILDINGS OF NEVADA

Introduction

Geography

To understand Nevada's architecture one must know its natural environment. Although indigenous peoples learned to survive in the harsh landscape, since Euro-Americans settled there in the mid-nineteenth century, Nevada has been regarded as a desert wasteland, rich in natural resources but inhospitable to humans. This view has permitted nineteenth- and twentieth-century inhabitants to extract what they could from the land with little concern for the long-term consequences. Much of Nevada's architecture, built for temporary uses, reflects this attitude toward the environment.

Jagged mountain ranges divide much of the state into narrow basins running north-south at an average elevation of 5,000 feet. This region of high-desert basins and ranges, known collectively as the Great Basin, covers most of Nevada. Most of the six to eight inches of annual rainfall evaporates immediately or drains into sinks—dry lake beds—where it eventually dries up, so there is no external drainage. The Sierra Nevada, along the western edge of the state, traps water from the Pacific storms heading eastward; most rain and snow fall on the Sierras rather than reaching the high desert beyond.

Vegetation in the state's mountain ranges is diverse, consisting of bristlecone pines in the highest elevations and ponderosa, sugar, and white pines; firs; and blue spruce at lower elevations. Along most of the ranges, piñon pine and juniper grow between 6,000 and 8,000 feet. Below 6,000 feet, sagebrush mixed with various native grasses blankets the desert floor.

Only the edges of Nevada fall outside the Great Basin. A strip along the northeastern border is part of the Columbia Plateau, where water from the Owyhee, Bruneau, and Salmon rivers reaches the Pacific Ocean via the Snake and Columbia rivers. In southern Nevada, the Mojave Desert—even drier than the Great Basin—is nevertheless home to myriad plants, including Joshua trees and creosote bushes. The region's Muddy and Virgin rivers both flow into the Colorado River and eventually to the Gulf of California.

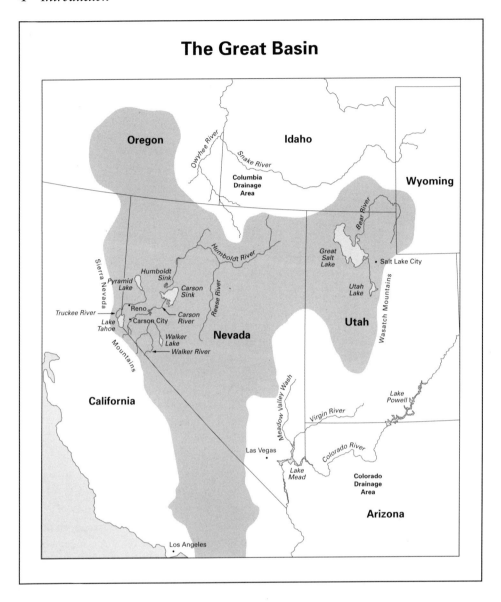

The Great Basin

Oregon

Idaho

Owyhee River

Snake River

Columbia
Drainage
Area

Wyoming

Bear River

Humboldt River

Great
Salt
Lake

Salt Lake City

Sierra Nevada

Humboldt
Sink

Pyramid
Lake

Carson
Sink

Reese River

Utah
Lake

Utah

Wasatch Mountains

Truckee River

Reno

Lake
Tahoe

Carson City

Carson
River

Walker
Lake

Nevada

Walker River

Mountains

California

Meadow Valley Wash

Lake
Powell

Las Vegas

Virgin River

Colorado River

Lake
Mead

Colorado
Drainage
Area

Arizona

Los Angeles

Though Nevada has several rivers, only the Colorado, located along the southeastern corner of the state, is navigable. The lack of major rivers has required other transportation systems across the state, such as trails, railroads, and highways. Minor rivers such as the Humboldt served first as paths for Native Americans and later for nineteenth-century emigrant trails because they were among the scarce sources of water for humans and animals. These trails in turn were the basis for nineteenth-century railroad routes and for twentieth-century highways because the rivers supplied water for railroad engines and for towns that were stopping points for motorists.

Trails and Railroads through Nevada

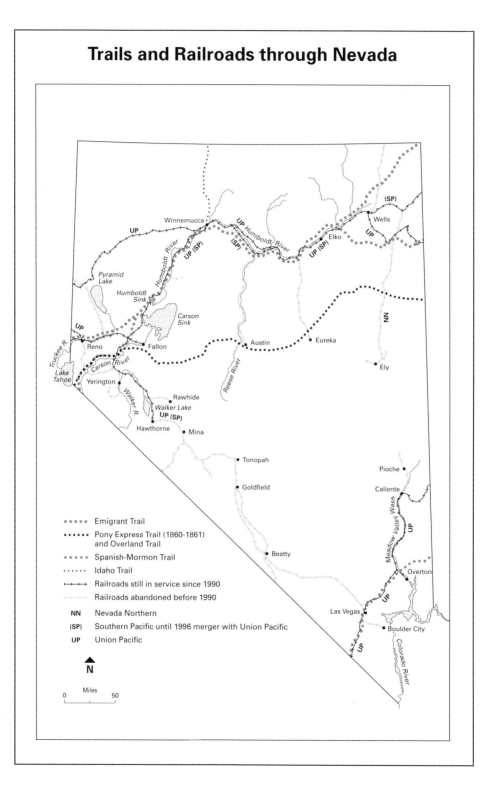

Emigrant Trail

Pony Express Trail (1860-1861) and Overland Trail

Spanish-Mormon Trail

Idaho Trail

Railroads still in service since 1990

Railroads abandoned before 1990

NN Nevada Northern

(SP) Southern Pacific until 1996 merger with Union Pacific

UP Union Pacific

N

Miles
0   50

Nevada Regions, Counties, and Major Highways

Nevada Regions, Counties, and Major Highways

NORTHERN

Humboldt

Elko

Washoe

Pershing

Lander | Eureka

White Pine

Churchill

Stoney

Carson City

CENTRAL

Douglas

Lyon

SOUTH-CENTRAL

NORTH-WESTERN

Mineral

Esmeralda

Nye

Lincoln

SOUTHERN

Clark

- - - - Counties
——— Regions

N

Miles
0   50

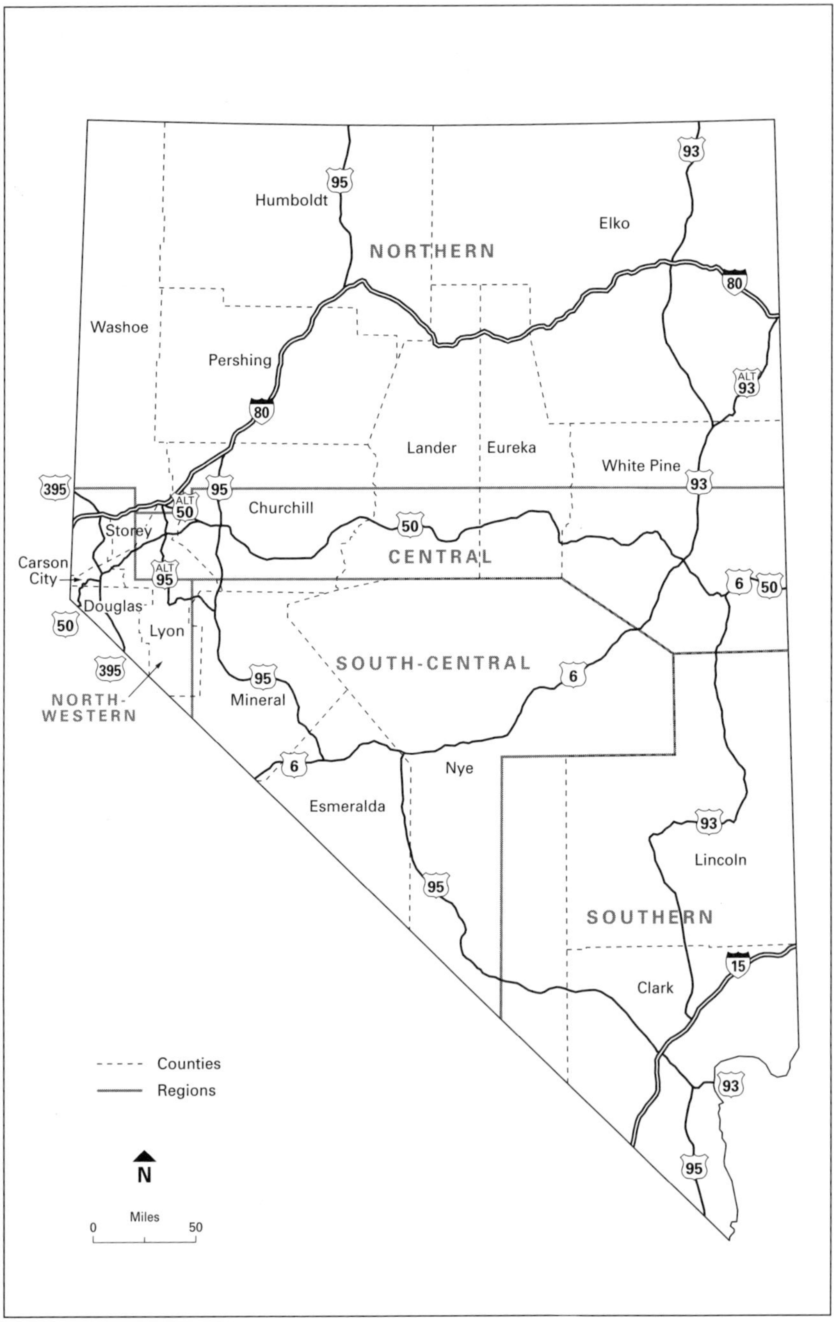

Since the beginning of human habitation in the region, much architecture has been created and used for temporary purposes. The prehistoric peoples who lived there found shelter in caves or among rocks. Their other structures—none of which have survived—were impermanent, usually made of wood and woven reed mats. The habitations of Nevada's later Native Americans, members of seminomadic groups, were made of ephemeral materials such as willow branches, erected and taken down each season.

During much of the nineteenth century, most Euro-Americans traveling through Nevada had no plans to settle there. Their aspirations lay in the states beyond—California and Oregon. Those who did stay to search for gold or silver hoped to return home with newfound wealth rather than remain in Nevada. Hundreds of nineteenth- and early twentieth-century mining towns, long abandoned, are scattered across the state; in some cases, no buildings remain where once hundreds or even thousands of people lived. Walking through these towns today gives the visitor a sense of the openness of the land and the isolation of these old settlements. The smell of sagebrush and creosote fills one's nostrils as the wind blows through empty buildings and over ruins. Sometimes the possessions and debris left by inhabitants remain, preserved in the desert sun, and the visitor can see old furniture, rusted carcasses of cars, and tin cans left behind when the mining boom failed and the residents moved on to what they hoped would be a more prosperous place.

Even in the twentieth century, this emphasis on the temporary persists. Modern gold and silver mines tend to have life spans averaging ten to fifteen years. While a mine is in operation, an entire town can develop around it, but once it has closed, the mine's employees move on to the next site. The same is true of the state's casino industry, which extracts money from gamblers in much the same way that mining companies extract natural resources. Few casinos are more than twenty years old, and many are altered or destroyed in fewer years than that. Despite a population numbering about 2 million, Nevada has not shed its reputation as a place of quick opportunity where life is always changing and the past can be reinvented. The general attitude toward habitation is still one that considers natural resources—water, clean air, and land—as expendable. This is perhaps best seen today in the endless rows of tract houses surrounded by lush lawns spreading across the Truckee Meadows around Reno or in the Las Vegas Valley. Developers build houses as quickly as they can, following the mid-twentieth-century model of laying out subdivisions, with little thought to the specific environment of the Great Basin.

Prehistoric and Later Native Americans

The prehistoric peoples who lived in the Great Basin depended on Lake Lahontan, which covered most of northwestern Nevada from 50,000 to 4,000 years ago. Since then, the enormous lake has gradually evaporated, although its legacy can still be seen in the alluvial fans along its edge. Pyramid Lake north of Reno, and Walker Lake near Hawthorne, are all that remain of this vast body of water.

Human habitation in Nevada began approximately 11,000 to 12,000 years ago—a time period established by findings at a number of sites throughout the state, including Tule Springs outside Las Vegas and Leonard Rockshelter in the Humboldt Basin. Another group of pre-historic peoples inhabited Lovelock Cave on the shore of Lake Lahontan from about 2,000 B.C. to about A.D. 1400.[1] The Lovelock peoples had a complex culture supported by the abundance of fish and waterfowl in the lake and surrounding wetlands. They created bas-kets, fishing nets, and duck decoys woven from willow and tule reeds. Their reasons for aban-doning the area are unknown.

About 4,500 years ago, prehistoric peoples from the Southwest settled in the southern part of the state, much of which is now covered by Lake Mead. The earliest groups lived in rock shelters and caves, giving way to the Basketmaker culture around 300 B.C. This group con-structed pit houses—circular, subterranean structures roofed with wood poles and mud. About 2,000 years ago the Anasazi moved into extreme southern Nevada, perhaps as part of an expanding trading network in the Southwest. By A.D. 500–700 they had created commu-nities with irrigated fields and adobe dwellings; however, these structures were much simpler than the pueblos typically found in the Southwest. The most famous of these communities was Pueblo Grande de Nevada (also known as the Lost City), named by the archaeologist M. R. Harrington. Harrington excavated the site before it was flooded by Lake Mead, which was created by Hoover Dam. The city, which included pit houses, pueblos, rock shelters, caves, and salt mines, covered both banks of the lower Muddy River.[2] Archaeological evi-dence shows that the Lost City was inhabited continuously from about 500 B.C. to A.D. 1150, when the Anasazi abandoned the area. The cause remains unclear but may have been over-population, conquest, or drought. Around this time the Southern Paiute moved into the area, becoming the dominant culture before the arrival of Euro-Americans.

The Native Americans succeeding these prehistoric groups encompass the Washoe, the Northern Paiute, the Southern Paiute, and the Shoshone. The Washoe, the smallest of these groups, historically inhabited valleys around Carson City in the winter and moved to the shores of Lake Tahoe in the summer to fish and harvest medicinal herbs. The Northern Paiute lived in the northwestern regions, centering on Pyramid Lake, nourished by Lahon-tan cutthroat trout, now extinct, and a once-abundant native fish, the cui-ui. The Southern Paiute continue to claim a relationship with Pueblo culture. They were the only Nevada tribe to practice agriculture, perhaps influenced by their Anasazi predecessors, though hunting and gathering dominated their daily life. The Shoshone lived in the eastern part of the state. All of these groups were nomadic hunter-gatherers. Their traditional lands covered thou-sands of square miles in which they moved in groups to take advantage of seasonal changes and animal migrations. The smallest economic unit, the nuclear family, consisted on average of six individuals.[3] Because of the harsh environment, these people formed bands ranging from one to twenty families during the winter; in the other months they would break off into single families or small groups of families to search for food.[4] In the fall they reunited for communal activities such as semiannual pine nut harvests or rabbit and deer hunts. Their numbers never grew large because of the sporadic quantities of food. Their nomadic lives motivated them to specialize in certain crafts, primarily basketmaking. Unlike pottery, bas-kets were lightweight and easy to move. Native Americans used baskets of various sizes, shapes, and weaves for water storage and catching fish. Washoe baskets are now highly prized by collectors and museums.

Native Americans of the Great Basin constructed temporary shelters that suited their lives as hunter-gatherers. Margaret M. Wheat photographed this grass house made by Mabel Wright, a Paiute, near Pyramid Lake in the 1950s. Grass woven into mats is tied to a willow frame to form the shelter; the sunshade is made of willow boughs.

Though these groups followed cyclical life patterns in the Great Basin, their nomadic existence prevented them from leaving permanent architectural forms. Winter dwellings were conical structures made of juniper or pine logs set directly on the ground or on a circular foundation of stones, with an opening at ground level. When shade was needed during the hot, dry summer months, local people made dwellings using a framework of narrow, bowed branches covered with brush to form a curved roof. Historians sometimes call them by the Apache term *wickiup*, referring to a circular structure of arched poles covered with brush.

These Native Americans managed to survive in an extremely unforgiving environment, but the first white men they encountered in the early nineteenth century considered them hardly better than animals because of their lack of permanent communities, buildings, and agricultural fields. The white settlers' attitude toward the Native Americans, whom they called Digger Indians, provided the ideology for justifying their mistreatment and even extermination. By the mid- to late nineteenth century the federal government had forced Nevada's indigenous people onto reservations consisting of the most uninhabitable land.

Euro-American Exploration and Settlement

With the arrival of European and American explorers and trappers, who in the last decades of the eighteenth century and the first decades of the nineteenth century began traversing what became Nevada, the region was opened to settlement, cultivation, and industrialization. In the late eighteenth century Spanish explorers and friars established the eastern and western approaches to a trail, defined by other Euro-American explorers in 1830–1831 as the Old Spanish Trail. It passed through today's Bunkerville, Moapa, and Las Vegas, connecting Santa Fe, New Mexico, and Los Angeles. In the early nineteenth century fur trappers searching for beaver followed rivers in the hope that they would lead to the Pacific. To their disappointment, they found that the Humboldt, which flows from eastern Nevada westward, eventually drained into the Humboldt Sink. Nevertheless, such ventures helped pave the way for emigrants moving west. The first group, the Bidwell-Bartleson Party, crossed Nevada in 1841 by following the Humboldt to its sink and then following the Carson and Walker rivers to the Sierra. The route along the Humboldt, with variations along either the Truckee River through present-day Reno or the Carson River through present-day Carson City, became the most popular because pioneers could find water and wild grasses to feed their livestock as they journeyed westward.

Two events in 1848 spurred westward migration. First, the discovery of gold in California in January 1848 brought prospectors through Nevada. Second, the signing of the Treaty of Guadalupe Hidalgo in February 1848 granted the United States all of Mexico's territory north of the Gila River, opening California, Arizona, New Mexico, Utah, and Nevada to settlement. The Mormons, who had migrated west to the Great Salt Lake in 1847, took control of the Utah Territory, which encompassed what later became the states of Utah and Nevada.

Only a few years after they settled in Utah, parties of Mormons began colonizing Nevada to establish trading posts. In 1851 they founded the first town in Nevada, Genoa, at the eastern base of the Sierra in Carson Valley, south of Carson City. By this time the discovery of gold in California had attracted westbound prospectors and pioneers, who stopped in Genoa to buy supplies before crossing over the mountains. The first Mormon structure, a log stockade and cabin, was soon followed by houses and farm buildings.

Mormons also began to settle the southern part of Nevada, following the Old Spanish Trail to send colonies as far west as San Bernardino, California. This trail became known as the Mormon Trail or the Spanish-Mormon Trail because of the Mormons' heavy use of it. In 1855 a small party established a fort near what is now downtown Las Vegas. Natural springs at the site provided water, but lack of wood forced the settlers to favor adobe for buildings. The settlement did not last long; in 1857 Brigham Young called all Mormons back to Salt Lake City in preparation for what he thought would be a war against federal troops. The Mormons left their homes and property to non-Mormon settlers, whom they called Gentiles. Though no war occurred, Mormons did not return to Nevada in large numbers until the late nineteenth century.

By the late 1850s a steady stream of emigrants passed through Nevada each year. The trade they provided, as well as the new logging operations in the mountains around Lake Tahoe, created a robust economy. Rather than continuing on to California, some prospectors searched for gold in the rivers and creeks of northwestern Nevada. Towns near Genoa, such as Carson City, were often settled with lofty aspirations. Abraham Curry, one of Carson City's founders, laid out the town's grid, including a plaza for the capitol. His forethought proved to be fortunate when Carson City became Nevada's capital in 1864.

Mining

One of the most famous mining rushes in the American West brought thousands to the Comstock, a mining district named after the Comstock Lode, a massive ledge of silver and gold ore that ran through what is now known as the Virginia Range, approximately fifteen miles northeast of Carson City. Throughout the 1850s placer miners in the canyons of the eastern Sierra hoped to replicate the success of their counterparts in the western Sierra Nevada gold country. Placer mining is used when gold is found in unconsolidated deposits of sand and gravel from which the metal, because of its high density, can easily be separated. The sand and gravel are suspended in moving water, and the much heavier metal sinks to the bottom. In the ravines of the Virginia Range, particularly in Gold Canyon and Six Mile Canyon, miners found enough gold flakes and nuggets to eke out a modest living as they searched for still richer claims.

A major discovery occurred in January 1859, when miners struck gold at the upper end of Gold Canyon, leading to the founding of the town of Gold Hill. Five months later other miners made a similar strike at the head of Six Mile Canyon, eventually giving rise to Virginia City. When an assay of the ore came back from California indicating that it would yield $876 in gold and $3,000 in silver, or nearly $4,000 a ton—the equivalent of nearly $85,000 a ton today—the district changed forever.[5] Because these metals were found in veins, or lodes, much of Virginia City's mining after these discoveries consisted of hard-rock mining, requiring the extraction and refining of gold and silver from ore.

News of the strikes inspired hundreds to swarm over the Sierra Nevada from California. By spring immigrants from throughout the continent, and indeed the world, had come to try their luck at getting rich. Like mining districts throughout the West, the Comstock had a high percentage of foreign-born residents; by 1870 over 44 percent of Nevada's population was foreign-born.[6] The largest ethnic groups were the thousands of Irish, Chinese, and Cornish immigrants, hundreds of German settlers, and numerous other new arrivals, including Canadians, Italians, and French. The towns that sprang up around this excitement and newfound prosperity became cosmopolitan cities, forming one of the largest urban chains west of the Mississippi. At its peak in the mid-1870s, the Gold Hill–Virginia City metropolis, sprawling across the slopes of Mt. Davidson, had a population of about 25,000 people. Discovery of the Comstock Lode lowered the price of American silver, making the United States the leading manufacturer of silver goods in the late nineteenth century. After 1860 or so, the abundance of this metal from mines in Nevada and California helped popularize the domestic use of silverware, making the late nineteenth century the "era of the sumptuous table."[7] However, the boom would not last forever.

Depletion of ores led to a local depression in the industry beginning in the late 1870s. A few limited strikes kept the mines open into the twentieth century, but the population and the economy of the Comstock fell into a downward spiral that left the area with fewer than a thousand people by the 1940s. Although mining has continued along the Comstock, tourism has taken its place as the principal industry. Today the Virginia City Landmark District is one of the nation's largest.

Most Comstock buildings are vernacular expressions of Italianate architecture, sometimes employing Greek Revival, Queen Anne, or Second Empire details and often made from mass-produced building components. Occasionally professional architects, some of regional importance, worked on the Comstock. A few structures, notably the Storey County Courthouse, the Fourth Ward School, and St. Mary in the Mountains Catholic Church, all in Virginia City, are distinguished examples of design of the period.

In his 1975 study of Colorado mining towns, Eric Stoehr identified three stages of town planning: (1) the settlement phase, characterized by small populations, log cabins and tents, and haphazard street layout; (2) the camp phase, characterized by larger populations, wood-frame buildings, town grids, and the establishment of local governments, utilities, and other amenities; and (3) the town phase, characterized by continued mining productivity, more elaborate architecture of brick and stone (including substantial public buildings), and the latest urban services.[8] These stages can be applied to most of Nevada's mining towns, along with a fourth phase, abandonment, which occurred when the mines were played out and most, if not all, of the population left for more prosperous places.

Like the habitations of other western boom towns, the Comstock's first buildings consisted of canvas tents with wood frames and foundations and canvas roofs and walls. More substantial structures—wood-frame houses and commercial buildings—were soon built. False-fronted buildings became characteristic of the nineteenth- and early-twentieth-century mining camp. These flat, rectangular facades provided ample space for signs and, more important, represented the promise that the camp would become an urban center.[9] The rapid, unplanned construction led to a town full of buildings of various styles and types. J. Ross Browne, a visitor to the Comstock in 1863, noted: "The oddity of the plan, and variety of its architecture—combining most of the styles known to the ancients, and some but little known to the moderns—give this famous city a grotesque, if not picturesque, appearance, which is rather increased upon a close inspection."[10] Virginia City's main streets were cut into the side of Mt. Davidson, creating steeply graded cross streets and building lots that backed right into the mountain. By the late 1860s buildings crowded the city, interspersed with mines and mills that continued to bring gold and silver ore from deep below the surface.

The Comstock region also featured industrial structures, including mine and mill buildings, scattered throughout the area as opportunity dictated. Along with having to build and maintain a large industrial complex to extract and process ore, the Comstock faced a number of logistical problems, which resulted in some technological achievements that became internationally famous. The Marlette Lake Water System brought water thirty miles from the Sierra Nevada mountain range, but its fame was due to the fact that it piped water 1,200 feet through an inverted siphon, down into the valley to the east and then back up the Virginia Range, 900 feet, to Virginia City. The construction of piping that could withstand the pressure of over 1,000 column feet of water was a remarkable engineering feat.

In addition to being responsible for transporting some of the richest gold and silver ore ever discovered, the Virginia and Truckee (V&T) Railroad became famous for the engineering of its right-of-way. Because it had to ascend over 2,000 feet in just over eleven miles, the railroad made the equivalent of thirty-seven complete turns. The Crown Point Trestle, bridging the depths of the Crown Point Ravine, was a tall wood structure that inspired awe among most of those who crossed it and demonstrated the accomplishments of the Comstock's businessmen, who built an infrastructure to facilitate the development of an industrial mining giant. Like most of the railroad line, the trestle is no longer extant.

Most of Nevada's mining towns of the nineteenth and early twentieth centuries follow the general plan of development in Virginia City. Ledges of ore were usually discovered and mined along mountainsides in Nevada, so towns grew up nearby along steep inclines or narrow valleys. Urban grids were dropped on top of the existing landscape with little regard for topography, resulting in steeply graded roads and awkward building lots. If the town survived to become a city, the main streets were lined with buildings displaying identifiable architectural styles with local or regional variations, crowding out earlier structures.

As many of the mining towns became prosperous, their architecture reflected local investment of this wealth. More of it, however, left the state, primarily for California, where large and powerful mining companies controlled most of Nevada's mines.[11] The uncertainties of the mining industry and the knowledge that the *borrasca*, or bust, would inevitably follow the bonanza prevented most prudent residents from pouring all their wealth into Nevada's mining communities. Other residents, particularly those who had profited from mining and real estate speculation, sometimes erected elaborate buildings despite rumors of an impending bust in order to maintain faith in the local mines.

The millions of dollars' worth of gold and silver pouring out of the Comstock swiftly brought statehood to Nevada. In 1860 Nevada broke off from Utah Territory to form a separate territory. By 1864 it had become a state. President Abraham Lincoln needed Nevada's electoral votes to ensure his re-election, and he needed the support of Nevada's congressional delegation for his Reconstruction program. Nevada telegraphed the text of its entire constitution to Washington, D.C., to expedite the process of entering the Union only days before the 1864 presidential election.

Although the Comstock played a pivotal role in Nevada's early history, other mining towns continued the process of settlement and exploitation of the state's natural resources. During the 1860s, for example, the towns of Austin and Aurora were established, and roads connecting them to agricultural areas were vital in ensuring the success of the mining operations there. Austin, which served as the seat of Lander County from 1862 to 1979, has lost most of its population over the years, but adobe, wood, brick, and stone buildings still line its streets. Aurora, on the other hand, peaked in the mid-1860s, thereafter struggling until the 1930s. At that time Aurora still had many historic buildings, but all of these were wiped out by the scavenging of materials after World War II. Today Aurora is a rich site for historical archaeology, but not a single building stands.

The Comstock boom continues to affect the environment and people living in the area today. First, the underground mines carved out of the earth beneath Virginia City are still there, creating a honeycomb whose parts occasionally collapse, creating dangerous sinkholes in town. Second, trains carried much of the ore from these mines to stamp mills along the Carson River east of Carson City, where it was processed. Though the mills disappeared long ago, their legacy remains in the form of mercury contamination along the Carson River. In the nineteenth century mercury was used to remove silver and gold from ore. Because the amalgam of gold, silver, and mercury required heating for separation, much of the mercury

Carleton Watkins, one of the West's most famous nineteenth-century photographers, took this view of Virginia City from the side of Mt. Davidson, looking east, in the late 1870s. The image shows the density of the prosperous mining town and the proximity of dwellings to milling and mining operations.

Opposite page. This 1876 engraving by T. L. Dawes delineates the system of square-set timbering used on the Comstock to shore up mines. The lumber came from the forests of the Lake Tahoe Basin, which was denuded by the turn of the century. Pictures of the Comstock's largest mills surround the diagram.

was lost into the drainage system. Consequently the Carson River's bed remains contaminated for a fifty-mile stretch between Carson City and Fallon.

The mining of the Comstock Lode transformed the Tahoe Basin. In the nineteenth century the mountains surrounding Lake Tahoe were covered with virgin forests of diverse species. Mark Twain, who camped on the shores of the lake in the early 1860s, commented on the striking clarity of the water in *Roughing It* (1872). However, by the turn of the century loggers had deforested the mountains, using the trees to satisfy the demands of the mining region to the east. Since the basin offered the nearest source of large trees, this area was logged first. Though some of the lumber was used for constructing buildings, most of it went underground to create a system of square-set timbering to support the mines as they went deeper into the earth to follow the veins of ore. To this day, much of Tahoe's old-growth timber remains underneath Virginia City.

Rather than replacing the original forest, which included sugar and Jeffrey pines, cedars, and some firs, lumbermen planted fast-growing varieties, mostly firs. The second-growth forest that stands today lacks diversity and is particularly susceptible to drought and fir beetles. Approximately one-third of the forest died as a consequence of a drought in the 1980s, leaving a dangerous threat of fire. The death of many trees and the process of removing them through controlled burns and bulldozing have also affected the lake's clarity. In addition, the lack of living trees has contributed to the runoff of soil and debris into the lake.

By the late 1870s Nevada's first big cycle of mining booms and busts had ended. Not only had the Comstock's lode played out, but mining towns across the state were abandoned. The extent of these busts is apparent in more than four hundred ghost towns throughout Nevada. Mining towns rose near the ore deposits, usually resulting in towns nestled in narrow mountain canyons, reachable only by rough roads or mule trails. When the inevitable bust came, miners and others who depended on the industry generally had to abandon their buildings, taking only what they could afford to move.

From 1880 to 1900, Nevada fell into a severe depression. During this period no new mineral strikes occurred. A series of severe winters hurt the ranching industry as well. Those who could leave the state did, and Nevada's population plummeted from 62,266 in 1880 to 42,335 in 1900. Many mining towns became ghost towns, and others, like Virginia City and Austin, limped along despite a drastic loss in population.

In 1900 the slump turned into another boom when Jim Butler discovered silver in Tonopah. Like the Comstock, Tonopah drew prospectors in huge numbers. By 1910 the state's population had nearly doubled to 81,875. The subsequent economic surge created new cities in the center of the state, led by Tonopah and Goldfield, located twenty-five miles to the south. For a short time Goldfield became Nevada's largest city, with a population of well over 15,000 in 1907–1908.[12] Other towns, such as Rhyolite, went through the boom-and-bust cycle in less than a decade.

Like earlier mining communities, these towns started out as tent camps, growing as more and more men arrived to strike it rich. Simultaneously, other men and women arrived to make their living by supplying the miners with goods and services such as housing, food, and mining equipment, as well as through prostitution. Within a few years, Tonopah and Goldfield had a number of solidly built hotels, banks, and public buildings. Both towns quickly be-

A panoramic view taken on 18 October 1907 by Welch and Tune captures Goldfield when it was briefly Nevada's largest city, with a population of over 15,000. In contrast to the gridded center of town, dwellings and mining structures on the edges sprawl at random across the valley floor.

"Moving day," Main Street, Manhattan, Nevada, c. 1906. All Nevada mining towns began as settlements filled with canvas tents and other rough forms of shelter. Many residents favored them for their portability.

In 1908 Rhyolite was home to 6,000 to 8,000 residents and a thriving mining town with many structures, including a few large concrete buildings on Golden Street, the main thoroughfare.

A photograph of Rhyolite in 1950 shows how a once thriving mining town could almost disappear in a little over four decades. The one-story building at the lower right appears in the same position in the preceding illustration. The Cook Bank Building (1908, George E. Holesworth) is at right center; the jail is in the center of the image.

came county seats, drawing away the population and economies of their predecessors. Such shifts were typical in Nevada, where county seats followed the boom-and-bust cycle of the mining industry.

Silver and gold were not the only metals that drove Nevada's economy in the early twentieth century. Discovery of copper in the vicinity of the small town of Ely in 1900 made the Robinson Mining District the richest such district in Nevada's history. The strike led to a strong and steady industry that lasted into the 1970s. Unlike relatively small veins of silver and gold, which can sustain a mining operation for ten to fifteen years on average, porphyry copper deposits can keep a mine going for decades. Because the copper is scattered relatively evenly throughout the rock, the resulting large deposits can be mined in great quantities over a long period of time. The Ruth Pit, near Ruth, seven miles west of Ely, became one of the largest open-pit mines in the world. Because of its excellent conductivity, copper is the material most widely used for electrical wire. The copper industry transformed Ely into a county seat and established the mining communities of Ruth, East Ely, and McGill. McGill, in particular, became the quintessential company town. The Nevada Consolidated Copper Company carefully planned industrial areas and residential neighborhoods to separate management from labor and to segregate other ethnic groups from Euro-Americans.[13] In the early 1990s Magma Copper Company began reworking the enormous piles of tailings sur-

The Ruth (Liberty-Eureka) Pit, located seven miles west of Ely, is one of the world's largest open-pit mines. Railroad cars, following tracks along the terraces inside the pit, hauled copper ore from the mine. In the 1950s huge ore trucks replaced the railroad.

rounding the pit to recover the precious and semiprecious metals left there by earlier, less efficient techniques. In addition, BHP Copper North America has been mining new sources of
copper ore. As a result of these recent initiatives, Ely and the surrounding area are experiencing a revival.

Though eclipsed by gambling and tourism since 1950, mining still contributes to the
state's economy and continues to shape land-use planning and architecture. Advances in
hard-rock mining in the mid-twentieth century have allowed mining companies to run gold-
mining operations that produce as little as .02 ounces of gold per ton. Instead of following
veins of ore underground, as was done in the nineteenth century, today's miners can exploit
entire mountains, blasting, sorting, and milling the ore into smaller pieces that are placed in
leaching pads. A cyanide solution circulates over the crushed rock, leaching out the gold and
silver. The Smoky Valley Common Operation in Nye County is gradually transforming Round
Mountain into a huge open pit as it extracts precious metals from the earth.[14]

In the second half of the twentieth century, mining continued to undergo boom-and-bust
cycles, though the industry was strong during the 1990s. Nevada's relatively few restrictions
and long-standing support of the industry have kept mining costs much lower than those in
many other parts of the world. Nevada is the nation's leading producer of gold, silver, and
barite and the only producer of mined magnesite.[15] It also produces other minerals, including copper, gypsum, and lithium. Gold production in particular has been a major part of the
state's mining industry. The country's first open-pit gold mine was opened near Carlin in

The McGill Smelter (1907–1908) processed copper ore from the Ruth Pit. To the right stands the trestle on
which cars carried ore to the top of the complex to begin the reduction process. The smelter closed in 1983,
and the last surviving smokestack was demolished in the early 1990s.

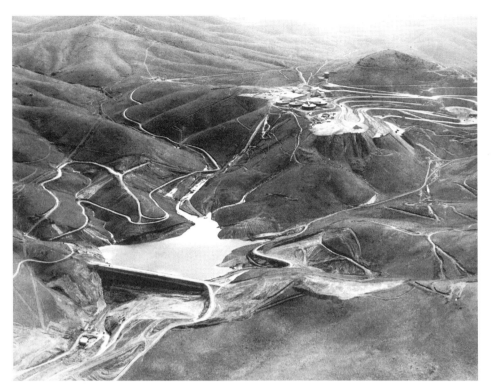

This 1960s aerial view shows the extent of Newmont Gold Company's open-pit gold mine near Carlin. The region has continued to be the richest gold-producing area in the United States.

1965. The Carlin Trend, the largest gold strike in North America in the twentieth century, has made the area around Carlin a major gold-producing region.

As in the past, mining has had both positive and negative effects on the state and local communities. Most operations are located largely on federal land and are highly regulated. Communities closest to the mines see the greatest economic effects, as highly paid workers move into the area. Rapid population growth, however, heavily burdens the infrastructure of small communities, whose populations may double or triple during the life of the mine. Many mining companies help relieve the burden by donating money to build additional roads, sewers, schools, and housing. Once the mine has played out, usually after ten to fifteen years, the mining company moves on, taking most of its employees with it. The once-bustling town falls into another economic slump, waiting for the next boom.

Because of the transitory nature of mining, as well as state and federal regulations, mining companies build structures based on the short term. Nevada and federal laws require that companies reclaim disturbed land once mining is ended. Though the open pit remains, tailing piles and other disturbances must be contoured and planted with native vegetation in order to support wildlife and new agricultural and industrial uses. All buildings erected for the mining operation must be removed as well. Mining companies and their employees therefore prefer prefabricated buildings, mobile homes, or trailers. When the mine closes, these buildings can be easily moved to another location, leaving behind only the open pits and waste piles.

Railroads

Since the 1860s, railroads have shaped the face of Nevada, creating opportunities for settlement and development. Their predecessors throughout the 1850s and early 1860s were road builders and telegraph companies. A route crossing the central part of the state, roughly followed today by U.S. 50, provided the path for the Pony Express, which carried express mail between St. Joseph, Missouri, and Sacramento, California. At regular intervals the Pony Express constructed stations for resting and changing horses, using local stone and sometimes wood if it was available. The express ended in 1861, after eighteen months, put out of business by the transcontinental telegraph. A telegraph line along the route kept many former Pony Express stations going, but the opening of a new telegraph line in 1869 along the recently completed Central Pacific Railroad to the north doomed the remaining stations. Crumbling piles of stones can still be seen today along U.S. 50. Nevada's only extant station still in its original location, a log cabin and wood-frame inn, stands in Stateline, near Lake Tahoe.

Fast on the heels of the mid-nineteenth-century mining boom came the construction of the transcontinental railroad across the state. After the arduous task of building the tracks over the Sierra Nevada, the pace of laying rails across Nevada accelerated. The tracks roughly followed the Humboldt River and the old Humboldt Emigrant Trail, as steam engines required frequent water stops to keep running. Although the Central Pacific was constructed to cross rather than specifically to serve Nevada, it proved to be an economic boon to the state. The towns established by the Central Pacific and later railroad companies have been among the most stable and prosperous in Nevada—Reno, Sparks, Winnemucca, Elko, and Las Vegas.[16] From 1868 to early 1869, the Central Pacific marched across the state, bringing a new industry and improved transportation for agricultural and mining products. In 1899 the Southern Pacific absorbed the Central Pacific, taking over its lines and building new tracks and towns in the early twentieth century.[17]

Railroad towns throughout Nevada and the West had similar physical characteristics.[18] The tracks ran through one end of town, with a grid of streets and lots stretching from them. In some instances a secondary grid would develop on the other side of the tracks, populated by shacks, bars, and brothels. The streets facing the tracks were lined with railroad structures, such as depots, warehouses, and water tanks, and commercial buildings largely catering to railroad passengers, including bars, stores, and hotels. Some towns, like Lovelock and Las Vegas (in its early days), had a main street running perpendicular to the tracks and terminating at the depot. Nearby the railroad built modest dwellings for its workers, which could range from wood-frame shacks to brick bungalows. In many former railroad towns the more substantial examples of these buildings still stand and are easily identifiable as identical structures set in an orderly row.

As in small towns across the country, the depot was an important fixture in small-town

Virginia and Truckee Railroad Engine House, Carson City, 1877. Built in 1872, the large stone engine house, which stood on Stewart Street near U.S. 50, served its purpose until 1950, when the V&T shut down. It stood vacant until its demolition in 1991.

Nevada, serving as the center of activity. It was the place where residents could get news beyond their town's borders and experience some of the hustle and bustle of metropolitan life when a train arrived or departed.[19] In Nevada most depots are side-loading, that is, oriented parallel to the tracks. Depending on the size of the town, a station might serve as both passenger and freight depot under one roof, as exemplified by the Gold Hill Depot. The combination station usually had space for passengers and freight depot located at opposite ends of the structure and separated by the agent's office, marked by a bay window that provided a clear view of the tracks. The freight end can often be identified by its greater size, large doors, loading platform, and a pattern of exterior sheathing that differentiates it from the passenger end.[20] Sometimes the depot included housing for the station agent. In larger towns, such as Reno, Lovelock, and Ely, separate stations were built to accommodate heavy passenger and freight traffic.

In addition to the transcontinental railroad, numerous short lines helped connect the state's major mining areas to supply centers that were linked with the main railroad. The V&T Railroad ran from Virginia City south to the Carson River, where it carried ore to a series of mills on its route to Carson City. A huge stone engine house dominated the railroad's center in Carson City. Constructed in 1872, it functioned until the demise of the V&T in 1950. The building stood vacant until 1991, when a developer demolished it. Other short lines connected mining towns to main lines, supply and population centers, and lumber sources. Examples include the Nevada Central Railroad, which connected Austin to Battle Mountain and the Central Pacific, and the Eureka and Palisade Railroad, which connected Eureka's smelters to the Central Pacific main line at Palisade south of Carlin. Both lines fell into disuse in the 1930s and were abandoned.[21]

Short lines also linked ranches and farms to major towns located on the railroad. The V&T Railroad, which initially served the Comstock mines and the ore smelters along the Carson River, built a connection from Carson City to Reno in 1872, connecting the line to the Central Pacific. The Truckee Meadows, the valley along the Truckee River and a longtime staging place for emigrant parties preparing to cross the Sierra, became an important trade and agricultural region in the later nineteenth century. Along the banks of the river, Reno served as the center for ranches in the meadows and to the north. In the early twentieth century the V&T's line to the fertile Carson Valley, running south from Carson City, created a link to agricultural communities there.

Railroad structures in Nevada included depots, engine houses, warehouses, workers' houses, and a variety of other structures such as water towers and bridges. The depots—the most visible railroad buildings—received the most attention from architects. The extant buildings constitute some of the best architecture in Nevada towns, usually displaying such popular styles of the period as the Stick Style in the late nineteenth century and the Mission Revival in the early twentieth.

Despite the significance of railroads in Nevada's history, relatively few structures from the nineteenth century survive today, particularly where cities favor growth over historic preservation. The car has long been the favored mode of transportation, connecting Nevada's far-flung towns and cities. By 1950 most railroads serving passengers had shut down. Today only Amtrak provides passenger service, with one line running through northern Nevada, stopping at Reno, Winnemucca, and Elko, the other line passing through southern Nevada, stopping at Las Vegas and Caliente. The historic depots continue to function as passenger stations only in Reno and Caliente.

Farming and Ranching

In the 1860s mining ventures and the railroad attracted more newcomers and increased the demand for food, thereby stimulating other enterprises such as farming and ranching. Although mining boosted these two industries, farming and ranching had their roots in the first phase of Euro-American settlement. Agricultural development played a vital role in the growth of Nevada in the late nineteenth century, not only providing food to sustain the state's growing population but also contributing to the characterization of Nevada as a place inhabited by self-sufficient, rugged, and rustic individuals.

Mormon farmers hoped to build stable communities in northwestern and southern Nevada as early as the 1850s. Each migrating family brought a few head of cattle.[22] Upon arriving in Nevada, the Mormons immediately built canals and ditches to irrigate their fields. Genoa, in particular, was on its way to becoming a prosperous agricultural community when Brigham Young called the Mormons back to Salt Lake City in 1857. In any event, the Mormons' efforts laid the groundwork for future farming and ranching. Agriculture continued and expanded on a small scale in valleys located near rivers.

Raising crops was often difficult in the desert, but cattle and sheep ranching throve because the Great Basin provided excellent forage in white sage, Great Basin wild rye, and wild

Ranchers and farmers constructed willow corrals throughout northern Nevada, and, though prefabricated wood and chain-link fences are more common today, many are still in use. This photograph, taken c. 1970, shows a corral on the Fort McDermitt Paiute-Shoshone Indian Reservation. Pairs of willow boughs hold narrower boughs in place. Euro-American ranchers also used the material for corrals.

grasses. Large, profitable sheep drives from New Mexico to the California gold country introduced sheepherding to Nevada in the 1850s. As California gold fields declined in the late 1850s, ranchers from California moved their cattle to the unexploited ranges of Nevada, Oregon, and Idaho.[23] The Comstock and other mining booms provided Nevada farmers and ranchers with a growing market for their stock and crops. The railroad helped expand these markets, primarily to California, where San Francisco and Sacramento became the primary destinations for Nevada products; in the 1870s, for example, half of San Francisco's beef supply came from Nevada.[24] The early presence of large cattle-ranching interests from other states quickly shaped this industry in Nevada. Since early Euro-American settlement, ranching in the state has been controlled almost entirely by a few large corporations, several dozen families, and the federal government.[25]

The open ranges of the intermountain West were considered well suited for raising sheep. In the late nineteenth and early twentieth centuries sheepherding became the province of Basque immigrants. Initially, most of them were young, single men from rural areas.[26] Often unable to acquire their own farms or ranches immediately, they turned to herding sheep, a common occupation in the Basque country of Spain and France. Many Basque farmers raised sheep in the western foothills of the Pyrenees Mountains. In the United States sheep-

herding was considered an undesirable career because of the low pay and long periods of isolation on the range, but it was one for which many Basque immigrants were well qualified.
They roamed the range, summering their small herds in the mountains and wintering them
in the low deserts. Over time, many sheepherders were able to add their own sheep to the
flocks, eventually going into the sheep-raising business for themselves. Though the range was
supposedly open, conflicts arose among Basque sheepherders and more established American ranchers, which helped to prompt the passage of federal laws creating a national forest
service and grazing districts with controlled access.[27] The loneliness of sheepherding and the
need for mobility led to an unusual type of dwelling known as the sheep camp. Compactly fitted out with built-in storage cabinets, these small trailers can be towed to sheep-grazing areas.
Shepherds now use modern prefabricated versions.[28] Some Basques continue in the occupation today, but most sheepherding is done by contract workers from Peru.

Ranching continues to contribute to Nevada's economy, but it has changed extensively
during the past sixty years. The Great Depression ravaged many independent ranchers,
opening the door for large corporations to take hold. In an attempt to conserve resources,
the Taylor Grazing Act of 1934 instituted the policy of restricting and controlling grazing on
public lands through leases.[29] Many large cattle operations are still run by ranching corporations that own thousands of acres of land and lease several thousand more from the federal

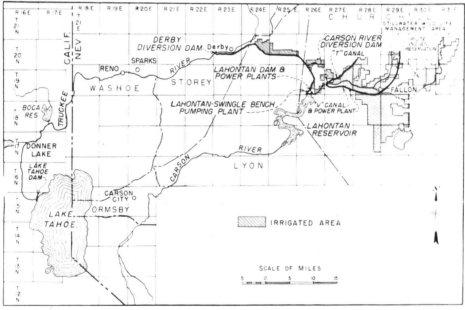

Diagram of the Truckee-Carson Irrigation District, Fallon. Created by the National Reclamation Act of 1902 and
one of the West's first major irrigation projects, this district promised to put 300,000 acres of desert into cultivation. The 60,000 acres actually irrigated fell far short of projections. In addition, the diversion of water from
the Truckee River led to the desiccation of Winnemucca Lake and the extinction of Pyramid Lake's Lahontan
cutthroat trout. In much of the West, water is used in the same way as mineral resources: used until it is exhausted.

government for grazing. Sheep ranching, once widespread in the state, has largely given way to cattle ranching; the decline in stock was so severe during the Great Depression that the sheep-ranching industry has never recovered. In urban areas developers have bought ranch land and subdivided it for tract housing.

Given the vast amounts of land required for grazing, ranches are often remote, relatively self-sufficient compounds. Large family-run ranches are centered around a home ranch, the base of operations where the family and hired hands live, livestock is kept over the winter, and new stock is branded. Home ranches consist of numerous buildings, including the main house, bunkhouses for cowboys—or buckaroos, as they are known in Nevada—storehouses, and corrals. During the summer months, when the herd is moved to higher elevations, smaller camps consisting of small corrals and perhaps a bunkhouse serve the buckaroos who watch the cattle. In the past, ranches have included such varied building forms and types as log cabins, adobe and mud structures, stone houses, and prefabricated buildings.

As in other western states, Nevada's ranching industry maintains a mythical status in its history. The decor of early casinos in Las Vegas—the El Rancho Vegas (c. 1943) and the Last Frontier (1942)—took ranching as its theme, with rustic furniture, lighting fixtures made of wagon wheels, and hunting trophies on the walls. Both complexes are gone, but their legacy remains in giant neon cowboy signs ornamenting casinos, such as Vegas Vic in downtown Las Vegas and Wendover Will in West Wendover. Even though few cowboys work in the state today, great interest in the culture of the buckaroo has persisted. The annual Cowboy Poetry Festival in Elko, established in 1985, has become a popular event, attracting thousands of people each January.

Nevada's lack of water remained a problem until the twentieth century, when the National Reclamation Act of 1902 provided for irrigation projects designed to put thousands of acres of desert into cultivation. Even with these federally subsidized programs, agriculture has never become a major industry in the state, and it probably never will because most available water is being diverted to urban areas to meet the demands of a rapidly growing population. The primary crops today are hay and alfalfa, grown to feed livestock.

Government

With mining the dominant factor in Nevada's economy and the driving force behind much of its architecture in the early years of statehood, federal, state, and local government had relatively little impact on the built environment in the late nineteenth century. Nevertheless, the most important building constructed during the last three decades of that century was the capitol. County courthouses erected throughout the state and two federal buildings of the era—the U.S. Mint and the federal courthouse and post office, both in Carson City— were the other most visible public edifices in Nevada. In general, the significance of these structures was expressed through solid materials such as stone and brick and the use of styles—particularly Beaux-Arts classical and Italianate—associated with public buildings. Architects or builders sometimes combined styles, selecting elements that they believed would suit a particular structure. When compared with similar structures in other states, Nevada's government buildings reveal a relative simplicity and small scale. As originally built, the capitol resembled county courthouses in larger, more populous states; likewise, Nevada's county courthouses tend to be modest compared with those in other states. Nonetheless, Nevadans have always considered these buildings important, and their recognizable styles and high-quality materials reinforce that perception. When a courthouse was erected in a mining town, however, it was never clear how long the town would survive, no matter how strong the initial boom. Though Nevada now has seventeen counties, thirty-four county courthouses have been erected since 1863, reflecting the frequent relocation of county seats to the town of the moment.30

Nevada's citizens also regarded school buildings as significant public structures. Schools often received large public expenditures to ensure that they would be well built and up-to-date. They range in form, materials, and style from one-room, wood-frame buildings to large brick edifices with classical elements. The school is often one of the few surviving structures in an abandoned town. Even in inhabited towns, the old school stands as a prominent symbol of residents' belief in the importance of public education.

Although the federal government would later play a major role in the state, its presence was minimal in the nineteenth century. Unlike the state and county governments, the federal government erected few buildings, except for such structures as military forts to protect settlers and mining operations from Native American uprisings. The first, Fort Churchill, was built along the Carson River near Silver Springs in 1860 in response to the Pyramid Lake War—two battles fought after settlers kidnapped two Native American women. As the only nearby wood came from cottonwood trees, the soldiers erected buildings of adobe and used wood for window and door lintels and roofs. The largest of the forts, it guarded the Comstock as well. Fort Churchill was abandoned only nine years later when the transcontinental railroad superseded mail routes through central Nevada that had also required protection. Several other forts stood at strategic locations across the northern part of the state, such as Fort McDermitt, Fort Schellbourne, and Fort Halleck. Fort McDermitt, established near the Nevada-Idaho border in Humboldt County in 1865, survived the longest, until 1888. Like Fort Churchill, it was established to protect settlers as well as stage routes and the main wagon road from Idaho to Winnemucca. Temporary forts dealt with local emergencies; Fort Ruby, for example, was built in 1862 to protect the overland mail route. These forts contained log cabins, adobe buildings, and stone houses, depending on the availability of materials. The military erected a total of twelve forts in northern Nevada to guard against Native American uprisings; portions of some of these buildings survive.

In addition to the forts, the federal government erected two buildings in Carson City in the latter half of the nineteenth century. The old U.S. Mint (1866–1869), now the Nevada State Museum, blends in with the early state government buildings in the capital, having been constructed of the same sandstone used for the capitol, the state prison, and the state printing office, among other structures. The old U.S. courthouse and post office, built two decades later, from 1881 to 1891, is a rare Nevadan example of Richardsonian Romanesque.

When Nevada entered the Union in 1864, its constitution contained a clause stating that the people of Nevada had to "forever disclaim all right and title to the unappropriated public lands lying within said territory, and that the same shall be and remain at the sole and entire

Public versus Private Lands in Nevada

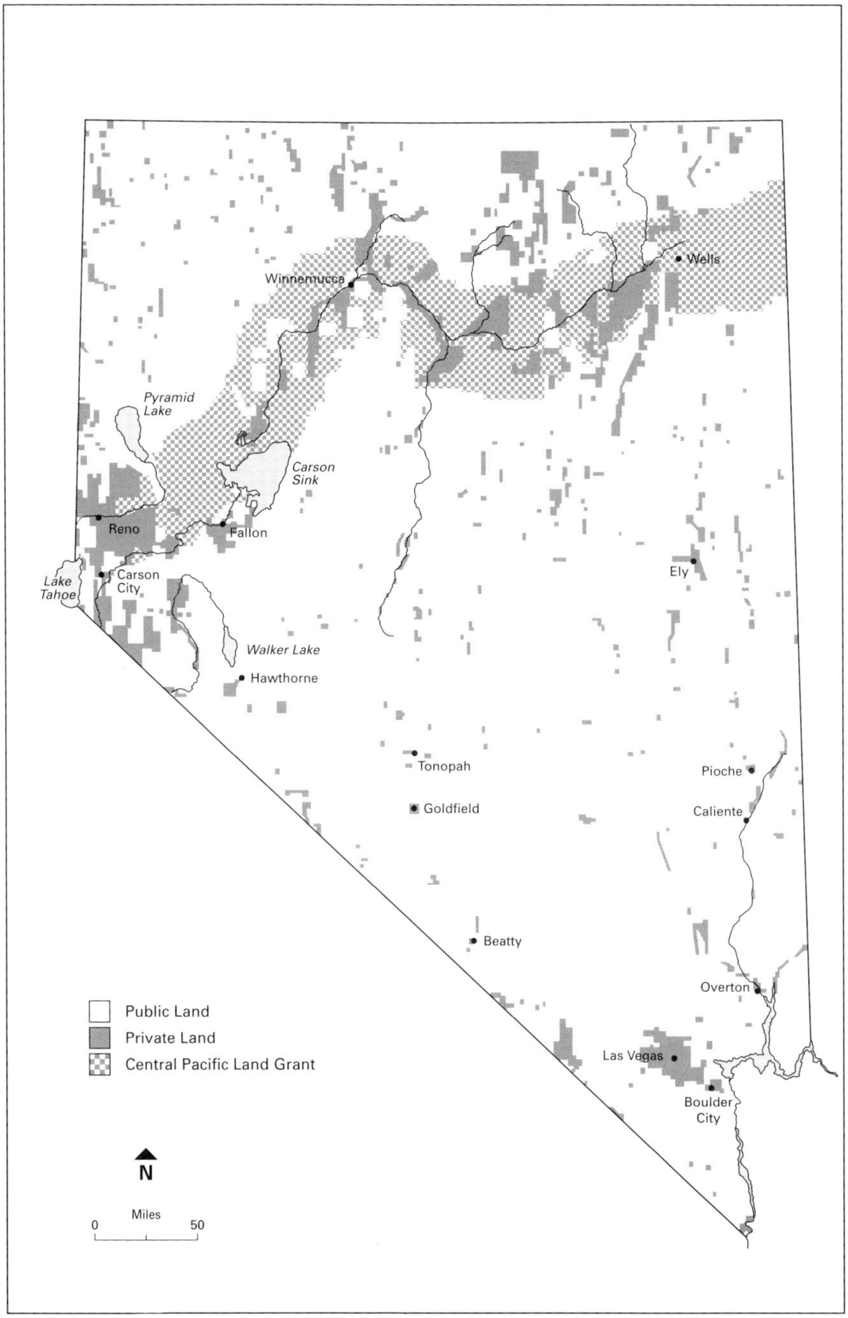
Winnemucca
Wells
Pyramid Lake
Carson Sink
Reno
Fallon
Lake Tahoe
Carson City
Ely
Walker Lake
Hawthorne
Tonopah
Pioche
Goldfield
Caliente
Beatty
Overton
Las Vegas
Boulder City
Public Land
Private Land
Central Pacific Land Grant
N
Miles
0
50

Black Canyon, 12 October 1931, looking upstream from the Nevada side toward the Hoover Dam site, located at the second bridge crossing the Colorado River. This photo shows the early stages of dam construction; tunnels built through the walls of the canyon diverted the river before the dam itself could be erected.

disposition of the United States." The act of Congress enabling Nevada to hold a constitutional convention required this clause for territorial land still held by the federal government.[31] Today these public lands amount to approximately 85 percent of the state.

In the nineteenth century the federal government used little of this land except for its forts. The biggest land exchange at the time involved handing over millions of acres to the Central Pacific Railroad for construction of the transcontinental line. This transaction resulted in a checkerboard pattern of private and public land ownership—a patttern largely intact today along the railroad right-of-way. However, the federal government increased its presence in the West in the twentieth century, primarily in large civil engineering projects and military establishments. Nevada, with the highest percentage of federally owned land of all the states, has seen growing federal involvement in much of its affairs. The federal presence in Nevada has created a love-hate relationship, as the state long ago became dependent on federal funds for its economic well-being. This reliance extends to almost every level of life in Nevada, from subsidies for mining ventures and cattle grazing on public lands to the construction of dams, highways, and military bases that put money directly and indirectly into the state economy and encourage growth by subsidizing water and electricity. At times Nevadans have attempted to gain control of the state's federal lands, but it is unlikely that these efforts will be successful.[32] The cost of managing those lands would likely require the state to sell the land to private owners. The consequent restricted access would be unpopular with the state's growing urban population, who consider open space a recreational benefit.

The federal government's first major project in Nevada, the Truckee-Carson Irrigation Project of 1902, was funded by the National Reclamation Act of that year, sponsored by Nevada's Senator Francis G. Newlands.[33] This project, which consisted of dams, canals, and hundreds of irrigation ditches, transformed a part of Nevada's desert into rich and productive agricultural land. The act also enabled the federal government, through the Reclamation Service (later the Bureau of Reclamation), to construct numerous dams throughout the West during the twentieth century. The construction of Hoover Dam (Boulder Dam), beginning in 1931, created Boulder City and helped transform Las Vegas from a small railroad town to a burgeoning city and tourist destination. The water and electricity provided by the dam have been critical to this city's rapid growth during the twentieth century. For example, low-cost energy in the Las Vegas area helped determine the location of the Basic Magnesium plant, constructed during World War II to produce this substance for incendiary

The entry of the United States into World War II brought increased industrial activity to southern Nevada. This aerial view, taken in 1970, shows the Basic Magnesium plant with Henderson in the distance. The subdivision at the upper right is Henderson Townsite (1941–1942), built to house white workers at the plant. To the upper left is Carver Park, a separate development built in 1943 and designed by Paul Revere Williams, for African American workers.

bombs. The town built to house workers became Henderson, now one of the nation's fastest-growing cities.

The construction of U.S. highways and interstates affected Nevada's development by bringing tourists and truckers through the state, boosting the economy of certain small towns along these roads. Two transcontinental highways were completed in the 1920s: the Victory Highway (U.S. 40), now largely superseded by I-80, and the Lincoln Highway (U.S. 50), passing through central Nevada. The two interstate highways, I-15 and I-80, have also played a significant economic role. I-15, paralleling the old Los Angeles Highway connecting Los Angeles to Salt Lake City via Las Vegas and cutting across Nevada's southern tip, has brought hordes of tourists by car and bus to gamble along the Strip. I-80 roughly follows the route of the old Central Pacific Railroad connecting Salt Lake City, Elko, Reno, and San Francisco. Some cities in northern Nevada welcomed the highway, but others fought it, viewing its completion and subsequent bypass as the death knell for local economies. This attitude has typified Nevadans' ambivalence toward the federal government. In the nineteenth and early twentieth century they welcomed federal policies and projects that supported mining, grazing, reclamation, and therefore the overall economy. During the twentieth century, however, Nevadans came to believe that the federal government often overlooked state interests in favor of national ones.

Though low in population, Nevada received a disproportionate amount of federal money during the 1930s. As historian Eugene P. Moehring notes, "By 1939, the state ranked first in per capita federal spending with public works programs taking the greatest percentage."[34] The Public Works Administration (PWA), the Works Progress Administration (WPA), the National Youth Administration (NYA), and the Civilian Conservation Corps (CCC) funded or provided labor to build a variety of structures. Each agency had a different purpose. In general, the PWA, formed in 1933, funded large-scale construction projects through private companies and contractors. The WPA, established in 1935, provided direct work relief through the construction of public buildings and hired writers and artists to document history and create public art. The NYA hired students for part-time jobs; the CCC enlisted young, single men to work on conservation and resource- development projects, often using CCC camps as home bases. In Nevada the WPA paved 142 miles of new roads and repaired another 900, in addition to building 50 bridges and 133 public buildings and renovating schools, courthouses, and recreation centers throughout the state.[35] The CCC helped construct U.S. Forest Service ranger stations and even assisted the National Park Service in reconstructing historic Fort Churchill.

Nevada's large percentage of federal land, arid climate, and relatively low population density encouraged renewed military involvement in the state. Approximately forty years after the closing of Fort McDermitt, the military returned to Nevada to establish an ammunition depot for the U.S. Navy near Hawthorne, just south of Walker Lake in western Nevada. As another decline in mining activity had occurred in the 1920s, the state welcomed the arrival of a large military installation. In the 1930s the base grew to a vast complex of more than 2,000 structures, most of them ammunition bunkers scattered across the valley floor.

World War II boosted Nevada's economy with the establishment of an auxiliary naval air station in Fallon and a gunnery range in north Las Vegas, now known as Nellis Air Force

The mushroom clouds of nuclear detonations eighty miles west of Las Vegas, on the Nevada Test Site, could often be seen from the city, as this view of Fremont Street shows. During the 1950s Las Vegas used the bomb as a marketing gimmick, advertising atomic drinks and even atomic bikinis.

Base. Both of these large bases closed after the war but were reestablished owing to the Cold War and the Korean War. Since the 1950s, the bases have grown in size, occupying millions of acres of federal land for the testing of aircraft and for bombing ranges.

Another product of World War II and the Cold War was the Nevada Test Site, carved out in 1950 from part of Nellis Air Force Base, located about eighty miles northwest of Las Vegas. The city and state welcomed this establishment as another means to encourage growth.[36] From 1951 to 1963, 126 atmospheric tests of nuclear bombs took place; the giant mushroom clouds of many of the detonations could be seen from Las Vegas. That city seems to have been unscathed by radioactive fallout, but many communities downwind of the blasts, in Lincoln County, Nevada, and southern Utah, have been less fortunate. Radiation killed sheep and has caused cancer in some residents of these areas. Underground testing continued until ratification of the 1992 nuclear test ban treaty.

Nevada, which once welcomed the atom bomb, now faces the possibility of becoming the final resting place for the nation's nuclear waste. Since 1987, the U.S. Department of Energy has been studying the development of a nuclear waste repository beneath Yucca Mountain on the Nevada Test Site adjacent to Death Valley. The repository would cover 1,500 acres with a maximum capacity of 70,000 metric tons of spent waste that would remain radioactive for at least 20,000 years. The site was selected in part because of its low average rainfall per year, approximately six inches. Another factor was Yucca Mountain's location on the test site—an unpopulated 1,350-acre area already managed by the federal government. An unacknowledged factor, however, is the continuing perception of Nevada as a wasteland. With its relatively low population and limited political influence, the state has been unable to prevent the planning and construction of the waste site, which is scheduled to open in 2010. It is ironic that Nevada, a place where few people planned to remain permanently, is now confronted with a project designed to last tens of thousands of years.

Tourism

Despite Nevada's founding as an industrial and agricultural state, the twentieth century has witnessed the development of the tourist industry through the exploitation of gambling and divorce, which were either illegal or heavily regulated in most other states. As a result, the state and its architecture have been irrevocably changed. Traditional industries, namely mining and ranching, continued to decline in the twentieth century. The century's first mining boom kept the economy going through the 1920s, but the halving of mineral production in 1930 intensified the Great Depression in Nevada. In an effort to attract more business, the state legislature liberalized divorce laws in 1931 by dropping the residency requirement from three months to six weeks—the lowest in the country; this put Nevada ahead of competing states such as Idaho and Arkansas, which had a three-month requirement.37 Another law enacted in the same year legalized gambling.

In the 1930s, however, the divorce industry was more important to the local economy than gambling. The six-week residency requirement meant a steady flow of money from out-of-staters to local residents and businesses. The demand for divorces was so high in the 1930s that Reno's hotels, auto camps, and nearby divorce ranches (dude ranches that catered to people waiting for divorces) remained full.38 Divorce was a large part of Reno's economy until the 1960s. By then, many other states had eased their divorce laws, and heavily populated states such as New York passed laws recognizing Mexican divorces; this measure shifted much of the market south.

The legalization of gambling has had more long-term effects on Nevada's economy. Passage of the law was not an entirely startling turn of events. Gambling had been legal in Nevada during most of the state's history from 1869 to 1909. From then until 1931, pressure from Progressive reformers made it illegal, but even during those years, sheriffs and police departments tolerated gambling in the back rooms of clubs.

As historian John Findlay notes, the legalization of gambling and the reduction in residency requirements for divorce were "part of a larger effort to attract people and capital" to the state.39 Having temporarily exhausted its mining resources, Nevada exploited its state's rights, granted by the federal government, to regulate, or deregulate, morals.40

Las Vegas, a town with a population of only about 5,000 in 1931, ultimately benefited the most from the legalization of gambling. Reno, with its nightclubs, bars, and back-room casinos, quickly capitalized on the influx of tourists coming to gamble or get a quick divorce. Served by the railroad and the Victory Highway, Reno was well located to receive tourists, mainly from the San Francisco area, who could make a short trip to gamble. Downtown nightclubs made alterations to accommodate casinos and continued to expand their gambling spaces to house an ever-growing number of tourists. As a means to control gambling, the city of Reno drew a boundary around—or redlined—the downtown area, thereby restricting gambling to a specific part of town. The density of construction there, as well as redlining, led to the erection in 1948 of the first high-rise hotel-casino in the country, the Mapes Hotel and Casino. Redlining remained in effect until 1971, when the city began to allow large casinos such as the MGM Grand (1978; now the Reno Hilton) to build in outlying locations.[41] Since then, casinos in the Reno-Sparks area have grown along I-80 and South Virginia Street, Reno's main north-south thoroughfare.

Gambling encouraged the rise of tourism in other parts of the state. Lake Tahoe, for example, had been a favorite recreation area in the early decades of the twentieth century, attracting Californians to its snow-capped mountains for winter skiing and to its blue waters for summer boating and fishing. With the legalization of gambling, popular resorts just over the California-Nevada border in Crystal Bay on Tahoe's north shore added casinos to draw larger crowds. This pattern would be repeated throughout Nevada in towns located at or near the borders of other states and served by highways, such as Stateline; on the south shore of Lake Tahoe; and in Mesquite, along I-15 at the Arizona border. Other towns have come to life simply to capitalize on a border location. Most of these boom towns are fairly recent, established in the 1960s to take advantage of increased automobile travel; examples are Jackpot and Laughlin. West Wendover, established during World War II on the border with Utah, where gambling in any form is prohibited, has also become a boom town. These towns developed around a few casinos, restaurants, and gas stations and have gradually expanded to include residential areas with schools and libraries. Other areas remain no more than large casino complexes, oases along major interstates, such as Boomtown, west of Reno along I-80, and Jean and Stateline (Primm), both in southern Nevada along I-15. These casinos crowd the interstate and can be seen from miles away. At night, when nothing else competes with the view, these brightly lit complexes are beacons to travelers passing through the mountains or desert.

Over the course of several decades, Las Vegas has fully exploited the legalization of gambling. Established as a railroad town in 1905, the city had a slow start in the decades before World War II. The construction of Hoover Dam in the 1930s provided the small town with a steady flow of customers, mostly dam workers living in Boulder City who came to drink, dance, and gamble. By 1931 an underworld figure from Los Angeles, Tony Cornero, had built the Meadows Club, a building in the Spanish Colonial Revival style, which was the first Strip-style hotel and casino resort built on a highway on the outskirts of Las Vegas.[42] The year 1931 also saw the completion of the Los Angeles Highway, connecting Las Vegas to southern California. Although train service was available to Las Vegas, the automobile soon became the preferred mode of travel.

By the 1930s the downtown area had been built up. Redlining restricted casinos to hotels and bars in the city center. The lack of space downtown encouraged development along the Los Angeles Highway to the south, beyond the city limits. This road eventually became the Strip. With the completion of the highway, Las Vegas was only a five- to six-hour drive from Los Angeles, which provided the major market for gambling in Las Vegas. Since the 1930s, and especially since World War II, Las Vegas and the Strip have attracted growing numbers of visitors from around the world.

Downtown Reno in the 1950s, lively at night, lined with casinos and bars. Neon lights lit Virginia Street, Reno's main thoroughfare. The Reno Arch, which celebrated "The Biggest Little City in the World," spanned the street from 1929 to 1963. Today a sign erected on New Year's Eve in 1963 arches over Virginia Street.

Fremont Street, Las Vegas, looking northwest, c. 1910. Las Vegas began as a small railroad town. For many years the depot at the head of Fremont Street signified the railroad's importance to the community. The Mission Revival depot, erected in 1905, was demolished around 1940 to make way for a Moderne station. The Union Plaza Hotel and Casino now occupies the site.

Fremont Street in 1998. In 1995 the Fremont Street Experience turned the street into a covered pedestrian mall. When lighted at night, this space frame competes with the older neon signs along the street.

Like the mining industry before it, the Las Vegas casino industry quickly became colonized, this time by hotel and nightclub owners from Los Angeles. These entrepreneurs hired architects in their own city who were already established designers of roadside coffee shops, diners, and drive-ins. The setting and architectural problems of Las Vegas were similar to those in Los Angeles and required similar solutions.[43]

Beginning in 1941, low-rise casino resorts based on the roadside motel prototype popped up at intervals along the highway. Resorts such as El Rancho Vegas (1941) and the Last Frontier (1942) set models for the next two decades. These casino complexes—a mix of the burgeoning ranch-farm style and the Spanish Colonial Revival—sprawled along the desert highway, catering to the visitor's every need. Buildings and parking lots were oriented toward the highway to attract motorists. Although World War II put a halt to casino construction, servicemen kept the gambling industry going during the war.

In 1946 mobster Benjamin "Bugsy" Siegel ushered in a new era of casino design with his sophisticated Hotel Flamingo. Siegel, along with architect George Vernon Russell of Los Angeles, looked to the modernism of that city's nightclubs, breaking with the earlier theme of the Old West.[44] Though the Flamingo resembled a motel in plan and scale, it was a new type of resort with a horseshoe plan enclosing a large pool, lawns, and tropical plants—an oasis in the desert crowned by a vertical sign featuring a neon flamingo.

In the 1950s and 1960s the sign became the identifying image of the Las Vegas Strip. As more resorts opened along the highway, their owners faced increasing competition to attract motorists. Most buildings remained low-slung, so the large sign by the roadside became the most effective means of advertising. Among the most striking signs were William Pereira and Charles Luckman's champagne tower of 1953 at the Flamingo. As part of a complete remodeling of the complex, they designed a 60-foot-high cylindrical tower with neon circles that blinked on and off, seeming to bubble upward. The Dunes sign of 1964, by Lee Klay of the Federal Sign and Signal Company, rose 180 feet high and remained the Strip's tallest sign until its demolition in 1993. The buildings served as mere backdrops for these exuberant signs.

Construction of the eleven-story Riviera Hotel in 1955, the first high-rise in Las Vegas, marked a shift in the perception of the Strip as having unlimited space. Although many casino owners in the 1960s continued to commission large, low buildings, the increasing density of the Strip soon required additional vertical expansion. This density also called for eye-grabbing forms. As in the 1940s, casino owners in the 1950s and 1960s turned mainly to architects from Los Angeles to create a Las Vegas Strip look. These architects continued to draw on roadside commercial vernacular architecture, dominated at that time by a style variously called Googie, Coffee Shop Modern, and Populuxe, and characterized by an organic expressionism employing boomerang and kidney shapes, starbursts, curved and cantilevered roofs, and abundant signage. The writer Tom Wolfe attempted to describe the Strip: "Boomerang Modern, Palette Curvilinear, Flash Gordon Ming-Alert Spiral, McDonald's Hamburger Parabola, Mint Casino Elliptical, Miami Beach Kidney."[45] Some entrepreneurs began to use themes to unify their hotel-casino resorts. Jay Sarno, for example, adapted ancient Rome for a popular audience for his Caesars Palace of 1966.

The success of casinos in Las Vegas has been a rich topic of discourse for architects since Robert Venturi's visit in 1968. In the fall of that year the Yale School of Art and Architecture offered a seminar entitled "Learning from Las Vegas, or Form Analysis as Design Research" taught by visiting faculty members Venturi, Denise Scott Brown, and Steven Izenour. They traveled to Las Vegas with thirteen architecture and design students, spending ten days studying the Strip and its architecture. The result was a celebration of the Strip. Venturi, Scott

Bugsy Siegel's Hotel Flamingo, designed by George Vernon Russell and built in 1946, brought a new era of sophistication to postwar Las Vegas with its angular, modern forms. The low-slung casino was surrounded by lush lawns, suggesting a desert oasis.

Caesars Palace, casino interior, 1960s. Casino owner Jay Sarno and architect Melvin Grossman drew from ancient Rome and mid-twentieth-century modernism to create a theme resort that would attract the average tourist. The large, domed casino with stylized Ionic columns reflects the sophisticated yet populist style of the exterior of the Caesars Palace complex.

By the 1960s the Las Vegas Strip had captured the attention of admirers and detractors alike. Commentators such as Tom Wolfe and Robert Venturi analyzed the organic forms of the Strip's Populuxe architecture and the preponderance of roadside signs, seeing in them a democratic form of architecture. The Strip at this time was still surrounded by open desert.

Brown, and Izenour published their findings in *Learning from Las Vegas*, which became the seminal book on the Strip and made the study of commercial vernacular architecture popular among architects. Considering the Strip as a phenomenon of architectural communication, the authors defined two types of roadside commercial buildings, which they called the duck and the decorated shed. The first, so called for a well-known Long Island poultry and egg shop (now a gift shop) in the form of a giant duck, represented the building as symbol, as architecture and sculpture combined. The second, a low, boxy building with oversized signage as ornament, represented the building as sign.[46] Venturi found both forms in Las Vegas, and they persist today in ever-changing incarnations.

Shortly after the group's trip to Las Vegas, major changes in Nevada's gambling industry began to affect casino architecture throughout the state. In 1969 the Nevada legislature passed the Corporate Gaming Act, allowing corporations to hold gambling licenses; previously only individuals could hold these licenses. Corporate consolidation began in 1969 with the construction of the International Hotel, now the Hilton. Architects began to work with corporate committees rather than with individual entrepreneurs, whose idiosyncratic personal tastes had often influenced the architecture. Examples of design by committee include the first MGM Grand Hotel (now Bally's; 1973, Martin Stern, Jr.) and the Flamingo

Hilton (c. 1977, Rissman and Rissman Associates), which resemble office towers pierced by small windows.

The national economic decline of the early 1980s showed that gambling—an industry the state had believed was recession-proof—was vulnerable to economic ups and downs. Since 1950, gambling has been Nevada's largest industry, far surpassing mining and ranching, and Las Vegas has become the center of the gambling economy. For much of the 1970s and 1980s, few new casinos were constructed. The opening of Steve Wynn's Mirage on the Strip in 1989 ushered in a new era of casino construction. Mega-resorts, with thousands of rooms and a variety of attractions besides gambling, have set a new standard of scale and entertainment for casinos. Thus far, the strategy has paid off; in 1999 over thirty-three million people visited the city, spending $7 billion. However, it has fueled a frenzy among major corporations in the gaming industry, which must create increasingly outlandish structures to attract new and repeat visitors. The result has been a constant reconfiguring of casino exteriors and interiors. For example, the second MGM Grand, built 1991–1993 as a big green box with a large cartoonish lion at its entrance, underwent a face-lift in 1998 that replaced the giant lion with one more regal in appearance. Other casinos, including Caesars Palace and Luxor, have added new hotel towers to accommodate more guests. Most important has been the increased density along the Strip, which forces visitors to walk rather than drive. Casinos have responded to rising pedestrian traffic by building out to the sidewalk, incorporating gateways and attractions to entice visitors.

Though much smaller than either Las Vegas or Reno, Stateline and Crystal Bay, on the Nevada side of Lake Tahoe, have also become gambling destinations, popular for their proximity to California. The eastern shore of Lake Tahoe is a strikingly beautiful place, where the steep mountains of the eastern Sierra's Carson Range meet the blue water of one of the world's deepest lakes. A few small communities dot the Nevada shore of the lake, beginning with Crystal Bay at the northern border with California and ending with Stateline at the southern border with South Lake Tahoe, California.

This basin was originally the home of the Washoe Indians, who spent their summers at the lake until being displaced. During the development of the Comstock, the basin's old-growth timber supplied raw materials for the massive square-framing used to support the walls of mines. Not until 1997 did the tribe win permission from the federal government to use parts of its traditional summer lands.

Beginning in the late nineteenth century, entrepreneurs began to exploit the lake as a recreational area for wealthy Californians. The trip to the lake from San Francisco was shortened in 1900 by the completion of a spur railroad from Truckee, California, where the transcontinental railroad stopped, to Tahoe City, California. In the 1920s resorts began catering to middle-class Americans with enough disposable income for vacations. New roads to the lakeshore, such as the Lincoln Highway (U.S. 50), made vacationing there increasingly convenient. The legalization of gambling attracted more tourists to the border towns of Crystal Bay and Stateline. Development quickly filled the California side, but much of the Nevada side, still in the hands of a few wealthy landholders, remained considerably less built up. Over time the federal and Nevada state governments acquired much of this land, managed in part within the Toiyabe National Forest and the rest in Lake Tahoe State Park.

After the 1960 Winter Olympics in nearby Squaw Valley, California, development in the basin exploded. Promoters used the long, snowy winters and dry, mild summers to sell the lake as a year-round recreation area. Construction of casinos accelerated. Although Crystal Bay has only a few casinos and high-rise towers, Stateline exploited its limited space along U.S. 50. To accommodate more visitors, the town's half-dozen casinos have erected high-rise hotel towers, which give the south shore of the lake a dense, banal, urban appearance that contrasts with the quieter, open spaces of most of the rest of the basin. The success of the casino industry has resulted in an increased number of permanent residents in the basin.

Rapid environmental degradation inspired Congress to create the joint California-Nevada Tahoe Regional Planning Agency (TRPA) in 1969. Although the agency has been able to restrict growth severely, runoff from roads and building sites, automobile traffic, and air pollution continue to threaten the clarity of the lake water. Growth has slowed, but not enough to ensure the lake's preservation.

Though overshadowed by gambling, other aspects of Nevada's tourist economy have helped to shape architecture in the state. The wedding industry has surpassed the divorce industry in both Las Vegas and Reno. Nevada requires no blood test or waiting period, and the abundance of chapels for both civil and non-denominational ceremonies has facilitated spur-of-the-moment weddings. In addition to wedding chapels in most major casinos, many small freestanding chapels line the main streets of downtown Reno and Las Vegas. Small chapels can also be found in other towns. In general, these structures are not striking, their forms ranging from replications of churches to boxy decorated sheds with neon hearts and wedding bells.

Nevada is the only state in the nation that has legalized prostitution, which also contributes to the state's tourist economy, though it is not clear to what extent. Brothels have always been part of the state's built environment because the largely male populations of mining camps and towns provided a ready market. Every town had its redlight district filled with large brothels, dance halls, and rows of cribs—small houses where individual prostitutes worked. The only exceptions were company towns such as McGill and federal towns such as Boulder City. Most towns tolerated redlight districts well into the twentieth century because the state had never officially made prostitution legal or illegal. Reno had a row of houses along the Truckee River, and Las Vegas concentrated its brothels in Block 16. Both districts attracted soldiers stationed nearby during World War II. However, health concerns became so great that military officials finally persuaded local governments to close the brothels in 1943. These towns did not wish to lose the income but were willing to cooperate with the war effort, thereby ensuring continued military spending in their communities.[47]

Today prostitution is legal in thirteen of Nevada's seventeen counties. In 1971 Joe Conforte, founder of the Mustang Ranch and the operator of brothels in Nevada since the 1950s, openly challenged the murky state and county laws governing prostitution. He convinced Storey County commissioners to legalize prostitution, making it the first county to do so. Other counties followed suit, and in 1973 the State Supreme Court upheld the right of counties with fewer than 50,000 people to license brothels.

In general, brothels cannot operate on main streets and must be located at least 300 feet from churches and schools. Brothels range from houses within a town to complexes of trailers and prefabricated buildings set back from the road outside of town. In small towns most brothels are located along alleys or on the edge of the town grid, as in Winnemucca and Wells. However, in both towns the brothels are clearly visible from the interstate, where they advertise to truck drivers and motorists.

The rise of tourism has had a major impact on all aspects of life in Nevada, especially on economics and politics. Northwestern Nevada, centered on Reno and Carson City, once was dominant because it had the largest population in the state, but southern Nevada surpassed the north in numbers and growth in the mid-twentieth century. Though the population of the Reno metropolitan area exceeds 300,000, that of the Las Vegas area is over 1.3 million, constituting about 65 percent of the state's total of approximately 2 million.[48] This huge imbalance has caused a greater portion of the state's revenue to head south to support social programs, education, infrastructure, and major construction projects.

Housing

Housing in Nevada has ranged from the simplest forms of shelter to ostentatious mansions. In general, the evolution of dwellings has paralleled that of other types of building, focusing mainly on the short term. Like Native American dwellings, the early shelters of Euro-Americans were small and easily movable, consisting of canvas tents or, if made from local materials, usually log or adobe brick cabins. If a community survived the initial settlement period, builders imported lumber from the mountains or from California, bought brick made at nearby kilns, or used locally quarried stone.

Given the transitory nature of Nevada's Euro-American settlements, nineteenth-century houses were rarely showy. Virginia City had its mansions, and those surviving from the Comstock era—most of them dating from the 1860s and 1870s and designed in the Italianate style—show a sophistication and knowledge of fashion in architecture. People who gained extraordinary wealth from the mines, however, such as James C. Flood, one of the Comstock's bonanza kings, often chose to build great houses in San Francisco. Flood's brownstone mansion, constructed in 1886, still stands on Nob Hill, where it houses the exclusive Pacific Union Club. Adolph Sutro, creator and developer of the Sutro Tunnel, a deep-level drain for the Comstock's mines, built public recreation and cultural areas such as the Sutro Baths, Sutro Heights Park, and the Sutro Library in San Francisco and served as mayor of that city in the 1890s.

Most housing was modest. Many Comstock miners lived in boardinghouses, ranging from single-family homes in which owners rented out rooms to three-story structures accommodating up to a hundred people. In Carson City the typical house had one story, with a front porch and mass-produced jigsawn ornamentation. Because of the economic cycles of the mining industry, many owners, or even building scavengers, moved houses to more promising locations. This predilection for mobility is reflected today in Nevadans' love of mobile homes and recreational vehicles. Indeed, modern mine workers frequently prefer mobile homes to more permanent dwellings because they want to be able to move their houses to the next mining job instead of being caught in a real estate collapse.

Mining towns, often built in narrow canyons or along mountainsides, were densely planned. Despite this initial density, Nevada's communities tended to sprawl outward from their centers in response to the automobile. Reno was the first town in Nevada to develop suburbs, beginning in the early twentieth century. Though the core of the town stands along the banks of the Truckee River, Reno's location in a broad valley encouraged outward growth. In the early 1900s Newlands Heights, set on a bluff overlooking the river and named for the home of Senator Francis G. Newlands—the first to be built there—became the most desirable neighborhood in the city and remains so today. All the major figures in Nevada politics and industry built mansions there in a variety of styles, employing the first group of professional architects in the state. For middle- and low-income residents the bungalow became the most popular housing form. Relatively inexpensive and designed for southern California's climate, bungalows were well suited to Nevada's early-twentieth-century suburbs. Since World War II, subdivisions of single-family houses have spread in all directions, gradually filling the Truckee Meadows.

The railroads also played a significant role in Nevada's housing stock, erecting orderly rows of identical dwellings in many towns. The federal government continued this pattern in the twentieth century. In southern Nevada, for example, the construction of Hoover Dam and then World War II brought an influx of workers who needed housing. The dwellings built by the federal government or its contractors were, in general, small and of one story. The housing erected in railroad and company towns helped establish a model that persisted in post–World War II suburban subdivisions.

With abundant land and subsidized electricity and water available in many parts of the state, suburban growth had few restrictions after the 1940s, when a postwar boom brought more people to Nevada. The growing tourism industry, as well as numerous federal projects, kept the demand for housing high. Since the 1960s, rapid growth around Reno and especially Las Vegas has resulted in the continued loss of open space to subdivisions of tract houses and ever-widening highways.

One example is Incline Village on Lake Tahoe. A single mobile-home park housed residents in the area until 1960, when a real estate developer created a master plan for a 10,000-resident community, including mansions along the lakeshore, condominiums in the flats beyond the shore, and chalets in the hills above. Limitation of the commercial strip to Nevada 28 and Southwood Road prevented the creation of a town center. The village is still privately owned, administered by the Incline Village General Improvement District rather than by a local government. Today this exclusive and affluent community has 7,000 year-round residents. Lakeshore Drive has some of the most expensive real estate in Nevada.

Much of the development of the last two decades has been conducted by large California firms, and the pattern follows that of Nevada's neighboring state. Public transportation has never played a large role in Nevada, though Reno, Las Vegas, and Clark County have small mass-transit systems. Dependence on the automobile and the construction of new freeways and arterials have encouraged development far away from urban downtowns.

As in the past, the perception of Nevada as a wasteland has helped fuel this construction boom. Developers and residents alike see open space as a vacuum to be filled rather than a resource to be preserved. Despite constant concerns about the lack of water, development

This view of a development in Henderson shows the wide streets and cookie-cutter houses of a typical suburb of the late 1990s in southern Nevada.

has continued. Las Vegas has experienced tremendous growth as a popular retirement area as well as a resort destination. In 1998 approximately 6,000 people per month moved into the Las Vegas metropolitan area. The region is the site of large master-planned communities, including Green Valley in Henderson and Summerlin, built by the Del Webb Corporation, developer of Sun City, Arizona. These continue the traditional pattern of suburban development, with restricted access, cul-de-sacs, and standardized houses. Even in smaller communities such as Elko and Winnemucca, recent economic growth has resulted in suburban sprawl, threatening the downtowns that distinguish them.

Indeed, development has been unable to keep up with demand, and houses remain out of reach for many Nevada residents. Construction of single-family homes has far outpaced that of less profitable condominiums or apartments, so low- and moderate-income housing is scarce. The mobile home has therefore continued to be a popular form of housing in Nevada. Trailer and RV parks are abundant, and in remote parts of the state, trailer homes far outnumber houses.

Ethnic Groups

Diverse ethnic groups have populated Nevada, but surprisingly few have had an identifiable impact on architecture in the state. The English, Irish, Cornish, French, Germans, Italians, Basques, Greeks, Slavs, Chinese, and Japanese, among others, came seeking work as miners, entrepreneurs, ranchers, or farmers. Like many other western states, Nevada had few African

American residents until the early twentieth century, when manufacturing jobs attracted southerners to the state.

Only the Basques, Italians, and Chinese have left much of a distinctive architectural imprint. The Basques did not introduce specific architectural styles or forms, but rather a distinct building type, the Basque hotel, found in many northern Nevada towns. Usually simple wood-frame or brick structures following vernacular American forms, these hotels served as centers for local Basques. Hotel owners often helped newly arrived Basques to find work and housing and obtain the required permits and papers. Many Basque sheepherders used the hotels as home base after spending months on the range. Few of the hotels continue to function in this way, though many maintain Basque-American culture through the hearty meals of lamb and beef served family style in their restaurants.

Italians came to Nevada to work in the mines and to run truck farms and ranches to support mining towns and government centers. Many of these immigrants came from northern Italy and, unlike their counterparts from impoverished southern Italy, had the resources to buy land and start farms. In most cases, their architectural legacy was small, except for freestanding ovens for baking bread. However, in the northern and central parts of the state Italian stonemasons left enduring reminders of their work. Howard Wight Marshall's study of Paradise Valley reveals that settlers from the Piedmont region of Italy built numerous stone structures for themselves and for others. Italian stonemasons worked with hand tools, erecting buildings with either finely finished ashlar walls and thin mortar joints or rough, random-coursed walls with thick mortar joints. Italian and Swiss immigrants who moved to mining regions often found work as *carbonari*, or charcoal makers, and used their expertise to build large stone charcoal kilns. Examples of these structures survive in Ward, near Ely; Bristol, near Pioche; and in the Spring Mountains near Las Vegas.

Although none of their extensive neighborhoods survive except in photographs and archaeological artifacts, Chinese immigrants helped shape urban landscapes. Like other immigrants, the Chinese initially came to Nevada to take advantage of the numerous mining booms, working as miners or as laborers and entrepreneurs in businesses that supported the mining economy. Soon after, many Chinese immigrated to the state to work on the Central Pacific Railroad. They were instrumental in building the railroad over the Sierra Nevada because of their expertise with dynamite and their willingness to take on the most dangerous tasks when Euro-Americans refused. After completion of the railroad, they looked for work in mining towns and on ranches. As in other western states, they were despised by whites and forced to live in ghettos that became known as Chinatowns. In the second half of the nineteenth century, Chinese lived in nearly every Nevada town; several towns had sizable, regionally important Chinese communities. By 1875 Virginia City's Chinatown numbered over 1,000 inhabitants, making it one of the most important Asian districts in the West. Carson City and Dayton also had large Chinese populations. In Virginia City the Chinese lived down the hill from the city center in an area bounded roughly by Union, G, L, and Taylor streets. They worked as domestic help in white households, in laundries, and on the construction of the V&T Railroad. After 1869, miners' unions persuaded the Bank of California to ban Chinese laborers from working on the railroad in Virginia City and Gold Hill. They had been banned from mining in 1859.[49]

Nearly every late nineteenth-century town in northern Nevada had a Chinatown. Though most Chinese left Nevada around the turn of the century because of racial persecution, many buildings from their neighborhoods remained for decades. At its peak, Carson City's Chinatown, located around East 3rd Street, had about 800 Chinese residents. Many of the buildings survived into the 1950s.

There is evidence that the Chinese practiced feng shui, the art of geomancy, shifting the orientation of streets in their neighborhoods from the main town grid to ensure the desirable siting of buildings. They also built distinct structures such as joss houses, which in China were used exclusively as temples or houses of worship serving Taoist, Confucian, or Buddhist devotees; in the United States these buildings also functioned as administrative centers and general meeting halls.

Economic depression in the 1880s and 1890s exacerbated the already uneasy relationship between the Chinese and Euro-Americans. The poor economy, as well as numerous riots and other acts of violence against the Chinese, drove most of them out of the state by the turn of the century. In some cases, Euro-Americans burned down Chinatowns to force out the residents. In other cases, these neighborhoods were abandoned and slowly deteriorated. Their loss is particularly unfortunate because some of them managed to survive more or less intact well into the twentieth century. Much of Carson City's Chinatown survived into the 1950s, when the state demolished the remaining buildings to make way for a new state office building.

Though not defined by ethnic origin, the Mormons have a distinct cultural identity that has helped shape Nevada architecture. The first white settlers in the state to establish farms and ranches, they returned to Utah in 1857. However, in the 1870s and 1880s groups of Mormons attempted new settlements in the Virgin River valley, founding Bunkerville as an agricultural collective with land held in common. The experiment lasted only two years, but Bunkerville survived. Buildings remaining from the nineteenth century include a house built for a polygamous family.

The Mormons' town plans for their communities are their greatest legacy in Nevada. In 1833, in Kirtland, Ohio, Joseph Smith and Frederick G. Williams devised a plan based on a grid, which formed the basis for all subsequent Mormon settlements. The main characteristics were "a grid pattern, wide streets, ample building lots, fenced or walled properties, church square, and open irrigation ditches."[50] The settlers named streets according to direction and number, such as 1st West Street and 2nd West Street. The order inherent in these plans helped the Mormons establish settlements in the wilderness of the nineteenth-century West. Today Mormons continue to shape the landscape through their churches and temples.

The Architectural Profession in Nevada

Given Nevada's relatively recent settlement, frontier character, small population, and economic ups and downs, it is not surprising that it took several decades for the architectural profession to become established. Nevada's historians have noted that the state served as a colony for larger, more populated states, especially California, in a number of industries, including mining, ranching, and, most recently, gambling. The architectural profession has been no different. Because of their proximity, California's architects received commissions for many of Nevada's early prominent buildings, including the state capitol, which was designed by Joseph Gosling of San Francisco, known as both an architect and a master builder. Local builders planned and erected most of Nevada's structures, using pattern books; prefabricated doors, windows, and trim; and their own ingenuity. In the twentieth century architects from Los Angeles shaped the look of the Las Vegas Strip.

By the early twentieth century only eleven men in Nevada called themselves architects.[51] Frederick J. DeLongchamps (1882–1969) emerged from this group to become Nevada's most influential architect in the first half of the twentieth century. After studying mining engineering at the University of Nevada, Reno, and graduating in 1904, he apprenticed as an architect in California. In 1907 he returned to Nevada to practice and over the years designed more than five hundred buildings, most of them in Nevada. DeLongchamps's ability to master a variety of styles and to build everything from small houses and large estates to county courthouses made him extremely prolific. Many of his projects survive.

Reno, as the largest city in Nevada in the early twentieth century, became the center for the architectural profession. It was here that most of the state's architects lived and worked, including the father-son team of George A. and Lehman A. Ferris, Edward Parsons, Russell Mills, and Graham Erskine. There was plenty of work, but Nevada's architects had to compete constantly against more prominent architects from neighboring states. Local architects were also at a disadvantage because the state had no licensing requirements. The low barriers to entering the profession caused many architects to lose commissions to out-of-state competitors who could impress clients with licenses from neighboring states. Nevada finally began to license architects in 1949, when it established the Nevada State Board of Architecture. The profession was further strengthened by the founding of the Nevada chapter of the American Institute of Architects that same year. In 1954 it became the Reno (later Northern Nevada) chapter, and two years later Las Vegas established its own chapter.[52]

Another problem affecting the advancement of the profession in Nevada was the lack of a school of architecture in the state. Nevadans who wished to become architects had to attend school elsewhere. In 1997 the University of Nevada, Las Vegas, School of Architecture received accreditation.

Since the mid-twentieth century, the architectural profession in Nevada has matured, supported by a strong economy and rapid growth that have ensured plenty of work for local architects. The current boom, centered in Las Vegas, has provided a variety of projects ranging from casinos to libraries. An increasing number of architects based in the state have won commissions for major public buildings, and most of the casinos in Las Vegas are now designed by in-state architects. Las Vegas has moved far ahead of Reno in creating a regional architecture. Despite the garishness of the new casinos, the city now has public and private buildings that respond to the desert environment. These structures, designed by local and out-of-state architects, may become more important than the casinos in defining a regional architecture.

Historic Preservation

The concept of historic preservation is relatively new to Nevada. The exploitation of natural resources and the land has shaped the economy since the mid-nineteenth century, and history has been of little importance to most residents. Nevada's rapid growth has hindered preservation because many businesses and residents believe that protecting historic structures impedes growth. New residents far outnumber native-born Nevadans, and virtually no collective memory exists to advocate for the significance of such structures. In addition, most of Nevada's historic resources date back no further than the early twentieth century—a period that is still not "historic" in the minds of most people. Nevertheless, in recent years the state has taken some steps to preserve its cultural resources.

There were few laws concerning preservation until the state took the momentous first step of establishing the Comstock Historic District in 1969. The towns and mines of the Comstock had already been designated a National Historic Landmark in 1961, but the state's recognition provided the foundation for establishing local ordinances and a design review commission. The district is one of the nation's largest, encompassing Virginia City, Gold Hill, Silver City, and Dayton and covering more than 14,000 acres.

In 1977 Nevada established a state historic preservation office, one of the last states in the nation to do so. Perpetually understaffed and underfunded, the office has struggled to survey Nevada's cultural resources as well as keep up with federal and state regulations. Nevada continues to suffer from the lack of a private statewide organization devoted to historic preservation, though the Clark County Preservation Association has had some success in preserving historic properties in Las Vegas.

A major victory for preservation occurred in 1993, when the state legislature approved a

The rapid growth of Las Vegas, combined with the frenzy of creating new casinos, has led to the demolition of many older ones. The Landmark Hotel, designed by Edward Hendricks in 1961–1962, was troubled from the start. It was not completed until 1969, when Howard Hughes bought it and opened it as a casino. In 1995, the Las Vegas Convention and Visitors Authority, the Landmark's last owner, demolished it to make way for a parking lot. Older casinos are considered too small and thus unprofitable in the age of the mega-resort.

$2.5 million bond measure to fund the rehabilitation of historic buildings throughout the state as cultural centers. In 1995 the legislature approved another $20 million to be spent over ten years to continue the program. This is the largest public expenditure to date for historic preservation projects in Nevada.

Even so, a number of factors make it difficult to promote preservation. The goals of major industries—gambling, mining, and rail transportation—often stand in direct opposition to those of historic preservation. In recent years large mining projects have been located near the sites of historic mining towns. Given the political and economic power of mining interests in the state, the most preservationists can hope for is to record historic buildings before demolition.

Likewise, the trend among casinos to remodel old structures or erect new ones has erased most traces of these buildings dating back even twenty years. Classic casinos such as the Flamingo have all been demolished. Imploding old casinos has become the latest gimmick of gambling corporations, which promote demolition, adding fireworks to ensure a memorable show. Even the famous Dunes (and its 180-foot-tall sign) was not spared; Steve Wynn of Mirage Resorts imploded the complex in 1993 to mark the opening of his new resort, Treasure Island. Other classic casinos including the Landmark, the Sands, the Hacienda, and the Aladdin have been imploded in the past few years. Given this record, preserving more recent gambling landmarks will be extremely difficult. Only buildings that are easily moved have survived the rapid stylistic and commercial changes of the Strip.

Nevada's extensive railroad resources have met a similar fate. Until its merger with Union Pacific in 1996, Southern Pacific owned the majority of Nevada's railroad structures. Despite preservationists' efforts to save and record historic depots, warehouses, and other buildings, Southern Pacific consistently opposed their efforts and demolished many of its buildings to avoid maintenance costs and liability.

In addition, the federal government, manager of more than 80 percent of Nevada's land, has not always been a good steward of the cultural resources in its care. Despite the requirements of the National Historic Preservation Act, some federal agencies in the state disregard the law, neither documenting nor protecting prehistoric and historic properties in their care. Given the lack of a large local constituency supporting preservation, these agencies know they can approve projects without following federal regulations. In addition, the National Register of Historic Places and National Historic Landmark programs of the National Park Service have had difficulty in evaluating Nevada's resources and their significance in the context of architecture in the state. Few reviewers in the Washington, D.C., headquarters

As in the past, mobility can be the key to survival for Nevada buildings. The Little Church of the West (1942, Walter Zick and Harris Sharp Architects), a wedding chapel that is the Strip's oldest extant structure, has been moved several times. This photo shows the chapel being relocated in 1954 on the grounds of the New Frontier Casino. It was moved most recently in 1996.

of these programs are familiar with Nevada architecture, and they often deny listing in the register, using criteria based on the study of eastern American architecture. Furthermore, many of Nevada's significant buildings, such as casinos, do not meet the National Register's age criteria, and therefore must be recognized in some other way.

Nevada has always been a pro-growth, pro-business state. Developers often consider historic preservation an obstacle to growth. They demolish historic and potentially historic buildings as quickly as possible to ensure that a project will proceed unimpeded. Finally, Nevada suffers from having few local governments that promote preservation through ordinances or planning. Only three municipalities, Carson City, Reno, and Las Vegas, and the Comstock Historic District, which includes Virginia City, have ordinances and design guidelines for historic districts, and local review commissions have few means to enforce these codes. Political and economic pressure for increased development and the desire of owners to alter their property as they see fit have resulted in districts that have lost much of their historic fabric.

Though Nevada has far to go in ensuring the preservation of many of its historic sites, there were successes in the late 1990s, particularly private initiatives. One example is the Golden Gate Hotel in downtown Las Vegas, the oldest extant hotel-casino in the state. In the 1950s the building's owners covered the Art Deco exterior with a modern facade. In 1990 a new generation of owners removed the modern sheathing, returning the Golden Gate to its earlier appearance and emphasizing the building's history.

Nevada has tremendous potential for developing a heritage tourism industry by preserving and promoting its historic sites. Hoover Dam, for example, attracts over one million visitors per year, though many of them view the site as an engineering feat rather than a historic landmark. Other sites such as Nevada's numerous ghost towns could be better marketed and interpreted to attract the public. An example is Berlin-Ichthyosaur State Park, in south-central Nevada, where the old mining town of Berlin has been protected and preserved in a state of arrested decay.

Given Nevada's continued growth, such success stories will likely remain exceptions to the prevailing rules of development. The state continues to draw fortune hunters who leave new ruins for the next wave of immigrants. Until Nevada builds a constituency that cares about the past, monuments of material significance will be routinely destroyed without opposition.

Notes

1. Russell R. Elliott, *History of Nevada,* 2nd ed. (Lincoln: University of Nebraska Press, 1987), 20.
2. Ibid., 22.
3. Donald K. Grayson, *The Desert's Past: A Natural Prehistory of the Great Basin* (Washington, D.C.: Smithsonian Institution Press, 1993), 36.
4. Ibid., 37–38.
5. Ronald M. James, *The Roar and the Silence: A History of Virginia City and the Comstock Lode* (Reno: University of Nevada Press, 1998), 11. The equivalent figure for 2000 and all other equivalents in this volume are based on the Composite Consumer Price Index in John J. McCusker, *How Much Is That in Real Money? A Historical Price Index for Use as a Deflator of Money Values in the Economy of the United States* (Worcester, Mass.: American Antiquarian Society, 1992), 323–32. As the index covers prices only to

1991, prices for 2000 have been adjusted, using an average of 3 percent inflation per year from 1992 to 2000.

6. Wilbur S. Shepperson, *Restless Strangers: Nevada's Immigrants and Their Interpreters* (Reno: University of Nevada Press, 1970), 13.

7. Charles H. Carpenter, Jr., with Mary Grace Carpenter, *Tiffany Silver* (New York: Dodd, Mead and Company, 1978), 51.

8. Eric Stoehr, *Bonanza Victorian: Architecture and Society in Colorado Mining Towns* (Albuquerque: University of New Mexico Press, 1975), 10.

9. Kingston Heath, "False-Front Architecture on Montana's Urban Frontier," in *Images of an American Land,* ed. Thomas Carter (Albuquerque: University of New Mexico Press, 1997), 22.

10. J. Ross Browne, *A Peep at Washoe and Washoe Revisited* (1863; reprint, Balboa, Calif.: Paisano Press, 1959), 181.

11. Hubert Howe Bancroft, *History of Nevada, Colorado and Wyoming, 1540–1888* (San Francisco: The History Company, 1890), 224; Michael W. Bowers, *The Sagebrush State: Nevada's History, Government, and Politics* (Reno: University of Nevada Press, 1996), 21–22.

12. Elliott, *History of Nevada,* 405.

13. Russell R. Elliott, *Nevada's Twentieth-Century Mining Boom: Tonopah, Goldfield, Ely* (Reno: University of Nevada Press, 1966), 228–31.

14. Robert D. McCracken, *A History of Beatty, Nevada* (Tonopah, Nev.: Nye County Press, 1996), 154.

15. Nevada Division of Mines, *Major Mines of Nevada 1996* (Carson City: Nevada Division of Mines, 1997), 23.

16. James W. Hulse, *The Silver State: Nevada's History Reinterpreted* (Reno: University of Nevada Press, 1991), 114.

17. Ibid., 180.

18. John Radzilowski, "Same Town, Different Name," *Invention and Technology* 10:3 (winter 1995): 20–21; H. Roger Grant and Charles W. Bohi, *The Country Railroad Station in America* (Boulder, Colo.: Pruett Publishing Company, 1978), 1–3.

19. John R. Stilgoe, *The Metropolitan Corridor: Railroads and the American Scene* (New Haven: Yale University Press, 1983), 193; John F. Stover, *The Life and Decline of the American Railroad* (New York: Oxford University Press, 1970), 98.

20. Grant and Bohi, *Country Railroad Station,* 22–23; Janet Greenstein Potter, *Great American Railroad Stations* (New York: John Wiley and Sons, 1996), 23.

21. Richard Adkins, *Steel Rails, Desert Vistas: Nevada Railroad Resources* (Carson City: Division of Historic Preservation and Archeology, 1992), 10.

22. Elliott, *History of Nevada,* 116.

23. Terry G. Jordan, *North American Cattle-Ranching Frontiers: Origins, Diffusion, and Differentiation* (Albuquerque: University of New Mexico Press, 1993), 247.

24. Elliott, *History of Nevada,* 121.

25. Howard W. Marshall and Richard E. Ahlborn, *Buckaroos in Paradise: Cowboy Life in Northern Nevada,* exh. cat. (Lincoln: University of Nebraska Press, 1981), 25.

26. William A. Douglass, "Basque-American Identity: Past Perspectives and Future Prospects," in *Change in the American West: Exploring the Human Dimension,* ed. Stephen Tchudi (Reno: University of Nevada Press, 1996), 184.

27. William A. Douglass, "Basques in Nevada," in *Towns and Tales, Vol. I—North* (Las Vegas: Nevada Publications, 1981), 64.

28. Andrea Graham and Blanton Owen, *Lander County Line: Folklife in Central Nevada* (Reno: Nevada State Council on the Arts, 1988), 20.

29. Elliott, *History of Nevada,* 290.

30. Ronald M. James, *Temples of Justice: County Courthouses of Nevada* (Reno: University of Nevada Press, 1994), 161.

31. Bowers, *Sagebrush State,* 20.
32. The first widespread effort was the much publicized Sagebrush Rebellion of the 1970s, which began with Elko County livestock owners who were angry at increased regulation by the Bureau of Land Management to control overgrazing and pollution on federal land. Though the rebellion failed, Nevadans in Nye County renewed the effort in the 1990s, attempting to gain control of public land within the county's borders. See Bowers, *Sagebrush State,* 118.
33. William D. Rowley, *Reclaiming the Arid West: The Career of Francis G. Newlands* (Bloomington: Indiana University Press, 1996), 103.
34. Eugene P. Moehring, "Public Works and the New Deal in Las Vegas, 1933–1940," *Nevada Historical Society Quarterly* 24:2 (summer 1981): 107.
35. Ibid., 107.
36. A. Costandina Titus, *Bombs in the Backyard: Atomic Testing and American Politics* (Reno: University of Nevada Press, 1986), xiii.
37. Elliott, *History of Nevada,* 285.
38. Mella Harmon, "Divorce and Economic Opportunity in Reno, Nevada, during the Great Depression" (master's thesis, University of Nevada, Reno, 1998), 41–44.
39. John M. Findlay, *People of Chance: Gambling in American Society from Jamestown to Las Vegas* (New York: Oxford University Press, 1986), 119.
40. Ibid., 119.
41. William D. Rowley, *Reno: Hub of the Washoe County* (Woodland Hills, Calif.: Windsor Publications, 1984), 76–79.
42. Alan Hess, *Viva Las Vegas: After Hours Architecture* (San Francisco: Chronicle Books, 1993), 20.
43. Reyner Banham, *Los Angeles: The Architecture of Four Ecologies* (London: Penguin Books, 1971), 124; Alan Hess, *Googie: Fifties Coffee Shop Architecture* (San Francisco: Chronicle Books, 1985), 109.
44. Hess, *Viva,* 43.
45. Tom Wolfe, *The Kandy-Kolored Tangerine-Flake Streamline Baby* (New York: Farrar, Straus & Giroux, 1965), 8.
46. Robert Venturi, Denise Scott Brown, and Steven Izenour, *Learning from Las Vegas,* rev. ed. (Cambridge, Mass.: MIT Press, 1977), 87.
47. Elliott, *History of Nevada,* 313.
48. "Population Trends," Nevada Statistical Abstract, Nevada Department of Administration, prepared by Budget and Planning Division, updated 29 December 1999; cited at *http://www.state.nv.us/budget/sapop.htm*, 21 January 2000.
49. Ronald M. James, personal communication with author, 13 August 1998.
50. C. Mark Hamilton, *Nineteenth-Century Mormon Architecture and City Planning* (New York: Oxford University Press, 1995), 31.
51. Maurice J. Nespor and Hyde L. Flippo, "Architects in Nevada: A Brief History" (manuscript, 1997, photocopy), 1.
52. Ibid., 4–5.

Northwestern Region (NW)

Although northwestern Nevada covers a relatively small part of the state, centered in the Reno-Sparks–Carson City–Lake Tahoe metropolitan area, it has the greatest range of architectural styles and types. The Truckee and Carson rivers and the Comstock Lode in the valleys and mountain ranges directly east of the Sierra Nevada and Lake Tahoe attracted settlers, initially to farming and later to mining and government-funded projects. The northwestern region has the state's earliest Euro-American and Chinese communities—Genoa and Dayton.

Although the depression of the 1880s and 1890s severely hurt the region, the communities of Reno and Carson City gradually gained population. Carson City's designation as the center of state government and Reno's acquisition of the University of Nevada in 1885 ensured the survival of these towns. Tourism, attracted by gambling and the availability of quick divorces, boosted the economy in the early twentieth century. During the 1890s Reno became Nevada's largest city but lost its lead to Goldfield for a brief period in the first decade of the twentieth century. By 1910 Reno was again the largest city, with a population of 10,687. The prominent role of state and federal government in the area supported the construction of large public buildings that represented, and often still represent, the best examples of Nevada's architecture.

The region's wealth supported much private construction of dwellings, churches, and commercial buildings. The concentration of building in this part of the state provided work for many of Nevada's professional architects in the early twentieth century. More fine buildings covering a range of architectural styles and periods can be found in this region than in any other part of the state. The greatest concentration is in Reno.

The tradition of vernacular building remained strong until recently. For over a century the region's low population and remoteness required builders to use their ingenuity when employing materials and styles for their structures. With the latest economic boom, however, people looking for inexpensive but functional buildings have turned frequently to prefabri-

Northwestern Region

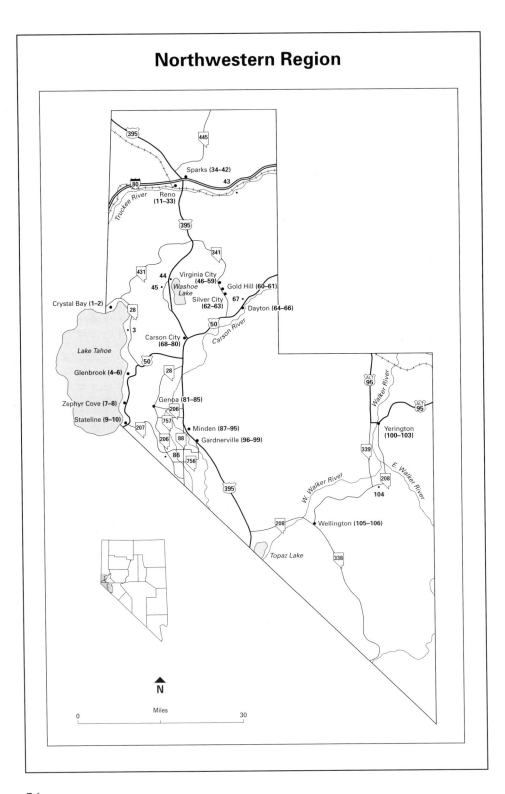

395
445
Sparks (34–42)
43
80
Truckee River
Reno (11–33)
395
341
431
44
Virginia City (46–59)
45
Washoe Lake
Gold Hill (60–61)
Silver City (62–63)
67
Crystal Bay (1–2)
28
Dayton (64–66)
3
50
Carson City (68–80)
Carson River
Lake Tahoe
50
Glenbrook (4–6)
28
Walker River
ALT 95
Genoa (81–85)
Zephyr Cove (7–8)
206
ALT 95
Stateline (9–10)
757
207
Minden (87–95)
Yerington (100–103)
206
88
Gardnerville (96–99)
339
86
756
E. Walker River
395
208
104
W. Walker River
208
Wellington (105–106)
Topaz Lake
338

N

0   Miles   30

cated buildings for commercial and residential use. Despite the urban nature of Reno and the surrounding area, northwestern Nevada has many farming and ranching communities dating back to the nineteenth century. Agriculture, concentrated in Carson, Mason, and Smith valleys, has given rise to a variety of vernacular buildings, including barns, bunkhouses, and stables that embody Nevada's rural way of life.

In the second half of the twentieth century northwestern Nevada's preeminence was eclipsed by Las Vegas and southern Nevada, which have become dominant economically, politically, and culturally. As more public and private money is spent in southern Nevada, this shift is reflected in the contemporary architecture of the two regions. With many more architecture firms and more visible commissions, Las Vegas attracts nationally known architects to participate in projects there more often than is the case in northern Nevada. This activity does not always ensure high quality, but it has encouraged a progressive attitude toward architecture and a willingness to experiment not seen in northwestern Nevada. With few exceptions, northern Nevada has become a region of unadventurous conservatism, neither preserving the past nor taking any risks designing for the future.

Crystal Bay

Crystal Bay, on the north shore of Lake Tahoe, experienced slower development than other points along the lake because only narrow, winding roads lead to it from California. Nevertheless, in the late 1920s residential subdivisions brought more people to the area. With the completion of the road around the lake in 1931 and the construction of resorts, Crystal Bay became a popular destination for Californians and Nevadans.

The first lodge erected here was the Cal-Neva in 1927. By the 1950s seven casino-resorts had been built as close to the state line as possible. Today the winding two-lane road leading to Crystal Bay still deters some visitors who prefer driving to the larger and more accessible Stateline–South Lake Tahoe area.

NW001 Cal-Neva Hotel and Casino
(Cal-Neva Lodge)

1937, many additions. 2 Stateline Rd., south of NV 28

Real estate developer Norman Henry Blitz built the first Cal-Neva in 1927 to house prospective clients for his nearby subdivisions. By the early 1930s the rustic lodge had become a popular resort. This building burned down in 1937 and was replaced by the present structure that same year. Over the decades, owners have altered the lodge, notably by the addition of a nine-story tower at the lake, but the original front portion of the complex, with its stone and timber peaked-roof entrance, retains some original features, including the Indian Room and the casino. The Indian Room has a cathe-dral ceiling with exposed beams and a huge stone fireplace. Across the entryway, the casino also suggests a lodge with its vaulted ceiling with heavy wood beams. The building actually straddles the border between Nevada and California; a line extending down the middle of the Indian Room, through the fireplace, and then through the middle of the swimming pool outside marks the boundary between the two states. The latest owner reduced the size of the casino by 30 percent to restore the ambience of the original lodge—a rare event in Nevada, where casinos generally increase in size.

NW002 **Border House Brewing Company**
(Cal-Vada Lodge Hotel)
1935, 1997. South side of NV 28 at Stateline Road

This bungalow, once part of the luxurious Cal-Vada Lodge (1927), is one of the few surviving structures from the early days of Crystal Bay's development as a resort. The building expresses its Craftsman roots in the porches, shingled walls, and clipped gable roofs. The old hotel was vacant for many years, but new owners recently converted it into a brew pub, adding a small extension to the north to contain brewing equipment but otherwise retaining the spirit of the original structure.

Sand Harbor Vicinity

NW003 **Whittell Estate**
1936–1941. 5000 NV 28, 2 miles south of Sand Harbor. Visible from the water

This was the last of the large private landholdings on the eastern shore of Lake Tahoe. Now covering 143 acres and nearly one mile of the shoreline, the estate encompassed more than 35,000 acres after George B. Whittell, Jr., heir to a San Francisco banking and railroad fortune, purchased several large parcels of land in the 1930s. For a time he controlled eighteen miles of shoreline from Crystal Bay to Zephyr Cove. Most of that land is now part of Lake Tahoe State Park.

In 1936 Whittell hired Frederick J. DeLongchamps to design the seven major buildings of the Thunderbird Lodge, as the owner called it. Stonemasons, including Paiute and Washoe craftsmen trained at Carson City's Stewart Indian School, erected the granite Tudor Revival buildings on a wooded hillside facing the lake. All the structures have steeply pitched, bell-shaped, side-gabled roofs covered with wood shingles, tall end chimneys, and ornamentation of hand-wrought iron. Much of the ironwork depicts wildlife found around the lake. The grounds have been left natural except around the main house, where stone terraces, paths, and fountains cascade to a small cove. Other features include a large man-made waterfall, a lighthouse, a gazebo, and a dollhouse. The landscaping seems to have been of Whittell's design—a whimsical fantasy played out in stone.

At the end of 1997 the American Land Conservancy negotiated an agreement between the property's owner, the Del Webb Corporation; the federal government; and the University of Nevada, Reno. By selling public land in southern Nevada to developers, the federal government was able to purchase the estate, and the university purchased the buildings to use as a research and conference center. Thus the eastern shore of Lake Tahoe has gained 143 more acres of public land, protecting it from private development and preserving the Thunderbird.

NW003.1 **Gatehouse**
1938, Frederick J. DeLongchamps

Beside the drive up the hill from Nevada 28 is the one-story gatekeeper's house, a miniature version of the main house. A front-facing gabled section contains an arched opening for the main entrance, which is flanked by iron lanterns. Small casement windows with diamond-shaped panes are at either side. Flat wrought iron deer decorate the chimneys. A wrought iron entry gate connects with the south side of the house.

NW003.2 Caretaker's House

1938, Frederick J. DeLongchamps

This one-and-one-half-story house has a partially exposed basement. The bell-shaped roof eaves hang low on the front and rear walls, nearly hiding the single-light casement windows. The building stands near another gate leading to the main house.

NW003.4 Whittell Estate, Main House

NW003.3 Garage (Elephant Barns)

1938, Frederick J. DeLongchamps

Whittell used this structure to house his elephants, which he kept at the estate as part of a menagerie of exotic animals to entertain himself and his guests. The spartan style and long, rectangular form of the garage set it apart from most of the other buildings on the estate. The one-story, flat-roofed stone building measures 18 by 50 feet and stands to the north of the main house. The west facade has three paneled metal double doors and irregular diagonal ends, one of whose randomly laid granite walls merges into a low stone wall along the driveway.

NW003.4 Main House

1938, Frederick J. DeLongchamps. 1985, Steven T. Sederquist

Winding down the hill toward the lake, the drive finally reaches the two-and-one-half-story main house, which combines elements of the Arts and Crafts and Tudor Revival styles. The random ashlar granite walls have thick mortar joints, enhancing the building's rustic appearance. A central gabled mass contains the recessed front entrance set in a round-arched opening. A wrought iron eagle with spread wings hovers above the entrance. Flanking this section are two massive stone chimneys with elaborately scrolled hand-wrought ironwork. Four blank gabled dormers are squeezed behind the chimneys and between them and the entrance bay. Two additional stone chimneys

rise along the gable ends of the house, and diamond-pane windows puncture the thick walls.

The interior has a large two-and-one-half-story living room with king-post trusses and 26-foot-long beams. A balcony with a balustrade of jigsawn wood boards extends around three sides of the room. On the fourth wall, a staircase leads to the balcony and second floor.

A two-story, wood-frame addition of 1985 doubled the size of the house, but its rooflines and massing are sympathetic to the original structure. Otherwise, the house and the rest of the estate are much the same as DeLongchamps's design. Located on a neck of land jutting into the lake, the house is clearly the focal point of the estate.

NW003.5 Card House

1938, Frederick J. DeLongchamps

Whittell built this structure as a clubhouse where he and his guests could play games late into the night. It stands about 200 feet east of the main house, overlooking a small cove below and the lake beyond. Paired curved side stairs with low stone walls lead to a large stone landing and patio in front of the house. As on the main house, an iron eagle marks the front entrance. An arched entry under the landing gives access to the tunnel running between the nearby boathouse and the main house. The original boathouse is built into the hillside under the terraces between the main house and card house. After Whittell bought a larger boat, he constructed another boathouse, located beyond the card house and its small cove.

Glenbrook

The area around Glenbrook was settled by Anglo-Americans in 1860, when prospectors traveled over the Sierra and around the southern end of Lake Tahoe on their way to the Comstock Lode. Entrepreneur Augustus Pray built the first sawmill here, exploiting the abundant forests to produce lumber for Virginia City and its surrounding mines. In 1862, with the completion of the Lake Bigler (Lake Tahoe) Toll Road (now U.S. 50) connecting Sacramento, South Lake Tahoe, Glenbrook, and Carson City, Glenbrook became an increasingly desirable location for hotels; both the Glen Brook House (no longer extant) and the Lake Shore House were erected in 1863.

In the late nineteenth century Duane L. Bliss brought an economic boom to the community by forming the Carson and Tahoe Lumber and Fluming Company. He connected Glenbrook by rail and flume to the eastern valleys, consuming the remaining timber in the area. The railroad carried logs to Spooner Summit, where a flume shot them down the mountain to a location just south of Carson City.

As logging quickly denuded the basin of trees, Bliss turned his attention to converting the milling complex at Glenbrook into a first-class resort. He established the Lake Tahoe Railway Transportation Company, which built a narrow-gauge railroad from Truckee to Tahoe City, California, in 1901. That same year he built the Tahoe Tavern, a luxury hotel, in Tahoe City. He launched several steamers to carry guests between the Tahoe Tavern and Glenbrook, where he built the Glenbrook Inn and Ranch Resort in 1906. Many small cabins soon followed to accommodate additional guests. An agricultural complex adjacent to a large meadow housed beef and dairy cattle and produced crops for the resort. The Glenbrook Inn remained in operation until 1975. Since then, private developers have converted the old estate into an exclusive residential resort community with a golf course and stunning lake views. Historic structures include the Lake Shore House, Jellerson House, Glenbrook Inn, a barn, and some cabins.

NW004 Lake Shore House

1863, 1906. 1960 Glenbrook Inn Rd.

One of the oldest remaining hotel buildings at Lake Tahoe, this wood-frame structure faces the lake along the original Glenbrook Road. The cornice returns, corner posts, and paneled window surrounds contribute to the eclectic Greek Revival and Italianate character of the building. Duane Bliss moved the structure a short distance to its present site when he built the Glenbrook Inn in 1906. The building functioned as a hotel until 1975, when it became part of Glenbrook Properties' development office. It now serves as a private vacation house.

NW005 Glenbrook Inn

1906, 1970s. Glenbrook Inn Rd., just north of the Lake Shore House

Unlike the Lake Shore House, the inn has no recognizable style. The two-story, wood-frame building, set slightly back from the road, became the anchor for the Glenbrook Inn and Ranch Resort. When built, the structure incorporated an old general merchandise store erected in 1877. Its long side faces the lake to take advantage of the view. A four-story, hip-roofed tower stands at the southwest corner. The success of the resort soon after its erection necessitated the addition of several bays at the inn's north end. Changes made during the 1970s include the enlargement of some of the second-story window openings, new chimneys, and the enclosure of the full-length front porch.

NW006 **Barn**

c. 1870. Glenbrook Rd., approximately .2 mile southeast of the Glenbrook Inn

One of the few agricultural buildings remaining in the Tahoe Basin, this large three-bay barn dominates the old ranch complex of the Glenbrook Inn and Ranch Resort. Oriented north-south to take advantage of winds off the lake, the barn has vertical board-and-batten walls that rise to broad gable ends with horizontal siding.

Zephyr Cove

Zephyr Cove was named after the Washoe Zephyr, the fierce westerly wind that occasionally torments the region. Anglo-Americans settled the area in 1862 about the time the Bigler Toll Road was constructed over Spooner Summit and down to Carson City. Like Glenbrook, Zephyr Cove and Marla Bay to the south were heavily logged during the late nineteenth century. Entrepreneurs built a few hotels during this time, but more extensive development did not occur until the 1920s. Since then, a popular resort and an exclusive subdivision have grown up along the shores of Lake Tahoe.

NW007 **Zephyr Cove Resort**

The resort encompasses about sixty acres of land between U.S. 50 and the lakeshore. Once part of George Whittell's estate, it is now owned by the U.S. Forest Service. Development began adjacent to the Lincoln Highway, which ran closer to the lake than does the current U.S. 50. The majority of buildings are small one-story cabins sited on paths leading toward the shore. The largest structure at the resort is the main lodge, which stands on the west side of U.S. 50.

The Bliss family's Carson and Tahoe Lumber and Fluming Company owned the land and in the late 1920s began to develop a resort. Individual one-room cabins had cedar bark siding and tar-paper roofs. Later structures had half-round pine siding to create a log cabin effect. Many of the original buildings have been demolished or moved, and new buildings have been erected, but the resort retains its rustic character with utilitarian but quaint cabins nestled among fir trees. Built to cater to middle-class vacationers, the resort continues to do so today.

NW007.1 **Lodge**

1931, early 1940s. 760 U.S. 50

The most prominent building at the resort is the wood-frame lodge, located just adjacent to the highway. Initially two stories tall with a gable roof and dormers, it was covered with half-round siding. After Whittell purchased the complex in 1937, he extended the lodge to the north, adding a hotel lobby, offices, kitchen, restaurant, and more guest rooms on the second floor. The building now measures 154 by 43 feet, with its long side parallel to the road. A one-story porch runs along most of the length of the facade. Irregular stones with raised mortar joints clad the wall under the porch. The restaurant in the north wing has numerous windows that take advantage of the lake view.

NW007.2 **Cabins 16–19**

1930–1931

These small identical buildings represent an early cabin form at the complex. One story tall, they have front-gabled roofs capping walls of manufactured half-round siding. Compared to later, larger cabins at Zephyr Cove, these seem spartan. Rear additions contain bathrooms and closets.

NW008 Zephyr Cove Subdivision

1920s–1930s

In 1925 Gertrude Church sold thirty acres of land to the Presbyterian Synod of California, which subsequently built the Zephyr Point Presbyterian Conference Center. A year later the first subdivision in Zephyr Cove was developed. The area still retains many houses from the early twentieth century, ranging from log cabins to large stone dwellings, set amid dense stands of pine trees. The high value of the lots, many of which have spectacular views of the lake, and late twentieth-century demand for more living space have encouraged property owners to enlarge or replace these structures. Many of them are still used only as vacation homes, but the increasing popularity of lakeshore dwellings as year-round residences also threatens the survival of smaller, older homes.

NW008.1 House

1926. 746 Lincoln Hwy. Not visible from the road

One of the original 1926 subdivision houses, this building stands on three lots facing the lake. Its shingled roof and first story made of square-cut logs typify the rustic look of vacation homes in this neighborhood. Wood shingles clad the upper story.

NW008.2 House

1927, Frederick Snyder? 684 Lake View Blvd. Not visible from the road

The summer home of Frederick Snyder, the first superintendent of the Stewart Indian School in Carson City, this building resembles many of the school's structures designed by Snyder. The T-shaped house has randomly laid walls of multicolored stone with dark gray mortar joints, metal casement windows, and wood-sided gable ends. James and John Christopher, stonemasons for the Stewart Indian School, constructed this dwelling, as well as two other houses in this subdivision in the same style (723 Cedar Street and 716 Lincoln Highway).

Stateline

Stateline stands right at the border of Nevada and California. It is difficult to say which side of the boundary is less attractive and more reflective of late twentieth-century throwaway American culture. Stateline's half-dozen high-rise casinos crowd the state line and sidewalks along the highway, exploiting as much of the available space as possible. South Lake Tahoe, California, is a banal strip with motels, shopping centers, fast-food restaurants, and gas stations lining the road for miles. There is rarely a season when this stretch of U.S. 50 is not clogged with cars, as the south shore area attracts skiers in the winter and boaters and campers in the summer. Residential areas are located on the mountainsides above the congestion.

NW009 Friday's Station

1860. 139 U.S. 50

Set on a large parcel of land, Friday's Station, the oldest surviving inn complex in this part of the Tahoe Basin, is now an anomaly in the glitter of Stateline. The property is surrounded by U.S. 50 and a golf course to the north, businesses to the east, and casinos to the west. To the south, undeveloped U.S. Forest Service land provides some relief from the congestion.

Martin K. "Friday" Burke and James Wash-

ington Small established a stage station on the site in March 1860 and a month later obtained a franchise to operate a Pony Express station there. The location had a natural spring and was on Kingsbury Grade, the new road leading from the lake down to Carson Valley. The station soon became a home base for a stage line and the Wells Fargo Express, which motivated the owners to build an inn. Although the Pony Express operated only eighteen months, the station had enough traffic to keep running until the opening of the Central Pacific Railroad in 1868. The station served as a resort in the late nineteenth century and is now a private residence.

NW009.1 Cabin

1860

This one-room log cabin was the first Pony Express station on the site. Logs meet at the corners in saddle-notched joints. The building has a gable roof with wood shingles, and vertical boards clad the gable ends.

NW009.2 Inn

1860

The inn's symmetrical exterior displays a frontier interpretation of the Greek Revival style, seen in the broad verandas and symmetrical facade and floor plan. Side lights and a cornice frame the central entrance. The eaves of the gable roof spread at the ends to cover full-length, two-story verandas front and back, articulated by square piers on each floor. The two-and-one-half-story, wood-frame building stands west of the log cabin.

NW010 Harvey's Casino

1970s, 1978, 1985, Stern Architectural Associates. Northwest corner of U.S. 50 and Stateline Rd.

The forerunner of this gleaming black glass-and-metal-clad 740-room hotel and casino—the largest on the lake—was a log cabin erected in 1944 by Harvey Gross as the south shore's first casino. The success of this venture after

NW010 Harvey's Casino

World War II coincided with increasing residential and commercial development around the lake. The casino gained notoriety in 1980, when an extortionist detonated a bomb that extensively damaged the hotel. Stern Architectural Associates of Beverly Hills, California, redesigned the complex, adding the seventeen-story Lake Tower. Martin Stern, Jr., firm principal, designed numerous hotels throughout Nevada but specialized in high-rise hotel-casinos. Metal-clad surfaces and reflective glass combined in boxy towers are typical of Stateline casinos, and Harvey's is no exception. Stern's use of zigzag angles for the hotel room windows in the Lake Tower takes advantage of the views and is similar to the motif he employed in the Riverside Hotel and Casino (1982–1983) in Laughlin, Nevada.

Reno

The second largest city in Nevada with a population of 165,940 (as of 1998), Reno sprawls across the Truckee Meadows, a fertile high-desert valley fed by the Truckee River just east of the Sierra Nevada range. The city started out as a small emigrant way station, the staging point for parties preparing to climb over the mountains. It was here that the Donner Party stopped briefly in October 1846 before embarking on its doomed crossing. Construction of the Central Pacific brought more traffic to Reno, and the completion of the Virginia and Truckee Railroad's line to the city in 1872 connected Reno to Carson City and the Comstock. Clustered around the railroad and along the Truckee River, the town's buildings were mostly wood-frame, with one or two stories and little architectural style or ornamentation. Numerous truck farms and ranches supplied nearby towns with agricultural products. The University of Nevada's move from Elko in 1885 established Reno—then a small town of a few thousand people—as an educational center in the state.

During this period Reno was also becoming a political center, drawing the rich and powerful from the fading mining towns of Tonopah and Goldfield. Influential people such as Senator Francis G. Newlands, Senator George Nixon, and financier George Wingfield built mansions near the downtown core. As the population of the city grew, Reno acquired political power that would not be eclipsed for half a century.

It was the divorce trade that brought a thriving economy during the 1930s. Until 1927, the residency requirement for a Nevada divorce was six months. The Washoe County Courthouse was the center of the burgeoning industry; the Riverside Hotel next door on the south bank of the Truckee River became known for offering the most desirable accommodations for those awaiting divorces. The legislature's reduction of the residency requirement in 1927 to three months and in 1931 to six weeks brought new surges in business.

The legalization of gambling in 1931 created an industry that surpassed even the divorce trade. Hotels, clubs, and bars quickly added casinos. Reno's downtown soon pulsed with neon lights and throngs of gamblers. By the 1940s Virginia Street had become the main thoroughfare, serving as the center of activity from its crossing of the Truckee to 9th Street. The railroad, passing through the center of downtown, disgorged tourists daily, and the completion of U.S. 40, which traveled along Reno's 4th Street, brought a steady stream of motorists.

By the 1950s, however, Las Vegas clearly posed stiff competition to its older, northern sister, and by 1960 it surpassed Reno in population. The popular Las Vegas Strip casinos and the already large and flourishing Los Angeles metropolitan area provided Las Vegas with a tourist base that Reno could not match. For thirty years after World War II, Reno had attempted to control the spread of gambling by restricting casinos to the downtown area. However, in 1971 the city threw out its redlining policy in order to compete with Las Vegas. New casinos quickly spread in all directions along Reno's main roads and highways, where sprawling complexes could be built based on the Las Vegas Strip model, surrounded by acres of parking lots. Recently some of Reno's downtown casinos, such as the Silver Legacy, have tried to compete with the Las Vegas mega-resorts by building enormous structures with diverse attractions and towering parking garages. Las Vegas, nevertheless, still far outpaces Reno in terms of growth and attracting tourists.

Like Las Vegas, Reno has grown at a rapid pace since the 1950s. Once bounded by vast stretches of open space, Reno now has subdivisions that are gradually covering the valley floor. Downtown has become the nearly exclusive domain of the casinos and is given over to tourists. Businesses and light industry have consequently grown along the freeways and on the edges of town, erasing the decades-old ranches. However, not all of them are gone; driving south or north of Reno, one can still spot an occasional collapsing barn or octagonal chicken coop—remnants of Reno's early days as an agricultural center.

Reno

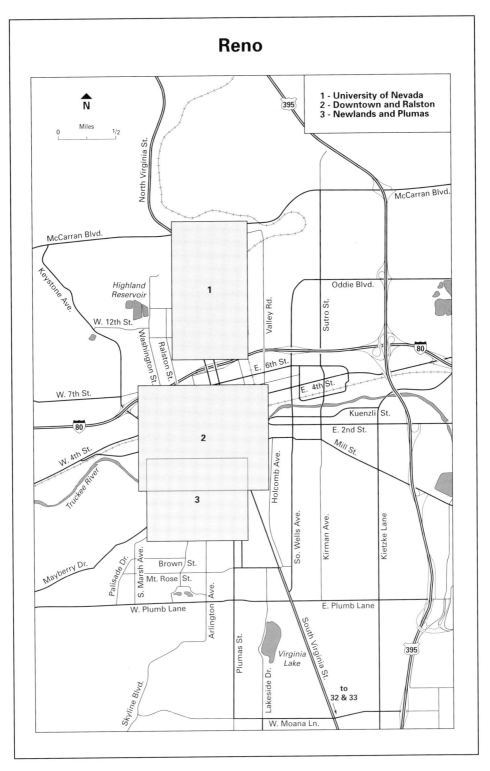

1 - University of Nevada
2 - Downtown and Ralston
3 - Newlands and Plumas

N

Miles
0   1/2

395

McCarran Blvd.

McCarran Blvd.

North Virginia St.

Keystone Ave.

Highland
Reservoir

Valley Rd.

Oddie Blvd.

Sutro St.

80

W. 12th St.

1

Washington St.

Ralston St.

E. 6th St.

E. 4th St.

W. 7th St.

Kuenzli St.

80

2

E. 2nd St.

Holcomb Ave.

Mill St.

W. 4th St.

Truckee River

3

So. Wells Ave.

Kirman Ave.

Kietzke Lane

Mayberry Dr.

Palisade Dr.

S. Marsh Ave.

Brown St.

Mt. Rose St.

Arlington Ave.

W. Plumb Lane

E. Plumb Lane

395

Plumas St.

Lakeside Dr.

Virginia
Lake

South Virginia St.

to
32 & 33

Skyline Blvd.

W. Moana Ln.

65

NW011   University of Nevada, Reno

1885, many additions. 9th and N. Virginia sts., roughly bounded by 9th St., N. Virginia St., N. McCarran Blvd., and Evans Ave.

The campus contains a historic district with buildings dating from the earliest period of academic development in the area. When the state government moved the university to Reno in 1885, it sited the campus on ten acres overlooking the Truckee Meadows, north of the Truckee River and the railroad. Both the university and the town expanded, the former purchasing surrounding land and the latter sprawling to the north until it finally met and then surrounded the campus. Throughout the nineteenth century, however, there was a clear division between town and university.

Morrill Hall dominated the early campus and maintains its prominent position on the historic quad. Although the university constructed several similar buildings over the course of its first decade in Reno, only Morrill Hall survives. Between 1894 and the turn of the century, the campus grew to eleven buildings and began to take shape.

Initially the campus lacked a cohesive plan, its scattered buildings tending to face Reno to the south. In 1906 Clarence Mackay, son of John Mackay, one of the Comstock's bonanza kings, commissioned the firm of McKim, Mead and White to design a school of mines and then develop a plan for the campus. William S. Richardson of the firm created a master plan as well as designs for the new school. With the Mackay School of Mines Building, the campus took a new direction, which included the creation of a central quadrangle between Morrill Hall and the Mackay School, complete with a program for landscaping. The plan arranged academic facilities along the sides of the quadrangle, facing the grassy, tree-lined open space bounded by brick walkways laid in a herringbone pattern. During the next quarter century much of the development of the campus followed a plan developed in 1908 by Bliss and Faville of San Francisco, architects who worked closely with the firm of McKim, Mead and White.

By the turn of the century the university had begun to build dormitories to the west of the campus, across the ravine created by a small creek. In 1911 the university dammed the creek's drainage system, creating Manzanita Lake, named for the oldest of the dormitories on its shores. Following the completion of the Mackay School of Mines, the university planted American elms along the quad, which, with other landscaping, soon produced a campus that was as striking for its trees and lush vegetation as it was for its buildings. American elms have fallen victim to disease throughout most of the nation, rendering the species nearly extinct. The remote nature of the Truckee Meadows, surrounded by desert, has inhibited the disease, preserving a type of landscaping that once was common in North America.

Between 1913 and 1930, the university undertook a building program directed by Frederick J. DeLongchamps, who designed thirty buildings for the campus. Several other architects contributed to the appearance of the university during those critical years of growth. Influenced by Beaux-Arts academicism, these brick structures bestowed on the campus an appearance of refined elegance.

Postwar construction has tended to extend the campus north. Occasionally new buildings called for the demolition of historic ones. Sev-

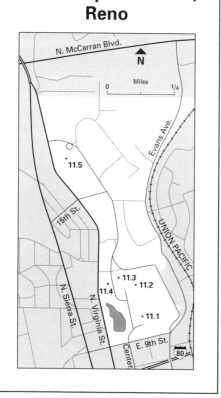

University of Nevada, Reno

eral buildings erected in the 1960s and 1970s stand on the site of the original Mackay Stadium to the north of the Mackay School of Mines. The turn-of-the-century Mechanical Arts Building on the quad fell into disuse, and in 1983 the university used this site for the new Paul Laxalt Mineral Research and Engineering Center. The Ross Business Building, replacing the old Chemistry Building on the quad, represents an intrusion of the International Style, not in keeping with the rest of the older campus.

Oddly enough, DeLongchamps is credited with the 1960s Scrugam Engineering Building, directly to the east of the Mackay School of Mines, but this International Style building is so uninspired, having been constructed late in DeLongchamps's life, that it was probably the product of his firm rather than of the principal architect. Since a flurry of construction in the 1960s featuring adaptations of the International Style, the university has returned to more classically inspired designs executed in brick. Many of the new buildings thus harmonize with the older campus.

NW011.1 **Morrill Hall**

1886, John M. Curtis

This four-story brick structure in the Second Empire style stands at the head of the university's historic quad. Its front entrance, however, faces south, away from the quad, reflecting the original orientation of the campus. The mansard roof has numerous pedimented dormers and is capped by a cupola with pointed arches and a cornice with dentils. A bracketed cornice lines the roof eaves, and brick quoins finish the corners. The interior incorporates accents in dark wood and wainscot in grained bird's-eye maple.

Morrill Hall was the university's only building during its first few years in Reno, providing space for classes, administration, and dormitories. By the mid-twentieth century it fell into disuse and disrepair. Using state grants, the university restored the hall, which now contains general meeting space and offices for the alumni association and the University of Nevada Press.

NW011.2 **Mackay School of Mines**

1906–1908, William S. Richardson, McKim, Mead and White. 1926, Frederick J. DeLongchamps

The only building in Nevada designed by the New York firm of McKim, Mead and White, the Mackay School of Mines is both architecturally and historically significant. Clarence Mackay built the school as a tribute to the life and career of his father, John Mackay, an Irish miner who found great success as one of the Comstock's four bonanza kings. In 1906 the son hired Gutzon Borglum, who later carved Mt. Rushmore, to erect a bronze statue of his father in front of the building. Located at the north end of the quad, the school and its statue provide a balance for Morrill Hall at the other end. These two anchors give the older campus its distinctive appearance.

The two-story brick building, with Georgian details, has a monumental pedimented stone portico supported by Tuscan columns. White tile in a herringbone pattern lines the portico's ceiling. Double oak doors open to a lateral hallway. The original U-shaped plan included one-story wings projecting from the front core of the building. In 1926 DeLongchamps's remodeling left the front section intact but modified the rear, adding a second story to the wings and filling in the central atrium. The new design included a second-story lightwell immediately behind the front section, providing light for the windows in the original building. DeLongchamps enlarged a mineral museum in the western wing, giving it a dramatic open, two-story space with a surrounding balcony, oak cabinets and balustrade. Overall, he executed the design around existing details so that the modifications did not compromise the original plan.

NW011.3 **Noble H. Getchell Library**

1962, Robert Alexander and David Vhay. 1977, David Vhay and George Ferrari

The third library built on the campus is located northwest of the quad. Robert Alexander of Los Angeles and David Vhay of Reno designed the modernist structure with a two-story entrance featuring floor-to-ceiling windows. A zigzag roofline of boomerangs, created by concrete folded plates, caps the structure and extends along the cover of the ramped walkway stretching to the east. Square piers, clad in highly polished red granite panels, support the roof, which projects over the main entrance. In the late 1970s the university attached a large black glass unornamented boxlike structure to the north elevation of the library, maintaining

NW011.1 Morrill Hall

NW011.2 Mackay School of Mines (above, left)

NW011.3 Noble H. Getchell Library (above, right)

NW011.5 Fleischmann Planetarium (right)

its roofline. This more than doubled the size of the library, also providing space for the growing collection in four underground levels.

NW011.4 Lincoln Hall

1896, Percy and Hamilton

Designed by a San Francisco firm, the two-and-one-half-story brick structure is adapted from several styles popular at the time and used for dormitories on eastern campuses. The whimsical design includes a long gable roof with gable wings crossing both ends, brick chimneys, Flemish gables along the parapet, and a central cupola in the Colonial Revival style. Rusticated granite accent blocks surrounding the entrance and rounded arches supporting the porch hint at the Neo-Romanesque. In the 1980s Lincoln Hall, originally a dormitory, became the center of the university honors program, providing rooms for participating students and space for related administrative offices.

NW011.5 Fleischmann Planetarium

1963, Raymond Hellmann. N. Virginia St.

Set into a hillside at the north end of campus, the Fleischmann Planetarium takes advantage of the slope with 40-foot-tall windows on its south facade. The showpiece of the planetarium is its butterfly roof—an 11,000-square-foot, concrete-shelled hyperbolic paraboloid supported at only two points although weighing 180 tons. The combination of a paraboloid longitudinal section and a hyperbolic cross section gives the roof its distinctive butterfly shape. The large open space created by its span contains a planetarium designed to give the viewer a sense of being inside a sphere. The window wall on the south facade floods this space with daylight, and at night the building glows when lit from the inside.

Downtown

Reno's urban core begins where Virginia Street crosses the Truckee River. In the 1860s this was the site of the Truckee Meadows' first bridge and a toll road to Virginia City, known as the Sierra Valley Road (Virginia Street). Myron Lake operated the bridge and toll-road franchise, and when the Central Pacific arrived, he donated sixty acres as a townsite, creating Reno. For several decades during the twentieth century, Reno's downtown prospered not only as a mecca for gambling and the divorce trade but also as a center for government and a variety of businesses. Several historically and architecturally significant structures stand at this intersection: the Reno Downtown Post Office, the Riverside Hotel, and the Washoe County Courthouse. Since the 1930s, however, casino interests have dominated downtown. Most of the area's businesses now cater to tourists who have come to Reno specifically to gamble rather than to local residents who seek a variety of services and entertainment. As casinos have become larger and parking has become more of a problem, many of Reno's historic structures have fallen under the wrecking ball, replaced by garish, multistory parking garages. The city's efforts to revitalize downtown with a riverside walk have proved somewhat successful in that the area offers space for cultural festivals, but much of the time downtown Reno's streets are devoid of pedestrians.

NW012 Bruce R. Thompson U.S. Courthouse and Federal Building

1994–1996, Casazza, Peetz, and Hancock. 400 S. Virginia St.

Part of a nationwide program to build new federal courthouses to keep up with increasing case loads in rapidly growing regions, this courthouse and federal building should have been one of the significant public architecture projects in Reno in the 1990s. Casazza, Peetz, and Hancock, a local architecture firm, won the commission to design a 197,000-square-foot, ten-story structure. Covering most of a city block, the building has a concave main facade, the recession providing some space between the entrance and Virginia Street. Granite clads the tower, contrasting with tiers of reflective glass windows. An unembellished two-story rotunda, supported by paired attenuated columns and centered on the west facade, projects to form the main entrance. The interior contains ten courtrooms, judges' chambers, libraries, and offices. Though the building's size is impressive, its office-tower appearance represents a missed opportunity to design a federal courthouse that reflects its function and responds to the surrounding buildings.

NW013 Washoe County Courthouse

1909–1911, Frederick J. DeLongchamps. 1946, 1949, 1963, Frederick J. DeLongchamps and George L. F. O'Brien. 117 S. Virginia St.

The Washoe County Courthouse was DeLongchamps's first major commission. In 1909 the county selected his plans in a competition, giving him a distinction that initiated a remarkable career. DeLongchamps went on to design six more county courthouses in Nevada, each stylistically indebted to Beaux-Arts classicism, although they show a steady move toward simplicity that culminates in the elegant lines of the Pershing County Courthouse.

The courthouse in Reno has clearly articulated components, strong Corinthian columns, and an ornate entablature. A sweeping staircase leads to the two-story Corinthian portico and a pair of paneled metal doors. Wide Doric pilasters flank windows with terra-cotta surrounds including bracketed pediments on the first floor and square moldings with keystones on the second. A large copper ribbed dome, rising from a stone drum embellished by pedimented dormers, crowns the building. Inside, DeLongchamps called for ornate metal balustrades, gray marble wainscot, pilasters with black marble bases, and multicolored tile

floors. The ceiling of the second-floor hallway has a shallow dome of colored, leaded glass that reveals the light from the dome above.

DeLongchamps's ability to create appealing buildings kept his practice active until his retirement in 1965, and the long span of his career gave him the unusual opportunity to add to buildings he had designed decades earlier. In the 1940s his firm designed matching wings for the courthouse and, in 1963, an addition to the rear in a modernist style that contrasts dramatically with the early twentieth-century building.

NW014 Riverside Hotel

1926–1927, 1931, Frederick J. DeLongchamps. 1950–1951, Frederick J. DeLongchamps and Frank W. Green. 17 S. Virginia St.

George Wingfield, one of Nevada's most prominent early twentieth-century financial figures, built the Riverside Hotel next to the county courthouse to accommodate people seeking divorces. Having made his money during the Tonopah and Goldfield booms, Wingfield turned his attention to other aspects of Nevada's economy. Viewing the divorce industry as a potential gold mine, he successfully lobbied the state legislature in 1927 to reduce the residency requirement from six to three months.

The six-story brick building has simplified Gothic details in cream terra-cotta, such as pointed-arched windows on the sixth floor, traceried parapets, and stacked bay windows embellished with panels and quoins. Although much of the rest of the exterior remains intact, the original storefronts at street level were bricked in during alterations in 1950–1951 to allow expansion of the main casino. The interior was virtually gutted after the legalization of gambling in 1931 fostered installation of the casino. In the 1950s DeLongchamps and his partner at that time, Frank W. Green, designed a large casino-restaurant-theater wing (demolished 1997) to the west of the original T-shaped structure. After standing vacant for several years and nearly being demolished, the Riverside was rehabilitated in 1999–2000 to accommodate retail space on the ground floor and artists' studios on the upper floors. This adaptive reuse project may signal a shift in the city's attitude toward preserving its historic buildings.

Reno — Downtown and Ralston

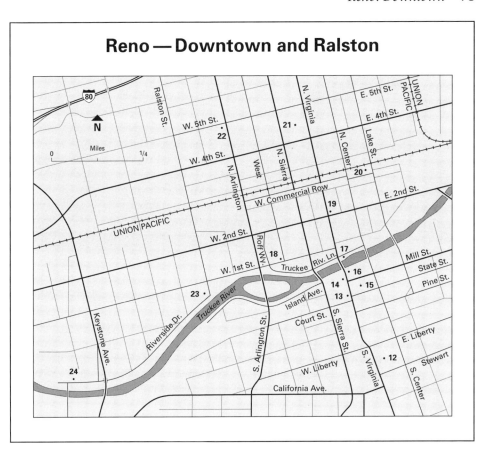

NW015 Pioneer Center for the Performing Arts

1966–1967, Bozalis, Dickinson, and Roloff. 100 S. Virginia St.

The Pioneer Center replaced a structure erected in 1926 as the "permanent" home of the Nevada Historical Society. The geodesic-domed center dominates the concrete and brick plaza lying immediately to its west. From the front, the building evokes a bird that has swooped down to the ground with its wings spread. The firm of Bozalis, Dickinson, and Roloff of Oklahoma City designed the dome, using the technololgical principles established by R. Buckminster Fuller for a lightweight but strong structure. The gold anodized aluminum roof, 140 feet in diameter, rests on five post-tensioned concrete arches. TEMCOR, a company in Torrance, California, fabricated and erected the roof, which consists of 500 faceted panels

supported by an interior steel-frame dome. The center's 1,428-seat theater provides a venue for most of northern Nevada's performing arts groups, as well as for traveling shows.

Washoe County's selection of the geodesic dome design displayed a conscious attempt by government leaders to build public structures that presented Reno as a modern, progressive city. At this time, other cities were also choosing the geodesic dome for public buildings, not only as a symbol of scientific and cultural progress but also because the structures were relatively inexpensive to erect.

NW016 Reno Downtown Post Office

1931–1934, Frederick J. DeLongchamps. 50 S. Virginia St.

Built as a combined post office and federal building containing offices for federal agen-

NW016 Reno Downtown Post Office, interior detail and exterior

cies, Reno's downtown post office stands across Virginia Street from two of its architect's other projects. DeLongchamps favored Beaux-Arts classical designs, but his use of Art Deco here demonstrates his willingness to modernize his work. Light green terra-cotta tiles, dark green terra-cotta spandrels, and aluminum-frame recessed windows and entrances contribute to the building's modern look. A broad fretwork band between the second and third floors provides horizontal emphasis, balanced by tall, fluted terra-cotta pilasters separating the first- and second-floor windows. Stylized bas-relief eagles embellish the roofline of each end projection, clearly denoting the structure as federal.

The Art Deco style continues in the lobby, with black marble walls inset with aluminum medallions, terrazzo floors, and geometric aluminum moldings. The interior is remarkably intact for a post office building; even the original marble and aluminum writing tables remain in use. In 1975 a new main post office, constructed two miles south, replaced the central function of this building, but it continues to operate as Reno's downtown postal center.

NW017 Mapes Hotel and Casino

1946–1947, F. H. Slocombe. 2000, demolished. 10 N. Virginia St.

For many years the Mapes flourished as "the place to be" in Reno. The first high-rise hotel and casino built in the United States, it became the prototype for later casinos in Reno, Las Vegas, and Atlantic City. Until the city of Reno imploded it on Super Bowl Sunday in January 2000, the twelve-story hotel occupied a prominent site in downtown Reno along Virginia Street and the Truckee River. Once the tallest building in Nevada, the Mapes in its later years was dwarfed by large, boxy office towers and casinos looming just to the north.

At its two-story base, the Mapes had large plate glass storefront windows and entrances surrounded by decorative terra-cotta. Above, the L-shaped reinforced concrete structure accommodated eight floors of guest quarters, a service floor, and a crowning sky room with floor-to-ceiling windows overlooking the Truckee River and Virginia Street. Curved, four-part window bays projected from three corners of the building, as well as from the center of the facades. The windows themselves, short, double-hung, and aluminum-framed, were characteristic of Art Deco. A zigzag brick cornice in high relief emphasized the verticality of the hotel, as did finials placed at intervals along the cornice.

F. H. Slocombe designed the building in the late 1930s, but World War II prevented construction until 1946–1947. The Mapes had been one of only three remaining large Art Deco buildings in Reno; the other two are the Reno Post Office and the El Cortez Hotel (1931). Of the three, the Mapes was the largest.

Patrons valued the hotel's size and modern simplicity. Hollywood also favored the Mapes; it appeared in numerous films, including *The Misfits* and *Desert Hearts*. Yet, as the casino industry matured, other characteristics, such as large, gaudy, and glittery interiors with little or no natural light, became popular with casino moguls. By today's standards, the Mapes was considered too small to be profitable. The hotel closed in 1982. Despite the interest of numerous potential buyers who proposed mixed uses, and its inclusion on the National Trust for Historic Preservation's list of the Eleven Most Endangered Places of 1998, the Mapes remained empty. Although the city has witnessed some preservation successes in recent years, the loss of the Mapes (the only structure on the National Trust's Most Endangered list to be demolished) bespeaks the city's continued lack of commitment to integrating preservation of historic structures into the planning process.

NW018 First United Methodist Church

1925–1926, Wythe, Blaine, and Olson. Northwest corner of W. 1st and West sts.

Designed by an architecture firm from Oakland, California, this Neo-Gothic church is unusual for Reno in that it is an early example of a poured-in-place concrete structure. Buttresses and pointed arches framing narrow round- and pointed-arched windows emphasize the verticality of the three-story church, as does the central bell tower. The main entrance, facing West 1st Street, is located in a recessed arched opening flanked by engaged Corinthian columns.

The exterior reflects the single-nave plan within the building and is loosely based on late nineteenth-century English churches and their American versions.

NW019 Planet Hollywood (Reno National Bank)

1915, Frederick J. DeLongchamps. 204 N. Virginia St.

This Beaux-Arts structure, its formality characteristic of much of DeLongchamps's early work, was the architect's first commission for George Wingfield. He used malleable terracotta to great decorative effect in reliefs high on the walls. The west facade has a double-height portico with Ionic columns, whereas the south wall has two-story Ionic pilasters because there was insufficient space for columns.

Wingfield used the building as headquarters for his statewide chain of twelve banks, from which he made extensive loans to support Nevada's livestock industry. However, the Great Depression led to the bank's collapse in 1932, followed by Wingfield's bankruptcy three years later. The building housed various banks until the early 1990s, when it was converted into a restaurant, part of the Planet Hollywood chain. Though the exterior remains largely intact, garish pink-and-green-striped awnings over the

NW017 Mapes Hotel and Casino

windows and palm fronds topping the Ionic columns somewhat obscure the building's classic lines.

NW020 Amtrak Depot (Southern Pacific Railroad Depot)

1925–1927, Southern Pacific Railroad. 135 E. Commercial Row

The current depot is the fourth to stand on the site; the Central Pacific built the first in 1869. This building served both the Southern Pacific and the Virginia and Truckee (V&T) passenger lines and now serves Amtrak's trains. Once a focal point of downtown Reno for thousands of arriving and departing tourists and divorce seekers, the depot has become a quiet place since the rise of the automobile. It stands parallel to the tracks, overshadowed by large structures, including a casino parking garage to the south and the National Bowling Stadium to the north. Neglect has caused the structure to deteriorate, but it remains in nearly original condition. Five large arches on the main facade contain windows and entry doors. Inside is a large waiting room with a 24-foot-high ceiling with exposed beams. The four large bowl-shaped lamps hanging from long chains, as well as the exterior fixtures, are original to the depot.

NW021 Silver Legacy

1994–1995, Mitchell Cohan. 407 N. Virginia St.

With the construction of the Silver Legacy, a joint venture of Reno's Circus Circus and the Eldorado Casino, the city finally acquired a Las Vegas–style mega-resort. The structure, designed by a Reno architect, covers two city blocks fronting Virginia Street, sandwiched between the Eldorado and Circus Circus. The

NW020 Amtrak Depot (Southern Pacific Railroad Depot) (left)

NW021 Silver Legacy (below)

casino's three-wing hotel tower—a common feature of contemporary Las Vegas casinos—rises next to the flat casino base, which supports a 200-foot-high dome framed by the two sections of the tower. During construction the owners switched the theme of the casino from sixteenth-century seaside port to nineteenth-century western mining town. The change mattered little, since the dome could accommodate either program. The casino's street-level exterior mimics a vaguely western Main Street, but does so in a colorful, self-conscious fashion that underscores the function of the buildings as false fronts for the casino within.

Skyways connect the Silver Legacy to its multistory parking garage to the west and to the Eldorado and Circus Circus casinos. Not just narrow walkways, these structures cover the entire street block and contain additional floor space for the hotel lobby and restaurants. They also serve to superimpose mega-resort scale on the existing old-fashioned urban grid of downtown Reno. The skyways have had a devastating effect on the streets below, turning them into dark, uncomfortable tunnels for pedestrians. Unfortunately other casino owners have easily persuaded the city to let them build their own skyways, destroying the streetscape below and privatizing increasing amounts of downtown space.

The dome is the most unusual aspect of the complex. It shelters the two-story casino, whose focal point is a towering headframe that "mines" coins and sends them to the "mill," a structure housing the cashier's cage. Lights transform the dome's ceiling into a stormy sky, and an occasional bolt of thunder strikes the top of the headframe, making a crash that barely startles the gamblers, who remain enthralled by the blackjack tables and slot machines below.

Ralston Neighborhood

This area west of downtown and north of the Truckee River is home to a variety of building styles and types. Divided by the Union Pacific Railroad, Ralston has a northern section historically characterized by industrial use and now given over to commercial and residential functions. The southern section, near the Truckee River, is more densely built up and has many houses converted to offices, as well as apartments, schools, and churches.

NW022 Humphrey House

1906, Fred M. Schadler. 467 Ralston St.

Designed by a local architect, the Humphrey House is a rare example of a Mission Revival residence in Reno. It combines such standard Mission Revival elements as stuccoed walls, curved roof parapets outlined by raised bands, and porches supported by squat paired columns. Other features include oriel windows resting on large carved brackets and small wood balconies with turned balustrades. The Humphrey family resided in the house until the 1960s, after which it was used as retail space. It is now in run-down condition.

NW023 **Lear Theater** (First Church of Christ, Scientist)

1938, Paul Revere Williams. 501 Riverside Dr.

Paul Revere Williams, the best-known African American architect in Los Angeles, designed this church during the height of the Colonial Revival in the 1930s. The church has a dramatic, rather theatrical entrance under a two-story portico, approached by twin curving stairs with flanking urns. The portico shelters three entrance doors, the central one marked by a pediment. Adamesque as well as Colonial Revival influences can be seen in the extremely attenuated Doric columns and the decorative detailing of the pediment.

Williams's Los Angeles commissions include the Theme Building at Los Angeles International Airport (designed with Pereira and Luckman and Welton Becket and Associates) and numerous mansions for movie stars and businessmen. He also designed a residence (589–599 California Avenue) in Reno's Newlands neighborhood and the Loomis Manor Apartments (see next entry).

The Reno-Sparks Theater Coalition, which acquired the church in 1998, plans to convert it to a theater as soon as funds for the renovation have been raised. The coalition expects more than thirty-five groups to use the facility for performances, workshops, and classes.

NW024 Loomis Manor Apartments

1939, Paul Revere Williams. 1045 Riverside Dr.

As a result of his design for Reno's First Church of Christ, Scientist, Williams received a commission for this building, which is dramatically different from the church. While in Reno working on the church, he met Anna Frandsen Loomis, who was impressed with his architectural skills and asked him to design an apartment building on the site of her home. Williams created a white, U-shaped complex facing the Truckee River. On smooth stuccoed walls, stringcourses emphasize horizontality, as do steel-frame casement windows arranged in bands and wrapping around the building's sharp corners. Semicircular canopies mark the entrances, and glass-block windows reveal the location of the stairwells. This complex and the Christian Science church display Williams's mastery of a variety of styles, an accomplishment that contributed to his long and successful career.

Newlands Neighborhood

This area atop a bluff overlooking the Truckee River and parts of Reno has been the city's most elegant and most desirable neighborhood since the early twentieth century. The majority of structures here were erected from the 1890s to the 1940s. Many of the oldest buildings along Court and Elm Court streets are visible from Riverside Park across the river. Breaking away from the downtown grid, winding streets follow the topography of the land. They are lined with a variety of building styles and types, including Classical Revival mansions, Tudor Revival cottages, bungalows, apartment houses, and duplexes. The largest dwellings stand along the bluff, whereas more modest structures are located inland. The district's proximity to downtown has encouraged owners with buildings closest to main roads to convert their structures to offices. Attempts to list the neighborhood as a National Register Historic District have been unsuccessful, defeated by a majority of property owners who incorrectly believe that the listing would infringe upon their property rights. This belief is commonly held in Nevada and has been a major obstacle to historic preservation. In fact, only local preservation ordinances can impose restrictions. A more recent development is the fear that listing on the National Register will encourage developers to convert residential buildings for commercial use, such as offices, in order to obtain a federal tax credit for the rehabilitation of historic properties. However, National Register listing and adherence to stringent rehabilitation guidelines are required in order to obtain the credits, which can be substantial.

NW025 Offices (Hawkins House)

1911, Elmer Grey. 549 Court St.

This brick Colonial Revival house stands back from the street, from which a curving white pergola supported by Doric columns leads to a one-story Ionic portico. The main entrance door, framed by a flattened elliptical fanlight and multipane side lights, opens into a central hall with a stylistically consistent stairway, wainscot, and Classical Revival ornament.

Prince Hawkins commissioned the design from Elmer Grey, a Los Angeles architect whose other projects include the Beverly Hills Hotel and the Huntington Library and Art Gallery. Members of the Hawkins family, longtime Reno philanthropists with ties to the Mackay family of Virginia City, lived in the residence until 1978.

NW025 Offices (Hawkins House)

NW026 **House** (Senator Francis G. Newlands House)

1889. 7 Elm Court. Visible from the Truckee River and Riverside Dr.

Senator Francis G. Newlands was the first person to build a residence in the neighborhood named for him. A major figure in Nevada politics, Newlands was responsible for the National Reclamation Act of 1902, which brought the state its first federally funded irrigation project. One of Nevada's few National Historic Landmarks, the building is an excellent example of the Shingle Style, which is rare in Nevada because its popularity coincided with a statewide economic depression that curtailed construction. Although the building is difficult to see from Elm Court, it is visible from the Truckee River.

The two-and-one-half-story house has a prominent cross-gable roof and shingle-sided walls. A one-story library wing on the southeast side of the building was added around the turn of the century. For a number of years the house stood alone on the bluff, but in the early decades of the twentieth century, when Nevada's economy hit a boom cycle, other mansions joined it. Near the gate of the property is a small stone English cottage (c. 1929), designed by Frederick J. DeLongchamps as his home.

NW027 **Duplex**

1920s. 602–604 California Ave.

This one-and-one-half-story brick duplex is among the more modest residences in the neighborhood. Designed in a simple Craftsman style, albeit in brick, the building has an unusual plan, with two main entrances located on opposite ends of the main facade on California Avenue. Gabled porches on brick piers with arched openings, outlined in brick of contrasting color, shelter the entrances. In the center, a large shed-roofed dormer with two triple windows meets the ridges of the entry porches. Brickwork is patterned to replicate quoins along the porch piers and around the window openings.

NW028 **House** (Senator George S. Nixon House)

1906–1911. 637 California Ave. Visible from the Truckee River and Riverside Dr.

The home of one of Nevada's most powerful men, this imposing Spanish Colonial Revival mansion of 21,000 square feet is among the neighborhood's largest. Nixon, a wealthy banker who increased his fortune in the Tonopah and Goldfield booms, became a U.S. senator in 1905, when senators were still elected by the state legislature, and he remained in office until 1912. Gates and trees obscure the view from the street, but the house commands a prominent position on the bluff overlooking the Truckee. A large porte-

Reno — Newlands and Plumas

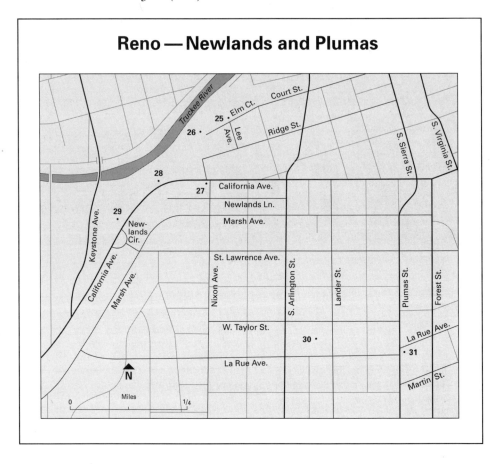

cochere adorns the main facade, and a one-story colonnaded portico extends along the river side. The red-tiled hipped roof offers a pleasing contrast to the creamy-colored stuccoed walls. A devastating fire in 1979 left the structure eerily empty, and the present owner has made no plans to rebuild or tear it down.

NW029 House

1942–1943, Edward S. Parsons. 745 California Ave.

Separated from the street by a green lawn and large mature trees, this Neo-Tudor house evokes a landscape far removed from that of Reno's high desert. Edward S. Parsons, a local architect who designed numerous buildings during his long career, used a variety of forms, textures, and materials for this skillfully executed residence. Front-facing gables break the solid line of the main roof's edge. The entrance is recessed in a narrow, brick-faced and

gabled central bay with a Tudor-arched opening of stone. Two larger gabled bays with stone-clad first stories and half-timbered second stories flank the entrance. Recycled brick from Virginia City buildings, interspersed with Carson City sandstone, creates a slightly rustic look.

Plumas Neighborhood

This area, east and south of the Newlands neighborhood, contains more modest structures than those found on the bluffs above the Truckee River. The Mount Rose Elementary School (1912) serves as the focal point, surrounded by small bungalows, larger homes in period revival styles, and later tract houses built over several decades.

NW030 Mount Rose Elementary School

1912, George A. Ferris. 1938, Lehman Ferris. 915 Lander St.

The Mission Revival Mount Rose Elementary School has served the surrounding community for nearly a century. Tall steps lead to the main facade, a U-shape enclosing a courtyard, formed by two projecting wings terminating in scrolled parapets decorated with mosaic insets. Two square towers capped by octagonal domes are the defining features of the school, visible from a few blocks away. Of four schools built about 1910, this building and the nearly identical McKinley Park School on Riverside Drive are the only two that remain, and Mount Rose is the only one that still functions as a school. Its survival is a rare example of preservation success in Nevada. Reno citizens, many of whom are alumni, supported the continued use of the building as a school and persuaded the school district to preserve the structure, which is in excellent condition.

NW031 Cathexes (McCarthy-Platt House)

c. 1900. 1925, Frederick J. DeLongchamps. 1000 Plumas St.

This Colonial Revival house exemplifies a style frequently used for middle- and upper-middle-class domestic architecture in early twentieth-century Reno. In general, such houses displayed the architect's or builder's knowledge of popular styles and forms, combined with the use of local materials to create modest, eclectic

structures. Hired to remodel the house, DeLongchamps attempted to unify its asymmetrical plan, cross-gable roof, and corner turret typical of late Victorian fashion by adding Colonial Revival elements, including Palladian windows and classical moldings. Today Cathexes, an architecture firm, uses the building as its offices.

South Reno

As the city has grown, ranches south of Reno have given way to subdivisions, the pace increasing drastically since the 1980s. With the opening of a new freeway parallel to South Virginia Street (old U.S. 395), business and industrial parks surrounded by asphalt parking lots have sprung up along the right-of-way. Always pro-growth, Reno and Washoe County have not been willing to manage the latest boom to prevent the Truckee Meadows from being engulfed by sprawl. Smog is a serious problem in the valley, and traffic jams are frequent. The foothills, where property owners take advantage of remaining open space and dramatic views, are considered the prime areas in which to build.

NW032 Damonte Ranch (Peleg Brown Ranch)

12945 Old Virginia Rd.

One of the last remaining nineteenth-century ranch complexes in the Truckee Meadows, the

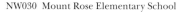
NW030 Mount Rose Elementary School

NW033 Stremmel House

Damonte Ranch once supplied agricultural products to the Comstock Mining District. The main house also served as a stage station along the road to Virginia City. Peleg Brown established the ranch, encompassing about 620 acres, in 1858. In addition to developing the alfalfa industry in the Truckee Meadows, he played a significant role in constructing irrigation ditches to bring Truckee River water to farms throughout the valley. He and his descendants erected most of the surviving buildings.

Since 1940, the ranch has been owned by the Damonte family. Its members were among the many Italian immigrants who came to the valley to make a living in farming and ranching, working for others until they had saved enough money to buy their own property. Over the years the owners subdivided the ranch. The property currently encompasses about three and one-half acres surrounding the historic core. In addition to the extant buildings, the complex once contained a hay barn, chicken coop, pump house, and outhouses. The Nevada Department of Transportation's construction of the south leg of U.S. 395 in the 1990s greatly degraded the site. The freeway passes very close to the historic complex; despite large berms constructed to shield the buildings from noise and pollution, the ranching landscape has been lost.

NW032.1 **Main House**

1864, 1940, 1955

This two-and-one-half-story, wood-frame structure is a rare extant example of the Greek Re-

vival in Nevada. At the time the house was constructed, many contemporary ranchers used Greek Revival elements for their houses, creating a simplified, frontier version of the style. The side-facing gables with enclosed pediments, symmetrical facade, and front entrance with narrow side lights and transom all reflect a vernacular interpretation of the Greek Revival. The owners have altered the house over the years. A square porch stands where a three-quarter-length porch once covered the main facade. In 1955 they combined twelve of the fourteen small rooms on the second floor that served as lodgings when the house functioned as a stage stop. The house stands in an enclosed yard shaded by mature trees facing the old Virginia Road and the freeway beyond.

NW032.2 **Outbuildings** (Play House, Foreman's House, Granary, Garage [Cold Storage])

The remaining outbuildings on the ranch represent varied uses. The play house (c. 1900) was most likely built for one of Peleg Brown's grandchildren. This tiny bungalow measuring 8 by 10 feet stands south of the main house within the enclosed yard. Also to the south, outside the yard and facing the old road, is the foreman's house (1860s), a modest one-and-one-half-story structure with a front-gable roof. A shed roof supported by square posts shelters the first floor of the main facade. Asphalt shingles cover original siding. The granary (1860s), behind the foreman's house, stands on a stone foundation measuring 16 by 25 feet. Tin lines the interior walls and floor to keep out rodents.

The garage, formerly cold storage (1860s), has heavy stone walls enclosing a 21-foot-by-26-foot space and supporting a front-gable roof with board-and-batten gable ends.

NW033 Stremmel House

1993–1995, Mack Architects. 339 Anitra Dr.

This colorful angular house perched on a hill south of Reno has understandably received a great deal of attention in the architectural press since its completion. Though the building stands out from the landscape (drivers on U.S. 395 can readily spot its bright red-orange and yellow walls), it responds to the rugged character of the site by using such industrial materials as steel and concrete blocks. Resting on a plinth, the house rises slightly above the ground; the surrounding landscape remains undisturbed, a dry terrain of sagebrush and rocks.

The design began as a collection of cubes sheltered by a large open shed, inspired by the architect's memory of metal canopies built to shield trailers from the sun. As the project evolved, the cubes became one mass covered by a hovering trellis, which is solid at the south end of the house, providing protection from the sun. The rear of the house backs into the hillside; the front opens up to an expansive view of the valley below. Designed as a residence in which the owners can display their collection of modern art, the house has large interior spaces flowing into one another. Concrete floors stained in earth tones meet plastered, wood-paneled, or glass walls. Mark Mack, an architect based in Venice, California, has expanded the boundaries of domestic architecture in northern Nevada. Despite Reno's libertarian views on divorce and gambling, the city's attitude toward architecture has been provincial. The Stremmel House may help to transform local architecture, pushing it toward more environmentally sensitive and economical forms of dwellings.

Sparks

Founded by the Southern Pacific, Sparks is one of a few twentieth-century railroad towns in northwestern Nevada. The Southern Pacific acquired the Central Pacific in 1899 and began upgrading the rails, relocating more than half of the old railroad's track to reduce grades and make curves easier to maneuver. The rerouting bypassed Wadsworth, the old Central Pacific division point, where the railroad had large repair and maintenance yards. Southern Pacific bought several ranches east of Reno as sites for large maintenance shops and in 1904 moved nearly all of Wadsworth's 700 residents and their buildings to the new railroad yard, thirty miles west. In that same year the new town adopted the name Sparks, in honor of John D. Sparks, a cattle baron and Nevada's fourth governor. The townsite, laid out in a grid north of the railroad tracks, is largely intact today. Houses dating from the early years stand among mid-twentieth-century ranch houses. The construction of I-80 in the 1970s and the ensuing development near the freeway have obliterated several blocks of the historic downtown.

Sparks grew steadily, eventually becoming contiguous with Reno. The railroad supported the economy until the 1950s, when the shops closed. However, in 1949 the state legislature passed a free-port law providing a property-tax exemption for goods in transit. Sparks jumped at the opportunity to attract companies to store and assemble products, successfully encouraging a large warehousing industry. The city's location near a major railroad line, interstate highway, and international airport has accelerated growth.

Sparks's urban fabric has suffered from this growth-at-all-costs policy. The former downtown has been carved up by huge casinos and urban renewal projects, which have killed most local businesses. In the late 1980s, in an attempt to create a more appealing public space, the city renamed B Street, the main road through downtown, calling it Victorian Avenue to capture an old-time feeling. The city curved the road, converted cross streets into pedestrian malls, added a small railroad park and amphitheater adjacent to the elevated freeway, reconstructed an old depot, and moved a historic school to the park. Casinos down the street built structures in an Old West style. Surprisingly, a few historic buildings survive to provide a semblance of the early commercial district. However, the city has moved on to a new project along C Street, demolishing several other historic buildings to erect a huge theater complex with a multistory parking garage. Both redevelopment projects are excellent examples of planners' attempts to revive downtowns by destroying historic buildings and streetscapes. Likewise, many older residential neighborhoods have been abandoned for developments on the edges of town. In this way, Sparks resembles many other booming late twentieth-century Nevada cities.

Sparks stands on the eastern edge of the Truckee Meadows. To the north, Nevada 445

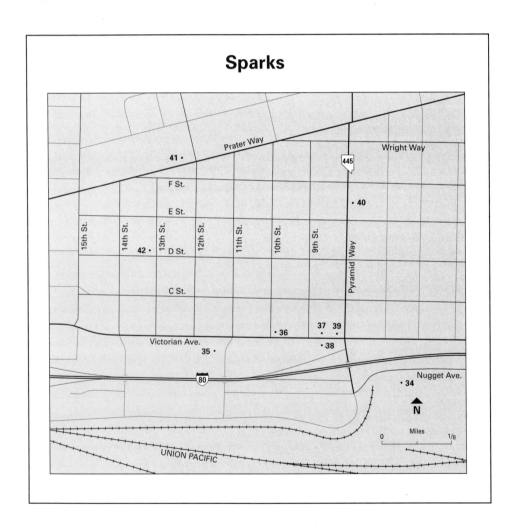

climbs out of the valley and heads to Pyramid Lake, passing numerous subdivisions along the way. I-80 east of Sparks parallels the railroad and the Truckee River, following both through a narrow canyon that quickly shuts out the traffic and noise of the Reno-Sparks area. Some ranches, scattered houses, power plants, junkyards, and brothels can be found here.

NW034 **Warehouse** (Southern Pacific Repair Shops)

1904, Southern Pacific Railroad. 599 Nugget Ave.

This rectangular warehouse, measuring 120 by 450 feet, is all that remains of the extensive railroad shops that helped create Sparks. Southern Pacific demolished most of the old railroad structures after the yards closed, and the state condemned other buildings to make way for I-80 and subsequent lane additions. The interstate separates the building from the rest of town, but its large size makes it easy to find. The brick warehouse has two levels of window openings, the top one segmentally arched, piercing recessed panels divided by pilasters. Steel posts and roof trusses support a metal roof. The building initially contained four separate shops: a tin shop, machine shop, blacksmith shop, and boiler shop. Although the shop's historical significance is obvious, Southern Pacific objected to attempts by the Nevada State Historic Preservation Office to list the building on the National Register of Historic Places in the early 1980s.

NW035 **John Ascuaga's Nugget**

1963, 1970s, 1984, 1994. 1996, Peter B. Wilday. 1100 Nugget Ave.

The Nugget, which is visible from many parts of the valley, competes with Reno's biggest casinos for customers. Like many other casinos, it began as a small operation, opening in downtown Sparks in 1955 as one of four coffee shops in northern Nevada. John Ascuaga, son of a Basque sheepherder, started out as general manager, eventually buying the business in 1960. In 1984 he added the first hotel tower, a concrete, rectangular block with 600 rooms. The second tower, completed in 1996, stands to the west of the first. An angular concrete, steel, and glass tower with 800 rooms, it complements the earlier tower in its use of materials, but its dynamic lines add more visual interest to the entire complex.

As Sparks grew, so did the Nugget. In 1973,

as I-80 plowed its way through the downtown area, Ascuaga persuaded the federal and state governments to give him a long-term lease of the space under the freeway. He expanded his casino under and around the interstate. Despite the addition of lanes to the freeway east and west of the casino, the roadway still narrows to a bottleneck as it crosses over the Nugget. Thus far, no casino has ever been demolished to make way for a road.

NW036 **Offices** (Bank of Sparks)

1904. 948 Victorian Ave. (B St.)

Like the other historic buildings on the north side of Victorian Avenue, this structure stood near the railroad tracks that ran through Sparks. This small corner building offers a vernacular interpretation of the Romanesque Revival style. Stone quoins, segmental arches, and parapets contrast with red brick walls in between. The main entrance is recessed in the building's corner, a single cast iron column supporting the wall above. Smooth stones carved with scrolls highlight the roof corner over the entrance. For many decades the building housed the only bank in Sparks.

NW037 **Antique Shop** (Hotel Abbay)

1920s. 834 Victorian Ave. (B St.)

When B Street was one of Sparks's main roads and passenger trains stopped nearby, buildings such as this former hotel were commonplace. The simple building has a flat facade laid in Flemish bond, with red and black alternating bricks adding texture and color to the structure. The facade rises to a central pediment and end piers; the roofline between these elements is decorated with ornamental ironwork. Now an antique shop, this structure has been altered, as have numerous surviving old buildings along the street.

NW034 Warehouse (Southern Pacific Repair Shops)

NW038 Glendale School (above)

NW039 Sparks Museum (Washoe County Library–Sparks Branch) (left)

NW038 Glendale School

1864. South side of Victorian Ave. (B St.) near Pyramid Way

Believed to be the oldest intact school in the state, the small wood-frame Glendale School has endured two moves during its history. The settlement of Glendale stood along the Truckee River at a crossing in what is now east Sparks. The building functioned as a one-room school until 1958. Over the years, the town added a gabled entrance to the facade and replaced the open belfry with an enclosed, vented cupola. In 1976 the building was moved to the Reno-Sparks Convention Center in Reno next to the Lake Mansion, another historic building relocated to the site. In 1993 the school was moved again, to Victorian Avenue. Although it is now closer to its original site than it had been previously, the plain building seems oddly placed, surrounded by a freeway, casinos, and fake Victorian street furniture.

NW039 Sparks Museum (Washoe County Library–Sparks Branch)

1931, Frederick J. DeLongchamps. 814 Victorian Ave.

This brick building in the Mediterranean Revival style is the most architecturally pleasing along the street. Alternating red and black bricks in a Flemish bond add color to the flat wall surface, continued in the color and texture of the tiled hipped roof. Although DeLongchamps preferred the Classical Revival style for public buildings, he designed several modest Mediterranean Revival structures for small towns in Nevada during the 1930s. The architect's love of order is apparent in the museum's symmetrical facade with a gabled central bay. The building functioned originally as the first Sparks branch of the Washoe County Public Library, occupying the second floor; the City of Sparks Justice Court occupied the first floor. The building became a museum in the 1990s.

NW040 Immaculate Conception Roman Catholic Church

1931–1932, Frederick J. DeLongchamps. 1970. 590 Pyramid Way

Though somewhat altered from its original appearance, this church in the North Italian Romanesque Revival style, loosely resembling Sant' Ambrogio in Milan, presents a counterpoint to the Sparks Museum. The cruciform brick building has a single nave with transept, all covered by a long red-tiled gable roof. Pairs of arched windows pierce the side walls flanked by brick buttresses. A brick-clad, shed-roofed vestibule with arched openings applied to the facade in 1970 has obscured the clean lines of the main elevation. The unadorned interior has a slightly vaulted ceiling from which hang six original black wrought iron chandeliers in a simple Mission Revival style. The bell that hangs in the tower at the rear of the building came from a firehouse in Virginia City and was purchased by Father William Devlin in 1938. The oldest extant Catholic church in Sparks, Immaculate Conception replaced an earlier structure, built in 1905, that burned down on Easter Sunday in 1930. Its construction coincided with the granting of diocesan status to Nevada by Pope Pius XI in 1931. The dedication of the church on 22 February 1932 marked a time of growth for the Catholic Church in Nevada.

NW041 Robert H. Mitchell School

1938–1939, Frederick J. DeLongchamps. 1216 12th St.

A Public Works Administration project, this large one-story, L-shaped structure, austere in style, has always functioned as an elementary school. Brick walls with generous windows rise to a slate-covered hipped roof with projecting eaves, exposed rafters, and a plain frieze. Most of the Art Deco details are confined to the main entrance on Prater Way. Fluted cast concrete pilasters culminating in chevrons flank the entry, rising to a flat canopy.

NW042 Robison House

1904. 409 13th St.

One of Sparks's earliest and largest houses was originally owned by George W. Robison, who bought his eighty-acre ranch in 1890. When the Southern Pacific decided to move its shops near his ranch, Robison subdivided his land and began to sell lots in 1903, using photographs of his house in advertisements for his land. The image of the two-story, wood-frame dwelling with its pedimented gables and bracketed eaves no doubt lent an air of respectability to Robison's speculative enterprise. The block on which this house

NW042 Robison House

stands has retained much of its original streetscape, with modest but attractive bungalows to the north. Looming over the neighborhood, however, is one of Sparks's latest redevelopment projects: an enormous theater complex and parking structure across D Street that puts the house in shadow for much of the day.

Sparks Vicinity

NW043 **Mustang Ranch**

1976. Approximately 5 miles east of Sparks at Exit 23 of I-80; follow signs to Fernley, cross railroad tracks and Truckee River

Since the mid-nineteenth century, brothels have been a part of Nevada's built environment. In a state where the main industries, mining and ranching, were dominated by men, prostitution developed quickly. Until the federal government shut it down in the summer of 1999, the Mustang Ranch was Nevada's largest, most elaborate, and most notorious brothel. Once visitors leave the interstate and cross the Truckee River to the south, they have entered Storey County, where prostitution is legal. The former brothel stands in an isolated area surrounded by a high metal

fence and gate. Two other former brothels are nearby.

Despite its hot-pink paint, the Mustang Ranch resembles a low-security prison. Built of concrete blocks with stucco on the exterior walls, the structure has a central circular section with radiating wings of bedrooms extending to the sides and rear, a plan reminiscent of a panopticon. A guard tower above the complex allows surveillance of the approaching roads and the brothel yard. Such security measures provided a means to control clients' access. A large parking lot in front of the "ranch" accommodated cars, trucks, and tractor trailers. Only customers were permitted inside. The entrance led to a parlor that served as a waiting area for clients. From there, hallways led to small bedrooms. Other spaces housed facilities for the prostitutes, including a cafeteria, a communal kitchen, and a hair salon. A branch next door, the Mustang II, provided additional accommodations in a warren of trailers.

Legalized prostitution in the state is highly regulated. The women must undergo weekly health examinations by doctors. They work as independent contractors, paying for their room and board in compounds such as the Mustang Ranch. Usually they work ten- to fourteen-hour-a-day shifts for three weeks, with one week off. During the three-week shift they cannot leave the compound.

Joe Conforte established the ranch here in the 1960s, housing the business in trailers. Its economic success and Conforte's influence persuaded the Storey County commissioners to legalize prostitution in 1971. Conforte operated the ranch until 1990, when the Internal Revenue Service seized it because of unpaid taxes. Ironically, the federal government operated the brothel for a few days until it was auctioned. The Mustang Ranch continued to be very profitable until the federal government closed it for a second time after the owners were convicted of fraud and racketeering. In another strange twist, the Bureau of Land Management is now considering converting the structure into an interpretive center for its Wild Horse and Burro Adoption Center.

Washoe Valley

This valley between Reno and Carson City is a microcosm of the strikingly rugged and beautiful landscape of the high desert. The Sierra Nevada foothills to the west provide a forest environment. From there the terrain flattens to a broad valley that in wet years has a large lake fed by the melting Sierra snowpack. In times of drought, the lake can dry up completely.

Mormons, drawn by the fertile soil and water for growing crops, settled the area in the early 1850s. The Comstock boom attracted ranchers in the early 1860s. Miners erected mills along the shore of the lake, and for a short time the valley prospered. Newly rich ranchers and miners erected impressive houses to display their success. Washoe City, located near the valley's northern edge, served as the Washoe County seat beginning in 1861. With the completion of the V&T Railroad line in 1869, the milling business shifted south to the Carson River, destroying the main economic basis of Washoe City. The Washoe County government's move to Reno in 1872 and the Comstock's decline beginning in the 1870s killed the town. Only a few stone ruins now remain alongside U.S. 395. By the late 1870s the valley had become home to a few cattle ranchers. Today, however, the growth of Reno and Carson City has encouraged developers to view Washoe Valley as a perfect location for commuters. As ranches are subdivided, houses and lawns are replacing barns and corrals.

NW044 Winters Ranch

1862–1864. 2000 U.S. 395 N., approximately 19 miles south of Reno

This Carpenter's Gothic house, which sits close to the road, is difficult to miss. The one-and-one-half-story, wood-frame building stands on a raised basement. Perhaps based in part on A. J. Downing's cottage designs, the dwelling has a steeply pitched roof broken by a front-facing central gable containing a Gothic lancet window. The side gables contain three lancet windows each. In a more classical vein is a veranda, supported by slender square posts, that covers the front and sides of the main floor. The interior has been altered over the years, but the second floor retains its large ballroom and wood-vaulted 20-foot-high ceiling. The interior includes Egyptian Revival motifs—a rarity in the state—which consist of slanted surrounds for doorways and fireplaces.

The members of the Winters family, the original owners, were among Washoe Valley's most prominent residents. Theodore Winters, a horse-racing aficionado, built a large racetrack behind his house, facing the valley. At one time the ranch encompassed approximately 6,000 acres. Since its heyday, the house has endured several periods of vacancy and deterioration, but it is now being restored as a residence by the current owner.

NW045 Bowers Mansion

1863, J. Neeley Johnson. 1967–1968, Edward S. Parsons. West side of NV 429 (old U.S. 395), approximately 20 miles south of Reno

Lemuel Sanford "Sandy" Bowers and his wife, Eilley, were among the first millionaires in the

Comstock area. They used their newly acquired wealth to build a two-story Italianate mansion against the foothills of the Sierra. Mrs. Bowers worked with J. Neeley Johnson, a builder and ex-governor of California, to create an imposing structure. The foundation and walls are composed of granite quarried from the hills behind the house and sandstone. Quoins finish the corners and surround the double-arched French-door openings on the second floor. A large veranda wraps around the front and sides, supported by beveled square posts and trimmed with balustrades. Pairs of brackets line the cornice, which is capped by another balustrade. Atop the shallow hipped roof stands an octagonal cupola.

After Sandy Bowers's death, which followed years of profligate spending, his widow added a third floor with a mansard roof so she could take in boarders. Nevertheless, she lost the house and the rest of her fortune in 1874. After changing hands many times, in 1966 the mansion was acquired by Washoe County and added to its park system. During the next two years Edward S. Parsons removed the old additions and returned the house to what he believed was its original appearance. The building is a visible reminder of the ephemeral quality of wealth and the boom-and-bust cycles in Nevada. Over the years period furnishings have been acquired for the house, which is open to the public during the summer.

Virginia City

At its height in the nineteenth century, Virginia City, often called the "Queen of the Comstock," was a large industrialized town that played an important role in western mining history. Its international population, both rich and poor, included at its peak thousands of Irish, over a thousand Chinese, almost that number of Cornish, and hundreds of Germans, as well as dozens of other groups. Since its early years Virginia City has been a center of government as an incorporated city and a county seat.

Mining and milling structures remain scattered throughout the Comstock, a legacy of the great efforts expended to extract ore from the mountains. In addition to industrial structures, numerous humble buildings, many of which survive, provided living accommodations for thousands of workers and their families, in both individual homes and boardinghouses. The upper hillsides of the cities and towns boasted mansions for the rich. Although these tended to be modest compared with their counterparts in San Francisco, for example, they nonetheless indicate the wealth of a place that produced what today would be billions of dollars in gold and silver. Commercial buildings and public structures add to the variety of architecture in the Comstock area.

Virginia City followed the standard pattern of mining town development from settlement to camp to town. Since the mid-twentieth century, the city has undergone additional changes, inspired in part by myth and media. Today the town has a year-round population of about 700, a mere fraction of the number in its heyday. A slow economy and remote location have helped preserve many of Virginia City's prominent structures as well as more modest buildings. However, preservation efforts have been threatened by occasional spurts of renewed mining activity and sometimes by publicity. For example, with the advent of the television show *Bonanza* in 1959, tourists from throughout the world came to see the hometown of the fictional protagonists. Local developers responded by altering buildings to correspond to the television image of the Comstock rather than the real place. Unpainted vertical boards cloaked several nineteenth-century brick Italianate buildings. Similar Hollywood western–style structures filled empty spaces where fires had claimed the original buildings. The new structures contradicted late nineteenth-century urban standards, which dictated construction in masonry or with painted horizontal pine board for wooden commercial buildings. This new "Cartwright era" approach to design reflected a twentieth-century misconception of what a western boom town looked like. In Nevada, as in other western states, stereotypical views of the West are used to attract tourists. "Frontier style" architecture still proliferates throughout Nevada in strip malls and casinos—and even in more far-flung places such as France's Euro-Disney, where it is the prevailing image of the American West.

Since the end of the *Bonanza* series in 1974, a growing preservation ethic has encouraged construction more in keeping with the Comstock's nineteenth-century heritage. The new interest in local history has led to the erection of large dwellings loosely based on late nineteenth-century styles in areas that one hundred years earlier would have had more modest homes.

NW046 Piper-Beebe House

1876. 2 S. A St.

Opera house owner John Piper once lived in this two-story, wood-frame Italianate structure on a street overlooking Virginia City. The house has a square bay window next to the front door, which is topped by an arched transom. Shiplap siding, a cornice with brackets and modillions, a paneled frieze, and elaborate door and window surrounds contribute to the Italianate appearance. The current owners recently painted the house yellow with red and black trim, based on what they believe were the original colors. During the mid-twentieth century, writers Lucius Beebe and Charles Clegg lived in the house. Their publications, and especially their resuscitation of the famed newspaper *Territorial Enterprise*, helped Virginia City to reclaim some of its earlier renown.

NW047 Miner's Union Hall

1876. 38 N. B St.

The Miner's Union Hall was home to one of the Comstock's most significant protective associations. Though the two-story brick building is small, it has an ornate curved parapet with a narrow, denticulated cornice. Decorating the parapet is a metal image of a beehive, which symbolizes communal labor, an appropriate emblem for a union. The Miner's Protective Association of Storey County, founded on 30 May 1863, was the first organization for miners in the West. It demanded a minimum standard

wage of $4 a day, equivalent to $56 today, and provided benefits for miners and their families. A few years later the Virginia City Miner's Union replaced the earlier organization. This group built the hall after the Great Fire of 1875.

NW048 Knights of Pythias Hall

1876. 30 N. B St.

The Knights of Pythias Hall was home to one of the Comstock's once-numerous fraternal organizations. It is a two-story brick building with square iron supports on the first floor and brick pilasters decorating the second story. The windows on the second story have graceful round arches. Protruding beams indicate where a metal cornice once decorated the roofline. The arched parapet bears the letters "K of P" in relief, commemorating the building's original use.

NW049 Piper's Opera House

c. 1861, 1885. Northwest corner of N. B and Union sts.

Opera houses were mainstays of western mining towns, being the main venues for traveling performers. Though called opera houses, these buildings rarely presented opera. Instead, they accommodated a variety of entertainers, from singers and bands to comedians and lecturers. During the boom days of mining towns many entrepreneurs operated opera houses because they provided much-needed entertainment in remote areas.

During Virginia City's heyday, John Piper's Opera House attracted famous artists on world tours. The building is notable for the preservation of its 1885 proscenium-arch, or picture-frame, stage, which was developed initially in the seventeenth century to heighten the illusion of the stage set and flourished in the late nineteenth century. The opera house is the third in a series of theaters operated by Piper in Virginia City. The two earlier ones burned down during the Comstock's heyday. After the first was destroyed in the Great Fire of 1875, Piper relocated his business to its present location, using a two-story brick business block built c. 1861 as a facade. After the opera house, located in the back, burned down in 1883, Piper erected a new building in 1885, incorporating once again his two-story brick structure. A blind arcade on the first floor frames doorways into the building and into a saloon formerly in the southeast corner of the lower floor. The front part of the building also provides a transition to the large wooden hall behind it, which contains the theater. Metal pilasters separate the doorways; their lotus capitals are a rare surviving example of 1860s Egyptian Revival architecture, subsequently to be seen in early twentieth-century movie theaters.

Virginia City, 1998

Seating on the main floor and in a U-shaped balcony can accommodate 500 people. The auditorium boasts a hand-painted stage curtain and boxes that once seated the bonanza kings, Virginia City's wealthiest and most powerful residents. Pulley systems and nineteenth-century backdrops stand ready at the rear of the stage.

The opera house functioned as a venue for the performing arts as well as a variety of other events. Buffalo Bill, Lillie Langtry, John Philip Sousa and his Peerless Concert Band, and others appeared there. Piper's also presented bear and cat fights, boxing matches, and basketball games. Some of the finest orators of the day, including nineteenth-century free-love advocates and Irish revolutionaries, spoke from its stage. In 1997 a private nonprofit organization purchased the structure and has revived it as a venue for the performing arts. Piper's Opera House is just one example of its type in towns across the American West in the nineteenth century. That Virginia City acquired an opera house in the early years of its existence speaks to the demand for cultural institutions even in sparsely populated, remote frontier towns.

NW050 Storey County Courthouse

1877, Kenitzer and Raun. Southwest corner of S. B and Union sts.

The Storey County Courthouse is the focal point of B Street. It was the most expensive county building erected in Nevada during its first sixty years, not to be outdone until Reno constructed the Washoe County Courthouse between 1909 and 1911. Testifying to the wealth of the Comstock, the Storey County facilities seemed to promise that its mines would continue to prosper. After the original courthouse burned down in the Great Fire of 1875, the county commissioners asked Kenitzer and Raun of San Francisco to provide design options. The architects furnished three designs, two with Gothic Revival details to be executed in stone or brick and iron. The commissioners selected the third and most expensive of the

proposals: a two-story Italianate stone structure with a fine brick facade and iron details. Though the exact reasons for their choice are unclear, the desire to display a prosperous appearance was certainly a major factor. Those with inside information knew that no new ore deposits had been discovered, indicating that a bust was imminent, so a new, monumental courthouse would help convince investors to keep funneling more money into the region.

The two-story building, still the county courthouse, provides office space for all the major agencies of local government. The interior retains much of the original fabric, including paneled doors, ornate gaslight fixtures, now converted to electricity, and gracious 18-foot-high ceilings on the first floor. Local judges still hear cases in the courtroom, which has been preserved in almost pristine condition with grained oak wainscot, marble fireplaces, and walnut furnishings and bar. The county used the double-tier jail until its closing in the 1980s because it did not meet federal standards.

NW050 Storey County Courthouse

Virginia City

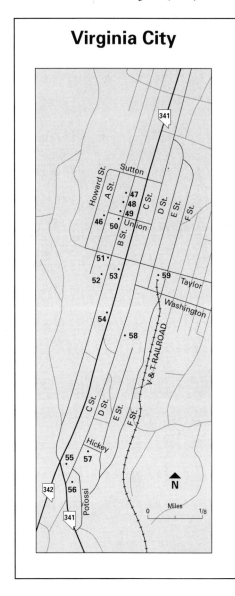

One of the principal curiosities of the Storey County Courthouse is the 7-foot zinc statue of Justice that stands in a recess above the main doorway. The only such freestanding statue to adorn the outside of a Nevada courthouse, it is also unusual because the figure lacks the customary blindfold, a depiction that is supposedly a testament to the wild nature of frontier justice. However, the statue has many counterparts elsewhere, and the choice of whether or not to blindfold Justice was simply a matter of taste.

NW051 Virginia City and Gold Hill Water Company Building

1874. Southwest corner of S. B and Taylor sts.

The Water Company Building is one of the more visual components of the Marlette Lake Water System, a considerable engineering feat that brought water from the Sierra Nevada to Virginia City. The two-story, wood-frame building stands on a stone rubble foundation, its elaborate Italianate doorway and window surrounds and brackets almost lost under many coats of white paint. Built by the Water Company in 1874 for corporate office space, it retains much of its original appearance and is one of the better examples of commercial architecture on B Street.

NW052 The Castle

1863–1868. West side of S. B St. between Taylor and Flowery sts.

Virginia City residents call this wood-frame Second Empire house the Castle. It stands high above B Street on a lot defined by stone retaining walls and a steep staircase leading from the street to the front porch. Mansions once lined this portion of B Street, giving it the name "Millionaires' Row." Like many other opulent Virginia City mansions, the Castle has as its crowning glory a three-story tower with a mansard roof and dormers.

Robert Graves, superintendent of the Empire Mine, began building the Castle in 1863 and completed it in 1868. He was from a prominent London publishing family, and it is apparent from the refined character of his house that he wished to bring a sense of luxury and civilization to the Comstock. The interior retains much of the original furnishings and trim, including black walnut finishes and silver doorknobs. Now a private museum, the Castle is open to the public for tours.

NW053 Old Washoe Club

Early 1860s. 46–48 S. C St.

The Old Washoe Club was one of the most celebrated commercial establishments in Virginia City. The brick building housed the club as well as Con Ahern's Capital Bar, both popular drinking establishments for prominent Comstock residents. The large building also featured a stock brokerage, a stationery store, and

NW052 The Castle, interior and exterior (above, left and right)

NW053 Old Washoe Club (left)

a hardware store. A rooming house occupied the second story, and the third story contained office space. The building's facade has mass-produced, fireproof ornamentation, including a metal cornice with brackets and dentils and a cast iron facade. Like most other commercial buildings on C Street, it has a one-story porch covering the wood sidewalk below.

NW054 First Presbyterian Church

1867. West side of S. C St.(near southwest corner of S. C and Flowery sts.)

This Carpenter's Gothic church is the oldest surviving religious structure in Virginia City. The congregation obtained land for the building through insider stock trading that yielded enough funds to obtain the site and pay for construction. The church's board-and-batten construction is formalized by the large size of the battens and the application of paint (for it is certain that the building was always painted). Few board-and-batten churches are found in Nevada, as this method of construction was usually reserved for utilitarian buildings such as stables or sheds. Little of the original interior remains, but the tall facade, culminating in a narrow bell tower, stands out on South C Street.

NW055 Fourth Ward School

1875–1877, C. M. Bennett. S. C St. at intersection with NV 341

The Fourth Ward School is an imposing, four-story Second Empire structure with a clock

NW055 Fourth Ward School, 1937 photo (top)

NW057 C. J. Prescott House (bottom)

school district never finished the fourth floor, which contained space for the school newspaper and gym classes; gymnasts' rings and basketball hoops remain in the northeast room on the top floor. The basement housed a cafeteria and general storage area. Although the school was built for 1,000 students and became the only public school in Storey County after the turn of the century, it never served many children because of the mining district's declining population.

The Fourth Ward School is the last surviving nineteenth-century school in Storey County. Under construction during the Great Fire of 1875, the building escaped the flames because of its location at the south end of Virginia City. The school admitted its first class in 1877 and closed its doors in 1936. After remaining empty for fifty years, it reopened as a local museum in 1986.

NW056 Chollar Mansion

1862–1864, 1870. 565 S. D St.

The mansion was the residence of Billy Chollar, superintendent of the Chollar Mine and one of the original prospectors who claimed the mine in 1859. Although he sold out early in the history of the mine, most likely before the mansion was erected, the operation kept his name. Initially built adjacent to the mine shaft, the two-story brick structure was moved a quarter mile to the north in 1870 when the sides of the shaft proved unstable, threatening the house. Since then, the mansion has stood on a lot below the Fourth Ward School, set into the hillside so the D Street entrance is at the second level. The plain brick building has wood Italianate details combined with classical elements, a wood veranda, a denticulated cornice, brackets, and a low hipped roof.

tower, a mansard roof, and large windows. C. M. Bennett, an architect based in Virginia City, designed the building and later attempted to establish himself in Nevada as a designer of public buildings. County commissioners rejected his proposal for the Eureka County Courthouse, however, and nothing is known about his subsequent career. Nonetheless, his Fourth Ward School is a monumental structure unique in a state with often modestly scaled buildings.

The old school rises on a coursed stone foundation and has drop siding. Each of the three main floors has a central hallway and staircase with two rooms on either side. The school included such innovations as central heating, indoor running water, and plumbed toilets attached to the north side of the structure. An all-purpose room on the third floor had sliding pocket doors that allowed it to serve either as a large space or as two separate classrooms. The

NW057 C. J. Prescott House

1864, 1867, C. J. Prescott. 12 Hickey St.

The Prescott House is one of the few territorial-era residences surviving in Virginia City and one of the most intact period houses in Nevada. C. J. Prescott, a timber merchant, built the one-and-one-half-story front-gabled house with a veranda on square piers, embellishing it with simple wood moldings. The original paint colors, oxblood with trim in gold and green, have been matched by the present owners. In

1867 Prescott built an addition to the house, which remains its only major modification since construction. During the 1980s the owners began a detailed restoration.

NW058 **Mackay Mansion**

1860. 129 S. D St.

Local tradition maintains that George Hearst built the Mackay Mansion, and it is possible that the future mining baron, who secured his start on the Comstock, was responsible for the construction of this three-story brick house. Built as the home and office of the superintendent of the famed Gould and Curry Mine, the building is one of the oldest substantial structures on the Comstock. Like the Chollar Mansion, this house has a hipped roof; a wraparound veranda with segmental arches, attenuated columns, and ornate jigsawn trim; and a cornice with dentils.

The structure became associated with bonanza king John Mackay after he won control of the Gould and Curry Mine. He probably lived in the house for a few months after the Great Fire destroyed his residence farther up the hill. After a visit to her husband's mine in

1874, Mary Louise Mackay supposedly came up with the idea of having a silver service made from some of the Comstock's silver. The Mackays commissioned Tiffany to design the service, which was made in 1877 and 1878. From one-half ton of silver sent directly from Virginia City to Tiffany in New York, a service of 1,250 pieces was produced. Although other affluent Americans, including the Vanderbilts, commissioned Tiffany to make silver services for them, the Mackay service received extensive publicity because of its size, opulence, and craftsmanship. It is now owned by the University of Nevada, Reno.

NW059 **St. Mary in the Mountains Roman Catholic Church**

1862, 1876–1877. Southeast corner of S. E and Taylor sts.

Virginia City's strong Irish community built St. Mary in the Mountains as the largest and most ornate church in the Comstock. During the Great Fire of 1875, John Mackay convinced Father Patrick Manogue to allow the church to be blown up as a means of slowing the fire's

NW059 St. Mary in the Mountains Roman Catholic Church

progress, promising to rebuild the church afterward. The current brick Gothic Revival structure, with a cruciform plan, stands on the granite foundation of the first (1862) church. Embellishments to the facade include buttresses with blind arches, the corner ones pinnacled, and, under crocketed gables, three sets of pointed-arched wood doors with raised tracery. Above these doors, a small rose window looks to the west, and a pair of arched windows admit light to the nave. Lancets on the sides light the aisles. St. Mary's octagonal spire, the tallest on the Comstock, can be seen from throughout the city. The church possesses one of Virginia City's most intricate interiors surviving from the late nineteenth century. A framework of wood columns and carved rafters supports the steep roof. Other features include large gas chandeliers and an elaborate altar and confessional.

Gold Hill

South C Street turns into Gold Hill's Main Street, snaking down the mountainside in a pair of hairpin curves known as Greiner's Bend. During the nineteenth century Gold Hill housed thousands of laborers for local industry. There were commercial buildings and a few houses for the affluent, but Virginia City provided many of the services for the area. When local mines began to fail, Gold Hill's population declined more quickly than that of its northern neighbor. As a result, fewer of its buildings have survived, but several dozen remnants of the nineteenth century testify to a time when Gold Hill was a bustling mining town on the Comstock.

NW060 **Virginia and Truckee Depot**

1869, Virginia and Truckee Railroad. Main St. at the railroad crossing

The Gold Hill V&T Depot, like its Virginia City counterpart, dates to the earliest period of railroad development. This passenger and freight station stands on a post-and-pier foundation. The one-story, wood-frame structure has vertical boards and battens on the southern, freight-handling end of the building and more refined horizontal drop siding on the northern half, which served passengers. Virginia City, the terminus of the V&T, had separate passenger and freight depots, whereas towns like Gold Hill, with less traffic, had one depot for both freight and passenger service. The finishing details on the Gold Hill Depot are typical of all-purpose depots. The V&T Railroad abandoned the facility in 1938 when it stopped service to that end of the line. Storey County assumed ownership of the building, which local groups have recently rehabilitated and operated on occasion as a museum. The V&T Railroad Company, an operating historic railroad constructed on the original V&T right-of-way, extended service from Virginia City to Gold Hill in 1991, bringing its historic locomotives once again to the depot.

NW061 **Gold Hill Hotel**

1859, 1986–1987. 1540 Main St. (NV 342)

The hotel, built as one of the first lodging houses in the Comstock, is visible to passersby heading to and from Virginia City. The simple stone and brick building contains a first-floor saloon and guest rooms on the second floor. A front porch on shaped balusters with balcony above embellishes the street facade. In 1987–1988 new owners renovated the original structure and added a large wood complex to the rear to provide more hotel rooms.

Silver City

Silver City stands to the south of Devil's Gate, a pass through tall rock outcroppings that mark the boundary between Storey and Lyon counties. Founded in 1859 near the original sites of placer diggings in the 1850s, Silver City never became as prosperous as its neighbors in Storey County. It managed a modest survival, benefiting from the free-flowing cash of prosperous times and weathering periods of depression. Silver City's population probably never exceeded several thousand people, and its buildings are typically unassuming, with limited references to Italianate and other styles.

NW063 Donovan Mill Complex

NW062 **Hardwicke House**

c. 1862. West side of Main St. (NV 342), about .2 mile south of northern Silver City limits

Originally a grocery store, the Hardwicke House is one of the best examples surviving from Silver City's nineteenth-century commer-

cial corridor. Built on a steep slope, it has one story on its front facade and two at the rear. A coursed ashlar facade rises to a stepped parapet; side walls are rougher random-coursed stone.

NW063 **Donovan Mill Complex**

1890. East side of NV 342, near intersection with Pedlar Rd.

The Donovan Mill is an industrial complex of wood-frame buildings sheathed in corrugated metal. Builders usually placed these structures on the slopes of hills so that gravity could help feed the ore through the system. The complex originally included a ten-stamp mill used to pulverize ore; it was enlarged to thirty stamps in the early twentieth century. The mill switched to cyanide processing around 1900 to retrieve microscopic gold and silver deposits. It remained in operation until 1959. The buildings are excellent utilitarian examples of the industrial architecture that played a major role in the state's mining history.

Dayton

One of the oldest communities in Nevada, Dayton was once known as Chinatown because of its large number of Chinese immigrants. In spite of their numerical importance, the Chinese tended to live in neighborhoods with humble wood buildings that were vulnerable to fire and the elements. Faced with prejudice and the failure of Nevada's economy in the late nineteenth century, almost all of the Chinese left for other states. Few Nevada towns have any visible remnants of a Chinatown.

Dayton became a commercial center for surrounding agricultural areas and in the 1850s for the placer miners to the north; it served as the seat of government for Lyon County from 1861 to 1910. Although it predated all other Comstock settlements, tiny Dayton never grew large, seeing its fortunes wane as Virginia City and Gold Hill grew into large cities. Nonetheless, Dayton's mills, using water from the nearby Carson River, provided an important component of the success of the area. Today Dayton is experiencing renewed growth as suburban development from Carson City spreads eastward.

W064 Odeon Hall

1863. 65 Pike St.

The Odeon Saloon and Billiard Parlor provided recreational space as well as a meeting room on the top floor for fraternal groups. Notables who stayed there include Mark Twain and Adolph Sutro, the mining entrepreneur. President Ulysses S. Grant spoke from the balcony in 1879 as part of his tour of the Comstock. The two-story brick Italianate structure has a large pedimented parapet. Four windows pierce the front elevation of the upper floor, which includes a wood balcony resting on a one-story porch consisting of thin posts joined by delicate brackets to the balcony floor.

NW065 Bluestone Building

c. 1862, F. Birdsall. Southwest corner of Main and River sts.

The one-story structure of native stone was home to the Bluestone Manufacturing Company, which produced materials used to mill ore. The business did well during the Comstock heyday of the 1860s and 1870s; but it ceased operation by 1895, and the building fell into disrepair. In the 1980s the Comstock Historic District Commission assumed ownership of the building and gave it to Lyon County. Since then, the structure has been extensively rehabilitated and currently houses a district court. The Bluestone Building is composed of a coursed ashlar facade with stone block quoins and randomly laid stone side walls. A low parapet on its front elevation rises above three bays, pilasters, and segmental-arched openings.

NW066 House (Chinese Residence)

c. 1865. 65 E. Silver St.

This modest wood house was situated in the midst of Dayton's Chinese neighborhood—home during the nineteenth century to Hep Sing and Ty Kim, immigrants from Canton. The simple gable-end structure has single-wall construction supported by wood and stone piers. The house originally included three rooms with dividing walls composed of wide planks covered with fabric, newspapers, and wallpaper.

Sutro

Adolph Sutro, a German immigrant, founded a town, which he named after himself, downriver from Dayton. He designed Sutro City as the home base for his tunnel project, which was to provide drainage and access to the Comstock mines three miles away. After overcoming political opposition, Sutro began construction on the project in 1869 and completed it in 1878. He planned that the tunnel would make it economically advantageous to move all the ore to mills that he would own. He also hoped that miners would prefer to use the tunnel for transportation to the mines, avoiding the more dangerous descent down Virginia City shafts. Sutro City would thus become home to thousands, transforming it into the most important economic and industrial center in the area. By the time the tunnel was completed, however, the Comstock mines had played out, and the town of Sutro was destined to house no more than a few dozen people. Recognizing early on that his plans would not be successful, Sutro sold his stock for a profit shortly before completion of the tunnel and moved to San Francisco, where he became mayor and established Golden Gate Park and the Sutro Baths.

NW067 **Sutro Tunnel**

1869–1878, 1888. Sutro Rd., approximately 3 miles north of Dayton along U.S. 50, then about 1 mile west of U.S. 50

Although several surviving buildings in the townsite of Sutro date from the nineteenth century, the most famous expression of the area's history is its much-photographed tunnel entrance. The tunnel continues to provide passive drainage to the 1,600-foot level of the mines beneath Virginia City, and it is possible to walk hundreds of yards into the precisely excavated tunnel. An elaborate brick facade, coated in plaster and whitewash, decorates the mouth of the tunnel. With its parapet and twin gated portals, the image of the Sutro Tunnel opening has become synonymous with the technological innovations and industrial might of the Comstock. This facade replaced a simpler one in 1888, long after the Comstock mines had slumped and the Sutro Tunnel had failed to realize its creator's expectations.

Carson City

Nestled in Eagle Valley against the Sierra Nevada Mountains, Carson City encompasses nearly 147 square miles of land, ranging from the eastern shore of Lake Tahoe to the Virginia Mountains to the east. The development pattern is densest along U.S. 395 and U.S. 50. As early as 1858, six years before statehood, one of Carson City's first settlers, Abraham Curry, laid out the town's grid. The flat basin of the valley suited Curry's linear plan. He reserved ten acres, bounded by Carson, Musser, Fall, and Third streets, for the capitol building. This area remained an open plaza until construction of the capitol in 1870. An 1875 bird's-eye view of the town shows the capitol surrounded by various residences and commercial buildings, many of which still stand. Today, the capitol complex includes land on both sides of Carson Street (U.S. 395), the main north-south thoroughfare. The grid is preserved in the center of town, breaking down into curving suburban streets as development extends the city's subdivisions to the edges of the valley in all directions.

In addition to being the center of government, Carson City became a commercial hub because of its proximity to the Comstock Lode and its access to the Carson River. Ore removed from the Comstock Lode and processed in mills in Virginia City and along the Carson River went through the U.S. mint in Carson City before heading to other parts of the country in the form of gold and silver coins. The V&T Railroad, the chief mode of transportation for people and supplies after 1872, built its main shops (demolished in 1991) in Carson City. Located in the eastern Sierra foothills, the city also became a center for the logging industry, which transported cut trees from the forests around Lake Tahoe to Carson via a system of flumes.

Today, with the mines of the Comstock and the V&T Railroad long closed, Carson City functions primarily as the center of state government, which provides the town with economic stability. Although tourism is on the rise, visitors perceive the city primarily as a stop-

Carson City

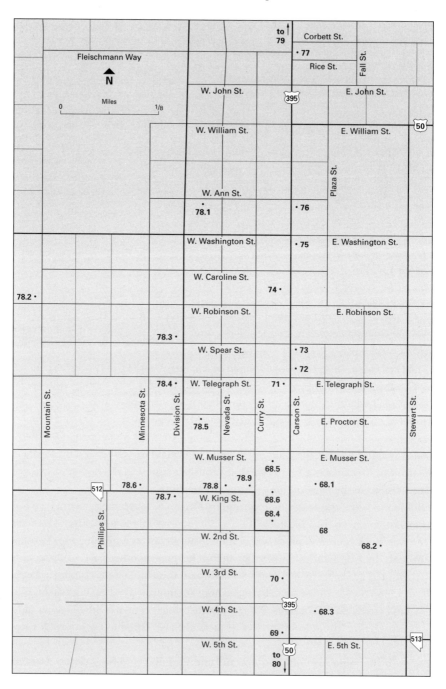

ping-off place on the way to Lake Tahoe or Reno. During the past two decades the population of Carson City has grown, largely as a by-product of development in the Reno and Lake Tahoe areas, and now exceeds 50,000. This growth and its associated sprawl stretching to the outlying edges of town are rapidly transforming Carson City from a small town to a suburb of Reno. The downtown area in particular has struggled for years, as more and more shopping centers and new housing developments pop up at the perimeter. It remains to be seen whether Carson City can retain a sense of place as it experiences rapid growth at its edges.

NW068 Capitol Complex

The Capitol Complex encompasses a large plaza in the center of the city bounded by Carson, Musser, Stewart, and 5th streets, as well as a block across Carson Street bounded by 2nd, Curry, and Musser streets. Although the capitol alone occupied the space set aside by Abe Curry, it now shares the plaza with an office building, the State Library, the Supreme Court, and the State Legislative Building. Directly across Carson Street from the capitol stands the Office of the Attorney General, flanked by the old Ormsby County Courthouse and the Attorney General's Annex, formerly the Heroes Memorial. Together these large public structures create a distinct, if slightly disjointed, district in Carson City.

NW068.1 Nevada State Capitol

1870, Joseph Gosling. 1905, John M. Curtis. 1913, Frederick J. DeLongchamps. 1970s, renovation. 101 N. Carson St.

The Nevada State Capitol stands in the center of Carson City. Early photographs show the building standing nearly alone, with only a few low houses and sheds in the background. Today densely planted mature pine and American elm trees on the capitol lawn prevent a full view of the structure. An iron fence, installed in 1875, still surrounds the grounds. Like many other buildings constructed in Nevada in the late nineteenth century, the capitol cannot be identified by a single architectural style; it presents a mixture of styles, dominated by the Italianate, with round-arched biforated windows, and the neoclassical, with its pedimented central section. This design reflects the lack of trained architects working in the West at that time; local builders seem to have consulted the abundant pattern books that encouraged a combination of architectural elements.

On 23 February 1869 state legislators authorized the construction of a state capitol. The following year the Board of Capitol Commissioners selected a design by Joseph Gosling of San Francisco, who was known as both an architect and a master builder. Gosling drew up plans for a building in the form of a Greek cross, which Peter Cavanaugh and Sons of Carson City erected. Standing two-and-one-half-stories tall, it is flanked by wings erected at a later date and capped by a gable roof and a white octagonal cupola with eight arched windows.

Rusticated sandstone blocks make up the load-bearing walls, measuring 8 feet thick at the basement level, 3 feet thick at the first story, and 2 feet 6 inches thick at the second story. The projecting central section, which has a large pediment trimmed with dentils and brackets, features a small porch projecting beyond the arched, recessed door and supported by four slender, fluted wooden columns with Roman Doric details. Similar but smaller porches cover the recessed entrances on the north and south sides. Quoins and protruding window surrounds add surface texture to the walls. A white balustrade extends along the roofline of the wings. The cupola rising above the main mass of the building was originally wood-framed and covered with tin. Granite blocks form the steps and door sills. The original interior walls were all constructed of brick. The capitol contains fourteen rooms on the first floor, originally including the offices of the governor, attorney general, controller, and treasurer. On the second floor are twelve rooms, among them the chambers of the Assembly and the Senate, the Supreme Court, and the State Library.

As Nevada's population grew, the number of legislators increased, requiring enlargement of the capitol. In 1905 the state commissioned John M. Curtis to design an octagonal sandstone library addition, which stands to the east of the capitol, connected to the main building by a breezeway. An enclosed second story over

NW068.1 Nevada State Capitol in 1876 (top) and today (bottom)

the breezeway, supported by eight fluted Doric columns, provides access to the annex's second level. A projecting vestibule, finished with two small octagonal cupolas and topped by lanterns, meets the passageway.

In 1913 the legislature approved the addition of two wings on the north and south sides, which provided larger chambers for the Senate and Assembly on the second floor and additional office space on the first floor. Frederick J. DeLongchamps designed the wings to match the original part of the capitol in materials and style, but he added numerous classical details and ornate finishes, lavishly decorating the first-floor halls and lobby with gray Alaskan marble for the wainscot, arches, and floors. His designs also called for a painted frieze along the first-floor halls, which depicts the industries and resources of the state, such as mining and silver, ranching and cattle. Pine cones, representing the landscape of the northern part of the state, form the top border, while grapes, representing the landscape of the southern part, line the bottom border. In the legislative chambers, DeLongchamps added Corinthian pilasters flanking the public galleries, modillions, and dentils.

The exterior of the building has changed little since 1913. In 1959 the Assembly passed a resolution to preserve and repair the capitol in response to the State Planning Board's proposal to demolish the building and replace it with a modern structure. Ten years later the state legislature decided to construct a separate legislative building to accommodate the growing Senate and Assembly and their staffs rather than add onto the capitol building itself. A major renovation of the capitol in the 1970s, however, resulted in the gutting of the interior. Workers carefully numbered and replaced all removed pieces after installing concrete shear walls to bring the building up to modern seismic codes. Fiberglass replicas of exterior wood features, including the cupola on the capitol and the window frames, were put in place.

The state capitol continues to house the offices of the governor, secretary of state, treasurer, state controller, and lieutenant governor. The Senate chamber now contains an exhibit on the history of the capitol, while the Assembly chamber functions as a meeting hall. The Supreme Court and State Library acquired their own building in 1937. The capitol remained the tallest building in Carson City until the completion in 1972 of the twelve-story Ormsby House Hotel and Casino, about two blocks south on Carson Street. The physical dominance of a casino rather than the capitol symbolizes the political power wielded by the gambling industry in Nevada.

NW068.2 Supreme Court

1989–1991, Eissmann-Pence Architects. 201 S. Carson St.

Although the Supreme Court was originally housed in the capitol, the latter's 1913 remodeling compromised office space for the judicial branch of government. In 1937 the Supreme Court moved across the street to what is now the Office of the Attorney General. By the 1980s the judicial branch had once again outgrown its quarters. The local architecture firm of Eissmann-Pence designed a new four-story facility, which was constructed in 1989–1991.

The west facade, looking onto the capitol plaza, has a stripped-down, pedimented portico with four bays on each side, defined by monumental but simple piers. The east facade has an imposing portico flanked by recessed wings. An elaborate system of staircases and landings on this side provides exterior access to the first two floors of the building. The main entrance leads into a three-story octagonal atrium below the rotunda—a monumental ceremonial space unlike most others in the state. Columns mark each of the eight corners, and the room is crowned with a shallow ribbed, glass dome. Embedded in the marble floor is a large brass image of the state seal. A concrete band above the second floor and below the rotunda features in relief the words "One nation under God, indivisible, with liberty and justice for all."

The courtroom is a large space decorated with pink marble and mahogany; the seal of the Nevada Supreme Court adorns the wall above the bench. The top floor provides office space for the justices and staff. Below the main floor is the ground-level Supreme Court Library. The building rests on a subterranean parking garage.

Like the recently renovated State Legislative Building and the State Library (1993) next door, the Supreme Court displays a late twentieth-century tendency toward the banal in public buildings in the Capitol Complex. Limited budgets and the desire on the part of architects and legislators to erect buildings that will not offend have produced results unworthy of the

NW068.3 State Legislative Building today (top) and in 1970

earlier tradition of small but elegantly designed structures.

NW068.3 State Legislative Building

1967–1970, Graham Erskine. 1996–1997, Dolven-Simpson/JMA Architects. 401 S. Carson St.

The history of the State Legislative Building reflects the changing tastes and aspirations of Nevadans. Originally built to provide additional space for the two chambers of the legislature, the structure has continued to grow. In 1995, in a move reminiscent of casino makeovers in Las Vegas, the legislature appropriated money to double the size of the building, making it larger than the capitol. At the same time, the architects gave it an exterior facelift.

A central three-story section containing a lobby is flanked by two one-story semicircular wings housing the two chambers of the legislature. The building's original appearance was monumental and geometric. Vertical beige and brown aggregate panels, divided by bands of white stucco, covered the walls. Narrow white precast concrete panels projected beyond the windows to allow some light inside the building while lending it a fortress-like character. Designed and erected in the late 1960s when public officials in Nevada feared riots, the shielded windows and cold materials created an intended expression of aloofness.

In 1995 the state legislature, less concerned about making the building more accessible than about providing more spacious offices for its members, sought to enlarge it. A five-story addition now looms over the original structure. The panels over the windows were removed, and the walls were refaced with concrete panels covered with pale pink stucco. An arcade articulated by plain engaged columns embellishes square window openings on the third story. Crucial to the remodeling was the addition of a dome, so that the legislative building would evoke the capitol and Supreme Court. However, the legislative dome, stuck awkwardly on the front of the building atop thin two-story-high columns, is disproportionately small. Beneath it is a small circular vestibule enclosed by glass. This area opens into the lobby, which has terrazzo floors and steel balustrades—survivors from the building's first incarnation.

The resultant renovation is not felicitous. The architects addressed the transition between the old and new sections by designing small gabled hyphens that are overshadowed by the rear addition. Disproportionately small "classical" arcades are stuck onto the walls seemingly as an afterthought, appearing more like the pseudoclassicism found in Las Vegas casino complexes rather than in public buildings.

NW068.4 Attorney General's Annex (Heroes Memorial Building)

NW068.5 Carson City Offices (Ormsby County Courthouse)

1920–1922, Frederick J. DeLongchamps. 100 S. Carson St. and 19 N. Carson St.

DeLongchamps designed these twin buildings across Carson Street from the capitol during one of his appointments as state architect (1919–1921). First he devised a plan for the Heroes Memorial, honoring those who fought in World War I. Then he suggested the same design to Ormsby County for its new courthouse just to the north of the state building. Both buildings have prominent porticoes with pediments and Tuscan columns. DeLongchamps, who had designed the Nevada buildings for San Francisco's Panama-Pacific Exposition (1915) and San Diego's Panama-California Exposition (1915–1916), may have wished to create an orderly plaza along the lines of the City Beautiful movement. The two coursed sandstone Classical Revival buildings originally flanked an open landscaped court centered on an ornate fountain. The Office of the Attorney General (NW068.6, formerly the Supreme Court and State Library) now stands in the middle of this court, and the fountain has been moved to a position in front of it. The state legislature has since dissolved Ormsby County, but its courthouse, together with its twin, continues to serve the public. Heroes Memorial houses additional offices of the state attorney general, while the courthouse accommodates Carson City's judicial functions.

NW068.6 Office of the Attorney General (Supreme Court and State Library)

1935–1937, Frederick J. DeLongchamps. 198 S. Carson St.

In 1937 the Nevada State Supreme Court and the State Library moved across the street from the capitol into new quarters. This austere structure stands between the identical Carson City Offices and Attorney General's Annex. As in his post office in Reno, DeLongchamps employed terra-cotta to clad the stone core of the walls. The sober dignity of the building is relieved only by occasional ornament, including a deeply incised Greek fret pattern on the cornice, simple fluted pilasters dividing the bays, and panels between the windows with incised chevrons and stylized sunbursts. The Supreme Court moved from the building to a new structure on the capitol plaza in 1991. Since then, the building has housed the Office of the Attorney General. Hyphens in the rear of the building connect it to the former Heroes Memorial Building to the south.

NW069 Jack's Bar and Saloon

1899. 418 S. Carson St.

The slightly leaning, rough-hewn sandstone walls of the town's oldest continually operating bar evoke an earlier urban architecture on South Carson Street. The walls rise to a low parapet that steps up from the rear toward the front. The main entrance to the bar, at the busy intersection of 5th and Carson streets, is set in the corner of the building for greatest visibility. Iron pilasters cast in Reno delineate the bays and entrance of the structure. The interior has changed little over the years. The ceiling still has its original narrow tongue-and-groove boards. The wooden bar was once housed in the Magnolia Saloon, located in the old Ormsby County Courthouse, which was demolished in 1920.

NW070 St. Charles Hotel

1862. 302–304–310 S. Carson St.

The St. Charles is composed of two abutting Italianate hotels, both constructed in 1862 as the first permanent hostelries in the town. The two-story Muller's Hotel, the smaller of the two, served working-class locals and visitors to town. The more imposing three-story St. Charles, capped by a heavy wood cornice decorated with brackets, quickly became popular among prominent residents. A one-story porch once ran along the Carson and 3rd Street facades; today a porch built in 1995 stands along the main facade.

In 1895 the two buildings were united as one hotel, which also accommodates commercial enterprises such as offices, saloons, restaurants, and shops. The hotel had fallen into disrepair by 1993, when a new owner began a major rehabilitation. At about the same time a developer added new facades to the one-story commercial buildings across 3rd Street. The brightly colored, frontier-style false fronts provide a jarring contrast to the worn brick of the St. Charles.

NW071 Justice Court (Nevada Bell Telephone Company Office)

1930, Frederick J. DeLongchamps. 320 N. Carson St.

This well-executed one-story structure has traces of the Spanish Churrigueresque style in its door and window surrounds. The warm-toned brick walls are vigorously ornamented with terra-cotta tile forming elaborately detailed window surrounds with quoins rising to pointed arches. The small but refined building enhanced the presence of Nevada Bell in the town and underscored the growing importance of the telephone in American life.

NW072 Nevada Commission on Tourism (U.S. Federal Courthouse and Post Office)

1888–1891, Mifflin E. Bell, Will Freret, James Windrim. 401 N. Carson St.

The only example of the Richardsonian Romanesque style in the state, this imposing brick and stone building commands attention. Planned and built under the administrations of three supervising architects of the U.S. Treasury Department, the structure reflects the style favored by the department for its buildings throughout the nation in the last two decades of the nineteenth century. Its impressive appearance attests to its significance as the state's first federal courthouse. In 1886 the federal government purchased the lot and demolished the town's opera house on that site. Upon completion, the new structure contained a post office, land office, weather bureau, and federal courts. The courts moved to Reno in 1965, and the post office was relocated in 1970 to a new federal building two blocks away. The state acquired the property for its library, which remained in the building until the opening of the new State Library behind the capitol in 1993. The building now houses the Nevada Commission on Tourism.

Dark red brick walls and asymmetrical massing characterize the structure, which stands on a granite foundation emphasizing its robustness. A four-story clock tower at the northwest corner rises high above the street. Horizontal bands add depth to the building's surface and counteract its verticality by delineating the separate levels of the structure. Carved sandstone capitals and lintels over the windows provide accents to the brick surfaces. An arcade of four arches resting on square columns leads to the recessed entrance.

Inside, Corinthian columns support the ceiling of the first floor. The courtroom was on the second floor at the east end. Its 20-foot-high ceilings, the tallest in the building, emphasize the room's importance. The building's long use has resulted in many alterations to the interior spaces.

NW074 Nevada State Museum (U.S. Mint)

NW073 **Carson Nugget**

1953, 1957, 1980s. 507 N. Carson St.

Built as a coffee shop in 1953 and converted to a casino in 1957, this structure is less important for its architecture, which has changed over the years, than for its large sign dominating the northwest corner. It copies the famous Las Vegas Golden Nugget sign, designed by Kermit Wayne of the Young Electric Sign Company (YESCO), maker of many of the most famous examples in Las Vegas. The Las Vegas sign is gone, a victim of that casino's latest facelift. The Carson City Nugget, a decorated shed built of concrete block, is typical of mid-twentieth-century casino architecture—a long, low, rectangular box to which signs could be attached.

NW074 **Nevada State Museum** (U.S. Mint)

1866–1869, Alfred Bult Mullett. 1971, Hewitt C. Wells. 600 N. Nevada St.

Like many of the structures of the Capitol Complex, the Nevada State Museum building, erected as a U.S. mint, is constructed of local sandstone. Millions of dollars of gold and silver bullion from the Comstock Lode passed through its doors. The mint produced both ingots and coins. The rough-faced stone walls and simple, stocky appearance of the building presented a facade of security. Mullett, Supervising Architect of the Treasury from 1866 to 1874, advocated large scale in government buildings to emphasize permanence and solidity. The two-story building has both Classical Revival and Italianate elements, seen in the front and rear pediments, symmetrical five-bay facade, and prominent brackets lining the cornice. A central section containing the entrance projects toward Carson Street. The entrance itself is sheltered by a stone porch with segmental-arched openings supported by wide piers with pairs of Tuscan pilasters. Both the porch and the cupola surmounting the hipped roof are constructed of smooth-faced sandstone to contrast with the rough walls of the main structure. In 1878 a one-story rear wing was added, followed by a second story in 1881.

The building served as the mint until 1893, when it became a federal office building. In 1939 the state of Nevada purchased the building for use as a museum. In 1959 it added a small wing to the southwest for exhibition space, and, in 1971, demolished the late nineteenth-century wing to make way for a boxy replacement with tall arched windows. The insensitive addition does not do justice to the venerable building.

NW075 **Masonic Temple** (Virginia and Truckee Passenger Depot)

1872, Virginia and Truckee Railroad. 729 N. Carson St.

Though it seems out of place today, the depot was once the main arrival and departure point for travelers to Carson City. The V&T Railroad tracks led from Virginia City and came down Washington Street just north of the depot. The one-story, wood-frame building is a rectangle oriented so that its long north side faced the tracks. The gable roof faces Carson Street; on that side a shed roof protects what is now the main entrance to the building. With its board-and-batten siding and wide overhanging eaves supported by crossed diagonal brackets, the depot is a classic example of railroad architecture of the period. The structure served as the depot until the closing down of the V&T Railroad in 1950. The Masons have used the building since 1952.

NW076 **Northern Nevada Children's Museum** (Civic Auditorium)

1939, Lehman A. Ferris. 813 N. Carson St.

The red brick walls and sandstone trim of this one-story building echo the materials used in the courthouse to the south, but the result is much more sedate. A gabled entry projects from the facade and features two pairs of octagonally paneled wood doors surrounded by a large sandstone arch. Engaged Ionic columns

flank the doors, dividing the two pairs at the center of the entry. A large fanlight window surmounts the doors, resting on a plain entablature. Adorning the facade gable is a corbeled brick arcade. The lobby leads into a large auditorium with a raised stage at the east end. The auditorium has been modified slightly with the installation of an elevator shaft, and the space now contains exhibits for the museum.

In the 1930s Carson City had no public meeting space. With a federal grant and funds raised locally, the Works Progress Administration erected the auditorium, using Ferris's design. At the time the style and size of the building were unusual for Carson City, which used the building as a library and later for city offices, vacating it in 1983. Since 1994 the Children's Museum has occupied the building.

NW077 **James D. Roberts House**

1859, moved 1873. 1207 N. Carson St.

The Roberts House is the only surviving example of a Carpenter's Gothic residence in Carson City. A front-facing gable roof covers the wood-frame building. Clapboards sheathe the walls, which rise to a roofline trimmed with bargeboards in the gables and drop molding hanging from the eaves. Pairs of slender wooden posts, embellished with carved brackets, support the porch. A balustrade of turned posts topping the porch and a stumpy, pointed-arched door opening onto the porch's roof appear to be later additions, as they do not match the lines of the house.

NW077 James D. Roberts House (left)

NW078.1 David Smaill House (below)

The door most likely replaced a window. On the north side is a small, two story gabled wing containing a secondary entry. Its rich jigsawn details include attenuated bargeboards and an ornate balustrade on the balcony, which rests on delicate brackets.

The dwelling was moved from Washoe Valley in 1873 on a V&T Railroad flatcar. Carson City and Carson Valley to the south have many homes relocated from Virginia City and the Washoe Valley after those areas fell into economic decline. Now standing on North Carson Street in an area of commercial strip development, the house, set in a small park, seems isolated and out of place. Owned by the Carson City Parks Department, it functions as a local museum.

NW078 Carson City Historic District

Bounded roughly by 5th, Curry, Mountain, and John sts.

Carson City's only residential historic district, on the west side of town, is characterized by short, straight blocks, mature trees, and a mixture of large and modest houses ranging in date from the mid-nineteenth century to the present. Once the primary residential area of town, the west side has a number of houses once inhabited by prominent individuals, including governors, state legislators, and Supreme Court justices, although many nearby houses were built for the middle and working classes. This intermingling of economic levels was not uncommon in small-town Nevada; however, since the mid-twentieth century, as settlements have grown rapidly, neighborhoods have become more segregated by class in the newer areas of towns. The district is historically significant for of its late nineteenth- and early twentieth-century architecture, which includes examples of many of the major styles of the period. Zoning laws established in the 1980s have allowed limited commercial use through the conversion of houses to offices. Although this action has promoted the use of historic buildings in the district, it has altered the original character of the neighborhood, as offices close in the evenings and on weekends. Off-street parking requirements for offices have turned many yards into asphalt lots. As the economy has accelerated in the 1990s, the district has lost an increasing number of historic structures to development.

NW078.1 David Smaill House

c. 1876, David Smaill. 313 W. Ann St.

This one-story gabled building represents a type of house commonly constructed in the late nineteenth century. Many miners and tradesmen in northern Nevada built individualistic, eclectic, and highly decorative houses. The Smaill House uses Eastlake-inspired wood porch trim and has an exuberant carved bargeboard; a gable pendant, often seen in houses of this type during that period; and a framed circular vent. Builders constructed the shell of a house and then applied prefabricated wood ornamentation.

NW078.2 Governor's Mansion

1908–1909, George A. Ferris. 1968, interior renovation. 606 Mountain St.

By the time Nevada finally agreed to construct a permanent governor's residence, it had been a state for over fifty years. Governors had had to build their own residences or live in existing houses. Several still stand in the district, including the Governor John E. Jones House at 600 West Robinson Street, the Governor Reinhold Sadler House at 310 North Mountain Street, and the Stewart-Nye House at 108 North Minnesota Street.

Of all the houses in the historic district, the one now called the Governor's Mansion is the most impressive. Set on a raised stone foundation, the two-story, wood-frame building spreads behind a broad, full-height portico supported by Ionic columns clustered in groups of three at the corners. Ionic pilasters flank the entrance and mark the corners of the mansion; dentils run along the cornice and the tympanum of the portico, adding further classical detail. The entryway has paneled double doors with side windows. Large double-hung windows pierce the clapboard-sided walls on both stories. A one-story porch, with Ionic columns resting on a brick wall and rising to a wooden balustrade, wraps around the front, south, and rear facades, giving the house a sense of formality and grandeur that is seen in few buildings in the state's capital.

Although the exterior is largely intact, the state drastically reorganized major interior spaces in 1968. Today the first floor contains a central grand entry hall with curving staircase, north and south reception rooms, formal dining room, governor's study, lunchroom, and kitchen. Upstairs are the family's living quarters. To the north of the mansion are a three-

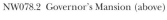

NW078.2 Governor's Mansion (above)

NW078.4 St. Peter's Episcopal Church (right)

car garage and a housekeeper's bungalow. Visible behind the house from Robinson Street are a circular Classical Revival fountain and pavilion donated in August 1969 by Harvey Gross, owner of Harvey's Casino in Stateline, Nevada, in memory of his wife. This structure is now crowded by a new garage, built in 1998, facing south onto Robinson Street.

NW078.3 Orion Clemens House

1862. 502 N. Division St.

Best known as the residence of the brother of Samuel Langhorne Clemens (Mark Twain), this house is an excellent example of early residential architecture in Carson City. The L-shaped structure has a gable roof with cornice returns lined with dentils, characteristic of the Greek Revival, whereas the brackets under the eaves and gables reflect the Italianate style. The wood-frame building originally stood on a foundation of timber posts driven into the earth. Like many other buildings in this part of the historic district, located close to state and local government buildings, the Clemens House now functions as a law office. The house has undergone many alterations over the years, including the application of stucco over the original drop-sided walls and the substitution of plain window surrounds for more ornate Italianate ones.

Orion Clemens went to Carson City in 1861 as secretary to the territorial governor of Nevada, an appointment received in return for supporting Abraham Lincoln in the presidential election of 1860. His younger brother, Samuel, accompanied him on the twenty-one-day overland journey by stage from St. Joseph, Missouri, to Carson City. Their trip and early days in Nevada are recounted in Twain's *Roughing It.*

NW078.4 St. Peter's Episcopal Church

1867, Corbett Brothers. 1873–1874, John G. Parker. 312 N. Division St.

This white clapboard church, the oldest extant Episcopal church in the state, looks as if it belongs in a New England town. In fact, many of the congregation's members had come from the East, and they constructed a building that reflected their roots. The tall, narrow steeple, the lancet windows, and the steep gable roof all contribute to the verticality of the structure. Narrow horizontal siding gives the church a severe but monumental aspect. Small carved brackets under the eaves and along the gables add Italianate detail to a building with Gothic-inspired arches, round vent, and steeple. The original part of the church measured 46 by 27 feet. By 1873 the congregation had outgrown the building, so a rear addition was constructed in 1873–1874, lengthening the church to 70 feet. Wings projecting from this addition housed the lecture and Sunday school rooms. The entry vestibule leads directly into a rectangular, four-bay nave that ends in a shallow, slightly elevated chancel at the west end. Four windows on each side, with colored leaded glass, let in a limited amount of light. An arcaded three-bay screen separates the nave from the chancel. The church is in excellent condition and has been altered little since 1874.

NW078.5 Dat-So-La-Lee House

1914, Abram Cohn. 331 W. Proctor St.

This modest building was once the home of the famous Washoe Indian basket weaver Louisa Keyser (c. 1861–1925), better known as Dat-So-La-Lee. Cohn and his wife, Clarisse Amy, collectors of Native American art, promoted Keyser's work and built for her the tiny, one-story, board-and-batten cottage with a gable roof adjacent to their own house. The Washoe Tribe of Nevada and California now owns the building and plans to open a museum in it.

NW078.6 Stewart-Nye House

c. 1861. 108 N. Minnesota St.

After the secession of the southern states, the federal government extended its control over the American West. From 1861 to 1864, Congress granted territorial status to every remaining unorganized area of the country except Oklahoma. The Stewart-Nye House thus gains some of its historical significance as the home of Nevada's only territorial governor, James W. Nye, later one of the state's first U.S. senators. The house was also the residence of William M. Stewart, Nevada's other first U.S. senator.

The house is typical of the simple structures built in Nevada's early years. A long rectangle broken by a bay window, it rises from a low stone foundation. Sandstone blocks are joined by raised mortar joints to form the walls. A full-length porch covers the first-floor facade, supported by double posts with simple molded capitals. The wood-frame roof has gable ends that were later stuccoed.

The Roman Catholic bishop of Sacramento purchased the house in 1917. It is currently owned by the Roman Catholic Diocese of Reno

and functions as the rectory of St. Teresa of Avila Church, across King Street from the house.

NW078.7 Brewery Arts Center (Carson Brewery)

1864. 102 S. Division St.

Originally the home of the Carson Brewing Company, founded in 1862, this utilitarian brick structure now houses the Brewery Arts Center. A bracketed cornice and low parapet edge the roofline of the hip-roofed rectangular structure. The cornice and segmental arches above the window and door openings offer some ornamentation on the otherwise plain brick exterior. The interior walls are wainscoted. The first floor housed a bar and saloon in the northeast corner, with the remaining space used for storage. The second floor, originally reached by a set of enclosed stairs attached to the rear of the building, has two rooms; the larger served as the Masonic Hall and still contains the raised dais used by the lodge master for meetings. The ceiling retains the original painted ornamentation of wreaths. The second room was used as a cooling room for beer. Despite Prohibition, the brewery survived until 1948. From 1951 to 1975, Carson City's local newspaper, the *Nevada Appeal*, was produced in the building, subsequently moving to new premises. The Brewery Arts Center now uses the space for exhibits, performances, and receptions.

NW078.8 Olcovich-Meyers House

1874–1875, Joseph Olcovich. 214 W. King St.

Two families prominent in the local Jewish community lived in this house for decades. Joseph Olcovich built the house but sold it to his brother, Bernard, one year later. The Olcovich family owned a store on Carson Street that helped supply the town and the Comstock with commercial goods. Many European Jews moved west in the nineteenth century, seeking their fortunes mainly as merchants in frontier towns.

The overall shape and facade of the wood-frame house, with its dominant front-facing gable and steeply pitched roof, reflect the influence of the Gothic Revival. Features added in the late 1880s indicate the builder's love of ornament typical of the late Victorian era. A front porch with spiral columns, a spindlework frieze, and a balustrade bring the facade toward the sidewalk. Other Victorian elements include ornately carved bargeboards in the peaks of the front and side gables. The bay windows on the front and sides of the house were added about the same time as the porch.

NW078.9 Rinckel Mansion

1875–1876, Charles H. Jones. 102 N. Curry St.

In its location on the east edge of the historic district, the Rinckel Mansion provides a transition between the large government buildings to the east and the smaller residential buildings to the west. The house is unusual for Carson City in that it was built of brick rather than wood or stone, the favored materials in the city at that time. It is one of the few nineteenth-century houses in Nevada known to have been designed by an architect. Jones, who trained at the Ecole des Beaux-Arts in Paris, provided an imposing house for his client, Mathias Rinckel, a German immigrant who made a fortune on the Comstock.

The impressive building stands two stories tall on a raised sandstone foundation. The pressed brick walls rise to a steeply pitched hipped roof decorated with ornate wrought iron cresting along the ridges. Large brackets support the cornice and gable. Two three-sided projecting bays flanking a porch and large double windows above dominate the facade. The porch extends from the corners of the bays, repeating their forms in its three-sided shape.

The house has accommodated a number of uses, including a wedding chapel and, most recently, a restaurant. The main floor, which contains dining rooms for the restaurant, is largely intact. The main entrance of double doors opens into a stair hall with grained woodwork resembling walnut. Woodwork in the rest of the house simulates oak and curly maple, except in the two parlors on the main floor, where the woodwork is painted white. Ornamental plasterwork on the ceilings and light fixtures remain from Mathias Rinckel's days.

NW079 Lakeview House

1873, Virginia City and Gold Hill Water Company. U.S. 395 south of E. Lake Blvd.

The Virginia City and Gold Hill Water Company erected the small house at the top of the hill dividing Washoe and Eagle valleys as part of the Marlette Lake Water System. The wood-frame building, now known as the Lakeview House, housed the water company's superintendent. Three water pipes nearby, laid between 1873 and 1887, brought water to the Comstock. The house remains nearly unaltered. Its L-shaped plan is embellished with a front-facing gable with jigsawn ornamentation in the gable peak. A porch nestled in the corner of the two wings has turned posts and spindlework along the roofline. Shiplap siding covers the walls.

NW080 Stewart Indian School

The Stewart Indian School is an intact complex of eighty-three buildings three and one-half miles south of Carson City. Although the 109-acre complex was once isolated from the town, new subdivisions now encroach upon the site. The school operated between 1890 and 1980 as Nevada's only nonreservation boarding facility founded to educate Native Americans. It began as the Stewart Institute, established by the Nevada state legislature in 1877. In that same year, U.S. Senator William Stewart of Nevada sponsored legislation requiring the federal government to provide funding for the school and to operate it to teach trades that would foster economic self-sufficiency. As was typical at the time, the school also promoted cultural assimilation by prohibiting the use of native languages and the practice of traditional religions and rituals.

The original two-story, wood-frame building no longer stands. The majority of the institution's surviving structures, erected from 1922 to 1944, were constructed of native rhyolitic stone in hues of pink, green, and brown joined with dark mortar. Frederick Snyder, school superintendent from 1919 to 1934, designed many of the stone buildings, drawing on the Craftsman style to establish a unifying form for the complex. In the 1930s the construction division of the U.S. Department of the Interior took over the design of the school's buildings, but the chief architect, Carl Sederstrand, continued to follow Snyder's basic design program in a simplified form. Stonemasons James and John Christopher constructed most of the masonry buildings at Stewart. Since the complex ceased to function as a school, it has been administered by a patchwork of federal, state, local, and tribal government managers. This arrangement has not always resulted in good stewardship of the structures, many of which are deteriorated or vacant. Others have been rehabilitated in recent years, showing possibilities for the site's adaptive reuse.

NW080.1 **Administrative Building** (Building 1)

1923, Frederick Snyder

This one-and-one-half-story structure was the first in the complex to be built of native stone. The building's H-plan has short wings ending in gables with stickwork. Window openings are marked by coursed masonry, flat arches, and slightly projecting cast concrete sills. Much of the interior has been altered, but it retains some rustic features reminiscent of the Arts and Crafts movement, including false beams and an ashlar stone fireplace with a solid rock mantel in the main room on the first floor.

NW080.2 **Stewart Indian Museum** (Superintendent's Cottage, Building 3)

1930, Frederick Snyder and the U.S. Department of the Interior

For his own residence, Snyder designed the most complete example of his interpretation of the Craftsman style established for the school.

NW080.1 AdministrativeBuilding (Building 1) (op)

NW080.3 Auditorium (Building 90) (bottom)

The one-and-one-half-story U-shaped house stands perpendicular to the administration building, forming an impressive entry to the complex. A long recessed porch along the main (east) facade and two wings projecting to the west form a courtyard at the rear of the house. Window and door openings are marked by coursed stone, flat arches, and rusticated stone sills. The Washoe tribe now uses the house as a museum.

NW080.3 **Auditorium** (Building 90)

1925, U.S. Department of the Interior

The auditorium combines a simplified form of classicism with the local characteristics of neighboring buildings. The rectangular structure has pedimented gable ends and a wide, banded cornice defining its major geometric elements. The multicolored stone walls end in cut sandstone quoins at the corners and rise from a rusticated sandstone water table. The two main entrances are approached by side-facing steps and a raised platform. Arches of sandstone set flush with the wall mark the entrances and windows. Built to serve as an assembly hall, the auditorium has a refined appearance that helped raise public awareness of the school and its position as one of Nevada's showplaces.

NW080.4 **Girls' Dormitory** (Building 16)

1942, Carl Sederstrand, U.S. Department of the Interior

This large one-story building is one of the simpler structures on the site, reflecting the increasingly spare designs of the federal government, which by this time was devoting its funds to the war effort. Instead of porches and stickwork details, the dormitory has flat surfaces. Nevertheless, it retains the characteristic multicolored stone walls and symmetrical form of the other school buildings. It is similar to other girls' dormitories at the school but has a U-plan rather than an H-plan. Dark wood shingles sheathe the upper gable ends, which are pierced by circular vents.

NW080.5 **Washoe Cultural Center** (Cottage, Building 26)

1937, Carl Sederstrand, U.S. Department of the Interior

Originally built as staff housing, this single-story, L-shaped stone building now serves as the Washoe tribe's cultural center. The modest structure has a main entrance sheltered by an open porch nestled in the junction of the wings. The wall flanking the entrance has board-and-batten siding. Wide horizontal wood boards trim the upper gable ends. The building represents a successful example of adaptive reuse, which could preserve the complex.

Genoa

Mormons founded Genoa, one of Nevada's earliest Euro-American settlements, in 1851. A year earlier members of the church had opened a trading post here to serve the Emigrant Trail. By the mid-1850s a few hundred families, both Mormons and non-Mormons, had established farms in this fertile part of Carson Valley. When the Mormons returned to Utah in 1857, they abandoned their land and property, losing their political hold over the valley. In a few years Genoa lost its prominence, as other towns such as Carson City and Virginia City benefited from the Comstock boom. When the V&T Railroad bypassed Genoa and instead went to nearby Minden in the early twentieth century, the town fell into a state of decline. However, the farms and ranches surrounding the town continued to thrive by supplying nearby cities with produce and other agricultural products.

Today Genoa's small village center, part of a National Register Historic District, retains remnants of its past; most of the empty lots once had buildings. Numerous historic buildings have been insensitively remodeled, drastically altering their original appearance. In addition, rapid growth in the valley threatens the town's peaceful existence by increasing density and encouraging unsympathetic development. Subdivisions of oversized, pseudo-Victorian houses abut the boundaries of Genoa's historic district. Historic structures have been demolished and others are threatened. Hollywood images of "the West" have gained prominence, overshadowing the authentic surviving architecture.

NW081 **Genoa Courthouse Museum** (Douglas County Courthouse)

1865, T. J. Furbee. 2300 Main St.

In 1864 the Nevada territorial legislature authorized Douglas County to raise taxes for a courthouse in Genoa. The local government commissioned T. J. Furbee, a mining superintendent, to design the structure, which was completed in 1865. It is the oldest standing courthouse in Nevada. A sturdy stone foundation supports the rectangular two-story brick building. Transoms and side lights surround a centered doorway, capped with an elaborate denticulated cornice. A later one-story addition to the northeast corner of the building elongates the facade, disrupting its symmetry. The interior includes a second-story courtroom and offices for officials. In the back of the first floor is a tin jail cell that is little more

than a metal box with two compartments. The courthouse partially burned down in 1910 but was quickly restored. Nonetheless, the local government soon moved to larger quarters in nearby Minden. The Genoa courthouse now serves as a local museum.

NW082 **Mormon Station State Park**

1947, Edward S. Parsons. 2295 Main St.

This one-story log cabin surrounded by a wood stockade is a mid-twentieth-century replica of the original cabin and stockade built in 1851 as a trading station. The original complex with its assemblage of additions and alterations burned down in 1910. In 1947 the state legislature appropriated money to reconstruct the cabin to promote Genoa's early history. Parsons, at the time the State Highway Department's architect, used historic photographs and archaeological findings to reconstruct the cabin as accurately as possible and to site it properly on its lot. Logs cut near Genoa recreated the rectangular, gabled central mass and the shed-roofed addition. A central stone chimney rises above the roof ridge. The excellent condition of the building and its surrounding two-and-one-half-acre park gives the complex an overrestored feeling that contrasts with the more rustic character of some of the older buildings nearby.

NW083 Main Street

West side of 2200 block of Main St.

The west side of Main Street has a number of mid- to late nineteenth-century structures. Among these, the two-story brick Masonic Hall (1862), 2286 Main Street, commands a prominent spot at the intersection of Main and Nixon streets and Genoa Lane. The facade is a simple and symmetrical gabled rectangle; two doorways covered with iron shutters pierce the first story. A one-story, full-length porch, supported by three square

posts, shelters the entrances. The one-story stone building (1870s), 2284 Main Street, abutting the Masonic Hall was built for use as a store and now contains an antique shop. The walls of rough-cut stone rise to a false front. Large iron shutters protect the entrances on the first floor. The wooden cornice along the roofline and the porch covering the first floor are recent additions. The brick of the Genoa Bar (1850s), 2282 Main Street, was made in a kiln north of town. The false front rises to a decorative brick cornice that hides the building's gable roof. A shed-roofed porch resting on four square posts protects three pairs of French doors, of which the central pair leads into the bar. The wood-frame addition to the north of the bar is a recently built structure intended to give the bar an "old West" look. Despite some modern alterations,

NW082 Cabin, Mormon Station State Park (right)

NW083 Main Street, Genoa (below)

this block remains the oldest and best preserved in Genoa.

NW084 Town Hall

1886, 1977. 2287 Main St.

The town hall stands on the east side of Main Street, a block away from the nineteenth-century commercial buildings on the west side. Initially built as the Raycraft Dance Hall, the structure has a large interior space that functions well today as a community meeting place. The one-story, wood-frame building has drop siding, now covered on the side walls by composition shingles. A stepped false front hides a steeply pitched gable roof. The bell tower and porch were added in 1977 in a clumsy attempt to make the building look more "Victorian." Even the balusters in the bell tower appear to be installed upside down. These additions have detracted from the original appearance of the hall. The interior, however, is in better condition. The large room has a barrel-vaulted roof. Wainscot, in alternating dark and light wood, lines the lower walls of the room. The upper walls and ceiling are sided with thin, vertical wood boards.

NW085 House (Kinney House)

1856. 196 Genoa Ln.

The brick house is a well-preserved example of Genoa's more prominent nineteenth-century dwellings, many of which have Greek Revival and Eastlake elements. The main facade is symmetrical, capped by a front-gabled roof trimmed with a delicate bargeboard. The front door, surrounded by side lights and a transom, stands to one side of the facade, with two pairs of French doors to the left. The front porch, supported by four square posts, covers the full width of the house. Over time, numerous additions have been built to the rear of the house, but the front has remained intact. The greatest threat to the building today is the encroaching development of new housing to the east, which has altered the dwelling's original setting and may continue to move eastward, ravaging historic structures.

Genoa Vicinity

NW086 Scossa Ranch

Foothill Rd., approximately 3 miles south of the intersection of Foothill Rd. and NV 207

Settled since 1859, the Scossa Ranch is one of many historic ranches in the Carson Valley. Wilson and Sophia Miller originally homesteaded the land. According to local legend, they were one of the first African American families in the valley, but no documentary evidence substantiates this. Although the 1860 U.S. Census documents ten African Americans in Carson Valley, the Millers do not appear in the records until the 1870 census. The Scossa brothers, immigrants from Switzerland, bought the ranch from Sophia Miller and her children in 1885 and raised beef cattle and a dairy herd. All buildings but the house date from the twentieth century. The complex consists of fourteen structures, five of which were built before 1921. The Scossa family continues to own the ranch and raise beef.

The large timber-frame barn (1908) is the most prominent building at the ranch as well as the most unusual. Although the broad gable roof and vertical siding on the walls are typical of barns, many of its first-floor doors have a parquet design terminating in a central diamond. This pattern appears to be of Swiss derivation and is unique in the valley.

Minden

Minden's quiet residential streets, large central square, and numerous well-designed buildings distinguish it from most northwestern Nevada towns. The Dangberg Land and Livestock Company founded Minden in 1904, naming it after a town in Westphalia, Germany. H. F. Dangberg, an immigrant from that region, became one of the earliest and most prominent landowners in Carson Valley, establishing the land and livestock company in the nineteenth century. Much of the early town developed on land donated by the Dangbergs. In 1906 the family lured the V&T Railroad to the town by granting land for the right-of-way. The railroad's presence encouraged more ranching and farming by providing a faster means of transporting products out of the valley.

Minden's town plan is an orderly grid surrounding a central square laid out to the west of the railroad. Because the railroad terminated in Minden, the town soon rivaled its older, southern neighbor, Gardnerville, which never acquired a railroad. In 1915 Minden captured the designation of Douglas County seat from Genoa, even though its population was only in the low hundreds. During this early period, Nevada architect Frederick J. DeLongchamps designed numerous buildings for the Dangbergs, which give the core of the town a unified appearance. Since the 1960s, Minden has grown dramatically. The old downtown, located along Esmeralda Street, one block west of U.S. 395, has been eclipsed by national and regional franchises and other businesses along the highway, the main thoroughfare through Minden. The sprawl at Minden's southern end has become contiguous with Gardnerville, originally settled two miles away.

NW087 Douglas County Courthouse

1915, 1956, Frederick J. DeLongchamps. 1964, Ferris, Erskine, Calef, Architects. 1616 8th St.

DeLongchamps designed a single-story courthouse in the Beaux-Arts Classical style for Douglas County after officials decided to move the seat of government from Genoa to Minden. Opened on New Year's Day 1916, the building cost $25,000, equivalent to $439,148 today. It has a raised concrete basement, walls of beige-colored brick, and an open concrete staircase leading to a portico with four Ionic columns. Pairs of simple brick pilasters terminate both ends of the portico. A denticulated cornice with full entablature supports a brick parapet capped with concrete. Glass and wooden doors lead to an entry hall decorated with black marble wainscot. In 1956 DeLongchamps designed an addition to the north side of the once symmetrical courthouse. Eight years later the county built an addition to the south side. These extensions exaggerate the broad, low-lying massing of the original design.

NW088 Offices (Minden Wool Warehouse)

1915, Frederick J. DeLongchamps. 1615 Railroad Ave. (U.S. 395)

DeLongchamps designed this building and the nearby Minden Butter Manufacturing Company (NW090) for the Dangbergs. These two structures, with the Minden Flour Milling Company (NW089) next door, form an agricultural and industrial complex along the old V&T Railroad right-of-way and U.S. 395. The rectangular warehouse testifies to the scale of the Nevada sheep industry at one time. The one-story building's long sides parallel the highway. As the road has been widened, the pavement has crept up to the concrete basement of the building. The gable roof ends in parapet walls flanked by square piers. Three rectangular vents in each peak seem almost decorative compared with the utilitarian simplicity of the structure. The building has been altered over the years; in 1997 the owners added a row of dormers along the street facade.

Minden

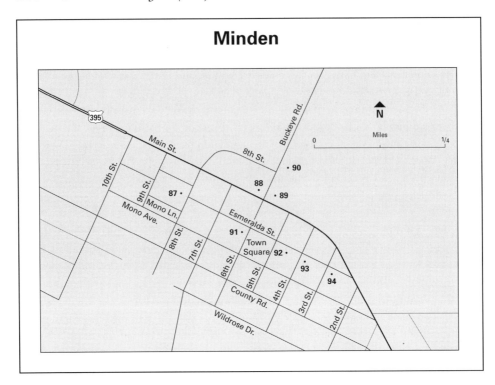

NW089 Minden Flour Milling Company

1906, F. G. Wezer. 1908, additions. 1609 Railroad Ave.

Built for the Dangberg company, the mill consists of two sections: a three-story brick mill building with a gable roof and stepped parapet gable end walls and a cluster of four 45-foot-high steel silos covered by a sheet-metal gable roof. A three-and-one-half-story corrugated sheet-metal enclosure connects the silos to the mill building. One-story

additions on the south and east sides of the brick structure were completed in 1908. Despite its utilitarian style, the mill has refined touches, including pilaster strips separating the walls into bays.

The oldest and most prominent of the three structures in the complex, the mill has a striking appearance, towering over U.S. 395. During the first decade of Minden's existence, it was the tallest building in town. It is now the only remaining flour mill of five that were built in the Carson Valley from 1854 to 1906. These structures played an important role in early Nevada, not only providing flour for emigrants heading west but also helping settlers to establish a local milling industry.

NW090 Offices (Minden Butter Manufacturing Company)

1916, Frederick J. DeLongchamps. 1970. 1617 Water St.

Set behind the warehouse and mill and located adjacent to the old railroad tracks, this one-story building provided storage and served as a clearinghouse for dairy products made in the Carson Valley. Its broad, asymmetrical facade has a main section that rises to a high parapet hiding a gable roof behind it. The brick is laid in decorative patterns on this wall around a cast concrete sign reading "Minden Butter Mfg. Co." Similar signs on slightly projecting bays flanking the central mass identify other parts of the structure: "Office" and "Storage." A one-story section at the west end of the building has a cast concrete sign reading "Eggs and Poultry." From 1970 until the late 1990s, the building, along with the old wool warehouse, provided office space for Bently Nevada, an electronics firm based in Minden.

NW091 **House** (Dangberg House)

1911, Fred Shadeter. 1600 6th St.

A rare example of the simplified Prairie Style in Nevada, this two-story, wood-frame house stands on the edge of Minden's large central square, making an impressive appearance in a town of modest houses and bungalows. As the home of John Dangberg, one of the Dangberg brothers who founded the town, the dwelling's unusual style displayed the wealth and progressive outlook of its owner.

On a raised basement, the rectangular house has walls covered with stucco. Thin vertical and horizontal boards divide the upper story into a grid in which fit five windows of two different sizes. A central front porch supported by heavy piers and capped by a pedimented gable roof covers part of the facade. Windows, symmetrically placed, balance the porch. A small enclosed, hip-roofed porch projects from the west side. A low-pitched hipped roof with a wide overhang emphasizes the horizontality of the house,

typical of Prairie Style buildings. The facade loosely resembles that of Frank Lloyd Wright's Ward Willitts house (1900–1902), suggesting that Shadeter was inspired by Wright's design.

NW092 **Carson Valley Improvement Club**

1912. 1606 Esmeralda Ave.

Anchoring one end of Minden's old downtown commercial district along Esmeralda Avenue, the Carson Valley Improvement Club has always been a meeting place for the town's residents. The two-story brick building measures 50 by 105 feet. Four piers divide the facade into three bays. The central bay, containing the main entrance, rises to a parapet. Decorative brickwork above the windows and along the cornice ornament the building. A sign reading "C.V.I.C." is recessed in the parapet. An electrified sign with the same letters rises on a metal frame above the building.

NW093 **Douglas County Offices** (Minden Inn)

1912–1916, Frederick J. DeLongchamps. 1992–1993. 1594 Esmeralda Ave.

This structure employs the restrained classicism of DeLongchamps's other buildings in town. The three-story building of buff-colored brick rises from a raised basement, culminating in an elaborate entablature with a cornice, brackets, egg-and-dart molding, dentils, and a frieze. The central section is slightly recessed and contains a recessed porch supported by four Doric columns. Five sets of multipane double entrance doors are each topped by a long multipane transom.

The Dangberg family built the structure as the Minden Inn to give the town a fine hotel with features including steam heat and an elevator. For most of the twentieth century the building functioned as a hotel and casino, but numerous alterations greatly diminished its appearance. In the 1990s the owner rehabilitated the building, which Douglas County now leases for use as offices.

NW094 **Minden Stables**

c. 1905. 1584 Esmeralda Ave.

This large frame structure appears out of place at the end of Esmeralda Avenue and facing U.S. 395. The survival of a utilitarian building is remarkable given Minden's recent rapid growth. The old stables resemble a barn with a broad gable roof and board-and-batten walls.

Minden Vicinity

NW095 **Dangberg Home Ranch**

1860–1880, 1915–1916. One mile southwest of Minden, off NV 88

One of the area's most prominent ranches in the late nineteenth and early twentieth centuries, the Dangberg Home Ranch remains in an excellent state of preservation, still in private hands. Both the state and county have discussed converting the ranch into a museum and park, but no concrete plans have beeen developed to date.

After arriving from Germany in 1856, H. F. Dangberg rapidly accumulated land for his growing ranching business. Between 1860 and 1880, he built a house, barn, slaughterhouse, bunkhouse, and supporting buildings. Under the Dangberg Land and Livestock Company, the ranch grew to 48,000 acres, the largest in the area. The complex served as the Dangbergs' base of operations, supporting line camps in more far-flung locations. Around 1915 Dangberg's heirs hired DeLongchamps to design a number of simple brick buildings to accommodate the variety of tasks on the ranch. The Dangberg company throve until the Great Depression, after which it limped along until the death of H. F. Dangberg, Jr., in 1946. The

NW093 Douglas County Offices (Minden Inn)

remaining Dangbergs sold the property in 1978. Today the home ranch covers 33.7 acres.

The buildings at the home ranch are clustered in two groups. The residential core, where the family lived, is enclosed within a fence and includes the main house, stone cellar, and garage as well as a laundry, where Native American women were employed to do the laundry for the ranch, and a pump house, which still contains the machinery that supplies the main house with water. Outside this compound are the working buildings: the bunkhouse, cook's quarters, slaughterhouse, hide house, barn, and a second garage.

NW095.1 **Main House**

1860s. 1915–1916, Frederick J. DeLongchamps

The simple wood-frame house features a large porch supported by twelve Tuscan columns. The round columns replaced square posts sometime after 1910. The house has grown over the years; the family erected a two-story addition at the rear containing a bedroom and a new kitchen, including a pantry and dining room for the ranch hands. Around 1915–1916 DeLongchamps designed a living room built of brick at the south side of the house.

NW095.2 **Stone Cellar**

1870s

The one-and-one-half-story stone cellar about ten feet behind the main house contained the large quantities of food necessary to feed the family and the hired hands on the ranch. The sandstone for the walls, from the Nevada State Prison quarry in Carson City, is laid in random courses and mortared with thick grooved joints. The building also has a sandstone floor and screened storage cabinets to store perishable goods.

NW095.3 Bunkhouse

1870s

The bunkhouse sheltered the men who lived and worked on the ranch to help with slaughtering, tanning hides, and other tasks. The one-and-one-half-story building, now dilapidated, has a gable roof and drop siding.

NW095.4 Slaughterhouse and Hide House

1915–1916, Frederick J. DeLongchamps

For these functional structures, DeLongchamps looked to western vernacular architecture, designing the slaughterhouse with a false front and the hide house with a flat roof and parapet. The two buildings replaced an earlier and smaller slaughterhouse located on the same site, enabling the ranch to expand its slaughtering business. The Dangberg company butchered not only their own animals here but also those belonging to neighboring ranchers. The slaughterhouse contains a cold-storage room, a smokehouse, an abattoir, a rendering room, kettles, and feeding pens. An overhead rail in the slaughterhouse was used to move carcasses into the cold-storage room.

NW095.5 Barn

Early 1870s

The three-bay barn is the largest of its type remaining in the Carson Valley. Its exterior form, with a broken roofline and three openings, reflects the three bays of the interior. The main posts and beams are hand hewn, with mortise-and-tenon joints pegged with wooden dowels. Vertical plank siding covers the exterior. Dangberg sheltered workhorses as well as his prized show horses here. The center bay has a wood-plank floor; the flanking bays have dirt floors.

Gardnerville

Lawrence Gilman, a settler in Genoa, founded Gardnerville in 1879, when he purchased land in the southern Carson Valley. He moved a house from Genoa and opened it as the Gardnerville Hotel. The construction of a road connecting the mining town of Bodie, California, and Carson City enabled Gardnerville to serve as a stage stop and agricultural center for surrounding mining communities. The town also became home to a few distinct and closely knit ethnic groups. In the 1880s a number of Danish immigrants settled in the area. At the turn of the century, Basque sheep ranchers moved to the valley; their architectural legacy is seen in Gardnerville's two Basque restaurants. Like Minden, Gardnerville has many brick buildings, reflecting a local preference for this material and local wealth. Uncontrolled development to the south in the 1980s and 1990s has changed Gardnerville, like its neighbor, Minden, from an agricultural community to a sprawling bedroom suburb of Carson City and Reno. Nevertheless, many historic buildings, including a number of old hotels, can be found along Main Street (U.S. 395).

NW096 Carson Valley Museum and Cultural Center (Douglas County High School)

1915, Frederick J. DeLongchamps. 1477 Main St. (U.S. 395)

This Classical Revival building is the result of a compromise between Gardnerville and Minden. In 1915 both towns vied to become the new seat of Douglas County; Gardnerville granted Minden the designation of seat and the new courthouse in exchange for the county high school. DeLongchamps won the commission for both projects.

The T-shaped brick building stands on a raised concrete basement approached by central steps. Though from the front the building appears to have only one story, it contains two stories above the basement. The symmetrical facade has a central projecting section with a porch supported by six Doric columns, with a pair at each corner. The columns meet a heavy galvanized iron entablature with dentils and cornice running along the upper section of the entire building.

In 1958, when the county erected a new high school behind the building, the old structure became the junior high school. In the mid-1980s the building was declared unsafe and was vacated because it did not meet current seismic codes. The Carson Valley Histori-

cal Society raised the funds to rehabilitate the structure and convert it to a museum, which opened in 1995. The property also contains a visitor center and rest stop for travelers on U.S. 395.

NW097 Netti's (Perry's Dry Goods)

c. 1880. 1448 Main St. (U.S. 395)

This wood-frame commercial structure is all that remains of Gardnerville's earliest mercantile buildings. The narrow two-story building rises to a gable roof, which is hidden by a tall false front trimmed with a prominent cornice. Narrow clapboards sheathe the walls. The facade is plain, with a central entrance flanked by two windows and two more windows above.

NW098 J and T Bar

1870s, c. 1895. 1426 Main St. (U.S. 395)

This popular Basque restaurant and bar is housed in one of the many buildings moved to Carson Valley. Built in Virginia City, it was relocated about 1895, at a time when the Comstock Lode had been depleted but Carson Valley was growing. Though the building's facade and interior have been heavily altered, many of its decorative features are still visible. The facade's second-story has three elaborately framed windows. The front entrance leads into an open barroom that leads to a large dining room. Like Basque hotels throughout northern Nevada, this one served the local Basque community, providing room and board and functioning as a social center. Most of the hotels that have survived are operated only as restaurants today.

NW097 Netti's (Perry's Dry Goods)

NW099 Nenzel Mansion (Arendt Jensen House)

c. 1910. 1431 Ezell St.

Danish immigrant Arendt Jensen built Gardnerville's most elaborate house a block east of Main Street. Arriving in Gardnerville in the 1880s, Jensen became one of the town's most successful merchants. His large two-story house in the Colonial Revival style displayed his wealth to the community. Ionic columns support the porch, which has a wide entablature with brackets under the eaves. A central entrance door

NW099 Nenzel Mansion (Arendt Jensen House)

with side lights is flanked by paired windows. Ionic pilasters flank the front edges of the central bay and edge the corners of the main mass. It has cornice returns, modillions lining the eaves, and Ionic pilasters at the corners. A large semicircular one-story porch, identical in style to the front porch, extends from the west side of the house. The interior has a central stairhall surrounded by large rooms.

By the time Jensen built this house, he had a successful store and had also opened Gardnerville's first bank. The stately house was the first of many homes the Jensen family built. Diagonally opposite at 1243 and 1235 Eddie Street are the modest bungalows that Jensen built for his son and parents, respectively.

Yerington

Yerington serves as the commercial and political center for the rural areas of Smith and Mason valleys. The Northern Paiute Indians first occupied the valleys, creating ditches to direct water from the East and West Walker rivers toward naturally occurring plants that sustained the tribe. Later, Euro-American settlers built ditches to enlarge the fertile agricultural lands. Like Carson Valley, these two valleys throve in the late nineteenth century by raising beef and produce for the mining centers of Aurora, Nevada, and Bodie, California, to the south and the Comstock to the north. Though the Carson and Colorado Railroad bypassed Yerington in the 1890s, the town survived to become a tightly knit rural community of about 2,900 residents. Even during the 1950s to the 1970s, when Anaconda Copper ran a huge mining operation to the west of town, Yerington retained its rural roots. The town stands on a small grid, with a thriving main street running through the center. To the east of Main Street are many older homes—mostly bungalows and ranch houses—and the town's public schools. Suburbia has, for the most part, been held at bay, though newer businesses have opened on the edges of Main Street rather than downtown.

NW100 **Lyon County Courthouse**

1911–1912, 1935, Frederick J. DeLongchamps. 31 S. Main St.

The Lyon County Courthouse was the second that DeLongchamps designed in Nevada. The concrete and brick structure in the Beaux-Arts classical style has a highly sculpted wooden cornice with dentils resting on a large pedimented portico supported by four paired terra-cotta Doric columns. Elaborate cornices with dentils and pediments adorn the main entrance and the first-floor windows. In 1935 the county constructed a large rear addition, which closely matches the original structure.

NW101 **Yerington Post Office**

1939, Louis A. Simon. 28 N. Main St.

The post office, a symmetrical rectangular box, continues to anchor downtown Yerington. Its PWA Moderne, or "starved classical," design, typical of federal buildings of the late 1930s, is nearly identical to that of Tonopah's post office. Fluted Doric columns support an entablature surmounted by a stylized eagle in bas-relief, whose open wings just fit inside the arch. The broad hipped roof rises above a cornice with dentils.

The post office was the first federal presence here, as was the case in other small towns in the state. The Yerington building follows one of nearly a dozen standardized plans produced by the Office of the Supervising Architect of the U.S. Department of the Treasury. The post office contains one of three federally funded Depression-era murals in Nevada, located in the lobby above the postmaster's door. Painted in 1941 by Adolph Gottlieb (1903–1974), who later became known for his Abstract Expressionist works, *Homestead on the Plain* depicts a small house to one side and, in the center, an old car, a windmill, and a rickety shack, all dwarfed by the jagged mountains of the eastern Sierra. Like the Lovelock and Winnemucca post office murals, this one was created under the auspices of the Treasury Department's Section of Fine Arts, which existed from 1934 to 1943.

NW102 **Main Street**

A number of historic public and commercial buildings remain on this street, though two large casinos have somewhat altered the character of the downtown. Frederick J. DeLongchamps's Odd Fellows Hall (1913–1914), 1 South Main Street, is one of the architect's simplest designs, displaying a quiet classicism in its symmetrical facade. This two-story concrete building, faced in brick, suits a small rural town. The small Bank Saloon and Deli (1917, c. 1955), 37 North Main Street, was initially erected as a bank. Though the structure is small, its restrained Beaux-Arts appearance lends it dignity and would have reassured depositors of the bank's security. The vacant

NW103 Yerington Cultural Center (Yerington Grammar School No. 9) (left)

NW104.4 Scatena Ranch Hay Derrick (below)

Lyon Market (1960), 120 North Main Street, stands out as a vernacular interpretation of modern architecture. The rectangular structure is brick with vertical bands of geometric cinderblock screening the windows. Its large footprint and parking lot along the street have disrupted the rhythm of the smaller one- and two-story buildings.

NW103 **Yerington Cultural Center**
(Yerington Grammar School No. 9)

1912, C. D. McDonald and J. J. Beatty. 1935, ell addition, Frederick J. DeLongchamps. 112 N. California St.

The Yerington Cultural Center is one of many historic preservation projects that the state of Nevada funded in the 1990s to convert historic buildings into cultural centers. This building, which functioned as a grammar school from 1912 to 1980, is one of the town's most impressive structures. Architects McDonald and Beatty of Reno designed the concrete and brick building. Projecting bays with front-facing, pedimented gables flank the central mass. The central section is slightly recessed and rises to a small pedimented gable surmounted by a hip-roofed bell tower. The lower eaves of the gable and of the tower roof have slender modillions. In 1935 DeLongchamps designed a two-story ell for the rear, making the school T-shaped. The recent renovations preserve the building's exterior and the front half of the interior, but open up the remaining space to allow for a two-story theater.

In 1911 Yerington residents campaigned for the school district to replace an old, inadequate facility with a new grammar school that "brings people into a community and makes it a home town," as the *Yerington Times* stated that year. The school was an important link in a chain of institutions for agricultural education in Mason Valley.

Yerington Vicinity

NW104 **Scatena Ranch**

1917, many additions. 1275 NV 208, approximately 12 miles south of Yerington

Like many ranches in Mason Valley, the Scatena Ranch straddles the main road, with residential buildings on one side and outbuild-

ings, including a bunkhouse, potato cellar, and stable, on the other. Unlike larger, sprawling ranches in more remote parts of the state, Mason Valley ranches resemble farmsteads; they are relatively compact and located close together on square plots of land. This ranch initially produced hogs, potatoes, hay, and beef; today it raises only hay and beef. Many ranches are now owned and operated by descendants of Italian and Portuguese immigrants who arrived in the valley in the 1870s and 1880s. Though Italian and Portuguese Americans still play active roles in the community, they have left virtually no architectural legacy in the valley.

NW104.1 **House**

1917, Frank Stickney

The Scatena house is one of the few in the valley that has not been replaced by a newer dwelling or drastically modernized. Frank Stickney, the ranch's previous owner, erected the house. Most dwellings built in the early twentieth century were plain vernacular structures. The two-story, wood-frame house, with a central hall, has narrow clapboard-sided walls and brackets lining the eaves.

NW104.2 **Potato Cellar**

1945, Louis G. Scatena

The long, narrow potato cellar, with its curved frame ceiling covered with metal, is clearly visible from the road. The subterranean structure has concrete retaining walls upon which the curved roof rests. Two wood doors open into the cellar's east end. Since the ranch no longer produces potatoes, the building is now used to store vehicles.

NW104.3 **Ditch**

1990s

The concrete-lined ditch runs along the north side of the road just inside the wire fence of the ranch and adjacent to a field of alfalfa. Small sluices open to allow water to flow down the rows of plants. This modern ditch continues the centuries-old tradition of using canals and ditches to irrigate naturally growing and cultivated plants.

NW104.4 Hay Derrick

c. 1900

Although hay derricks were replaced by mechanical haying equipment over fifty years ago, they are still common features of the landscape in Mason Valley, as well as in Smith and Carson valleys and in Dayton and Fallon. In her study of ranches in Mason Valley, folklorist Andrea Graham documents that the derricks found in these areas are all of the same type. The tall central mast has a boom fastened halfway up its height. To stack hay, this boom can be raised or lowered with a cable. The mast rotates, enabling stacks to be made without moving the derrick.

Wellington

A small village near the West Walker River on Nevada 208, Wellington is a service center for Smith Valley. The area was settled in the 1860s and, like Mason Valley, became a rich agricultural region. Wellington also functioned as a stage stop for the mining town of Aurora. Despite recent development in the form of mobile homes and prefabricated houses scattered across the landscape, the small town center remains largely intact.

NW105 Wellington Inn (Hoye Hotel)

c. 1883. South side NV 208, approximately 1.5 miles west of the intersection with the Wellington cutoff

An Irish couple, John and Mary Hoye, built this large building, four bays long, as a hotel and stage stop along the road from Dayton to Aurora. The building is in excellent condition and appears to have changed little over the years, except for the screening of the front porch and the addition of a small side porch over the east entrance. The cornice returns and corner boards ending in capitals are among the few ornamental touches. The Hoyes also built the Wellington Mercantile (c. 1883) next door.

NW106 Wellington School

1898. South side NV 208, approximately 2.5 miles west of the intersection with the Wellington cutoff

Wellington School is a simple structure with board-and-batten siding terminating in a boxed cornice. Above the entrance on the gable ridge is a bell tower supported on short square posts. The one-room, wood-frame schoolhouse with a front-facing gable roof was once a common sight in small-town Nevada. By the early twentieth century, ambitious towns, no matter how small, wanted prominent school buildings to enhance their communities. Many of the buildings, however, have been demolished or moved to museums for preservation; this one may have been moved from its original site.

Northern Region (NO)

Northern Nevada, one of the state's least populated regions, is home to national forests, wilderness areas, Native American reservations, and small, isolated towns with populations ranging from thirty to 25,000 residents. The remote northwest corner of the region, which contains the Black Rock Desert and the Sheldon Wildlife Refuge, is the most sparsely settled. Native Americans, including the Shoshone and Northern Paiute, once roamed the mountain ranges and basins. The landscape changed after the arrival of Euro-Americans, who increased the number of transportation routes and travelers across the region and established agriculture and industry.

The Humboldt River provided the earliest connecting thread through this region. Fed by mountain streams arising near Wells, it cuts across northern Nevada, finally draining into the Humboldt Sink southeast of Lovelock. Though it seems a creek compared with the Mississippi or the Columbia River, the Humboldt was important as a source of water for Native Americans and later for travelers along the Emigrant Trail, the Central Pacific Railroad, and highways.

The transcontinental railroad transformed this region, creating towns along its route and drawing more people to Nevada (or at least through it). The river and the railroad determined the paths of later transportation routes—Victory Highway (U.S. 40) and I-80. Victory Highway, like the railroad, brought traffic through northern Nevada's small towns, but the interstate highway has proved to be a boon for a few towns and a catastrophe for many others. Towns advantageously located for motorists have benefited from the highway; others were bypassed, losing a steady source of commerce. Secondary highways and railroads leading to towns north and south of the Humboldt River have brought some trade, but towns along Nevada's northern border and nestled in valleys to the south remain fairly isolated.

Most of the towns along the tracks display common characteristics introduced by the railroad company, including town grids and commercial rows fronting the tracks. At one time, each of these communities had a prominent depot; most of these structures, as well as many

Northern Region

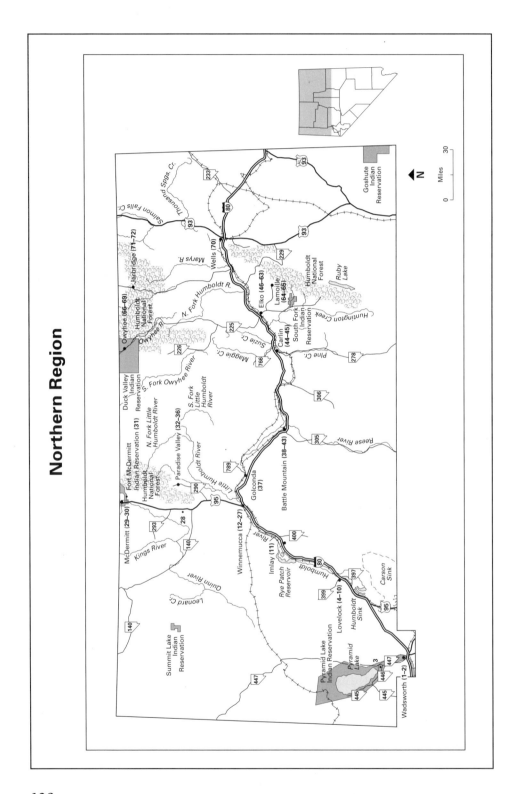

other railroad buildings, have been destroyed. The interstate introduced new commercial and tourism-related structures clustered at the freeway exits. Hotel, gas, and fast-food franchises have drawn business from every downtown along the interstate. Motorists using these easy on-and-off services rarely venture into the downtowns. Communities have done little to stem this tide, seeing the short-term revenues brought in by such commercial ventures as an asset rather than a detriment to the long-term survival of local businesses along the main streets.

The buildings in this region vary in style, type, and material. Ethnic groups, particularly Italians and Basques, have contributed to the built environment through specific building techniques and forms, such as well-executed stone construction (Italians) and hotels (Basques). Farming and ranching have left a rich legacy of agricultural structures, including bunkhouses, barns, and mills. The region includes three county seats; in these communities the county courthouses and public schools rank among the most elaborate buildings. Housing generally consists of a mix of modest structures ranging from log cabins to mobile homes.

Wadsworth

Initially part of the Pyramid Lake Indian Reservation, granted to the Pyramid Lake Paiute tribe in 1859, what would become Wadsworth was soon overrun by Euro-American settlers and the Central Pacific Railroad, which illegally took the best land along the Truckee River from the tribe. At the time, the federal government supported these actions as part of a larger program to encourage Euro-American settlement of the West.

The town of Wadsworth, like its counterparts along I-80, began as a railroad community in 1868, when the Central Pacific reached the area. Wadsworth's site on the Truckee River made it a suitable division point, as well as a supply base for builders continuing the tracks eastward across Nevada. Wadsworth grew to a peak of about 1,300 residents but languished after 1904, when the Southern Pacific Railroad moved its maintenance facilities and most of the town to Sparks. The Southern Pacific razed many buildings and removed others, but Wadsworth persevered. A few vacant structures survive from the town's railroad-era past, accompanied by some new houses and a mobile home park along the Truckee River.

After a century and a half of supporting the rights of white property owners in the Wadsworth area, the federal government has shifted its policy in order to return land rightfully belonging to the Paiute. The Truckee River Negotiated Settlement Act (1990) authorizes the U.S. Department of the Interior to buy any land within the reservation from non-Native American residents who wish to sell their property. In recent years the Bureau of Land Management has sold public land to developers in rapidly growing southern Nevada, and the Interior Department has used some of the proceeds to buy privately held land on the reservation.

NO01 **Wadsworth School**

1898. School St.

The tallest and largest building left from the railroad days, the old school is a reminder of the thriving town Wadsworth once was. The two-story building, built of brick and covered with tan stucco, stands on a large lot near the Truckee River. Its H-shaped plan gives it a stable and orderly appearance, enhanced by the central section with a recessed porch marked by three open arches. Above, three arched window openings face a balcony created by the porch roof. A small hexagonal cupola with six vents tops the hipped roof. Though it has been boarded up for years, the Wadsworth School, with its simplified echoes of Renaissance villas, displays the townspeople's high esteem for public education.

NO02 **Southern Pacific Baggage Car Apartments**

c. 1911, Pullman Car and Manufacturing Company. 411 Main St.

Though Wadsworth is no longer a railroad town, remnants of its past can be found. One example is this Pullman baggage car converted to apartments. In 1863 George M. Pullman built the first modern sleeping car, which had a folding upper berth and seat cushions that could be extended to create a lower berth. The success of this car enabled Pullman to build a manufacturing empire, crushing many of his competitors. The Pullman company retained a monopoly in the sleeping-car business into the 1940s. It also produced other types of railroad cars, including dining and baggage cars and combination cars (divided into two or more compartments for different classes of traffic).

Railroad cars of various types and vintages have been recycled in Nevada to provide architecture for residential or commercial use. This car was produced for the Southern Pacific Railroad, a leader at the time in using all-steel cars. Much of the car's original fabric remains, such as the handles on the roof and sides, the roof vents, and the right-hand window. One of the

two large baggage doors on the long side has been filled in, but the other serves as an entrance, now covered by a small porch. This car has been removed from its undercarriage and rests on a foundation. A gabled porch covering an entrance has been added to the side. In its form and materials the structure resembles trailers and mobile homes used as dwellings across the state.

Wadsworth Vicinity

NO03 **Pyramid Lake Cultural Center and Museum**

1976, Dennis Numkena. 1997–1998, Ganther, Melby, and Lee. Northwest corner of intersection of NV 446 and 447

The dramatic sweeping forms of the cultural center and museum rise out of the stark desert surrounding Pyramid Lake. Local multicolored stone covers the exterior walls of the round building, which has a curved roof rising to a triangular entry section. Inside is a central area for ceremonial dances, surrounded by stepped seats. The Hopi architect Dennis Numkena designed the structure after winning a national competition. Because the Paiute do not have a tradition of permanent architecture, Numkena relied on universal forms, such as the circle and triangle, and used native materials to reflect the building's connection with the tribe's ancestral land. Compared with much of the contemporary architecture erected on other reservations in Nevada, this structure makes a strong statement for Native American cultural identity.

For reasons that are unclear, the building was not completed in the 1970s and has stood neglected for over twenty years. However, the Paiute received a federal grant in 1997 to complete the building as a center for heritage education for Paiute children and as a visitor center. Ganther, Melby, and Lee of Reno are completing the project, following Numkena's original scheme with some modifications.

NO02 Southern Pacific Baggage Car Apartments (left)
NO03 Pyramid Lake Cultural Center and Museum (below, left)
NO04 Lovelock Depot (below, right)

Lovelock

The area surrounding what is now Lovelock was settled by Euro-Americans in the early 1860s, when several individuals established ranches near the Humboldt River. The eponymous George Lovelock purchased hundreds of acres in 1866, as well as the stage stop located along the Emigrant Trail. When the railroad arrived in 1868, he donated eighty-five acres to the Central Pacific as a townsite. The railroad provided Lovelock's ranchers and farmers with a ready means of shipping hay, alfalfa, sugar beets, wheat, and cattle to California.

Mining had little effect on Lovelock until the 1907 discovery of ore deposits at Seven Troughs and Vernon to the northwest. Lovelock flourished for the next two decades; buildings from that time represent the second period of the town's development. Growth culminated in Lovelock's selection as county seat for the newly formed Pershing County, carved out of Humboldt County in 1919. The construction of U.S. 40 in 1916 brought additional traffic through town. The railroad slowly declined, however, and I-80, completed in 1983, bypassed Lovelock. Despite new mining operations in the area, Lovelock is a quiet place, and many of its commercial buildings are vacant. This economic decline has, however, helped preserve many buildings in the downtown area and has discouraged the subdivisions that have transformed many other towns. On the other hand, it has also left many historic buildings vulnerable to neglect and demolition.

NO04 Lovelock Depot

1889, Central Pacific Railroad. 1917, Southern Pacific Railroad. Northeast corner of Main St. and W. Broadway

The original L-shaped depot of 1889 at the east end of Main Street is one of the more architecturally significant depots in the state, built in the popular Stick Style seen in many nineteenth-century depots throughout the United States. Although the building is dilapidated, it is largely unaltered and retains much of its decorative stickwork. The main section of the building has two stories, with a one-story wing projecting along the tracks to the southwest. Board-and-batten siding covers the gable ends; drop siding clads the rest of the building, embellished with vertical, horizontal, and diagonal flat stickwork. A three-sided bay window marking the ticket office projects from the two-story section toward the tracks. In addition to the ticket office, the first floor includes a waiting room and baggage room; offices were on the second floor. In 1917 Southern Pacific expanded the baggage and office areas. Though it is a focal point of Lovelock's Main Street, the building is currently vacant.

NO05 Motor Cargo (Southern Pacific Freight Warehouse)

c. 1912. 1090 W. Broadway

This one-story, wood-frame structure next to the depot was built as a freight warehouse. The side-facing gable roof has wide overhangs supported by diagonal brackets covering elevated loading docks on both sides of the building. Horizontal beveled boards clad the exterior walls. One of three railroad buildings still standing in Lovelock, the structure represents the utilitarian approach to railroad warehouse construction as compared with the more elaborate approach used for passenger depots.

NO06 Main Street

Main St. between W. Broadway and Cornell Ave.

From the railroad tracks, Main Street runs northwest for two blocks, terminating at the

Pershing County Courthouse. Dating from 1889 to the 1940s, the buildings along the street represent the second period of Lovelock's downtown development. During that time, banks, offices, bars, stores, a pool hall, a dance hall, and a post office lined the street. Today the businesses are less diverse, but Main Street remains Lovelock's downtown core. Despite some infill, the blocks are fairly intact, lined with simple one- and two-story structures expressing the town's modest prosperity. Most buildings retain large storefront windows and simple metal cornices along the roofline. Good examples of Lovelock's commercial buildings from the period run along the east side of the street, including the old First National Bank Building (1905), now a store; the Soroptimist Club (1925); and Davin's Dining (1926 and 1930). The old bank building and club have facades with large storefront windows on the first floor, two segmental-arched windows on the second floor, and narrow cornices above. Both facades are stuccoed; the bank's facade is scored to resemble coursed ashlar. The restaurant consists of two wood-frame structures with facades of cast concrete rock-faced blocks that originally contained the Marcucci and Brunetti Store, a pool hall, and a dance hall.

NO07 Lovelock Post Office

1937, Louis A. Simon. Northeast corner of Main St. and Dartmouth Ave.

Of the many U.S. post offices erected in Nevada during the 1930s, Lovelock's brick building is one of the more modest, designed in a spare but massive geometric style commonly known as PWA Moderne, also called "starved classical" because of its stripped-down classical look. During the New Deal era the Office of the Supervising Architect of the U.S. Treasury Department designed many public buildings in this style across the country. Flanking the steps on two concrete piers are tall bronze lamps, each with a slender shaft flaring at the top and a cage holding a bowl-shaped glass. A stylized aluminum eagle stands above the door. In the lobby, over the postmaster's door, is a mural, *Uncovering of the Comstock Lode* (1940), by Ejnar Hansen (1884–1965), which depicts three prospectors in

NO07 Lovelock Post Office, exterior and interior (above)

NO08 Pershing County Courthouse (left)

1859 examining gold from a wooden sluice while another pans for gold. The mural, painted in the simplified realist style favored for public art in the 1930s, was completed under the auspices of the Treasury Department's Section of Fine Arts.

The building, which retains much of its original appearance, is an example of a small-town, single-purpose post office still located in a downtown area. The Treasury Department typically constructed such buildings in small towns and in neighborhoods of large metropolitan areas served by a main post office. Like other Nevada post offices built during the 1930s, the Lovelock building was the first and only federal building in town and represented an amicable link between the local community and the national government.

NO08 Pershing County Courthouse

1921, Frederick J. DeLongchamps. 400 Main St. (southwest corner of Main St. and Dartmouth Ave.)

The people of Lovelock have one of the nation's only round courthouses. Pershing County officials approached Frederick J. DeLongchamps, by then the architect of six Nevada courthouses, and asked for a design that would be low in price but distinctive in appearance. As a solution, DeLongchamps designed a round courthouse, patterning it after Thomas Jefferson's library on the University of Virginia campus. The circle-over-hexagon design includes a circular interior hallway and a round courtroom decorated with Corinthian pilasters. A broad, sweeping concrete staircase leads to the main floor of this Beaux-Arts classical structure. Its entrance includes a pedimented portico supported by six Ionic columns. Doric pilasters separate the main-story windows. Cream-colored brick and terra-cotta finish the exterior. A shallow dome crowns the roof and provides the courtroom with a dramatic, soaring ceiling.

NO09 Pershing County School District Building (Vocational-Agriculture Building)

1941, Russell Mills. 1150 Elmhurst St.

The National Youth Administration (NYA) built the structure to house vocational education programs run by the Pershing County School District. One of only two New Deal–era buildings associated with the NYA in Nevada, the long, low structure stands near the high school, which was also designed by Mills and built in 1950. Stucco over wood frame gives the building a smooth finish. Lines incised in the upper portions of the walls emphasize the building's horizontality. A low parapet hides the double-arched wood-frame truss roof. The main entrance is set to one side, marked by a slightly projecting bay that breaks above the parapet. The placement of the entry permitted the building to accommodate a large workshop area. The building was used for its original purpose until the early 1990s, when the school district converted it into offices, replacing all the original windows with reflective glass. This alteration has marred what was an exceptionally well-preserved building.

NO10 Marzen House (Big Meadows Ranch House)

1875, 1981. 25 Marzen Lane

This large two-story house is one of the oldest remaining from Lovelock's early ranching period. Joseph Marzen, a German immigrant, worked as a butcher in Virginia City and Reno during the 1860s. In the 1870s he arrived in the Lovelock area, where he established himself as a cattle breeder and rancher. The house he built functioned as the center of a prosperous ranch encompassing over 3,500 acres at the turn of the century. The five-by-two-bay wood-frame house has a hipped roof with eaves decorated with pairs of elaborately scrolled brackets. The window surrounds, corner boards, and porch supports also have ornate jigsawn cutouts. The main entrance contains ornate double doors with a transom above, and the symmetrical floor plan has a central hallway running the length of the house, with four large rooms on each floor.

Although the house has been altered little over the years, it no longer stands on its original rural site. In 1981 the county moved it to a lot at the edge of Lovelock, near a freeway on-ramp, where it now serves as the Pershing County Museum.

Imlay

NO11 Thunder Mountain

1969–1973, Frank Van Zant (Chief Rolling Mountain Thunder). Frontage Rd., south of I-80

Thunder Mountain, in the tiny village of Imlay, was built by Frank Van Zant, an Oklahoma-born Native American, environmental folk artist, and spiritual healer who moved to Nevada in 1968 because he believed that a mountain of the same name, part of the Humboldt Range, held spiritual powers. He took the name Chief Rolling Mountain Thunder and named his creation after the nearby peak. The three-story main structure is made of found objects, including bottles, rocks, auto parts, animal bones, wood scraps, railroad ties, and tiles, all held together by concrete. Inside are nine rooms and a staircase—made of bicycle wheels and handlebars—that provides interior structural support. The irregularly placed windows are glazed with windshields and television picture tubes. Human faces and figures incorporated into the construction seem to gaze at the visitor. Metal pipes rise to form a curving framework like a giant basket handle, so that, in Van Zant's words, "the Great Spirit [could] pick the whole thing up and just carry us away."

Van Zant said that he built Thunder Mountain to commemorate the Native Americans who came before him and to celebrate their closeness to the earth. By using discarded objects, he commented on the wastefulness of modern Euro-American society. The five-and-one-half-acre site is owned by Van Zant's family and is open to the public.

Winnemucca

The development of Winnemucca and surrounding Humboldt County, unlike that of most other settlements in Nevada, was not tied exclusively to the boom-and-bust cycle of the mining industry. The Humboldt River Valley served much of the westward migration to California as a natural path across the Great Basin. The arrival in 1868 of the Central Pacific Railroad, which ran through the valley, enabled the community to avoid complete dependence on mining. Once just a ferry crossing on the banks of the Humboldt River, Winnemucca, named for the great Paiute chief, became the county seat in 1872. The courthouse and the railroad established the settlement as a commercial center.

The construction of other transportation routes through town helped shape its development. The Western Pacific Railroad, which arrived in 1908, ran along the Humboldt River in the northern part of town, bringing commercial activity to Bridge Street. In the early twentieth century U.S. 40, locally known as Winnemucca Boulevard, shifted activity to the center of town between the two railroads. With the completion of I-80 in the 1980s, Winnemucca—approximately halfway between San Francisco and Salt Lake City and halfway between Reno and Elko—became a popular stopping point for truck drivers and tourists.

Although Winnemucca was not a mining town, it did feel the effects of great mining booms, particularly the bonanza of Jim Butler's famous strikes in Tonopah in 1900. After the discovery of silver and gold ore in the nearby hills and canyons, Winnemucca became a supply and shipping center for mining. This activity, along with growth to the north, bolstered commerce and precipitated three decades of strong building activity. Many structures from this period remain in downtown Winnemucca.

The town has prospered again with renewed mining activity in the region beginning in the mid-1980s. Since the last decade, its population has more than doubled, from approximately 3,000 to 8,800 (as of 1998). This growth is visible in development at either end of Winnemucca Boulevard and in new housing subdivisions on the north side of the Humboldt River. Nevertheless, the core remains vibrant, with a wide variety of architectural styles and building types represented in a mixture of modest houses, railroad buildings, Basque hotels, casinos, and brothels.

NO12 Old Winnemucca Electric Power and Water Company

1910. 93 Bridge St.

This charming building of stucco over poured concrete was constructed in the Mission Revival style to match the nearby Western Pacific Railroad Depot (1910; demolished 1980s). In the early twentieth century many regional railroads favored this style for their buildings as a symbol of the West. Despite the popularity of the style during this period, these were the only two examples in Winnemucca. The building served as the power and water company's offices and

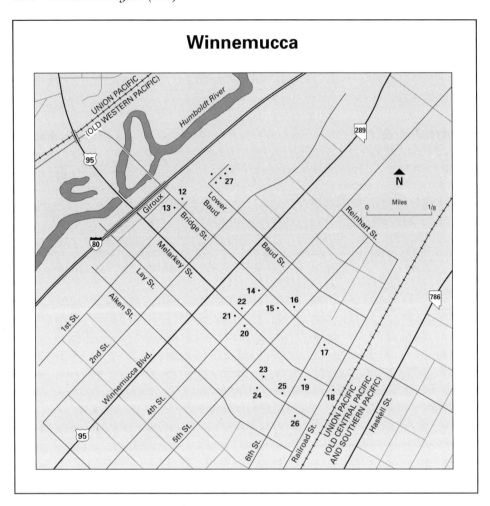

Winnemucca

generating and pumping station. A curved parapet, with a plain inset disk for ornamentation, crowns the one-story structure.

NO13 **Winnemucca Hotel**

c. 1863, 1866, Louis and Theophile Lay. 95 Bridge St.

Winnemucca's oldest extant building also houses its oldest continually operating business. Located at the corner of Bridge and West 1st streets, the Winnemucca Hotel and its saloon took advantage of ferry traffic crossing the Humboldt River. It grew quickly in the 1860s, resulting in an L-shaped structure. Today the building consists of four distinct sections, the oldest at the corner. Owners have altered the wood-frame building over the years, removing

the nineteenth-century porch after 1910 and adding brick-patterned composition siding over the original drop siding. The inset entrance at the east corner of the building leads into a large room with an ornately carved bar dating from the late nineteenth century. Behind the bar is a large dining room, and upstairs are rooms for boarders. The remaining three sections of the hotel were constructed in 1866. Built of brick rather than wood, and with arched rather than rectangular windows, these structures are somewhat more elaborate than the original part. The hip-roofed section flanking the main part of the hotel along Bridge Street has two large oriel windows on the second story.

In 1867 Louis and Theophile Lay and Frank Baud built a cottonwood-pole toll bridge 100

NO13 Winnemucca Hotel (top)

NO15 Humboldt County Courthouse (bottom)

yards downstream from the ferry crossing, which increased traffic at the hotel. The building also housed the first stage stop and post office in Winnemucca. Around the turn of the century, Basques took over the business. Today the structure is one of the last Basque hotels in the state to house boarders and serve food.

NO14 Offices (First National Bank)

1886. 1915, Frederick J. DeLongchamps. 352 Bridge St.

DeLongchamps, who designed four of Winnemucca's handsomest buildings, added a second story and modified the first-story facade of the First National Bank in 1915, giving the original brick building a dignified solidity. Stucco, scored to look like coursed ashlar, covers the exterior walls. Two Doric columns supporting a

short entablature of triglyphs and metopes stand at the clipped corner of the building at Bridge and 4th streets. The entrance on the 4th Street side is flanked by pilasters and capped with a heavy cornice and ornament made of scrolls and a crest topped by a sphere. DeLongchamps could not, however, overcome the awkward overall composition in which the long south-facing wall turns the corner and ends abruptly on Bridge Street.

NO15 Humboldt County Courthouse

1919–1921, Frederick J. DeLongchamps. 1976, rear passageway. Northwest corner of Bridge and 5th sts.

A long, wide concrete staircase leads to the Beaux-Arts classical courthouse, which has a massive pedimented portico supported by six Corinthian columns, with the entablature continuing around the building, above which is a parapet. Corinthian pilasters separate bays on side-elevation projections. The first-floor windows on the front elevation feature stone pedimented caps, contrasting slightly with the buff-colored brick of the walls and pilasters. Cream-colored terra-cotta details include eagles above the doors on the main and north entries. The interior of the building is the most monumental of DeLongchamps's commissions in Nevada, featuring a sweeping marble staircase and a two-story atrium with Ionic columns and a leaded glass ceiling. In 1976 the county constructed a passageway linking the courthouse with a newer county office building to the rear.

NO16 Winnemucca Fire Department

1935, Andrew P. Weidman. 437 Bridge St.

The fire-department facility is one of many Moderne buildings in Winnemucca. In the 1930s the style swept through the town, encouraging many owners to remodel their structures to look more up-to-date. These include the Turin Brown Mercantile (355 Bridge Street), built in 1898 and remodeled c. 1937, and the Nixon Opera House, built in 1906 and remodeled in 1937 but destroyed by fire in 1992. Designed as a cube with a symmetrical facade, the well-proportioned, two-story concrete fire station has a facade of superimposed rectangular planes that suggest the architect's acquaintance with cubist paintings or the geometric works of the De Stijl movement. The recessed garage doors and windows above provide depth to the facade, and the visual variety is enhanced by the stepped edges of the parapet, side piers, and window surrounds. Only the large garages, flanking the building and added at a later date, disrupt the balance. Many of Nevada's historic firehouses have been demolished, but this one continues to be used for its original purpose.

NO17 Shone House

1901, R. F. Hoy, builder. 602 Bridge St.

Located just a block away from the old Central Pacific tracks, the Shone House was one of many hotels serving railroad traffic at the turn of the century. Today only two modest hotels from the period remain in the neighborhood (the other is the Martin Hotel at Melarkey and Railroad streets). Though damaged by fire in 1980, the building was fully restored later in that decade. The two-story, wood-frame hotel has a false front capped by a narrow cornice decorated with pairs of small brackets. Shiplap siding and a front porch enhance the building's frontier appearance.

NO18 Old Central Pacific Freight Depot

c. 1880, c. 1905. Railroad St. opposite the end of Melarkey St.

The oldest extant structure associated with the Central Pacific Railroad in Winnemucca, this freight depot, now owned by Union Pacific, still retains the ochre paint characteristic of Central Pacific and Southern Pacific buildings. The long, narrow depot stands on a lot between Railroad Street and the tracks. This site was originally occupied by a wide loading platform with one small, gable-roofed freight shed at

NO18 Old Central Pacific Freight Depot (top)

NO20 Apartment Building (bottom)

each end. Around 1905 Southern Pacific filled the space between them with a large, gable-roofed shed, forming one long, continuous building. Wide eaves supported by diagonal brackets extend unevenly over the loading docks on both sides of the building. The Railroad Street side has a 20-foot-wide dock, requiring longer eaves. Economical board-and-batten siding, used frequently on railroad warehouses, clads the walls.

NO19 3-R Building (MECO Storage Building)

c. 1905–1910, c. 1920. 620–650 Melarkey St.

Located near the old Central Pacific Railroad, the 3-R Building, erected to store freight, is one of the largest in downtown Winnemucca. A large gambrel roof was added around 1920 to the two-story, poured-in-place concrete building, giving it the appearance of a giant barn.

Large diagonal brackets line the gambrel eaves. Along Melarkey Street, two entrances covered by gable roofs on brackets lead into the first floor. After the alterations, the building was used as a parking garage. Since the 1980s, it has functioned as an office building—an interesting case of adaptive reuse twice over. The owner named it the 3-R Building after his three sons, whose names begin with that letter.

NO20 Apartment Building

1940, J. C. Nicholson. 416 Melarkey St.

This unpretentious Moderne apartment building is unique in style among houses in Winnemucca. The cream-colored, two-story building on a corner lot has an L-shaped plan, with small projections from the first story to accommodate entry doors with porthole windows. Modern features include recessed and projecting wall panels and multipane, steel-frame casement windows. Some of these windows wrap around the outer corners of the building—perhaps a nod to the International Style. Other touches include stepped parapets and a fin projecting above the roofline and over an entry bay on the 4th Street side. H. P. Aste, proprietor of the Winnemucca Laundry, had the apartments built in a modern style to advertise the newness and modern conveniences of the complex and thus attract tenants. The style was popular for apartment complexes built at the time in larger western cities such as Reno (see NW024, Loomis Manor Apartments) and Salt Lake City.

NO21 St. Paul's Catholic Church

1924, J. J. Foley. 350 Melarkey St.

The most architecturally significant church in the area, St. Paul's combines a Neo-Romanesque body with twin towers in a late Renaissance style. With its stuccoed reinforced concrete walls, painted a brilliant white in a 1990 renovation project, and its tall towers topped by octagonal cupolas, the church can be seen from many points in Winnemucca. Above both towers rise louvered belfries topped by crosses. The church follows a cruciform plan, with a short transept and a curved apse projecting from the altar end of the nave. Above the main entrance a rose window admits light to the nave.

An influx of Italians and Basques in the late nineteenth and early twentieth centuries

NO21 St. Paul's Catholic Church

strengthened the Catholic community in Winnemucca. By 1926 Roman Catholics constituted the largest denomination in the state, according to the WPA *Guide to Nevada*. When the congregation decided to erect a large new church, it considered a style blending medieval Italian and Spanish Renaissance forms appropriate to display the size and aspirations of the local Catholic community. It also hired an out-of-state architect experienced in the design of churches—J. J. Foley of San Francisco. In the early twentieth century Catholic churches in the West often employed styles that evoked medieval and Counter-Reformation religious devotion. The monumental scale of the church also imparted legitimacy and longevity to a congregation that may have wished to counter the anti-Catholic sentiment widespread in the United States in the nineteenth and early twentieth centuries.

NO22 Winnemucca City Hall
(Winnemucca Post Office)

1919–1920, James A. Wetmore. 1940–1941, Louis A. Simon. 90 W. 4th St.

The one-story brick city hall was originally Winnemucca's post office and federal building. The city had fought for many years to acquire a federal building and finally, with the help of Nevada's U.S. senators, received a post office in

1920. Designed by the Office of the Supervising Architect of the Treasury, the building is small but refined, with a symmetrical facade receding slightly behind a projecting central section. The main entrance is embellished with a fanlight and flanked by two small multipane windows. A plain wood entablature has a simple frieze, a cornice with dentils, and a low parapet. An addition, designed by Louis Simon, the Supervising Architect of the Treasury in the late 1930s and early 1940s, nearly doubled the size of the building.

In 1942 Polly Duncan painted a mural, *Cattle Round-up*, on the north wall of the lobby. It depicts cowboys guiding cattle into a shed, while in the distance other cowboys drive in the rest of the herd from a broad valley framed by mountains. Like the post-office murals in Lovelock and Yerington, this one was painted under the auspices of the Treasury Department's Section of Fine Arts. The agency encouraged artists to work in a realist style and use themes relating to local history and customs. In 1991 the city of Winnemucca acquired the building, which became the city hall the following year.

NO23 House

c. 1915. 517 Lay St.

This one-and-one-half-story house is an exceptionally intact example of the California bungalow. The hipped roof has gently curving eaves and ends in a projecting gable at the facade. Wood shingles and large brackets decorate the gable. A central balcony with double doors projects over the front steps to the porch below.

The asymmetrical facade, with its generous front porch, typifies the informal lifestyle the bungalow was intended to enhance. In the early twentieth century the bungalow was popular throughout Nevada and the West as an inexpensive housing form providing quality of design and construction as well as comfort.

NO24 Winnemucca Grammar School

1927–1928, Richard Watkins. 522 Lay St.

The grammar school's relative grandeur reflects its prominence in the community. The WPA *Guide to Nevada* (1940) reported: "This school has a wide reputation for its practical equipment and for the instruction it gives; it is significant that, among the periodicals and papers in its teachers' library, the *New York Times* and *Harper's Magazine* are particularly well-worn." Winnemucca continues to use the building as a grammar school.

The design emphasizes horizontal lines, flat roofs, parapets delineated by projecting moldings, and original ornamentation based upon geometric or organic models. Stringcourses, cornices, and ornamentation of white cast stone decorate the red brick walls. One-story classrooms surround a central two-story, three-bay mass containing the main entrance. The second story above the entrance has large windows in the recessed center bay.

The interior is both remarkably ornate and intact. Opposite the entry doors, the foyer leads to a grand stairway that divides at an intermediate landing, then continues upward to the second floor. Shortly after the building was

NO24 Winnemucca Grammar School, exterior and interior

completed, local civic groups donated the half-size statues for the four corner niches of the foyer. Representing the importance of classical learning and civic duty, these include copies of two classical statues, of Hebe, the Greek goddess of youth, and Venus, and replicas of the Statue of Liberty and the Concord Minuteman. Portraits of George Washington and Abraham Lincoln are also installed in the foyer.

Considered the most modern in the state when it was built in 1927–1928, the Winnemucca Grammar School boasted self-ventilating cloakrooms, a heating and ventilating system with individual thermostats in each room, classrooms lighted from the pupils' left sides (assuming right-handed penmanship), and brick partitions between classrooms to fireproof the rooms and deaden sound. The architect, Richard Watkins, was well versed in school design, having served as Utah's architect of state schools from 1912 to 1920. During his career he designed more than 240 school buildings.

NO25 Kluncy's Apartments

1912, Bert Kluncy. 583 Lay St.

Lay Street has many houses representative of popular styles, but it also has some exceptional structures that display the creative spirit of vernacular builders. Kluncy's Apartments is one of these. Bert Kluncy, a German immigrant and one of Winnemucca's most prosperous ranchers in the early twentieth century, built the apartments in the form of a large single-family residence, perhaps to fit better into the streetscape or to allow tenants to give the impression that they were prosperous homeowners. Stock construction materials account for the building's

unusual appearance. The two-story-high walls are made of rock-faced concrete blocks, seen in other residential buildings in town. Iron tiles made to resemble red clay tiles cover the gambrel roof. Two porches, one on each side, run across the facade. A small porch with a mansard roof topped by a wrought iron railing projects from the east side of the building on the first story. Ornate cast concrete columns with fluted and banded shafts and Ionic capitals support the two first-floor porches; an ornate wrought iron railing decorates the second-story porch. Pressed metal shingles line the pediment of the front gambrel. The only alteration is the addition of a roof and posts on the second-story porch. The iron gate surrounding the lot is original.

NO26 House

c. 1890. 612 Lay St.

The asymmetrical plan of this wood-frame house is seen in many Victorian-era residences in the West. A large, gabled projection stands to the left of the main entrance, the gable decorated with alternating paired rows of scalloped and diamond shingles, with a king-post truss in the gable peak. A narrow bargeboard trims the roofline of the gable. Sheltering the front entrance is an elaborately decorated porch with a variety of carved and scrolled trim. Using presawn, mass-produced wood trim, carpenters could embellish such simple buildings. This picturesque example is one of the oldest remaining residences dating from the heyday of Winnemucca's "Uppertown," the area along the Central Pacific tracks.

NO27 Brothels

c. 1914, many alterations. Alley at the end of Baud St.

The brothels in Winnemucca are not significant in terms of architectural style, but they are important as a building type in Nevada—one- and two-story wood-frame buildings with little decoration. Like the brothels in Wells, Winnemucca's are tucked away, their backs turned to town. In 1914 the city moved them from a location on East 2nd Street because a new ordinance required brothels to be a certain distance from schools and churches. With the construction of I-80 adjacent to the buildings, the brothels could advertise directly to passing motorists. At night, the lights of My Place, Simone de Paris, Villa Joy, and Penny's Cozy Corner can be seen clearly from the highway. These four brothels stand in a row, leading to a large parking area for trucks.

Winnemucca Vicinity

NO28 **Andorno Ranch**

1899–1900, 1922. 9535 U.S. 95 N., approximately 36 miles north of Winnemucca

Andorno Ranch comprises 320 acres near the farming and ranching community of Orovada, thirty-six miles north of Winnemucca. Situated along the old Idaho Trail, roughly paralleled today by U.S. 95, the complex originally served as a stage station. Its builder and first owner, Alfonso Pasquale, capitalized on the mule trains bringing hay and produce south into Winnemucca and carrying finished goods to the northern ranches. (The modern highway now runs one-tenth of one mile southeast of the site.) The property also functioned as a ranch, producing hundreds of tons of hay each year. The complex is significant not only as a well-preserved example of turn-of-the-century vernacular ranch architecture but also for its examples of Italian stonemasonry. Italian immigrants moved into the Paradise Valley and Orovada areas in the late nineteenth and early twentieth centuries, and some of their buildings remain in the region. Many of these have regular- or random-coursed granite or sandstone walls with hipped roofs.

NO28.1 **Main House**

1899–1900, Alfonso Pasquale

Built as a hotel for the stage station, this structure is now used as a single-family dwelling. Measuring 74 by 25 feet, it originally contained forty-eight 8-foot-by-5-foot rooms for travelers. Later owners reconfigured the interior space,

creating fewer, larger rooms to accommodate a twentieth-century family. Italian stonecutters quarried the granite for the basement in Paradise Valley.

NO28.2 **Barn**

1899–1900, Alfonso Pasquale

This one-story barn with a gable roof measures 210 by 18 feet. Vertical boards and battens clad the walls; corrugated metal covers the roof. The largest building on the property, it could accommodate up to 300 horses when the ranch served as a stage station.

NO28.3 **Bunkhouse**

1899–1900, Alfonso Pasquale

The simple wood-frame bunkhouse provided rustic accommodations for ranch hands. The building measures 33 by 19 feet and is covered by a gable roof. It is connected to an open shed, now used as a carport.

NO28.4 **Shop and Cellar**

c. 1922, Antone Ramasco

This structure across the old road from the rest of the complex has two sections, one a granite cellar, the other a wood-frame shop. The cellar, which has thick stone walls under a shed roof, exhibits the stonemasonry of immigrants from the Piedmont region of Italy. Antone Ramasco constructed many buildings in Paradise Valley and in the Orovada and McDermitt areas. Attached to the north side of the cellar is a one-story, two-room shop with a gable roof and exterior stone chimney. Inside is a trapdoor leading down into a second stone cellar. Unsubstantiated legend holds that the room was used either as a jail for prisoners being transported along the Idaho Trail or as space for bootleg liquor during Prohibition.

McDermitt

The town of McDermitt straddles U.S. 95 just south of the Nevada-Oregon border. It began as a stage stop on the Idaho Trail between Boise and Winnemucca and later served as the community center for people living on vast sheep, cattle, and horse ranches. In the twentieth century the McDermitt Mine, eleven miles southwest of town, bolstered the local economy. Once among the world's largest producers of mercury, the mine shut down in the late 1980s.

Today McDermitt is a sleepy town, providing minimal services to travelers between Idaho, Oregon, and Nevada. A small neighborhood of modest houses and trailers stands along the east side of U.S. 95.

NO29 Jail

1890. East side of U.S. 95 near the Nevada-Oregon border and next to the post office

Situated close to the main road through McDermitt, the old jail holds a prominent place in the town. The stone building has a single entrance through the west facade. An iron door that bolts into the door frame provides access to the one-room interior, which contains a single iron cell. One window on the north side of the jail, covered with an iron grate, allows some light inside. This small structure was possibly built by Italian stonemasons from Paradise Valley, as the stonework is similar to that of buildings there.

Today the building stands as a reminder of the past and a curiosity for passersby.

NO30 Ore-vada Club

c. 1880. The Lane

Located on the major crossroad in McDermitt, the pink-painted wood-frame bar is believed to be the oldest functioning building in town. Made up of two sections, it features a main building two stories tall, with a one-story porch topped by a balcony along the length of the facade.

McDermitt Vicinity

Located near the town of McDermitt, the 34,650-acre Fort McDermitt Indian Reservation is currently the home of about half of the 8,000-member Fort McDermitt Paiute-Shoshone tribe. The reservation occupies the site of a nineteenth-century U.S. Army fort. A thirteen-mile loop road, east of U.S. 95, passes through the reservation into a small green canyon with alfalfa farms and ranches that produce horses and some cattle. Along this road are simple, early twentieth-century vernacular houses, late twentieth-century prefabricated dwellings, various outbuildings, and even some willow corrals.

The U.S. Army began patrolling the area in the summer of 1865 in response to conflict between settlers and Native Americans. Lieutenant Colonel Charles McDermit, commander of Fort Churchill and of the Nevada Military District, led his troops against the Native Americans in several battles that summer. After his death in battle in August 1865, a military post was established and named Camp McDermit. Soldiers built the first structures of stone and wood the following year. In 1879 the camp became known as Fort McDermit. (The spelling was changed to McDermitt with the establishment of a post office in 1891.) The longest-surviving active army fort in all of Nevada, the post was converted into a reservation in 1889.

Sarah Winnemucca, daughter of the Paiute Chief Winnemucca, came to the fort in 1870 with 500 starving Paiute and members of other groups from the Truckee River reservation to beg the army for food. She remained at the fort during the 1870s, where she worked in the hospital. An eloquent writer and fluent speaker of English and several Native American languages, she dedicated her life to improving living conditions and securing rights for all Native Americans.

The administrative complex of the tribe is adjacent to the only two remaining fort buildings. In an interesting twist of history, the tribe now uses these buildings for community activities.

NO31 Senior Center (Officers' Quarters)

c. 1866–1870. 5.1 miles east along North Road from the intersection with U.S. 95

The better preserved of the two remaining fort structures, this one-story stone building with a gable roof stands across the driveway from the tribe's modern, unassuming one-story community and administration building. The older facade has a single entry door with two windows to the left and three to the right. The original windows have been replaced with smaller double-hung windows, the lower portions of the openings having been closed up with wood panels. Two interior brick chimneys rise above the roof near the gable ends. A later wood-frame addition projects from the rear of the building at its east end. The rubblestone walls have been whitewashed.

Paradise Valley

Paradise Valley is located between the Santa Rosa Mountains to the west and the Bloody Run Hills to the east. Its fertile, flat lands, surrounded by steep mountains, form one of the most beautiful valleys in Nevada. Settlers, including Euro-Americans, Germans, Italians, Hispanic Californians, Chinese, and Basques, quickly crowded out Native Americans after 1864. The total population of about 300 residents has remained fairly stable since the late nineteenth century. The town of Paradise Valley lies in the northern part of the valley on a grid oriented to Cottonwood Creek, the main local water source. The town and surrounding valley prospered from raising cattle and sheep and growing hay, barley, and wheat. The two major intersecting streets, Main and Bridge, were laid out as broad avenues to accommodate anticipated herds of animals, as well as people and equipment traveling to mines in the Santa Rosas, although most of this traffic bypassed Paradise. Today these streets seem unnecessarily wide for the quiet town.

Trailers and prefabricated houses on the edges of town attest to new growth in the area, but a number of older buildings remain. Many were built by northern Italians who settled the area in the late nineteenth and early twentieth centuries. Their skill in stone construction has left a lasting architectural legacy. A few older adobe buildings survive, a reminder of the early pioneers of the region.

The major institutional complex in Paradise, the Paradise Valley Ranger Station, built in 1935 by the U.S. Forest Service and the Civilian Conservation Corps, stands at the south end of town. Despite its early twentieth-century character, its wood-frame vernacular buildings blend smoothly with the overall character of others in town.

NO32 Micca House

1880s. 1902, Alfonso Pasquale. South side of Bridge St. at Cottonwood Creek

Alfonso Pasquale purchased this small adobe store (built in the 1880s) in 1902 to expand it into a hotel and saloon. The building, containing a post office, land office, bar, dining room, and kitchen, soon became a center for town business. Pasquale made extensive additions to the original adobe store, adding a wood-frame false front and a framed upper story with cross gables on top of the adobe walls. Beneath the painted letters reading "Korral Bar," one can still see the words "Micca Saloon." (Sagliano Micca was Pasquale's native town in Italy.) A narrow cornice is supported by small brackets on both facades. At the rear is a granite basement housing an oven for baking bread, an element often found in Italian settlements in this region. Micca House has been vacant for decades and has deteriorated. Abutting a creek

NO32 Micca House (left)

NO34 Paradise Valley Ranger Station (below)

to the west of the building is a granite retaining wall, built by Augusto Ramasco and his son Antone in the early twentieth century, with granite steps leading down to the water. The Ramascos constructed numerous buildings in Paradise Valley and other nearby places.

NO33 **Protestant Church** (formerly Methodist Church)

1895. 285 S. Main St. (northeast corner of S. Main and S.3rd sts.)

The town's Methodist congregation built this white-painted, wood-frame structure, but it now serves Protestants of all denominations. Shiplap siding covers the walls and bell tower. Gothic Revival details include simplified pointed windows with multipane, double-hung sashes and ogee-arched entrance doors. The tower rises from a gable-roofed entry vestibule to an unusual triple-hipped roof covered with shingles. An open belfry, supported by posts and decorated with large scrolled brackets, tops the roof.

Though the builder is unknown, Italian stone-masons probably built the granite foundation and front steps.

NO34 **Paradise Valley Ranger Station**

1933–1941. 355 S. Main St. (northeast corner of S. Main and S. 4th sts.)

With few alterations and all seven original buildings and a cistern intact, this still-functioning U.S. Forest Service (USFS) ranger station provides an unusually well-preserved example of such a complex constructed during the 1930s in Nevada. The eighth building, a barn constructed by the Civilian Conservation Corps (CCC), was moved to the site in 1948 and converted into a bunkhouse. The CCC constructed the station to serve the Santa Rosa Division of the Humboldt National Forest. The CCC also constructed a grammar school and improved roads in Paradise. The design of each of the eight buildings on the site, not including the concrete and masonry cistern, followed standard USFS plans.

Simple and practical, the wood-frame buildings retain their original color scheme of white with green trim. Displaying the influence of bungalow design, all of them have drop siding and medium-pitched gable roofs of cedar. Several other USFS ranger stations in Nevada erected by the CCC in the 1930s have buildings constructed according to the same plans; one is Baker Ranger Station near Great Basin National Park.

NO34.1 Office

1934, U.S. Forest Service and Civilian Conservation Corps

The office is a one-story, wood-frame structure with a rectangular plan measuring 16 by 40 feet. Built following USFS Plan R-4 #51, it features a gable roof extending the length of the building; at each end the gable projects to cover an open, full-length porch supported by three square columns. The interior has two rooms of equal size used year round by USFS employees.

NO34.2 Ranger's House

1940–1941, U.S. Forest Service and Civilian Conservation Corps

With its irregular plan (USFS Plan R-4 #1) and cross-gabled roof, this station's house differs from the square and rectangular office and utilitarian structures on the site. A small gable-roofed porch shelters the front entrance. A Forest Service ranger and his or her family live in this building throughout the year.

NO34.3 Bunkhouse (Barn)

1930s, U.S. Forest Service and Civilian Conservation Corps; moved 1948–1949

The CCC erected this building (USFS Plan R-4 #13-A) as a two-horse barn near Paradise Valley. The USFS moved it to the station for use as a bunkhouse, removing the horse stalls and adding a bathroom and kitchen counter. The building retains many of its original windows, doors, and interior wood paneling. Seasonal USFS employees sleep here from May to October.

NO34.4 Warehouse-Shop

1935–1936, U.S. Forest Service and Civilian Conservation Corps

One of the larger buildings on the site, 20 by 40 feet, this shop (USFS Plan R-4 #33-A) stands east of the bunkhouse at the southeast corner of the complex. It is divided into two equal rooms, one for the warehouse, the other for the shop. The heavy wood-plank bench and bins in the shop are original. The USFS stores tools, camping supplies, and other equipment here.

NO34.5 Horse Barn

1934, U.S. Forest Service and Civilian Conservation Corps

The one-and-one-half-story, wood-frame barn stands at the northeast corner of the property adjacent to a corral and a hay yard and across from the warehouse-shop. Covered with drop siding and measuring 31 by 18 feet, it features a large door with cross braces painted in green. A hay door pierces the gable above.

NO35 St. Alfonso's Catholic Church

1906, Augusto Ramasco. Southeast corner of S. Main and 4th South sts.

The only building in Paradise Valley constructed entirely of granite, the Catholic church combines excellent craftsmanship with a simple design in keeping with that of other buildings in town. The treatment of the granite defines the three sections of the building's walls. The surfaces of the foundation stones are left rough-hewn, but the three courses above, rising to the windowsills, are smoother, creating a break between the foundation and the smooth stone blocks that make up the rest of the walls. The church itself is a narrow rectangle with an open interior plan and a tower at a rear (northeast)

corner. According to Howard Wight Marshall's *Paradise Valley, Nevada: The People and Buildings of an American Place* (1995), the location of the tower is similar to that of the church in Sagliano Micca, Italy, the native village of many of Paradise Valley's Italian stonemasons. The belfry of the tower, however, is similar to that of the Protestant church (NO33) in the treatment of the posts and brackets supporting the hipped roof above and may indicate other influences as well. Round-arched openings for the doors and windows are finished with tightly fitted voussoirs. A cropped biforated window pierces the front gable end, endowing the church with a restrained Romanesque appearance.

NO36 Silver State Flour Mill

c. 1868, Battiste Recanzone? Casinelli Ranch, 7 miles east of Paradise Valley, off NV 8B

This was the site of the first flour mill in Humboldt County and one of the earliest in Nevada. Following its construction, farmers in the sur-

rounding area began to grow wheat, which could finally be processed locally; previously flour had been shipped from California. Charles Adams, the first owner of the mill, sold the property to Battiste Recanzone, an Italian immigrant, in the early 1880s. Recanzone's son Lorenzo continued to operate the mill into the early twentieth century.

The mill consists of two structures: the original mill building and a stone warehouse, both probably built by Battiste Recanzone before he bought the property from Adams. The original two-story mill measured 60 by 30 feet, but the addition of the 51-foot-by-31-foot warehouse considerably enlarged the complex. The lower portion of the mill is made of cut sandstone from a nearby quarry; the wood-frame upper portion is clad with rough-sawn horizontal planks. Traces remain of heavy black tar paper once nailed to the exterior. The cut sandstone walls of the one-story warehouse rest on a rubble foundation. The milling equipment survives, though the facility has not functioned as a mill since the early 1930s.

Golconda

Golconda was settled during the 1860s when mining commenced in the nearby mountains. The town's founders optimistically took its name from a city in Hyderabad, India, once famed for its wealth in diamonds. In 1862 Louis and Theophile Lay, who had helped settle Winnemucca, began construction of the Humboldt Canal. Originally intended to irrigate lands to the south and to power ore mills as far east as Unionville, the canal was completed only as far as Golconda. As a result, agriculture and ranching flourished in and around the town. When the Central Pacific Railroad arrived in 1868, it provided Golconda with a new and faster way to export its products.

Once a prosperous mining, agricultural, and railroad town, Golconda is now sparsely settled, with one-story houses and trailers. The small commercial center consists of a row of gas stations and stores along old U.S. 40. Along the north end of town are the railroad tracks, now owned by Union Pacific. A few structures stand along Stanford Street, across the tracks from the main part of town. Today, despite profitable mining operations nearby, most mining employees choose to live in larger towns like Winnemucca or Battle Mountain. I-80 has also kept most passersby away, leaving Golconda a quiet place.

NO37 Golconda School

1888, J. L. Donnel. 1929, C. A. LaGrave. Morrison Ave.

The tallest, most elaborate building left in Golconda, the wood-frame school reflects the late nineteenth-century prosperity of the town. The school, with two classrooms, was larger and more elaborate than most of its rural one-room counterparts. The building consists of three sections: the front-porch mass, containing the entry and supporting the tower; the central mass, containing the original classrooms; and the rear ell, built in 1929 to house the high school addition. The school's masses make a harmonious whole; the double gables of the classroom section frame the front-porch mass and the tower above. The flared-eave mansard roof provides a base for the bell tower.

Battle Mountain

Battle Mountain is located at the north end of Lander County in the Reese River Valley. The small settlement, established in the 1860s, served as a supply center for the Battle Mountain Mining District, then one of the most active in the state. It also became a railroad town upon the arrival of the Central Pacific in Battle Mountain in 1869. Later, in 1880, the Nevada Central Railroad connected Austin to the south to the transcontinental railroad in Battle Mountain, making the town a hub for the county.

The most recent mining boom in the area began in the 1960s when the Duval Company's Copper Canyon operation reopened. Several mines are now yielding gold, silver, copper, barite, turquoise, iron, and mercury. In 1979 Battle Mountain's boom and subsequent growth allowed it to wrest the designation of county seat from Austin, 100 miles to the south.

Unlike other railroad towns in northern Nevada, Battle Mountain has a commercial center that still faces the old Central Pacific railroad tracks along Front Street (U.S. 40). Few railroad structures remain; the old depot, for instance, was demolished in the 1980s. Smaller buildings associated with the railroad survive, including sheds and station masters' houses. Residential streets of mostly modest bungalows stretch away from the tracks to the southwest. I-80, however, has shifted the latest development away from the old town center to Battle Mountain's two highway exits, leaving the future of the old commercial district in doubt.

NO38 Lemaire's Grocery

c. 1882, 1990s. 6 Front St.

This large store fronting the railroad tracks is one of the earliest commercial buildings remaining in town. Built after a disastrous fire in 1880, the two-story building, purchased by A. D. Lemaire, has been in business ever since.

Recent alterations obscure the fact that the store is actually composed of three structures: a two-story building at the corner of Front and Broad, which was the original Lemaire Store, and two one-story buildings to the west. All the buildings are constructed of brick and originally had flat roofs with parapets instead of the present gable roofs.

NO39 Nevada Hotel

1872, 1882, 1950s. 36 E. Front St.

The Altenberg family, early settlers of Battle Mountain, built the Nevada Hotel across the street from the railroad depot, and the business has remained in operation ever since. In the mid-twentieth century the owners installed a modern facade of alternating aqua- and cream-colored metal screens, but the original brick walls can be seen along the sides and rear. The interior has been substantially altered.

NO40 Louis Lemaire House

c. 1900. 215 S. Broad St.

The Louis Lemaire house represents a simplified interpretation of the Shingle Style. It is the kind of dwelling a well-to-do businessman in this part of the state would have built—comfortable but not immense or ostentatious. The Lemaire family, among the first to settle in Battle Mountain, participated in business and politics. Shingled walls, prominent gables, and a full-length porch reflect the Shingle Style.

NO41 Lander County Courthouse (Lander County Grammar School)

1916, Dan P. Bell. 315 S. Humboldt St.

This structure was originally built as a school, although it looks as if it had been designed as one of Nevada's many Classical Revival courthouses. In 1979, when Lander County government shifted from Austin in central Nevada to Battle Mountain, elected officials sought a dignified setting for their duties. The old school needed only a few minor modifications to serve their purpose well. The one-story brick structure has a full basement rising to a water table. Above this, the facade has five bays on either side of a central portico approached by steps and supported by two pairs of Tuscan columns.

NO42 Grace Orthodox Presbyterian Church (St. Andrew's Episcopal Church)

Late nineteenth century. 45 4th St.

An unusual two-story porch covering the full length and height of the front-gabled facade gives this wood-frame church a distinctive appearance lacking in most of Battle Mountain's structures. Set behind the porch on the roof ridge is an open belfry with a flared, shingled hipped roof. The building is one of three historic churches remaining in Battle Mountain.

NO43 Well Tower

c. 1917–1923. Behind the house at 232 E. 2nd St.

One of two well towers in the old residential neighborhood of Battle Mountain, this structure, containing a holding tank, stands atop a

NO41 Lander County Courthouse (Lander County Grammar School) (below)

NO43 Well Tower (right)

rectangular one-story building with a shed roof. Both components have board-and-batten siding, painted bright green, and corrugated metal roofs. The tower was probably used as late as 1931, when the town built its municipal water tower.

Carlin

Unlike Battle Mountain and Winnemucca, which were towns in their own right before the arrival of the Central Pacific, Carlin was founded by the railroad as a division point. Set in a small valley, it was the first spot where the Emigrant Trail met the Humboldt River after a long detour. The river made this a logical place for the railroad to build switching and maintenance yards, repair shops, and a large icehouse. The tracks remain, widening to several sidings along the old Main Street before narrowing to two tracks on the edges of town.

Main Street, Carlin's first commercial center, developed across from the railroad yards, complete with hotels, saloons, shops, and a depot, all facing the tracks. By traveling from Main Street and the railroad north to I-80, one can see how the automobile gradually replaced the train as the primary means of passenger transportation, and how this change affected the town's development. Chestnut Street (U.S. 40) now serves as the main street, though its buildings, dating from the early to mid-twentieth century, look neglected and run-down. Just one block north is I-80. New development along Carlin's interstate exits has drawn business away from the old commercial centers.

Carlin has enjoyed some economic prosperity in recent years because of the opening of several gold mines to the north. The influx of new residents can be seen in the subdivision of prefabricated houses at the west end of town and the trailer park at the east end.

NO44 **Union Pacific Railroad Yards**
(Southern Pacific Railroad Yards)
Bounded roughly by 1st, 13th, Hamilton, and Main sts.

No railroad buildings remain from the Central Pacific period (late nineteenth century), but two brick buildings from the early twentieth century remind visitors of Carlin's importance for the Southern Pacific. These structures were part of the railroad's upgrading of facilities. The yards are now used by Union Pacific, though the buildings themselves are vacant.

NO44.1 **Engine House**
1916, Southern Pacific Railroad

The massive appearance of the old Southern Pacific engine house underscores the central function of this building, which provided storage and work space to maintain the railroad's engines. It stands parallel to the railroad tracks on an east-west axis. The broad, slightly pitched gable roof

is hidden by stepped parapets at the ends of the building. Long windows set in recessed bays terminate in heavy concrete sills at the bottom and corbeling at the top. On the west side, a pair of large wooden doors sheathed with sheet metal provides access to the interior. Tracks west of the building led to a turntable (demolished) where engines were rotated to other tracks.

NO44.2 **General Storehouse**
1916, Southern Pacific Railroad

The storehouse stands parallel to the engine house and adjacent to the main tracks. This long building is considerably smaller in size than the engine house but echoes many of the architectural characteristics of its neighbor. Each gable end has a single door opening, now boarded up, centered in the wall and elevated above ground. Along the track side, a series of single elevated door openings, now boarded up, allowed the loading of boxcars. The opposite wall has several similar openings, as well as a large sliding door at the west end and, to the left, a pair of wood doors. Though deteriorated, the building is largely unaltered.

NO45 Main Street

West side of Main Street between 6th and 7th sts.

Main Street runs along the south side of the tracks for several blocks, eventually becoming a rural county road. Though many buildings have disappeared or have been unsympathetically altered, the block between 6th and 7th streets retains some of its former character and obvious charm. Most of the buildings were constructed in the late nineteenth or early twentieth century. Typical of the buildings along the tracks is the Colonial Hotel (1911), 609 Main Street, which continues in operation as a rooming house. Stucco now covers its brick walls, and later alterations have obliterated the first floor. The Overland Bar and Cafe (c. 1900), which was destroyed by fire in 1998, had the most architecturally elaborate facade on the block, with a pedimented parapet and pilaster strips.

Elko

Elko is one of Nevada's more complex towns. In the 1990s it became one of the fastest-growing places in one of the fastest-growing states in the country, with a population that doubled, to 25,000 people, within a decade. Its history, however, is similar to that of other towns settled along the Humboldt River.

Elko was established in 1868 as a railroad town when the Central Pacific laid out a townsite, with the tracks defining the south end of the grid. Railroad workshops, sheds, railroad workers' housing, and the commercial and residential areas of town developed to the north, while a commercial row quickly rose along the south side of the tracks. As time passed, more structures developed on this side of the tracks so businesses could be near the railroad and take advantage of the traffic it created. These included hotels, brothels, and bars. Mining in the mountains outside Elko brought prosperity to the town as a supply and transportation center in the late nineteenth century. Many cattle ranches were established in the outlying areas, transforming Elko into a cowtown. In 1874 the state established the University of Nevada campus here, but the boom-and-bust cycle of the mining industry soon brought decline to Elko, and the university moved to Reno in 1884. The railroad and the town's role as the seat of Elko County kept the economy alive until the early twentieth century.

The arrival of the Western Pacific in 1907, on tracks about one block south of the Central Pacific, and the opening of U.S. 40 along Idaho Street in the 1920s brought renewed prosperity from tourism and spurred more development in the southern part of town. Growing cattle ranches also fueled Elko's economy, though much of the area's ranching in the early twentieth century concentrated on raising sheep tended by Basques. The WPA guide to the state describes Elko in the 1930s as "anything but provincial," with "shops selling clothes bearing trademarks of prominent designers, fine tweeds, and even Lalique glass." As the largest town between Salt Lake City and Reno, and between Boise and Las Vegas, Elko served, and continues to serve, an area as large as Connecticut, Rhode Island, and Massachusetts combined.

In the past decade, new gold-mining ventures have brought rapid growth; mining now accounts for almost 60 percent of the economy, with gambling and ranching providing the rest. The downtown, with its brick and concrete commercial structures, is holding its own, but sprawl around the I-80 exits and subdivisions on the north side of the highway and to the south threaten to draw away business. Elko has nonetheless managed to maintain its character as a small town with a sophisticated edge. This sophistication is evident in some of the town's prominent historic buildings, as well as in the Western Folklife Center's annual Cowboy Poetry Festival, held since 1985. Old residential neighborhoods have quiet, shady streets with houses in recognizable styles interspersed with small plainer dwellings.

Centered on Idaho Avenue and bordered by 2nd, 13th, Water, and Elm streets, Elko's downtown thrives with a mix of casinos, bars, Basque restaurants, a saddle shop, an espresso bar, and the Western Folklife Center. The northern part of downtown contains Elko's oldest residential

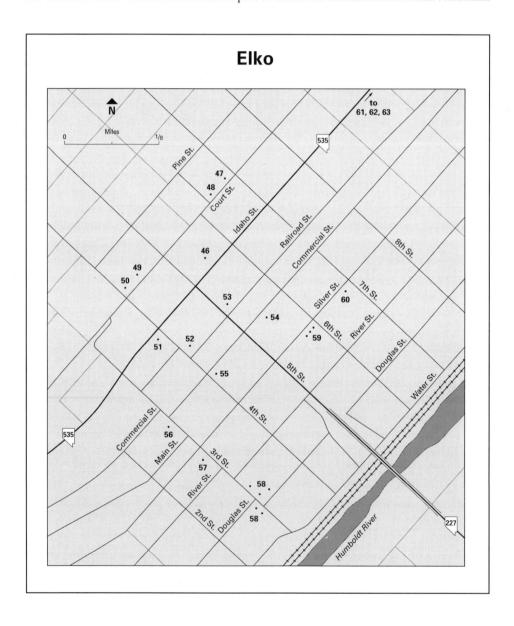

neighborhood, with many large homes and churches dating from the late nineteenth and early twentieth centuries. The streetscapes remain largely intact, though the facades of many late nineteenth-century commercial buildings have been covered with metal siding.

Between 1978 and 1983, Elko used federal funds to move its railroad tracks from the center of town to the southern edge of the old grid, alongside the Humboldt River. The city paved the old railroad right-of-way and converted it into a large parking lot between Railroad and Commercial streets. The removal of the tracks and subsequent loss of railroad buildings in the center of town have erased most of Elko's railroad roots. Only a small park with a Western Pacific engine and caboose reminds residents of this part of Elko's past. Although removal of the tracks irrevocably altered Elko's urban fabric, the vast asphalt spaces subsequently created may have helped preserve downtown Elko, as abundant parking has slowed the flight of businesses to strip malls outside of town.

NO46 Elko County Courthouse

1911, William H. Weeks. 571 Idaho St.

This two-story masonry Beaux-Arts classical structure, designed by California architect William H. Weeks, is one of the most monumental in the state. A massive two-story portico supported by four Tuscan columns ending in capitals with a prominent egg-and-dart motif projects from the symmetrical main facade, elevated on a masonry foundation. An ornamental cartouche decorates the pediment over the portico; above the door is a bas-relief of a female face personifying Justice. Terra-cotta quoins adorn the corners of the building; on the side elevations, engaged columns echo the full columns on the facade. The courthouse features a full entablature capped with an ornate balustrade, and a flat roof with a shallow dome. The building stands on a large lot that also contains Elko's first high school, a small building now used as county offices.

NO47 Bradley House

large front-facing gable with more decorative scalloped shingles influenced by the Shingle Style. A large shed-roofed porch supported by square columns shelters the main entrance. The house was built by John R. Bradley, one-time owner of the Commercial Hotel, Bradley Opera House, and various ranches in the area.

NO47 Bradley House

1904. 643 Court St.

This is one of many fine homes built in the early twentieth century along Court and Pine streets in Elko's earliest residential neighborhood. The two-story brick and wood-frame structure has a large corner turret topped by a conical roof, adding variety to the building's blocklike form. The first story of the tower and house is made of brick; the tower windows on this level have segmental-arched openings emphasized in the brickwork. The second story of the tower is faced with plain wood shingles, the

NO48 Reinhart House

1927. 627 Court St.

Like its neighbor, this brick Neo-Tudor house was built by a prominent and wealthy resident of Elko, Edgar Reinhart, owner of Reinhart's Company Clothing and Dry Goods. The Reinhart family, German immigrants, ran one of the largest and most successful mercantile enterprises in northern Nevada during the late nineteenth and early twentieth centuries. The one-and-one-half-story house incorporates such Tudor Revival elements as a steeply pitched gable roof, half timbering in the front gable, and tall brick chimneys.

NO49 Chilton Engineering Building
(Knights of Pythias Hall)

1927. 421 Court St.

This compact building in a Renaissance Revival mode is a little jewel in Elko's downtown district. The Knights of Pythias erected the one-story, brick-walled building as their meeting hall. The large arched windows and entry and the red-tiled gable roof are major features, enlivened by a ceramic tile frieze and ceramic escutcheons in the spandrels of each arch.

The Knights of Pythias was formed in Washington, D.C., in 1866 as a fraternal order adhering to the principles of loyal friendship, based on the ancient story of Damon and Pythias. Condemned to death by the tyrant of Syracuse, Pythias was to receive a furlough before his execution if someone would take his place in jail. Pythias's friend Damon offered to do so. Instead of leaving his friend to be executed, Pythias returned, and the tyrant freed both men. The Knights of Pythias, based on this tale of brotherhood, became a particularly popular organization in the years after the Civil War. In late nineteenth-century Nevada the Knights, with a largely Protestant membership, had lodges in many towns and were known for taking care of their members and aiding orphans and widows. Other fraternal organizations such as the Masons and the Odd Fellows were also commonplace, providing camaraderie and community service for a transient and scattered population.

NO50 Map House

1869. 405 Court St.

The oldest house still standing in Elko is now used by Chilton Engineering to store and sell maps. The one-story, L-shaped building is typical of mid-nineteenth-century vernacular architecture in the area, when residents erected modest wood-frame dwellings. The house has drop siding, a full-length porch supported on posts, and window surrounds with simple moldings.

NO51 Commercial Hotel

c. 1893, 1941. 345 4th St.

Though much of its original facade is hidden by signs, stone veneer, and metal cornices, the Commercial Hotel houses one of the oldest casinos in the state. The three-story brick structure stands at the corner of 4th and Idaho streets on the site of the Humboldt Lodging House, a one-story frame building with a false front and porch, built in 1869. After J. B. Abel bought the Humboldt in 1893, he rebuilt it, erecting a two-story brick building, the core of which still stands.

The hotel is a simple commercial structure, enlivened by decorative brickwork including quoins around some of the windows. The largest sign, mounted over the corner entrance to the building, displays a giant polar bear standing atop letters that proclaim "Coffee Shop Always Open." Neon and flashing signs on every side of the hotel attract customers from all over downtown.

The Commercial added a casino soon after Nevada legalized gambling in 1931. Ten years later the hotel became the first in the state to feature famous entertainers to attract customers to its casino. Among the stars who performed there during the 1940s were the Andrews Sisters, Sophie Tucker, and Chico Marx. This tradition of providing entertainment in casinos has continued ever since, taken to its greatest heights in the elaborate shows presented in Las Vegas.

NO52 U.S. Bank (Henderson Bank)

1929, George W. Kelham. 1979, interior renovation. 401 Railroad St.

Built for George Wingfield, president of the bank and a major figure in Nevada's early twentieth-century mining and banking industries, this structure was designed to impress the public. At four stories, it is still downtown Elko's tallest building. Constructed of reinforced concrete, with a facade of Boise sandstone and brick, the bank is also notable for a decorative

NO52 U.S. Bank (Henderson Bank, left)

NO53 Western Folklife Center (Pioneer Hotel) (right)

cornice loosely evoking late medieval or early Renaissance motifs. The brick is laid in a repeating-arch pattern that runs around the parapet of the structure. Terra-cotta tiles are used as contrasting elements in the design. Providing another decorative touch are the evenly spaced colored terra-cotta tiles above the round-arched door and window openings of the first floor. The main facade along Railroad Street has a large central entrance marked by two receding arches faced with terra-cotta. Large medallions with stylized foliage flank the central arch.

The interior of the main floor is still largely intact, revealing architectural details and surface finishes in a classical mode. The banking room has high ceilings and tall arched windows with columns forming two rows along the sides of the room. Gray marble covers the walls of the office lobby and the lower portions of the corridor walls throughout the building.

The bank opened in February 1929 to much fanfare, only to fail in 1932. A 1979 renovation consisted mostly of interior work.

NO53 Western Folklife Center (Pioneer Hotel)

1912–1913, 1950, 1994–present. 501 Railroad St.

This former hotel and bar along the railroad tracks has been the home of the Western Folklife Center since 1992. Since 1994, the center has been restoring the building to serve as a major cultural institution and the main venue for the annual Cowboy Poetry Festival. The front entrance is located in a clipped corner at Railroad and 5th streets. Another entrance on 5th Street leads to the upper floors. A wide frieze of colorful ceramic tiles separates the main floor, containing a gallery, shop, and performance area, from the upper floors, which are now offices converted from hotel rooms. Both facades originally rose to a cornice set on brackets. A previous owner removed the cornice topping the Railroad Street side in order to construct a penthouse in 1950.

The center has acquired the two adjacent one-story buildings to create the Pioneer Room and a music hall. A mirrored and elaborately carved wood bar, taken from the old Pioneer Saloon, formerly on the site, has been installed in the Pioneer Room. Both spaces are used for poetry readings, meetings, and other programs.

NO54 Club Brandin' Iron

1930s. 548 Commercial St.

One of Elko's vintage bars, the Brandin' Iron displays a simple but integrated example of Moderne styling. The facade serves as a backdrop for the large sign over the main entrance. Two plate glass windows flank the entrance, which is marked by curving glass block walls receding to the door. The entire entry is covered by a canopy trimmed with aluminum. Above, the backdrop for the neon appears to be a rugged cliff or a broken down fence. The words "Club Brandin' Iron" float above two branding irons with the brands "El" and "Ko."

NO54 Club Brandin' Iron

NO58 Brothels

NO55 Silver Dollar Club

c. 1920s. 400 Commercial St.

Erected to house the first Henderson Bank, this one-story brick building is a modest structure, but it has some fine details in its denticulated cornice and arched window openings. After the bank moved to new quarters on Railroad Street, the building became a bar. The arches were filled in with glass blocks and plywood. Red tiles were applied to the lower part of the facade to suggest modernity in materials and color. Crowning the building, a large neon sign announces the "Silver Dollar Club." A number of other vintage neon signs are displayed inside.

NO56 Elko Downtown Post Office

1933, James A. Wetmore. 275 3rd St.

Elko's main post office was one of several designed by the Office of the Supervising Architect of the U.S. Treasury Department that were built in Nevada during the Great Depression. The two-story building stands on a concrete foundation, the raised basement wall faced with granite and the upper walls with buff-colored brick. The symmetrical facade has seven bays with two slightly projecting end bays. The main entrance and flanking windows are set in arches defined by terra-cotta surrounds with slender twisted columns and tiles displaying stylized flora and fauna. The post office is an example of the rich architectural design and construction that the federal government supported in the early 1930s. Later, the desire to economize, combined with the influence of the

Moderne and the International Style, diminished the role of decoration and fine materials.

Although this building, the first and only federal building in Elko, represents the success of local efforts for a stronger federal presence—and more jobs—in the 1930s, the planning process for the structure did not go smoothly. The location of the proposed building became a major point of contention between the town and the government when local residents demanded that the post office be centrally placed downtown. After considering several possibilities, both parties agreed on the present site. This debate foreshadowed more recent disputes between Elko residents and the federal government, largely over the management of public lands. Nevertheless, the post office, now an anchor for the downtown, remains a symbol of the cooperation between the local and federal governments in the past.

NO57 Star Hotel

1910. 246 Silver St.

Built by a Basque couple, Pete and Matilda Jauregui, the Star serves as a social center for the Basque community but is well known to the entire town for its Basque-American cooking and attracts a diverse clientele of local residents and tourists. The hotel is unusual in that it still has Basque boarders who eat in the dining room every night.

Until the railroad tracks were relocated, the Star had the advantage of being close to both the Central Pacific and Western Pacific lines. Time has taken its toll on the hotel's exterior. The two-story, wood-frame building originally had a balcony supported by brackets running along the second floor on the Commercial Street facade. Composition siding now covers the original drop siding. The main entrance, set in the corner facing the intersection of Silver and 3rd streets, leads directly into the barroom. Against the interior wall stands a bar of red lacquer and chrome, installed in the 1930s. Beyond is the dining room, recently remodeled to turn what was a dark, crowded space into a brighter and airier room. Guest rooms are on the second floor.

NO58 Brothels

3rd and Douglas sts.

Unlike Winnemucca's brothels, which are some distance from the town center, Elko's are near the downtown in a modest neighborhood of houses and mobile homes. Although none of the brothels displays a particular architectural style, they have some common features. All are one-story buildings and have long, rectangular footprints. The only exceptions are Mona's Ranch (1915, many alterations), 103 South 3rd Street, and Sue's (1970), 171 South 3rd Street, each of which has a two-story main section with a long one-story ell. The first floor of the main section contains a large room with a bar, where clients are served drinks and look over the women. The ells contain small bedrooms indicated on the exterior by the closely spaced windows in the upper half of the wall. One of Elko's oldest brothels, Mona's Ranch, has been extensively remodeled inside and out over the years. Though the buildings are undistinguished, their neon signs, lit up at night, bathe the street in a warm glow intended to attract customers.

NO59 Railroad Cottages

c. 1907, Western Pacific Railroad. Southwest corner of Silver and 6th sts.

Another reminder of the Western Pacific Railroad, these three identical one-story, brick cottages with hipped roofs provide an odd note of uniformity on an otherwise typically varied street. Each house has a central entrance flanked by double-hung windows. Low segmental arches topping windows and doors are the only decorative feature. The roof overhang projects forward to create a porch at the front.

The city's relocation of the railroad from downtown has altered the cottages' original physical context, but their identical appearance indicates their original function as railroad workers' housing, usually a simple expression of domestic architecture. These three dwellings are unusual for Nevada in that they are constructed of brick rather than wood. They were located near the tracks and yards for the convenience of the railroads, which used identical plans to facilitate rapid construction. In their symmetry and regular placement along the road, these cottages reflect the order that the railroads wished to impose on their towns by means of the linearity of the urban grid and the order of the railroad yards. They continue to provide modest-income housing.

NO60 Hay and Grain Store

c. 1907. 672 Silver St.

This storehouse stands next to the original location of the Western Pacific tracks that ran along Silver Street. The building rests on a raised basement, with doors positioned at the height of a loading dock, now missing from the front of the building. Goods could be loaded onto boxcars waiting on the adjacent tracks. A shed roof projects over the front to protect the dock from rain and snow. The frame building has a gable roof, with both walls and roof covered with tar paper. The painted sign reading "Hay & Grain" is still visible on the front of the building.

NO61 Ruby Valley Pony Express Station

c. 1860. 1960, moved. 1515 Idaho St.

This small log cabin, measuring 11 by 18 feet, looks out of place on the front lawn of the Northeastern Nevada Museum. It is the only surviving cabin of several built for a Pony Express station in remote Ruby Valley, about sixty miles southeast of Elko. Concerned about the cabin's possible destruction, the museum moved the building in 1960, the centennial of the Pony Express. Although the move destroyed the cabin's physical context, the building remains today as one of only two surviving Pony Express log stations in Nevada; the other is Friday's Station at Stateline.

Vertical logs form the walls, which are topped by smaller logs placed perpendicularly to support the slightly sloped shed roof. Two posts inside the building also support the sod-covered roof. An exterior stone chimney stands at one end of the cabin. The only opening into the building is the front entrance, centered in the main facade. Although many Pony Express stations consisted of rudimentary cabins for shelter, they were critical to the survival of the route during its eighteen months of existence in 1860 and 1861.

NO62 Sherman Station

1902–1903, Valentine Walther. 1997, moved. 1515 Idaho St.

This two-story, 4,700-square-foot log house is an unusual structure in Nevada, where log buildings tend to be small cabins. In 1997 the Elko Chamber of Commerce moved the house in one piece by flatbed truck to the grounds of the Northeastern Nevada Museum for use as its offices and as a visitor center. The building's original site, in Huntington Valley, about sixty miles south of Elko, was on a ranch homesteaded by Valentine Walther in 1876. Walther, a Bavarian immigrant, ran the ranch as a stage stop along the road between Elko and Hamilton in White Pine County. He built ten log buildings on the ranch, using round logs and saddle notches for all the structures except the main house and blacksmith's shop, which have square logs and dovetail notches. Of these, the creamery, blacksmith's shop, and schoolhouse were also moved to Elko to serve as part of the visitor center. Walther made the house of pine logs from Sherman Peak, part of the Ruby Mountain range, near the original site of the station. He cut them in 1902 and began con-

struction the following year. With the help of two men, he hewed the logs by hand, completing the building in 1903.

Despite the harsh winters and hot summers, the building has weathered the climate well. Its dovetailed joints hold the massive timbers in place, and chinking of mud, plaster, cement, wood, and other materials keeps the elements at bay. Dormer windows break the eaves of the broad hipped roof at several places. A small porch on the east facade covers the main entrance. A bay window on the south elevation, probably ready-made, adds a note of refinement. The interior, inhabited until the 1970s, has a kitchen, living room, and dining room on the ground floor and one large room on the upper floor.

NO63 Elko City Hall

1972, Arne Purhonen. 1751 College Ave.

Representing the misguided decision of city governments to relocate away from downtown areas, the city hall stands several blocks away from Elko's core, near the convention center. Purhonen, a local architect, designed a modern structure of steel, brick, and glass featuring a curving wall facing the street. Thin piers, separating tall, narrow windows, rise to a metal cornice. Two low brick sections project from the central mass, connected to it by low hyphens that contain the building's entrances.

Lamoille

The town of Lamoille, in the quiet and isolated Lamoille Valley at the foot of the Ruby Mountains, about sixteen miles southeast of Elko, has a pastoral atmosphere. Along its one main road are a general store, bar, and old school. Euro-Americans settled Lamoille around 1865 and established a few farms and ranches. The valley provided an alternative to the main route of the Emigrant Trail from Wells to Elko, following an old Shoshone trail.

NO64 Community Presbyterian Church

1905, 1982, 1994. NV 227

The white church with its Gothic Revival details is unexpected in this isolated environment, and yet the contrast of height and firmly spreading solidity gives the church some of the variety of its natural surroundings, where flat lands rise to nearby mountains. From its pointed-arched, paired doors at the base to the tall conical steeple above, the corner tower strains to touch the sky. Large stained glass windows, set within pointed arches, punctuate the broad gable ends.

In 1982 the congregation added a one-story wing to the rear by extending the rear gable back from the church. Another wing, two sto-

ries in height, extends from the 1982 addition to provide increased meeting space. Both wings blend with the style of the church, although in an energy-conscious age the congregation seems to have been reluctant to include large windows.

NO65 Railroad Tie Sheds

c. 1900. NV 227, just west of the Presbyterian Church and NV 227 at the bend in the road

The two railroad tie sheds in Lamoille are typical of the genre. Relatively small, simple structures, they utilize ties as if they were logs, interlocked at the corners with abutting ends. Both have gable roofs covered with corrugated metal and pairs of doors facing the road. Salvaged ties became a popular building material, often the only ready source of lumber. When the Central Pacific began repairing its tracks in the 1890s, thousands of ties became available for reuse in a variety of buildings, from sheds and garages to cabins. In areas such as mining towns, which tended to be more prosperous, tie cabins were rare.

NO64 Community Presbyterian Church

Owyhee

The small town of Owyhee, near the Nevada-Idaho border, is the center of the Duck Valley Indian Reservation, established in 1877 for the Shoshone and Paiute. The reservation, a huge square of land, half in Nevada, half in Idaho, is situated in the beautiful Owyhee River Valley. Driving north on Nevada 226, one gradually leaves the Great Basin and enters the Columbia Plateau. Until around the turn of the century, salmon from the Pacific Ocean swam up the Columbia and Snake rivers and tributaries to spawn in the nearby Owyhee River.

After the establishment of the reservation, Native American residents lived in a variety of dwellings, ranging from wickiups covered with blankets or canvas to log cabins and adobe houses. Until fairly recently, many tribal members continued to live in log cabins, but new housing, built by the tribe's own housing authority under the aegis of the Bureau of Indian Affairs (BIA), is replacing these structures. In the 1930s the BIA and other federal agencies constructed a number of vernacular stone buildings consisting mainly of institutional structures and housing for its employees. Many of the houses and cottages were built from standard plans prepared in the construction division of the Office of the Commissioner of Indian Affairs in Washington, D.C. The Public Works Administration (PWA) funded construction of some of the larger buildings, as well as structures built to support an improved electrical power supply for the town. In style and materials, particularly their native multicolored stone, these buildings resemble those at the Stewart Indian School in Carson City, though no evidence directly connecting the architecture of the two complexes has been found. Although the buildings are serviceable, they constitute an ambivalent legacy as reminders of white oppression.

Reservation residents continue to use many of the old BIA buildings and even plan to restore some of the stone structures, but others are deteriorated and vacant. Traditional architecture, such as wickiups made of willows and brush or pieces of wood, can also be found in Owyhee, although they are used for storage or summer shade rather than as year-round dwellings. Contemporary architecture, in the form of prefabricated houses and a new tribal headquarters, provides another counterpoint to the earlier federally constructed buildings on the reservation.

NO66 Gymnasium

1936–1937, Mayers, Murray, and Phillip. West side of NV 226

Mayers, Murray, and Phillip of New York, employed as architects for several reservations, designed the reservation gymnasium to PWA specifications and a program determined by the BIA. The superintendent of the reservation had requested a community building that the tribe could use for vocational education, sports, and an assembly hall. The resulting two-and-one-half-story stone gymnasium is an appealing structure whose large mass, emphasized by its broad clipped-gable roof, resembles that of a barn. The walls are made of reddish-brown, random-coursed rubble stone contrasting with naturally square-shaped stones used as quoins. A two-story, gable-roofed bay, projecting from the center front of the building, contains the main entrance, marked by a segmental-arched opening. Although the building is currently boarded up, tribal leaders plan to rehabilitate it as a museum.

NO66 Gymnasium (above, left)

NO67 Barn (above, right)

NO69 Duck Valley Indian Reservation Tribal Headquarters (left)

NO67 **Barn**

1930s, Bureau of Indian Affairs. One block west of NV 226

One of the tallest buildings in Owyhee, this large barn has stone walls rising one story to meet the flared edges of a steep, shingled gambrel roof. The faces of the gable ends are sheathed with short horizontal wood boards. Above the south door in the gable is a closed-up opening for a hay door, flanked by two small square windows. Above the hay door, the gambrel roof projects to a point at which a pulley could be attached to hoist hay.

NO68 **Old Hospital**

1936–1937, Schmidt, Garden and Erikson. East side of NV 226

The most elaborate of the federal government's stone buildings in Owyhee, the hospital displays architectural details and a level of craftsmanship that surpass anything seen in many of the town's other structures. Although some local whites and Native Ameri-cans worked on the project, the BIA and PWA used contractors and materials from all over the West, in part because of Owyhee's remote location and limited resources. The firm of Schmidt, Garden, and Erikson in Chicago designed the building.

The one-story, C-shaped building stands on a rise above the highway, its long side facing the road. Two short wings extend to the rear. The walls, made of stones of varying shades of brown, are set off by white cut-stone quoins. The gable roof is covered with red tile, unusual in this part of the state. Multicolored stone steps and a retaining wall define the setting. After the tribe built a new, modern hospital on the hill above, the old building was closed.

NO69 **Duck Valley Indian Reservation Tribal Headquarters**

1979–1980, James Gibson. East side of NV 226 at the Nevada-Idaho border

The broad, one-story headquarters building straddles the Nevada-Idaho border to indicate that the reservation is located in both states. Compared with the BIA-constructed buildings in Owyhee, this structure asserts the modernity of the Shoshone and Paiute government today in an era of greater self-determination. Angular forms, horizontal wood siding, and interconnected exterior and interior spaces demonstrate that natural materi-

als, favored by Native Americans, can be used in striking new ways, just as innovation can enhance traditional lifeways. The wall facing the highway is painted with a basket-weave pattern that reflects some of the traditional arts of the tribe. Inside the tribal council's chambers, large windows open to views of the hills beyond.

Wells

The site of numerous freshwater springs, Wells was first known as Humboldt Wells, as it is the easternmost source of the Humboldt River. The abundant water attracted westward settlers, who made it an important campsite on the Emigrant Trail. When the Central Pacific Railroad came through in 1869, it built a division point here, around which the town of Wells grew up.

Like other towns along the railroad, Wells exemplifies the effects of shifting modes of transportation on urban form. On 7th Street, facing the old Central Pacific line, is one of the best-preserved railroad rows in Nevada. One block south of the tracks is 6th Street (U.S. 40). The rise of the automobile brought new development to this strip. With I-80 came franchised truck stops and motels clustered at the exit ramps, pulling people even farther from the earlier commercial centers. Many people leave the highway at Wells but never bother to enter the heart of town. Not helping matters is U.S. 93, now rerouted to bypass Wells and intersect with U.S. 40 west of the town center. South of 6th Street and north of the tracks are two residential neighborhoods.

NO70 7th Street

7th Street between Starr and Clover aves.

Until a decade ago, several businesses occupied this row of one- and two-story buildings dating from the late nineteenth and early twentieth centuries, but most of them are now vacant. Built to take advantage of railroad traffic, the row, originally called Main Street, contained stores, bars, and hotels. Later some of the buildings were converted for use as a liquor warehouse, bowling alley, and thrift shop, reflecting the decline in real estate values as traffic shifted from trains to cars. The city of Wells has conducted surveys in the hope of preserving the street and making it a tourist attraction, but this plan is unlikely to succeed as long as development continues unabated around the freeway exits.

Wells Bank (1911), a white one-story concrete building in the Beaux-Arts classical style, on 7th Street between Starr and Lake avenues, lends a level of sophistication to the commercial row facing the tracks. Pairs of Ionic pilasters frame the facade, below a wide entablature with a frieze decorated with dentils and topped by a heavy cornice. The building served as

Wells's first and only bank until the 1960s. Though recently renovated, it appears forlorn, standing alone on the block.

The buildings in the 400 block of 7th Street are some of the railroad row's most significant structures. Anchoring the southeast corner of 7th Street and Lake Avenue is the Bullshead Bar and Wells Hotel (1900). The wood-frame hotel, one of three wood buildings remaining on the street, was clad in brick in 1945. Next door stands Quilici's Market (1871, 1950s), opened in the 1920s by John Quilici, an Italian immigrant. He extensively remodeled the structure in the 1950s, applying brick and stucco to the wood-frame building. The two-story Nevada Theater (1902) has one of the best-preserved turn-of-the-century brick facades on the block. Large arched openings rise to a decorative cornice flanked by pilaster strips projecting just above the roofline.

Jarbidge

One of Nevada's remotest towns, Jarbidge is located in the Jarbidge Wilderness, part of the Humboldt National Forest. Access from Nevada is along one of two dirt roads, both of which are snowed in during the winter, sometimes for as long as eight months. The road from Idaho is open year round, but is also unpaved. Telephone service did not arrive until 1984. The inaccessibility of the place gives Jarbidge a strikingly independent spirit in this state of independent spirits.

The town was settled in a narrow valley created by the Jarbidge River. Prospectors had been roaming through the area well before the turn of the last century, looking for gold and silver. When they discovered gold in 1909, just south of the present location of the town, a boom brought 1,500 people to the area. Jarbidge was founded on U.S. Forest Service land, and conflicts over land have been a part of its history. In 1911 the Department of Agriculture set aside ten and one-half acres in the Humboldt National Forest for Jarbidge, declaring it an independent town. At its peak, in 1919, the Jarbidge Mining District was the largest gold producer in the state. The boom lasted into the 1930s, when the town hit hard times.

Although mining continues in the region today, Jarbidge has changed from a boom town to a small tourist town with a year-round population of about thirty-five. Unlike other remote mountainous mining towns, however, Jarbidge has been continuously inhabited. After a devastating fire in 1919, the townspeople rebuilt their homes. Abundant trees provided the materials for log cabins, which are still numerous and add to Jarbidge's rustic character. A single street running through the town is lined with these cabins and wood-frame buildings—some inhabited, most decaying. Although the town is quiet, it serves as a center for tourists who come to camp, hike, and ride mountain bikes in the Jarbidge Wilderness. Most of the inhabitants are retired; a few run small businesses, which include the local store, a café, a bar, and a bed-and-breakfast.

NO71 **Jarbidge Community Hall** (Jarbidge Commercial Club)

1910. Main St.

One of Jarbidge's oldest buildings, the hall survived the fire of 1919 and continues as the town's community hall and museum. Measuring 23 by 60 feet, the one-story building is constructed like a barn, with bent trusses creating bays from front to back. Logs and chinking fill in the spaces between the bays to create the side walls; the same materials are used to complete the front and rear walls. A small, wood-frame gabled front entry replaced an earlier shed-roofed vestibule. Corrugated metal covers the roof.

The anteroom leads into a large meeting room with unfinished interior walls, exposed logs, and chinking. The ceiling has been left open, so that the truss system and rafters are visible. The interior of the roof is lined with sheets of tin to keep out rain and snow, and they also create a decorative patchwork effect. At the far end of the hall is a stage with a hand-painted backdrop. The curtain has a framed scene of a harbor with boats, surrounded by advertisements for local businesses. The vaguely Venetian harborscape on the curtain closely resembles the scene depicted on the stage curtain in the Eureka Opera House (CE17), suggesting that it dates from the same period, the 1920s.

NO72 Jail

c. 1910. Main St.

NO72 Jail

Though small and rough-looking, this jail is one of the more picturesque in the state. The jailhouse proper has poured-in-place concrete walls topped by a gable roof. A door with a plain wood frame, centered below the gable peak, leads inside. Abutting the door is a wood-frame shed addition, its roof continuing the line of the gable. The jail is famous in Nevada history for having housed the three men arrested for the last horse-drawn stage robbery in the United States, which occurred outside Jarbidge in 1916.

Central Region (CE)

Linear features connect the towns of central Nevada in much the same way that the towns of the northern region are linked. In the nineteenth century the Pony Express and Overland Trail routes carried mail and immigrants across the state. In the twentieth century U.S. 50 linked central Nevada (from Baker in the west to Stateline in the east) with the rest of the country. As many of the region's towns developed around mines, the trails and roads shifted to pass through them.

Of the routes across the region, U.S. 50 provides the most vivid impression of the basin-and-range landscape. The highway crosses several mountain ranges, passing through piñon pine and juniper and dipping down into narrow valleys watered by small rivers. Unlike the Emigrant Trail–Central Pacific–I-80 corridor to the north, U.S. 50 never had a railroad stage of development. Central Nevada's relative isolation has prevented its four main towns, Fallon, Austin, Eureka, and Ely, from attracting large populations. Because U.S. 50—dubbed the "Loneliest Road in America" by Nevada's Commission on Tourism in the 1980s—still passes through the center of each town, main streets remain intact, lined with banks, hotels, churches, schools, and public buildings.

The isolation also kept architecture relatively modest. Only public buildings, large commercial structures, and the occasional house were designed by architects. The difficulty of obtaining wood in Austin, Eureka, and Ely led builders to use locally fired brick and locally quarried stone. As mining towns, these three places have had their economic ups and downs, but each has always retained a small core population that has survived until the next upswing in mining activity. Fallon is an anomaly in the region, an agricultural community created by one of the federal government's first reclamation projects. Its stability and proximity to Reno, Carson City, and California allowed builders to obtain lumber, so Fallon has a greater variety of structures than do the other towns in the region.

Central Region

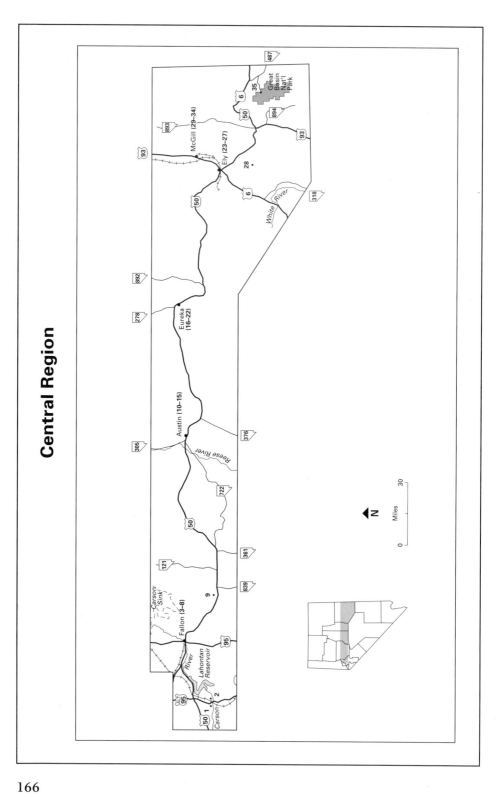

Silver Springs Vicinity

The area south of Silver Springs is rich in early Nevada history. The area may have been named for the glistening spring waters in the vicinity. Several routes passed through this region, the most famous of which were the Overland Trail and the Pony Express.

CE01 Fort Churchill

1860, U.S. Army. Early 1930s, National Park Service and Civilian Conservation Corps. U.S. 95 Alt., 8 miles south of U.S. 50

With the largest collection of adobe ruins in the state, Fort Churchill stands as a reminder of the early federal presence in Nevada, dating back to territorial days. The fort was built in the summer of 1860, shortly after the Pyramid Lake War. Fearing Native American attacks, the army stationed the soldiers of the Carson River expedition at the fort to protect the newly discovered mines of the Comstock Lode, as well as the Pony Express, settlers, and emigrants traveling through the area.

Soldiers and civilians built the fort near the site where the Overland Trail crossed the Carson River. The buildings were made of adobe brick covered with layers of adobe mud, built on stone foundations and topped by gable or hipped roofs. The officers' quarters, barracks, stables, shops, a laundry, hospital, and bakery were arranged in a large square surrounding a central parade ground. When the army abandoned the fort in 1869, Samuel Buckland, a local rancher, purchased the site and its structures. The fort quickly deteriorated into ruins as Buckland salvaged building materials.

After conducting historical and archaeological investigations, in the early 1930s the National Park Service (NPS) supervised the reconstruction of several adobe buildings at the site, using labor furnished by the Civilian Conservation Corps (CCC). The CCC also built the nearby visitor center and park headquarters at this time. Much of what can be seen today at Fort Churchill is the work of the CCC and later reconstruction efforts under the Nevada Division of State Parks, which acquired the site in 1957. Although partly filtered through the lens of the 1930s, the reconstruction and the ruins of the old fort evoke the era of Nevada's early settlement.

CE02 Buckland Station

1870. U.S. 95 Alt. at the Carson River

This stage station was the third structure Samuel Buckland built on this site on the cottonwood-lined bank of the Carson River. In 1859 he established a tent hotel to serve travelers on the Overland Trail. The following year he built a house

CE01 Fort Churchill

CE02 Buckland Station

that included a trading post, tavern, and hotel, which also served as a Pony Express station and stage stop. Buckland's flourishing business required another expansion by 1870.

The current two-story, wood-frame building has a T-shaped plan with a long rectangular section facing the road. Cornice returns and symmetrical facades lend order to the simple exterior. The rear ell is a composite of small one-story additions including an adobe structure, which was probably an extant springhouse. Built a year after the abandonment of Fort Churchill, the station undoubtedly contains materials from the fort, such as doors and windows and the adobe nogging on the first floor. The Nevada Division of State Parks acquired the old station in 1994 and has rehabilitated it as a visitor center.

Fallon

For centuries the site of Fallon and the environs were inhabited by prehistoric cave-dwelling peoples who left behind baskets, woven mats, and a variety of petroglyphs, the most visible of which can be seen at Grimes Point off U.S. 50 just east of town. In the nineteenth century the Pony Express and pioneers passed through the area. By the time they arrived in what is now Fallon, emigrants had crossed the Nevada desert and set their sights on climbing over the Sierra Nevada, staying in the Fallon area only long enough to discard possessions in order to lighten the load for the last big push west.

Fallon's isolated location and lack of readily available water prohibited development until the creation of the Truckee-Carson Irrigation District in 1902. This was the first of many federal reclamation projects in the West set in motion by Senator Francis G. Newlands of Nevada, who pushed through the passage of the National Reclamation Act of 1902. Newlands made sure that one of the first five irrigation projects under this act would benefit his state. Workers diverted water from the Truckee River to the Carson River to irrigate land provided free to farmers, along with heavily subsidized water rights, for cultivation of alfalfa and cantaloupes, Fallon's major agricultural products. The town quickly became an oasis in the desert.

Fallon is still a fairly quiet agricultural town, but it is changing quickly. In recent years farmers have lost many legal battles over water supplies to the Pyramid Lake Paiute tribe and the urban population of Reno. However, another federally funded boost to the local economy has arrived in the form of the Fallon Naval Air Station. Originally a World War II airfield, the base has expanded since the Korean War. The relocation of the Navy's "Top Gun" school to Fallon has brought an influx of money and people. Fallon's center retains a number of older public and private structures, but most of the new development has occurred on the edges of town.

CE03 **Lahontan Dam and Power Plant**

1911–1915, U.S. Reclamation Service (later known as U.S. Bureau of Reclamation). 16 miles west of Fallon on U.S. 50

This earthen dam plays a pivotal role in the Newlands Reclamation Project, which includes the Derby Diversion Dam, the Carson River Diversion Dam, 104 miles of canals, and 335 miles of open drains, all bringing water from the Sierra Nevada by way of the Truckee and Carson rivers. The main embankment of the dam is built into the Carson River and has a length of approximately 1,300 feet. Five reinforced concrete arches with 50-foot spans carry the roadway that runs along the top of the dam, adding a graceful element to the robust, functional structure. The massive reinforced concrete outlet tower contains twelve gates that release water from Lahontan Reservoir behind

CE03 Lahontan Dam and Power Plan

CE04 Churchill County Courthouse

the dam. The stone and concrete powerhouse contains three generators that continue to supply electricity to the surrounding area.

The dam is an excellent example of an early twentieth-century federal project that attempted to transform a desert environment into a vital farming community. The Newlands system put many fewer acres into cultivation than intended—barely 60,000 acres rather than the projected 300,000. Other western reclamation projects on the Columbia and Colorado rivers were similarly unsuccessful. Nevertheless, the Newlands project served as a precursor to the massive federal projects that dammed rivers all over the West. It also points to the problems involved in taking substantial amounts of water from fragile ecosystems and creating economic dependence on one industry. Providing water to Fallon has resulted in dangerously low water levels in Pyramid Lake and the Stillwater Wildlife Refuge, northeast of Fallon, and the complete drainage of Winnemucca Lake. Fallon's farmers have been gradually forced to relinquish their water rights in order to preserve these areas.

CE04 Churchill County Courthouse

1903, Ben Leon. 1973, Raymond Hellmann. 10 Williams St. (U.S. 50)

The Churchill County Courthouse is the only monumental wood-frame court building in Nevada, standing as a symbol of a local economy unusual in the state because it is largely dependent on agriculture. Ben Leon of Reno designed the structure with one-over-one windows flanking a large entry. A two-story pedimented portico with paired Ionic columns and a second-story deck with a turned balustrade enhances the front facade. The cornice includes shallow brackets, and the front pedimented gable features dentils and raised letters reading "Churchill 1903." A cupola with stylized fanlights caps a hipped roof.

Although Frederick J. DeLongchamps designed a Moderne addition in 1948, the county did not add a new wing until the early 1970s. This nondescript two-story structure behind the old building contains the courtroom and law enforcement facilities. The courthouse serves as the ceremonial entrance and houses offices.

CE05 Offices (Fallon Post Office)

1928–1929, James A. Wetmore. Southeast corner of N. Maine (U.S. 95) and E. A sts.

Like other federal post offices in Nevada's small towns, the one in Fallon lends a refined character to downtown, owing to its simple Classical Revival style, which was favored by James A. Wetmore, then the Supervising Architect of the Treasury. The steel-frame building stands two stories tall with brick-clad walls. The main facade is symmetrical, with a slightly recessed central section containing the main entrance and two large flanking windows—all set into arched openings with keystones and semicircular filled panels above. A denticulated cornice caps the building.

CE06 Fallon City Hall

1930, Frederick J. DeLongchamps. 55 W. Williams St.
(U.S. 50)

During the 1930s DeLongchamps designed a
number of public buildings for small towns,
among them Sparks and Fallon. He frequently
used a Neo-Romanesque style, which could be
executed inexpensively in brick and red tile yet
imparted a dignity suitable for public edifices.

The city hall stands across the street from the
county courthouse. Its main mass is a hip-
roofed structure with a gabled entry bay projecting toward Williams Street. An arched entryway is set into a slightly recessed panel trimmed
with an arcuated corbel table. The side facing
South Carson Street has two projecting wings,
one with a hipped roof, the other gabled, flanking a central section containing a side-gabled
entry. A tower with three arched windows on
each side rises to the south of the entry.

CE07 Western Nevada Community College, Fallon Campus

1981, Maurice J. Nespor. Northeast corner of Auction
Rd. and Campus Way

The community college campus has three
buildings adjacent to Fallon's convention center in the north part of town. The angular, low-
lying structures employ the same forms and
materials and are arranged roughly in a row
from west to east. Nespor designed a cost-effective campus, in terms of both construction and
operation, by using simple finishes and orient-
ing the buildings to take advantage of winter
sunlight but screening out summer sun. Large
concrete triangular and rectangular members
at the corners of the buildings meet roofs dominated by wide cornices of vertical wood
boards. These supports allow the walls to be
made primarily of large glass panes in steel
frames.

CE08 Oats Park Grammar School

1914–1915, 1920–1921, Frederick J. DeLongchamps.
167 E. Park St.

Although DeLongchamps designed Classical
Revival buildings at the time this school was
built, the Oats Park Grammar School is a plain
building with only a few classical elements.
The one-story brick building has a broad, horizontal layout and symmetrical massing and

fenestration. The principal classical form, a
pedimented pavilion centered on the main facade, contains the front entrance. Five years
later DeLongchamps designed the north and
south wings. The building is currently under-
going a major renovation that will transform it
into an arts center containing a gallery and
theater.

The school stands at the edge of Oats Park,
an open area in the center of the Oats Park Addition, an early twentieth-century subdivision
located at the east end of town. Constructed at
the time of the completion of Lahontan Dam,
the school was poised to accommodate an influx of children as part of Fallon's rapidly growing population.

Fallon Vicinity

CE09 Sand Springs Pony Express Station

1860. Sand Mountain access road off U.S. 50, approximately 27 miles east of Fallon

In ruins, the low walls of undressed rhyolitic
stones mark the site of one of the numerous
Pony Express stations that dotted Nevada in the
mid-nineteenth century. The six-room station
is roughly rectangular, with the long axis oriented east-west, measuring approximately 102
by 56 feet. The rocks for the walls were found
locally and laid up dry. A stone corral stands at
the east end of the ruins. The British writer and
explorer Sir Richard Burton described the station in 1860, noting that the structure had no
roof, but archaeological evidence suggests the
existence of a roof made of thatched willow,
used because of the scarcity of lumber. The
building functioned as a Pony Express station
from 1860 until the express service ended in
1861. The station then became a stop along the
overland mail route from 1861 to 1863 and also
a telegraph station, which closed in 1869.

Desert sands quickly buried the station,
which was unearthed by archaeologists in 1976.
Today the Bureau of Land Management maintains the old station and has posted interpretive
signs around it. Approximately thirty-five miles
to the east along U.S. 50, the stone ruins of the
Cold Springs stage and telegraph stations are
visible from the highway. The Cold Springs
Pony Express station ruins are located about
one and one-half miles east of these ruins.

CE06 Fallon City Hall (left)

CE07 Western Nevada Community College, Fallon Campus (below, left)

CE09 Sand Springs Pony Express Station (below, right)

Austin

Despite its location near the geographic center of Nevada, Austin is far from just about everything. At one time it was a booming mining town that rivaled the silver production of Virginia City. In 1862 a former Pony Express rider familiar with the area discovered silver in Pony Canyon in the mountains near the Reese River Valley; Austin was founded in the canyon shortly thereafter. Within two years, 3,000 to 4,000 people lived in the town, occupying buildings of wood, adobe, brick, and stone. Even Virginia City's International Hotel was moved to Austin in 1863 (demolished 1873). Despite Austin's large population, railroads did not serve it until the arrival of the Northern Central in 1880, a little too late to capitalize on the once-thriving economy. The town's remoteness and lack of good transportation during its peak years prevented the construction of large or elaborate edifices.

Like other mid-nineteenth-century mining towns, Austin saw its boom end in the late 1870s. Since then, economic stagnation has helped preserve many of its historic buildings. Few new structures have been built, and with a population of 420 as of 1997, Austin seems almost a ghost town. The entire town is a National Register Historic District.

CE10 **Stokes Castle**

1897. Castle Rd. .5 mile from U.S. 50

Anson Phelps Stokes, a financier from New York who owned the Austin Silver Mining Company, built this three-story tower as a summer residence for his sons, but it was used only once, in 1897. Constructed of hand-hewn native granite, the castle possesses a commanding view of the Reese River Valley from its location at the west end of Austin. Although the structure resembles southwestern Native American towers such as Montezuma's Castle in Arizona, it was probably modeled after the towers of medieval Italian hilltowns. Certainly its heavy, irregular coursed-rubble walls, narrow windows, and crenellations give the building an ancient air. The remnants of balconies, constructed of wood with simple cross rails for balustrades, are visible in the metal supports projecting from the facade's second and third floors. Documentation of the original interior is scant, but the "castle" is said to have had ample indoor plumbing and rich furnishings. Each floor had a fireplace, and window openings had plate glass to take advantage of the spectacular views. Vacant since 1897, the building has slowly deteriorated. A chain-link fence surrounds the structure, and its interior has been almost completely gutted.

CE11 **House**

1860s. Northwest corner of Virginia and Union sts.

This one-story brick house is among the more elaborate residences remaining in Austin. The remoteness of the town dissuaded most wealthy residents from constructing ostentatious dwellings; these would have been built in more accessible, established places such as San Francisco. Nevertheless, this house shows the use of contrasting materials and colors to dress up the otherwise simple exterior. The two main sections, with decorative parapets, follow the rise of the steep hill on which the house stands, supported in front by a stone retaining wall. Two large bay windows project from the front facade. A corner vestibule, lined with multipane windows and a door with side lights and transom, contains the front entrance.

CE12 **Town Meeting Hall** (Methodist Church)

1866. North side of Court St.

The construction of the former Methodist church is related to one of the more interesting mining stock swindles in Nevada's history. After an unsuccessful attempt to gather donations from his congregation, the minister turned to local interests, who gave him mining claims. He then created the Methodist Mining Company and went east to sell stock in order to raise capital to build the church. Fortunately the church was erected before the stock venture collapsed.

The brick edifice is one of three churches in Austin dating from the nineteenth century. Typical of church architecture in most mining towns, the building is solid and simple, with a few details such as the double-bracketed cornice on the tower. In the 1980s the town converted the building into a meeting hall.

CE13 **Lander County Offices** (Lander County Courthouse)

1871, Dan P. Bell. South side of Main St. (U.S. 50)

This structure is a late manifestation of the Greek Revival style. Such time lags were typical of nineteenth-century Nevada. Dan P. Bell, a mining engineer, designed the two-story brick courthouse, which features a stone foundation, five-bay facade, and double-door entry with transom. Windows and doors are arranged symmetrically on both stories. The gable roof rises above a brick denticulated cornice, and a small oculus decorates the pediment.

Over time, the mines around Austin failed. In the mid-twentieth century U.S. 50 helped the economy to a certain extent by bringing travelers through central Nevada, but with the opening of I-80 to the north, fewer people passed through this old mining town. In 1979 the county government moved to Battle Mountain but retained the old courthouse for use as county offices.

CE14 **St. George's Episcopal Church**

1878. South side of Main St. (U.S. 50)

Unlike the Methodist church, which it resembles in massing (including a corner tower), materials, and elevation, this brick structure was built with generous donations from the congregation. The last of Austin's three churches to be built, it is the most elaborate

CE10　Stokes Castle (top)

CE14　St. George's Episcopal Church (bottom)

and continues to house the town's Episcopalian congregation. Side buttresses, lancet windows, and a steep gable roof express the Gothic Revival, differentiating it from the rectilinear Methodist church. Wood brackets just

beneath the spire and along the side cornices reveal Italianate influences. The church still possesses its original pipe organ, which was made in the East, shipped around Cape Horn to San Francisco, and then delivered to Austin by wagon.

CE15　Gridley Store

1863. Northwest corner of Main (U.S. 50) and Water sts.

Representative of the early commercial buildings erected in Austin's boom period, this one-story granite structure is simple in form and unadorned. The store is famous for its association with one of Nevada's legends, Reuel Gridley, who lost a bet and had to carry a fifty-pound flour sack across town. He then auctioned off the sack and sent the proceeds to the Sanitary Fund to help wounded Union soldiers during the Civil War. So successful was the auction that Gridley auctioned the sack several times in Nevada, California, and New York, raising thousands of dollars. Mark Twain recounts these exploits in *Roughing It.* In the 1980s the building's owner rehabilitated the old store with a grant from the federal government, adding a new roof and installing multipane doors.

Eureka

Like Austin, Eureka began as a mining town nestled in a mountain canyon. In 1864 prospectors fanning out from Austin discovered silver-lead ore, but its composition was such that it took nearly six years to devise a milling and smelting technology to refine the ore. Once the smelting process was improved, Eureka quickly became a boom town. By 1872 fifteen blast furnaces filled the canyon with smoke, amid the frenzy to produce more and more silver and gold. Many Italian and Swiss immigrants found employment as *carbonari*, skilled artisans who made charcoal to fuel the furnaces. In a few years the need for wood to fuel the smelters led local inhabitants to denude the mountains around Eureka. Although the smelters are gone, slag heaps around town are a reminder of Eureka's industrial past. Up the hill, west of Main Street, is the primary residential area with houses of wood and brick.

Today Eureka retains many structures made of locally fired brick, as well as some stone and wood buildings. A number of the commercial and public buildings that line Main Street date from around 1880–1881, built after fires in 1879 and 1880. Mines developed in the 1980s and 1990s have brought tremendous prosperity to this county seat, generating a new wave of development seen in subdivisions of prefabricated houses and new schools on the edges of the old town. The town's population as of 1997 was 510. Like Austin, all of Eureka is contained within a National Register Historic District. The town and county, cognizant of the value of their old buildings, have spent millions in recent years to restore many of the most significant structures—one of the few attempts to develop heritage tourism in Nevada.

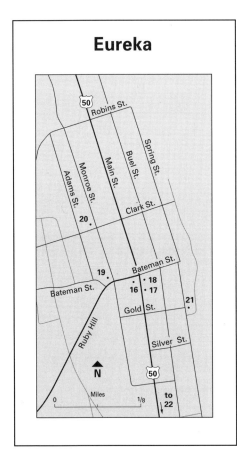

CE16 Eureka County Courthouse

1879–1880, George F. Costerisan. 1997–1998, renovation. 10 S. Main St. (U.S. 50)

The Eureka County commissioners called for local architects to submit plans for the construction of a courthouse in 1879. The three designs submitted ranged in style from Greek Revival to Italianate in vernacular interpretations. The county selected George F. Costerisan's proposal, but his design ultimately incorporated elements from the other two. Costerisan, a native of Pennsylvania, apprenticed as an architect in the Midwest and designed numerous structures in Wisconsin, Iowa, and Minnesota. After working in Eureka, he moved to California, where he won commissions for several buildings, mostly schools, in the 1880s and 1890s.

The courthouse is a two-story brick Italianate structure. The five-bay front facade includes windows with pediments on the first floor and arched caps on the second, all resting on brackets. Simple brick pilasters separate the bays. A second-story door opens onto a wooden balcony. The courthouse has an ornate cornice with paired brackets and an elaborate parapet wall featuring round arches in brick. The interior, one of the best-preserved public spaces in the state, includes original pressed metal ceilings and unpainted carved woodwork.

In 1997–1998 the courthouse underwent an

CE17 Eureka Opera House exterior (top) and interior (bottom)

extensive renovation to bring it up to current codes. Though the project left much of the original fabric intact, including the courtroom, a vestibule was added to the front entrance, substantially altering the appearance of the main facade.

CE17 **Eureka Opera House**

1880. 10201 Main St. (U.S. 50)

Like the courthouse across the street, the opera house was erected after the fire of 1880 and designed to be completely fireproof, with 2-foot-thick masonry walls, a brick and iron facade, and a slate roof. A full-length porch with balcony above, supported by four columns, shelters the first floor. The brick facade rises to a stepped and scrolled parapet displaying in paint the words "Eureka Opera House." The interior is equally impressive, with a horseshoe balcony suspended from the ceiling and a stage curtain painted in Minneapolis in 1924, on which old-time advertisements for local businesses surround a framed depiction of an exotic-looking sailing ship in a seascape resembling a Venetian harbor. In the early 1990s Eureka County, rich with revenues from gold mines, spent over $2 million to restore the structure as a performing arts and conference center. In 1994 the project won a National Trust for Historic Preservation Honor Award—the only project in Nevada to receive one.

CE18 **Jackson House**

1877. 11 S. Main St.

Though gutted in the fire of 1880, this building was repaired and continued to serve as a hotel through the early twentieth century. After many years of vacancy, it has been restored and is now operated as a hotel by new owners. The two-story brick structure consists of two adjacent buildings unified by a single bracketed cornice and long porch that curves around the northwest corner of the hotel. With its Italianate details, porch, and red brick walls, the hotel harmonizes with the nearby courthouse and opera house, making this block in Eureka one of the most attractive and best preserved in the state.

CE19 **Sentinel Museum** (Eureka Sentinel Building)

1879, C. M. Bennett. Northwest corner of Monroe and Ruby Hill sts.

From the time of its construction until 1960, this two-story building was home to the Eureka *Sentinel*. Since 1982, the sturdy block has been the town's museum, retaining much of the old printing equipment used by the newspaper. The arch stones and capitals of the piers were quarried from local volcanic tuff and contrast with the buff-colored brick walls. An elaborate cornice crowns the facade.

CE20 **House** (Wren House)

1880. Northwest corner of Monroe and Clark sts.

This one-story brick rectangular box is typical of the homes of professionals in Eureka in the

CE19 Sentinel Museum (Eureka Sentinel Building)

late nineteenth century. The porch, with jig-sawn brackets, is the most ornate part of the house. Thomas Wren, the building's second owner, was an attorney. In ever-changing nineteenth-century mining towns, however, neighborhoods were often mixed. Just to the south of Wren's house stood Eureka's China-

town, a collection of closely spaced wood-frame huts.

CE21 St. James Episcopal Church

1872. East side of Spring St. between Bateman and Silver sts.

Eureka's first church is built of local volcanic tuff, cut in irregularly sized rock-faced ashlar. The building stands two blocks east of Main Street in a quiet area of churches and houses dating from the nineteenth century. Several trailers and a railroad-tie garage are also on the street.

CE22 Tannehill Log Cabin

c. 1865. Main St., approximately .5 mile south of the courthouse

Believed to be the oldest dwelling in Eureka, this log cabin has been moved and altered a number of times. It contrasts markedly with the town's brick houses, which replaced log cabins and tents as Eureka became more settled. The cabin's massive logs, rarely seen in Nevada, came from old-growth limber pines cut and transported from high elevations around Eureka.

Ely

The enormous waste piles of the Ruth (Liberty-Eureka) Pit near the town of Ruth are visible from a distance on U.S. 50, heading east toward Ely. This pit, created during the first half of the twentieth century, was the site of one of the most prolific mining operations in Nevada's history. Ely was founded around 1872, but most late nineteenth-century mining activity in the region occurred west and south of Ely in the Hamilton and Ward areas. As the latter towns failed, Ely became the seat of White Pine County in 1887, drawing more people to town. Then, beginning in the first decade of the twentieth century, a copper boom transformed Ely and created the nearby towns of Ruth and McGill.

The town is divided into the distinct areas of Ely and East Ely. The main part of Ely contains the courthouse, city buildings, schools, churches, and early residential neighborhoods arranged around Aultman Street (U.S. 50). The Nevada Consolidated Copper Company (NCCC) laid out East Ely's townsite in 1904. Intended to be the site of the NCCC's smelter, East Ely instead became the base of operations for the Nevada Northern Railroad. The line carried ore from the pit in Ruth to the smelter, which was finally built in McGill, twelve miles north of Ely. Ely's various stages of development have resulted in a patchwork of small grids oriented more or less to the railroad.

Kennecott Copper took over operations in 1933; the long-lived copper boom lasted until the late 1970s. Fortunately for Ely, the cessation of mining operations did not last long. Magma Copper Company entered the scene in the 1990s, followed by BHP Copper North America, to start up a new mine in the area. Until mid-1999Ely was experiencing another economic surge, but with a drop in metal prices, BHP has shutdown operations.

CE23 White Pine County Courthouse

1908, George T. Beardslee. Campton St. near 10th St.

The courthouse is an eclectic building with a few Italianate and classical details. The massive two-story stone structure rests on a concrete basement, from which stairs lead to a heavy porch supporting a balcony. Rusticated stone facing blocks extend over the entire surface, even on the shallow pilasters that accent the corners of the building. A bracketed cornice meets a pediment over the main entrance. During construction the county commissioners modified the design to include a single-story rectangular cupola with a copper dome and flagpole. Surrounded by mature trees, the courthouse stands on a low rise at the head of a park in the center of Ely.

CE24 Centennial Fine Arts Center (Ely L.D.S. Stake Tabernacle)

1927–1928. 900 Aultman St.

This is a prominent reminder of the presence of the Church of Jesus Christ of Latter-day Saints in Ely. The two-story brick tabernacle is T-shaped, with a gabled nave extending toward Aultman Street and a rear transept capped by a hipped roof. Brick and concrete quoins and a frieze embellish the walls. Cornice returns, a Palladian-arched main entrance, and keystones in the semicircular-topped window openings are details taken from the Colonial Revival style. The Mormons built tabernacles (of a lesser order than temples) as houses of worship for local congregations, or stakes. In his study of nineteenth-century Mormon architecture, C. Mark Hamilton defines the stake as a Mormon ecclesiastical unit "roughly equivalent to a diocese," which often included an entire town and outlying areas. Ely, like other eastern Nevada towns, attracted increasing numbers of Mormons in the late nineteenth and early twentieth centuries as they moved westward from Utah. A late twentieth-century church located nearby replaced this tabernacle, which is now used as a community arts center.

CE23 White Pine County Courthouse (top)

CE24 Centennial Fine Arts Center (Ely L.D.S. Stake Tabernacle) (bottom)

CE25 Hotel Nevada

1929, H. L. Stevens Company. 501 Aultman St.

The six-story red brick hotel, once the tallest building in the state, memorializes the boom times Ely experienced as a copper mining capital. Built to be fireproof, the hotel has a steel frame and concrete between the floors. Although the walls of the ground level have been obscured by new construction or the addition of panels of aggregate to cover street-level windows, the upper stories of the exterior remain intact. The building has a main facade of five bays. The two outer bays, containing a single double-hung window on each floor, are edged with ornamental brickwork of small raised rectangles running from the base of the third story and ending at the roofline. A set of three narrow blind arches terminates the top of each end bay. The center bay follows this overall pattern, but contains pairs of double-hung windows on each floor and has a set of five blind arches at the top. The windows along the sixth story are capped by flat arches emphasized by decorative brickwork and a background of tan brick. Most eye-catching are the vintage neon signs, including the two-and-one-half-story-tall "Unknown Prospector," reflecting the mining base of the local economy. The hotel has been renovated recently but retains many of its original exterior and interior features, including wooden walls bearing the brands of local ranchers dating from the 1960s.

CE26 **Capital Theater**

1916, C. O. Fleming and Percy W. Hull. 1938, interior redecoration. 460 Aultman St.

The Capital Theater is located on the main thoroughfare through town near other early twentieth-century buildings erected during Ely's first boom decades. Designed by its owners, the theater has a brick facade displaying an eclectic assortment of features taken from several periods of Spanish architecture, an idea popular in American cinema design in the 1910s and 1920s. Renaissance elements include the two stacked door surrounds carved of stone in low relief with elaborate pilasters and capitals. Classical urns occupy niches directly above the entablature of the lower surround. The curvilinear cornice is a late baroque form that contrasts with an arcade of medieval proportions immediately below. Much of the wall surface flanking the surrounds is covered with recessed brick panels containing a pattern of slightly projecting headers. Replacement of doors and windows has substantially altered the street-level facade.

CE25 Hotel Nevada

The interior received an Art Deco remodeling in 1938.

Fleming and Hull built the theater at a time when the nation was beginning to embrace moving pictures as a form of entertainment. For Ely, an up-and-coming mining town, the arrival of the theater symbolized a growing sophistication and connection with trends across the country. The Capital served its original function as a movie theater until the mid-1960s. The theater remains vacant, but two small commercial spaces flanking the theater entrance on the ground floor contain retail businesses.

East Ely

CE27 **Nevada Northern Railroad Yards**

1907, many additions and alterations. Avenue A at the north terminus of 11th St. E.

Although the Nevada Northern shut down in 1982 as an operating railroad, it is still a conspicuous presence in East Ely. Currently the complex consists of fifty-two structures and several pieces of vintage rolling stock. Running roughly southeast from the passenger depot, 11th Street once served as the main commercial thoroughfare; today most of the activity has moved to the main highways running through town.

The passenger depot is the most visible and public of the buildings. Most of the remaining structures are located to the northwest of it. Flanking the depot are the old communications building to the east and the freight depot to the west. The communications building once housed a telegraph office and now accommodates a souvenir shop and the offices of the Nevada Northern Railway Museum. The massive engine house anchors the yards at their west end. Emanating from it are several tracks leading to other structures, including the paint and car repair shops located to the east. Across the tracks from the passenger depot stand the coal tower, sand house, and water tower. Their isolated location allowed for easy loading of coal, sand, and water into the engines. The chief engineer's office is at the far east end of the yards, allowing the occupant a clear view of the yards all the way to the engine house.

In the 1980s Kennecott donated the land, buildings, rolling stock, and thirty-two miles of track to the White Pine County Historical Railroad Foundation, a nonprofit organization. The foundation now runs the Nevada Northern Railway Museum and operates train rides with vintage engines and cars in the summer months.

CE27.1 East Ely Passenger Depot

1907, Frederick Hale

Visible from U.S. 50, this Mission Revival depot and the tall water tower behind it serve as a focal point for East Ely. A number of similarly styled depots from the early twentieth century survive in Nevada, attesting to the popularity of the curvilinear gables derived from Spanish Colonial models. The rectangular, two-story building has a steep hipped roof embellished with central scrolled parapets facing north and south. On each are projecting roundels framing stone letters spelling out "East Ely." The upper story is stuccoed, whereas the main floor is constructed of rusticated stone quarried in Cherry Creek, about forty-six miles to the north. As a relatively large passenger depot in Nevada, this structure housed men's and women's waiting rooms, the agent's office, and a baggage and express room on the first floor. Railroad offices were located on the second floor. The depot served passenger traffic until 1941; it continued to function as an office building for Kennecott until 1985. In 1990 the state of Nevada acquired the building for use as a museum.

CE27.2 Freight and Express Building

1907, Nevada Northern Railroad

This one-story, wood-frame building, measuring 40 by 160 feet, contained the freight and express shipping facilities of the railroad, located in the west and east ends respectively. The building stood just to the west of the passenger depot—a typical arrangement when a station had separate passenger and freight depots. Vertical boards and battens cover the long north and south sides. Little used since 1985, the structure, now a storage area, contains a wide range of railroad documents, equipment, and fixtures dating back several decades.

CE27.3 Engine House

1908–1915, 1917, c. 1941, Nevada Northern Railroad

The focal point of the railroad yards is the massive engine house, which continues in use as a maintenance and repair shop, now for the Nevada Northern Railway Museum's engines. Originally a rectangular 175-foot-by-225-foot masonry building, it was extended over the years by wings to the west, northwest, northeast, and southeast corners. The interior has five work areas—the machine shop, engine room, air room, boiler room, and blacksmith shop. Multilight, industrial steel sash windows running along the north and south sides let light into the building. Out of use for a few years after Kennecott shut down the building in 1983, it was reopened in 1987 when the museum began operations.

CE27.4 Paint Shop

c. 1915, Nevada Northern Railroad

Large forty-four-light, steel sash windows serve as walls in this two-story building set north of the engine house. Like many of the other buildings in the yards, the paint shop has a long rectangular plan (45 by 210 feet). Its function required a great deal of natural light; to supplement daylight from the window walls, a gable-roofed clerestory with thirty-two-light steel sashes rises above the standing-seam, metal-clad roof. Because of the structural weakness of the windowed walls and years of neglect, the building has become dangerously unstable. The museum is slowly restoring it.

CE27.1 East Ely Passenger Depot (left)

CE27.4 Paint Shop (below)

Ely Vicinity

CE28 Ward Charcoal Ovens

1876. NV 486, 6 miles south of Ely off U.S. 50

These six identical conical stone structures would stand out anywhere, but their appearance in a quiet, empty landscape makes them seem like mysterious apparitions. By no means the only collection of stone charcoal kilns in the state (others can be found in Bristol and in the Spring Mountain National Recreation Area near Las Vegas), these structures are the best preserved and most accessible.

Charcoal was necessary to fire up the smelter furnaces used to process ore. Various methods and structures were employed to make charcoal for furnaces in Nevada; in the Eureka area, *carbonari* used primitive platform kilns. Cords of stacked wood, covered with sod or more wood, smoldered for several days until the wood became charcoal. Stone or brick kilns could greatly improve the process. These six ovens were built to supply the Ward Mining District, opened after the discovery of silver and gold in 1872 but shut down seven years later.

The kilns at Ward are believed to have been built by Italian stonemasons. Many Italian and Swiss immigrants worked as *carbonari*, having brought their charcoal-making skills with them from Europe.

The ovens measure 25 feet in diameter at the base and 30 feet in height. The stones are laid up dry, with vents around the bottom of the wall. A large arched opening with voussoirs gives access at the base of the oven, and an arched window pierces the upper rear wall. A hole at the top allowed smoke to escape. Thirty-five cords of wood, usually piñon or juniper, were stacked inside through the door and window; these openings were then sealed with iron doors and a fire was started. *Carbonari* controlled the temperature of the fire by plugging and unplugging the vents at the base of the oven.

McGill

Once a thriving company town, McGill has struggled to survive since the closing of the Kennecott Copper plant in the late 1970s. The smelter (built 1907–1908) with its 750-foot-tall smokestack is gone, but much of the town's fabric remains. The Nevada Consolidated Copper Company (NCCC) laid out the townsite in 1906; by 1910, 2,000 employees lived and worked in McGill in a rigid hierarchy based on rank in the company and ethnicity.

The NCCC used the relative quality of buildings as a means to distinguish higher-ranking employees from those of lower status. The first permanent houses for high-level employees were erected in mid-1907. A cluster of administrative buildings and five large houses stands on a hill above a park in an area called The Circle. South of this area was Upper Town, for salaried employees and their families, who lived in concrete-block houses. By 1909 the company had completed construction of its industrial complex and had established a commercial district along 4th Street (U.S. 93), known as Middle Town. The residential areas known as the Lower Town, where workers' wood-frame dormitories and mess halls stood, had also been built. Finally, the company established separate ethnic communities for "foreigners"— Jap Town and Austrian Town (including Serb, Croatian, and other Slavs), located on the east side of 4th Street, at the north end of McGill, and Greek Town at the south end of town— thus institutionalizing segregation as a way to manage its employees. In 1955 Kennecott Copper, which had taken over the NCCC's operations in 1933, sold off all townsite house lots, ending total company ownership of McGill.

CE29 **House** (Kennecott General Manager's Residence)

1907, 1928. 3 Circle Dr.

Set near the head of the circular road overlooking McGill, this two-and-one-half-story house of poured concrete was the largest in town, indicating the prominence of the general manager. The building has Craftsman details such as a broad hipped roof with boxed eaves and dormer windows projecting from all four sides of the main roof. In 1928 the NCCC added two one-story wings to the north and west sides, creating a front porch and side porte-cochere.

CE30 **Apartments** (Dormitory)

c. 1916. 4th St.

In contrast to the houses on the hill, this one-story, wood-frame building typifies the simple style of architecture used to house single male workers in the Lower Town. The clapboard-sided dwelling stands close to the road, its double-entry vestibule extending straight out from the center of the front. In the 1930s Kennecott

McGill

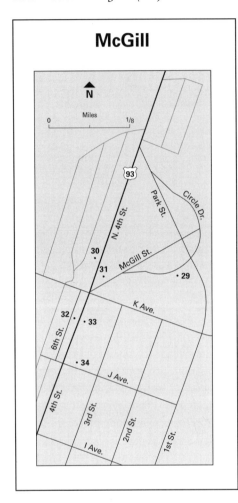

stories give the building a simple classical appearance. The Mormons acquired the building in 1958 and used it as a church until they erected a new house of worship nearby in the 1980s.

CE32 McGill Theater

1929, Albert Collins. 8 4th St.

The theater stands in the middle of McGill's commercial district, which is characterized by early twentieth-century one- and two-story buildings of brick, concrete, or wood. Despite its simplicity, the theater is one of the more noteworthy structures on this street. Rectangular concrete panels, decorated with bricks laid in a diamond motif, relieve the brick facade, which rises to a curved parapet. A hexagonal ticket booth stands between two pairs of wooden doors. Like most of the other businesses along 4th Street, the theater has been empty for several years.

CE33 Odd Fellows Hall

1926. 21 4th St.

The Odd Fellows Hall continues to serve as one of two large meeting places in town, though it is now in poor condition. The two-story main mass has brick walls rising to corner parapets and central shed roofs with wide overhangs. Four shields decorating the second-floor facade contain letters spelling out "IOOF." The front-entry vestibule, one story tall, has a curved parapet topped by concrete coping. Inside on the first floor are a kitchen and dining room–meeting room. The upper floor is more ornate, with wainscot, a stage, and a tabernacle used during lodge ceremonies.

converted most of these dormitories into apartments for married workers, who had largely replaced single men by this time. The building is located in what was a row of dormitories across the street from the old McGill Clubhouse.

CE31 McGill Clubhouse

1915–1918. 8 N. 4th St.

This massive brick building is located in an area of McGill that was primarily residential. In addition to housing single men, it served as a clubhouse and community center for employees and their families. The third story was added in 1918 to the original two. Brick piers rising a full two

CE34 American Legion Hall

1918. 24 4th St.

The wood-frame American Legion Hall originally functioned as a one-story lodging house for single women employed by the NCCC. In 1925 the company moved the structure from Lower Town to its current location in Middle Town. At this site the building served as a staff annex before becoming the American Legion Hall in 1932. The interior was then converted into a large meeting space, with smaller areas for a card room, kitchen, and rest rooms.

Great Basin National Park

Nevada's only national park encompasses 77,000 acres on the remote central eastern edge of the state. The park contains the entire range of ecosystems found within the Great Basin. Main attractions include the Snake Range, with thirteen peaks rising over 11,000 feet; a stand of bristlecone pines—the oldest living things on earth, having survived 3,000 to 4,000 years; and the Lehman Caves, formed from quartzite limestone.

The federal government established the park in 1986 after heavy lobbying from the state to help support the depressed economy of White Pine County following the decline of copper mining. A few conservationists, including William Penn Mott, Jr., who later became director of the National Park Service, initiated efforts to establish a park in the 1920s, when the caves were designated a National Monument. Over the next six decades mining and ranching interests stymied these efforts because of the fear that such a designation would prohibit those uses of the land. Only a severe economic depression swayed local opinion; the park's boundaries, however, were drawn to exclude private mining land. The National Park Service has kept grazing permits in force but is monitoring the environmental effects of ranching.

The tiny town of Baker stands at the entrance to the park. On the main road nearby is a U.S. Forest Service ranger station, built in the mid-1930s to supervise part of the Humboldt National Forest, now contained within the park. The Civilian Conservation Corps erected the buildings, following the standardized plans also used at the Paradise Valley ranger station (NO34), north of Winnemucca.

CE35 Rhodes Cabin

c. 1928, C. T. Rhodes?. Near the visitor center and entrance to Lehman Caves

Absalom Lehman discovered the underground maze of caves and their remarkable formations about 1885. He and a few successors gave tours until the caves attained National Monument status in 1922. Rhodes Cabin is the only one remaining of several believed to have been built by C. T. Rhodes, a proprietor of the site, to shelter tourists near the entrance to the caves. The one-story, one-room structure, measuring 11 1/2 by 20 feet, is built of white fir and Englemann spruce logs notched at the corners, with ends projecting 8 to 12 inches. This cabin survives as one of the oldest tourist accommodations in the area.

South-Central Region (SC)

As in central Nevada, this region's remoteness has preserved small-town life. No interstates or railroads connect places here, although the main highway, U.S. 95, carries some traffic between northwestern Nevada and Las Vegas. Mining has always been the driving force in this part of the state, supplemented by county government work and jobs at military installations. The built environment is primarily characterized by mines and mining towns dating from the mid-nineteenth century. The great impact of the industry is evident in the landscape, in wood and steel headframes, brick mill smokestacks, waste piles, and modern open-pit mines. Severe housing shortages occurred in the initial camp phase of towns such as Tonopah and Goldfield. Dwellings and other buildings were made of available materials, including bottles, barrels, and oil cans, either filled with earth or flattened to serve as siding or roofing material. Most mining booms in south-central Nevada faded quickly, but they survived long enough to leave a legacy of more permanent structures of stone, brick, and concrete. The temporary aspect of mining towns continues today in the form of recreational vehicles and mobile homes, favored by many regional residents as inexpensive and practical housing.

Hawthorne

Settled just south of Walker Lake in a broad, flat valley, Hawthorne has always been tied economically to the boom-and-bust cycles of mining, politics, and the military. The arrival of the Carson and Colorado Railroad in 1881, which bypassed Yerington to the north, made Hawthorne a service center for nearby mining towns. Two years later Hawthorne gained the designation of Esmeralda County seat from Aurora, a nineteenth-century mining town to the west that had Nearly died out by the 1880s. When boom times hit Tonopah and Goldfield, Hawthorne lost to the selection of Goldfield as the county seat in 1903 but regained its status in 1911, this time in the newly created Mineral County. This cycle of fluctuating county poli-

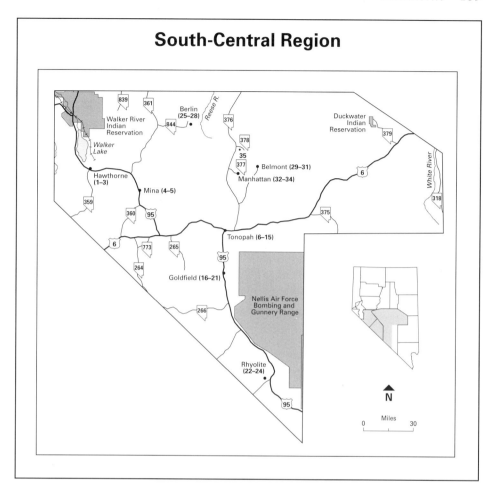

South-Central Region

Walker River Indian Reservation
839
361
Berlin (25-28)
Reese R.
376
844
378
35
377
Belmont (29-31)
Manhattan (32-34)
Walker Lake
Hawthorne (1-3)
Mina (4-5)
359
360
95
6
773
265
95
264
Goldfield (16-21)
Tonopah (6-15)
375
266
Nellis Air Force Bombing and Gunnery Range
Rhyolite (22-24)
95
Duckwater Indian Reservation
379
White River
6
318

N

Miles
0   30

tics and the shutdown of the Carson and Colorado Railroad in 1904 left Hawthorne in a slump. The town got a much needed boost in the late 1920s, when the U.S. Navy relocated its Lake Denmark, New Jersey, ammunition depot there. Since the end of the Cold War, activities at the depot, now run by the U.S. Army, have slowed, but it is still the major local employer. Nevertheless, Mineral County remains one of the poorest regions of the state.

SC01 **Hawthorne Army Ammunition Depot** (Hawthorne Naval Ammunition Depot)

1928, many additions and alterations. U.S. 95. Access by permission only

This enormous complex, encompassing 2,905 structures on 148,517 acres, is the largest ammunition depot in the Western world. The U.S. Navy erected most of the buildings and struc-tures between 1928 and 1945, the majority of them during World War II. The core of the base, the Personnel and Industrial Area, stands among clusters of trees and wide lawns, including administrative and industrial buildings, officers' houses, and a barracks. Most of these buildings date from the initial construction period (1928–1938) and have Colonial Revival features. This style, popular at the time, gave a unified appearance to the base and, with the planting of lawns and trees, helped transform the western desert into an area that looked more like rural Virginia. To the north is the Conelly Housing Area, a collection of one-story, wood-frame duplexes built in 1969.

Architecture from the World War II era is more utilitarian in style, revealing the need to increase production rapidly by erecting mass-produced buildings. During this time the Navy erected an entire housing area, Babbitt (demolished 1960s–1990s), to accommodate thousands of married workers and their families. Nearly 600 prefabricated wood-frame duplexes and community buildings were built quickly in an area between the Personnel and Industrial Area and the town of Hawthorne. Many of these buildings were salvaged during the dismantling of Babbitt and now stand in Hawthorne, Tonopah, and other parts of the state.

The largest part of the base is the Production Area, where the collection of ammunition magazines is arranged in an orderly configuration across the desert valley floor, approached by miles and miles of railroad tracks. The Production Area is located on the east side of U.S. 95, well away from houses and administrative facilities. To anyone who sees them from a car or an airplane, these identical earthen and concrete structures convey the extent of the military presence in Nevada. Though public access is not permitted, the magazines are easily visible from the highway.

SC01.1 Headquarters-Administration Building

1930, U.S. Navy Bureau of Yards and Docks

The one-story concrete building stands at the head of a U-shaped drive between the administrative-industrial and the housing areas. The simple structure has a symmetrical, five-bay facade with a side-facing gable roof. Concrete quoins cast with the walls add a decorative touch. Two slightly lower wings project from the sides of the central mass.

SC01.2 Theater (School)

1930, U.S. Navy Bureau of Yards and Docks

The one-story structure shares the simple Colonial Revival elements of the headquarters building, expressed in brick rather than concrete. A small vented cupola rises above the center of the roof. Originally an elementary school, the structure stands in the center of the old housing area, surrounded by trees and a lawn. The Navy converted it into a theater in 1963; it is now used for meetings.

SC01.3 Commander's Residence (Inspector's Quarters)

1929, U.S. Navy Bureau of Yards and Docks

The largest house on the base, set apart from the other officers' residences, is clearly the home of the commander of the depot. Brick walls rise two-and-one-half stories from a concrete foundation to a side-gabled roof. The symmetrical facade has a central entrance flanked by multipane, double-hung windows. The front door, set in a recessed arch defined by cast stone, is capped by a fanlight. Shutters, dormers, and brick quoins complete the Colonial Revival detailing.

SC01.4 Company Grade and Warrant Officer Housing (Petty Officer Quarters)

1930, U.S. Navy Bureau of Yards and Docks

This one-and-one-half-story brick house is one of sixteen similar dwellings arranged along a U-shaped street in the residential area of the depot. Though much smaller and simpler than the commander's residence, this house, with its brick walls, side-gabled roof, and small front dormer window, continues the Colonial Revival theme of the oldest part of the base. A recessed porch located within a corner of the house has arched openings, now screened, with a door inserted in the central arch.

SC01.5 Fuse and Detonator Magazine

1943, U.S. Navy Bureau of Yards and Docks

This single-arched concrete and earthen structure is one of 112 similar magazines built during World War II. The magazine measures 26 by 21 by 13 feet. The roof and three sides are covered with earth, while the fourth side, facing an asphalt road, is made of concrete. The building is designed to direct the force of any accidental explosions one way, limiting damage to other magazines. Entry into the magazine is through a double-leaf door in the concrete facade.

SC01.3 Commander's Residence (Inspector's Quarters) (top)

SC01.5 Fuse and Detonator Magazine (center)

SC02 Old Mineral County Courthouse (bottom)

SC01.6 High Explosive Storage Magazine

1943, U.S. Navy Bureau of Yards and Docks

These large triple-arched magazines, 167 in all, were designed to store highly explosive ammu-

nition. Each arch section measures approximately 25 by 80 feet. As is true of the other magazines at the depot, earth covers the roof and three sides of the structure; reinforced concrete facades face a long concrete loading dock. A pair of doors pierces the facade of each section.

SC01.7 Cat Creek Dam

1932, U.S. Bureau of Reclamation. About 2.5 miles west of Personnel and Industrial Area

This reinforced concrete dam, built with its concave side downstream, impounds a 50-million-gallon reservoir for the depot. The dam is 120 feet high and approximately 180 feet wide and has a thickness of 6 feet at the top and 24 feet at the base. It is one of four dams built in the 1930s to supply the depot with water and one of six dams in the area built for the depot.

SC02 Old Mineral County Courthouse

1883, A. C. Glenn and D. R. Munro. 551 C St.

Hawthorne's first courthouse originally served Esmeralda County. When the seat of government moved to Goldfield in 1903, officials vacated the structure. In 1911, however, when the state legislature created Mineral County, with Hawthorne as the county seat, the two-story brick building was called back into service. It was abandoned again when Mineral County erected a new courthouse in 1970. Now surrounded by a chain-link fence, it is a forlorn reminder of the past.

The structure is fronted by a five-sided entry porch with wood columns. Above a simple cornice with brackets is a cross-gable roof with narrow gable ends that flatten out to the edges of the cornice on each of the elevations. The courthouse stands in one of Hawthorne's few green spaces, shaded by mature trees and flanked by other public buildings, including the school district's offices and the local gymnasium.

SC03 Mineral County Arts and Culture Center (Sixth Street School)

1936, 1942. Northeast corner of 6th and C sts.

Built as a PWA project, this simple, one-story building served as a primary school until 1980. The WPA guide to Nevada noted: "As elsewhere in the State, a school is one of the most impressive buildings. . . . The low building of very modern design is up to date even to the Venetian shades at its windows." In 1942 the school district added five rooms in two wings off the east and west sides to accommodate a rapid influx of students. Hawthorne's population jumped at the beginning of World War II because of the expansion of the ammunition depot. Today the school is being renovated by a local organization as a cultural center.

Mina

The Southern Pacific established Mina in 1905 to serve as the terminus of its Hazen branch. The town gained its small share of prosperity as the junction for the Southern Pacific Railroad, the Tonopah and Goldfield Railroad, and a Southern Pacific narrow-gauge line to California. Never a large town, Mina began losing population in the 1920s and 1930s as local mining ventures declined. The Southern Pacific kept the line to Mina open until about 1990. Today most of Mina's railroad buildings are gone. The town itself straddles U.S. 95, with the residential area located on the opposite side of the highway from the old railroad grade.

SC04 **Railroad Cottages**

c. 1905, Southern Pacific Railroad. Along U.S. 95 and 7th St.

The railroad erected these identical one-story houses for its workers. The simple wood-frame bungalows rise to hipped roofs, each with a single front-facing hipped dormer containing two multipane windows. Most of the cottages are still occupied as dwellings or are abandoned. One was converted to a community chapel, gaining a small open belfry. The most common alteration in these houses is the addition of a screened porch and a side dormer.

SC05 **Municipal Building**

1939. 945 U.S. 95

This one-story structure displays a spare modern style typical of buildings of the period in small Nevada towns. Its main mass steps back to two side wings, while engaged vertical piers rise to a slightly stepped parapet. Despite its small size, the building houses a number of city offices, including the water and police departments, the justice clerk, and a courtroom.

Tonopah

Tonopah was settled when Jim Butler discovered a rich vein of silver ore in 1900. Within a year, the rush was on with such fervor that it pulled Nevada out of a twenty-year depression. The boom lasted off and on until about 1915, when the mines began to play out, but Tonopah has endured over the years as the seat of Nye County.

The town is nestled between Mt. Brougher and Mt. Oddie. Atop Mt. Oddie stands a relic from the mining bonanza—the headframe of the Mizpah Mine, one of the most productive

Tonopah, 1998

in the area. The town itself is laid out in a rather haphazard fashion, generally following the topography of the land, with one small grid stretching toward the southwest. Its early isolation favored the use of local materials for buildings; Tonopah had abundant supplies of granite, found in many surviving buildings. Tonopah's economic slumber since the 1910s has protected many early structures. Contrasting sharply with them, mobile homes and trailers also occupy town lots today.

SC06 Nye County Courthouse

1905, J. C. Robertson. 1960s, additions. McCullough St.

The two-story Nye County Courthouse is a sturdy, rusticated stone structure with at least two features unusual in Nevada's architecture: it has an ornate Romanesque Revival entrance and a bullet-shaped metal dome. The five-bay facade has round-arched windows on the first floor and segmental-arched windows on the second. A simple denticulated cornice supports a pyramidal hipped roof, in turn surmounted by a dome with four dormers for vents. The courthouse has not been treated well over years of continual use. The county has marred the building with a series of concrete-block additions to the sides and rear, and with the installation of a steel-frame and glass vestibule that obscures the elaborate arched entrance.

SC07 House (Samuel C. Dunham House)

1904. 406 Belmont Ave.

This one-story bungalow is typical of those built by businessmen in Tonopah during the town's first boom period. A hipped roof extends forward to enclose a front veranda supported by six shingled, tapered columns. The veranda curves around the building's southeast corner. The main entrance has multipane side lights

SC08 St. Mark's Protestant Episcopal Church (above, left)

SC10 Mizpah Hotel (above, right)

SC09 Silver Queen Motel (left)

and transom; a bay window with multilight sashes projects from the west side of the house next to a massive stone chimney.

SC08 St. Mark's Protestant Episcopal Church

1906–1907, G. B. Lyons. 210 University St.

Like many of Tonopah's other buildings, this church has rock-faced granite ashlar walls. The one-story building on a raised stone basement has a steeply pitched gable roof with a small king-post truss and two lancet windows flanking the main entrance. A gabled entry porch rests on a wood framework forming pointed arches. Local architect G. B. Lyons

and local stonemason E. E. Burdick collaborated on the church, which is one of the best-constructed stone buildings in Tonopah.

SC09 Silver Queen Motel

1963, 1971. 255 Main St.

The fantasy of the Silver Queen Motel provides a striking contrast to the solid Classical Revival forms of the Mizpah Hotel down the street. The round office (1971) stands near the street, distracting the eye from the bland motel-room blocks behind. Because the motel was built on the site of the Queen Silver Mine, the steel-frame structure was meant to look like a crown. Stuccoed piers curve up and outward. The ends terminate in upside-down hooks, from which hang round white lamps that look like beads. The piers support a tilting, scalloped cornice that hides the base of the saucer-shaped roof rising over the structure. A large modernistic finial thrusts upward from the center of the roof. Full-length plate glass windows between the piers open up the interior to the outside.

SC10 Mizpah Hotel

1907–1908, George E. Holesworth. 100 Main St.

The Mizpah Hotel, one of the tallest structures in Tonopah, exemplifies the prosperity of the early twentieth-century mining boom and suggests the aspirations of its financiers, George Wingfield, George Nixon, Cal Brougher, and Bob Govan, to bolster faith in the continued success of the region. Many hotels, like rooming houses, provided accommodations for the hundreds or even thousands of new arrivals to mining towns in the nineteenth and early twentieth centuries. More elegant hotels, however, pro-

vided opulent accommodations for businessmen and travelers rather than miners and laborers and thus were expected to be prominent buildings. Construction of the hotel was halted by the Panic of 1907, which hurt Nevada's mining towns as San Francisco's investors shifted their money to more stable investments. The building opened to much fanfare the following year, however, featuring amenities such as an electric elevator. Ironically, it was the last major construction project in Tonopah before the economy went into a tailspin.

The five-story reinforced concrete building has a veneer of stone on the main facade and brick on the side and rear walls. Stone piers mark the street-level facade; windows above are grouped in three pairs on each floor. George Holesworth, a Reno architect and contractor, designed the building, as well as a number of other structures in town and in nearby Goldfield. The Mizpah is still a hotel, now with a casino on the main floor. It also encompasses the three-story building next door, the old granite Brougher-Govan Block, designed by

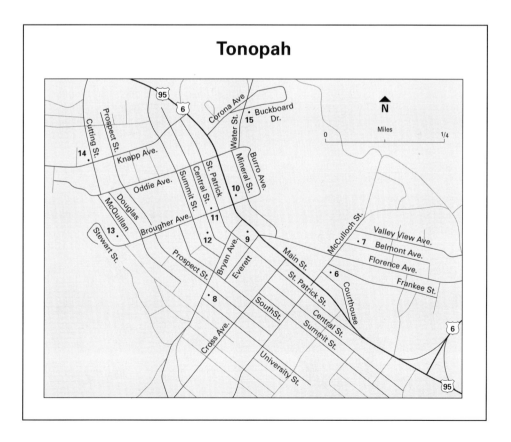

Tonopah

John M. Curtis and constructed in 1905 as a bank. Masons from San Francisco executed the stonework. By 1909 the hotel had taken over two upper floors for additional rooms.

SC11 **Senior Center** (Brokers Exchange–Tonopah Divide Mining Co. Building)

1905, 1919. 209–251 Brougher Ave.

This one-story structure of coursed granite ashlar has rock-faced stones that give it a robust appearance. The building was originally constructed with two stories that contained offices. It was remodeled in 1919 by the Tonopah Divide Mining Company after a fire destroyed the upper floor. The main entrance faces the intersection of Brougher Avenue and St. Patrick Street, set in a cutaway corner of the building. Four storefront bays with large windows face Brougher Avenue. All the window and door openings had prism glass transoms, now covered by wood siding. A cast plaster frieze, with a pattern of repeating pointed arches and geometric forms, caps the walls.

SC12 **Tonopah Public Library**

1906, John J. Hill. 171 Central St.

The third public library established in Nevada continues to serve Tonopah. Few changes have been made to this small one-story, hip-roofed stone building except for enclosing the front porch with screens. Grace R. Moore and Marjorie Moore Brown, two local residents, led the move to erect a building to house a gift of 200 books from Tonopah resident George F. Weeks. Unlike many earlier mining towns, Tonopah quickly changed from a camp to a community of families. Many women organized social and service groups that helped to stabilize mining town society.

SC13 **Old Knights of Columbus Hall** (George A. Bartlett House)

1907. Northwest corner of McQuillan and Brougher sts.

This large Shingle Style house stands near the end of the town grid on the slope of Mt. Brougher, commanding a sweeping view of Tonopah. It is a well-executed example of a style rare in Nevada. A massive stone foundation, built into the hillside, supports the building. Its rambling, asymmetrical plan is contained in shingled walls under broadly spreading roofs. Entry is under a large porch held up by stone piers. The rear of the building has another deck supported in the same manner. Designed by an unknown architect, the house is one of Tonopah's most architecturally prominent residences. Its original owner, George A. Bartlett, a lawyer and later a U.S. congressman, lost the house in the Panic of 1907. After serving as a Knights of Columbus Hall for many years, the now vacant house is quickly deteriorating.

SC13 Old Knights of Columbus Hall (George A. Bartlett House, left)

SC14 Sierra Pacific Power Company Substation (Nevada-California Power Company Substation) (right)

SC14 **Sierra Pacific Power Company Substation** (Nevada-California Power Company Substation)

1905, 1912. Northwest corner of Knapp and Cutting sts.

Surrounded by power lines, the stone substation creates a small industrial zone at the end of a residential street. Though the building is simple, details such as the stone water table, plinth, and parapet lend it dignity. In the early twentieth century the Nevada-California Power Company supplied all the south-central mining towns with electricity, which was vital to operating the mines.

SC15 **Dugout**

1900s. South side of Burro Ave. just before Buckboard Dr.

Like tents, dugouts served as dwellings during the first stages of the mining boom. They could generally be built of local materials and required relatively little effort, as a hillside provided most of the structural support. In this typical example, two rough stone buttresses support the front of the gable roof. Side walls of horizontal wood boards are built into the hillside to support the rear of the roof. A narrow door between the buttresses and a small side window provide the only light into the interior. Corrugated metal sheets cover the roof. This dugout is in good condition and has probably been used fairly recently.

SC15 Dugout

Goldfield

In 1902 Jim Butler, the discoverer of valuable ore that set off Tonopah's first boom, sponsored two young prospectors searching for new veins of gold and silver. About twenty-five miles south of Tonopah they found a ledge of gold ore that turned out to be more valuable than any previously mined in Nevada. As Tonopah boomed in silver, Goldfield attracted thousands more people looking for gold. By 1907 Goldfield had become the largest city in Nevada, with a population of well over 15,000, while Tonopah had 10,000, Rhyolite 6,000 to 8,000, and Reno 8,000.

Publicity and speculation—a feature of all the early twentieth-century mining booms in south-central Nevada—were strongest in Goldfield. The speedy construction of numerous fine stone houses and public buildings not only satisfied residents but also helped promote the idea of continued economic success. In 1907 the town won the designation of Esmeralda county seat from Hawthorne. However, Goldfield's star faded quickly; by 1910 the decline had begun, later exacerbated by natural disasters. Set in a valley, the town endured a devastating flood in 1913. An enormous fire in 1923 wiped out much of what remained of Goldfield's built environment. Today a few landmarks stand as relics of the booming past in a quiet town of about 400 people.

SC16 Library (West Crook Street School)

1908. Northeast corner of W. Crook Ave. and 5th St.

This one-story stone building is a box with a central arched entrance projecting from the center of the facade. Stone quoins, windowsills, and lintels relieve the rough stone surface. A squat stone arch resting on low stone piers creates an entry under the gable roof of the entrance. In addition to functioning as a school, the building has been a garage and is now a library.

SC17 Goldfield Hotel

1907–1908, George E. Holesworth. Southeast corner of Crook Ave. and Columbia St.

Built concurrently with the Mizpah Hotel in Tonopah, the Goldfield Hotel outdid its counterpart in size and luxuriousness when it opened. The four-story brick structure faces Columbia Street with a tripartite facade comprising a recessed central section and two flanking room wings. Stone piers define the bays of the street-level facade; above, brick pilasters divide groups of windows. The central bay contains the main entrance and lobby and features two levels of balconies resting on brick columns. A large cornice completes the simply articulated exterior.

When the hotel opened, local newspapers praised its elegant mahogany-trimmed lobby with gilded columns, glass chandeliers, and black-leather-upholstered furniture. Guest rooms had red carpets, velvet draperies, and brass beds. The interior is still largely intact but has deteriorated dramatically since the hotel's heyday.

George Holesworth designed this building and the Mizpah Hotel at the same time. Similarities between the two are evident in the stone piers at street level and the symmetrical facades and floor plans. The Panic of 1907, as well as serious labor disputes in town, slowed construction of the Goldfield Hotel. By the time it opened, the town was at its peak, but the mining bust a few years later denied the building its anticipated status as a grand hotel. The Goldfield survived the terrible flood and fire of later decades and remained in operation until 1946. Despite attempts to restore it, the building has remained vacant.

SC18 Esmeralda County Courthouse

1907, John Shea. Northeast corner of Crook and Euclid aves.

As soon as the seat of Esmeralda County moved to the mining boom town of Goldfield in 1907, the town set to work erecting a courthouse. The rusticated stone structure stands two stories tall, with a jail wing at the rear. The crenellated corner parapets and a central stepped parapet make the courthouse look like a castle, albeit one with windows too large for any medieval building. In the nineteenth and early twentieth centuries crenellations were popular for buildings that needed to look solid and fortress-like, such as prisons and armories. The courtroom is well preserved, retaining its colored glass lamps on the bench and original furniture and fixtures.

SC19 Old Bottle House (E. A. Byler House)

1905. 406 Crook Ave.

This small house constructed of bottles and adobe mortar is a rare example of its type. Some residents in south-central Nevada mining towns built bottle houses because beer bottles were plentiful, whereas conventional building materials were locally scarce and expensive to transport. In addition, the method of construction did not require the level of skill necessary for erecting brick or stone buildings. E. A. Byler, a mining engineer, constructed this house as his residence.

SC20 House (George W. Durgan House)

1905. 408 Crook Ave.

This simple one-story house with restrained volumes and decorative elements survives as the best remaining example of vernacular residential stone architecture in Goldfield. Though modest, the building has a mixture of well-executed details, especially the light-colored quoins, which contrast with the darker walls of the house; bell-shaped eaves; and enclosed soffits.

SC21 House (G. L. "Tex" Rickard House)

1906. 420 Crook Ave.

Unlike the house next door, this eclectic residence displays a profusion of forms and mass-produced trims. Brick walls rise to a steeply pitched hipped roof with intersecting gables, one on the north (facade) side and the other on the east side. Narrow hipped roofs top these gables and are edged with crenellated cresting. An inset porch stands to the left of the front

SC17 Goldfield Hotel (top, left)

SC16 Library (West Crook Street School, top) (right)

SC18 Esmeralda County Courthouse, interior and exterior (middle)

SC20, SC21 Houses (bottom); George W. Durgan House at right; G. L. "Tex" Rickard House at left.

gable, trimmed with turned posts and jigsawn brackets and dentils. The house was built for "Tex" Rickard, a gambler, saloon owner, and promoter of prizefights. He later moved to New York City, where he managed Madison Square Garden.

Rhyolite

Located near the Nevada entrance to Death Valley, Rhyolite is one of Nevada's most visited ghost towns. Its sparse ruins provide little evidence of the town's size in the 1900s. Within one year of the discovery of gold in the area, Rhyolite was a booming mining center. Residents constructed buildings of wood, adobe, concrete, and stone, replacing the canvas tents of the initial settlement phase. At its peak, around 1907, Rhyolite was the third largest city in Nevada, with a population between 6,000 and 8,000. The nationwide Panic of 1907 signaled the beginning of the end, and by 1911 the town was abandoned by the people who had recently created it. Few buildings remain, and most of them are falling victim to deterioration or vandalism. The Las Vegas and Tonopah Railroad depot and the bottle house are the only extant intact buildings. The ruins and waste piles, standing starkly against the landscape, are evocative reminders of the fleeting nature of mining wealth and the towns that it built.

SC22 Bottle House

1906, Tom Kelly

Though deteriorated, this three-room, one-story structure is the finest remaining example of a bottle house in Nevada. It was erected by Tom Kelly, an Australian-born stonemason. Kelly used about 20,000 beer bottles, along with some medicine bottles. Because of their fragile construction and attraction for bottle collectors, few such houses have survived in the United States.

The building's plan is L-shaped, with a gable roof and eclectic details on the porch and gable ends. Bottles make up the foundation and walls, laid in regular courses, bottoms to the exterior. Adobe mortar holds the bottles together. Kelly differentiated the foundation from the walls by

SC22 Bottle House, in photo possibly from 1940s (left) and today

using dark amber bottles for the foundation and bottles of various colors for the walls.

Paramount Pictures used the building in the 1920s as a set for a western film, *Wanderer of the Wasteland*. Since then, the building has deteriorated, though various owners inhabited the dwelling until the 1980s. The on-and-off operation of nearby mines during the twentieth century has posed the greatest danger to the survival of the house and to Rhyolite's ruins. In addition, the difficulty of affixing the adobe to the smooth surfaces of the bottles has remained a problem in stabilizing the house. The Bureau of Land Management, which now manages the property, has worked diligently with a local preservation group to keep the house standing.

A favorite of locals and tourists alike, the bottle house has inspired others to use glass to create their own objects. A wishing well and miniature village comprising about thirty-six structures made of glass, ceramic fragments, and bottlecaps stand near the house. Tommy Thompson, a former resident of the house, created the folk-art village from the 1950s to the 1970s.

SC23 Cook Bank Building

1908, George E. Holesworth. Golden St.

The largest structure in Rhyolite, the three-story, reinforced concrete Cook Bank Building fell into ruin decades ago. Among the details still visible are quoins, piers scored to look like stone, an arched first-floor facade, and the remnant of a metal cornice near the roofline. A movie company that used the building as a film set in the 1940s added wrought iron balconies and frame and plaster arches and cornices.

SC24 Porter Store

1906. Golden St.

This one-story store reveals the high-quality stonework found in some of the buildings in Rhyolite. Though the rest of the structure is gutted, the facade of coursed rock-faced ashlar is largely intact. A large opening in the facade, supported by a concrete lintel and cast iron column, accommodated plate glass windows and a front entrance. Side walls are made of rough stone. One of the last businesses to leave Rhyolite, the store remained open until about 1915.

Berlin

Though the region around Berlin had been prospected in the 1860s, miners did not establish the Berlin Mine until 1896 and the town of Berlin until the following year. The name may have been given to the town by German prospectors, but no evidence exists to substantiate this story. The mining discoveries at Berlin predated the major finds at Tonopah and Goldfield, but Berlin never had the ore deposits required to thrive as those towns did. It always remained a mining camp, with scattered buildings and a population of less than 300. Abundant trees in the nearby mountains allowed the construction of wood-frame buildings. The Panic of 1907 hit Berlin hard. Despite a short revival in 1909–1910, the town declined. By 1911 most residents had left, abandoning numerous wood-frame, board-and-batten-sided structures, including the large mill and several smaller buildings. Berlin became a ghost town. The Nevada State Parks system acquired Berlin in 1957 to create Berlin-Ichthyosaur State Park. It has preserved a portion of the old mining town as well as North America's greatest concentration of ichthyosaur fossils. The park system stabilized the remaining structures, including the mill, which remains the finest example of its kind in the state.

SC28 Berlin (mill at right)

SC25 **Park Office** (Mine Supervisor's House)

c. 1896

The largest of the remaining houses in Berlin, this building is located on the main road leading to the mill near the intersection of the road along which most of the town's houses stood. Thus positioned, the structure bridged the industrial and residential zones. A side-gabled roof of wood shingles tops the main portion of the building; a shed addition extends from the rear, and a partially enclosed shed-roofed porch covers the front entrance.

SC26 **Assay Office**

c. 1896

Like the park office, this building is a simple long box with a gable roof. The multilight, double-hung windows have flat wood frames. The assay office, where the value of ore was determined, was an important structure in every mining town.

SC27 **Machine Shop**

c. 1896

The machine shop, located uphill from the assay office, not far from the mill, has large openings to allow for the movement of machinery. A metal roof with standing seams kept out rain and snow and helped reduce the risk of fire. Pieces of rusted equipment stand in the sagebrush nearby. This type of structure, built to shelter workers repairing, assembling, and taking apart mining and milling equipment, was common in late nineteenth- and early twentieth-century mining towns.

SC28 **Mill**

c. 1896. c. 1974, Edward S. Parsons

This timber-frame structure set into the hillside overlooks Berlin. A wood trestle supported carts transporting ore to the top of the building, where the ore passed through a thirty-stamp mill that broke it into smaller pieces. Gradually the ore was crushed to a pulp, heated, then mixed with mercury, which adhered to the gold and silver in the ore. The precious metals were then separated from the mercury and converted into bullion. A long shed roof covered with standing-seam metal slopes over the board-and-batten-sided walls, terminating at the base of the mill. In the 1970s the state undertook a major stabilization of the building, hiring architect Edward S. Parsons of Reno, who had worked on other historic preservation projects in the state, to reconstruct the roof.

Belmont

Most of Nevada's hundreds of ghost towns have no inhabitants. Belmont has about ten residents, though most of its main street has fallen into ruin. The town was settled after the discovery of silver deposits in 1865 started a rush. Within two years, Belmont had a population of several thousand. In 1867 it became the seat of Nye County; the large Italianate courthouse, completed in 1876, still stands. As was typical of many Nevada boom towns, the boom was over by the time the courthouse was built. Tonopah replaced Belmont as county seat in 1905.

C29 Main Street

Belmont's main street is a mix of old and new. The most intact historic facade is that of a former brick-faced bank building. Next to it are the ruins of two saloons—a mangled mass of stone, wood, and corrugated metal. At the end of Main Street, where the road curves south, is a large stone house with a two-story porch and side ell. A road veering north from Main Street is lined with small stone houses and ruins and a wooden water tank. The other end of Main Street has some modern houses, trailers, and the Belmont Saloon, a one-story, wood-frame structure composed of parts of old buildings, including a bar from a collapsed hotel down the street. Near the entrance to the town are the ruins of the Belmont-Monitor Mill, its square smokestack visible from the road. Main Street passes through town, then heads up a hill toward two of Belmont's three surviving mills.

SC30 Old Nye County Courthouse

1875–1876, J. K. Winchell. Court St.

This impressive building can be seen either as a symbol of faith in the town's survival or as a denial of the cyclical nature of mining booms and busts. Set on a rise, the two-story, red brick Italianate structure looms over the town. Corner pilasters with simple cornices provide some of the only detail in the spare but elegant design. A rear ell contained the jail, which was ripped open so the metal cells could be removed and used in the jail at Gabbs. The cells were returned in the early 1990s and stand outside the courthouse, awaiting placement in the jail. In 1974 the Belmont courthouse became a state historic site managed by the Nevada Division of State Parks and has since undergone extensive restoration.

SC29 Main Street

SC31 Combination Mill

SC31 Combination Mill

1868

Little remains of Belmont's largest mill except for the brick smokestack towering over the deserted hills. Despite the utilitarian nature of the structure, raised brick arches and a cornice encircle the top. Stone ruins once contained the forty-stamp mill, which was removed when the operation closed in the early twentieth century.

Manhattan

The remaining buildings of this town, named after the old Manhattan Mines southwest of Belmont, stand in a narrow gulch in the Toquima Mountains not far from Belmont. Though mining began in the area in the nineteenth century, only after major discoveries spurred by the mining booms in Tonopah and Goldfield did Manhattan become a boom town in 1905. Its prosperity was short-lived, as many obstacles slowed development, but Manhattan experienced a forty-year period of production, much longer than that of many mining towns and camps in this part of the state. Like Tonopah and Goldfield, Manhattan fell on hard times in 1907. The San Francisco earthquake of 1906 forced investors living there to shift their money to rebuilding the city, thereby draining money from towns in Nevada and starting a bust exacerbated by the Panic of 1907. However, Manhattan persevered as the result of new discoveries. At its peak, the town had nearly 1,000 inhabitants.

Today about sixty year-round residents live in Manhattan, mostly in trailers and old houses, interspersed with abandoned dwellings, commercial buildings, and a few new structures. Some old cabins display a form of exterior sheathing popular in the region—tin cans flattened and nailed onto the building's frame. Headframes atop the hills are a potent reminder of Manhattan's past.

SC32 Main Street (NV 377)

Driving into Manhattan from the east, the visitor passes numerous ruined stone and wood-frame buildings. The most impressive is the simple but solid former Nye and Ormsby County Bank (c. 1906–1907), a one-story, coursed ashlar structure with a main entrance set into the corner facing the once-busy intersection of Main and 1st streets. Farther along the street stand a number of abandoned wood-frame buildings with false fronts, covered by a variety of materials, including clapboards and sheets of corrugated metal.

SC33 Manhattan School

1912, Joseph Cook. Dexter Ave.

The Manhattan School, on a hill above Main Street, is a one-story, hip-roofed building measuring 30 by 75 feet, with a projecting gabled entry vestibule and four interior rooms. Pressed metal originally covered the wood-frame structure. These metal surfaces replicated a variety of patterns, including coursed stone, wood shingles, and cornices on the exterior and wainscot, friezes, and cornices on the interior. The exterior has been plastered over, but the plaster could be removed to restore the school to its original condition. Though unusual for a moderately large public building, the use of metal for sheathing small houses and commercial buildings was common in mining towns, as can be seen in the small cabin on Dexter Avenue behind the school. Perhaps the material—a precursor of aluminum and vinyl siding—was seen as a modern and inexpensive way to give the school building a finished appearance.

SC34 Catholic Church

1874. 1908, moved. Mineral St.

The church was moved from Belmont, after that town's virtual abandonment in the early twentieth century, to a hilltop in Manhattan.

The simplicity of the building and its lone position add to the picturesqueness of Manhattan's almost ghostly state. The church is in good condition, retaining its drop siding, multipane lancet windows, pointed-arched entry, and small cupola topped with a large cross. The tongue-and-groove floors and interior wainscot remain, though the original canvas wall covering has been removed.

Round Mountain Vicinity

sc35 Smoky Valley–Round Mountain Gold Operation

1906, continual alterations. Junction of NV 376 and NV 378

The extent of this enormous open-pit gold-mining operation is visible from miles away. The vast bronze and silver-colored tailings and waste piles of the pit—8,000 feet long, 7,200 feet wide, and 1,200 feet deep—surround the site. This operation is the culmination of over ninety years of mining in the area. Prospectors discovered gold here in 1906. Operations began with placer mining, then graduated to gold-gravel washing, using a dredge in the 1920s. Hard-rock mining, using a method that could process 500 tons of ore an hour, began in the 1950s. Technological advances now allow the mining of microscopic amounts of gold; as much as 300 tons of ore are processed to retrieve one ounce of gold. This type of mining was impossible in earlier years, but the efficiency of the newer process makes such ratios cost-effective. The effort to recover such small amounts of gold relies on the quick processing of huge amounts of ore and on a favorable regulatory environment. The results are the enormous open pits we see today. In 1983 the mine produced 92,000 ounces of gold at a cost of $265 an ounce. In 1999 the mine produced 510,504 ounces of gold from 16 million tons at a cost of $198 per ounce.

The nearby town of Round Mountain has been affected by the changing fortunes of the mining operation. Few people live in the town today, and most of its historic buildings are gone. Instead, the majority of mine workers live on the other side of Nevada 376 in Hadley, a residential subdivision of trailers.

SC34 Catholic Church

Southern Region (SO)

Southern Nevada is a place of contrasts. Much of the region is uninhabited, yet nearly two-thirds of Nevada's population live in the Las Vegas metropolitan area. Though Las Vegas is the region's economic and political center, small mining and farming towns, with their own strong identities, are scattered throughout the southern part of the state. In a state dominated by the federal government, southern Nevada has the greatest federal presence in military installations, defense-related sites, and reclamation projects. Tourism, focused on Las Vegas and to a lesser extent on a number of border towns near Arizona and California, has become the biggest industry.

The lack of adequate water supplies prevented much settlement in the region until the construction of Hoover Dam in the 1930s. Unlike the northern part of the state, southern Nevada could not support extensive ranching, as the native vegetation of creosote and Joshua trees provided poor forage. Farming was also difficult except in the region's few valleys fed by creeks or rivers, such as the Muddy and Virgin river valleys, where Mormon settlers managed to establish a few small, well-planned agricultural communities in the late nineteenth century.

The mountains around the Las Vegas Valley, however, contained a variety of minerals that supported a small mining industry. To the north and northeast, the Pahranagat Valley and the hills along the Meadow Valley Wash experienced nineteenth-century mining booms. At the turn of the twentieth century, a few gold mines led to the establishment of the towns of Goodsprings and Searchlight, southwest and southeast of Las Vegas respectively. Though mining in these areas ended decades ago, the towns survive. Other mines in the region continue to produce limestone, gypsum, and dolomite.

Development for tourism was ideally suited to an area with few natural resources to exploit. The legalization of gambling, roughly coinciding with the completion of Hoover Dam, provided tourist attractions and inexpensive water and electricity to supply a growing city. Like the Mormons before them, hotel and club owners from Los Angeles colonized southern

Southern Region

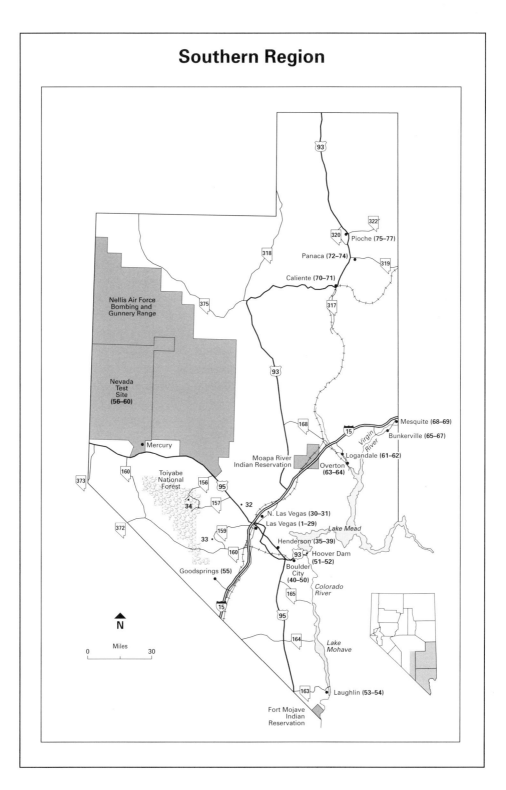

93

322
320 Pioche **(75–77)**
318
Panaca **(72–74)**
319
Caliente **(70–71)**
317

Nellis Air Force
Bombing and
Gunnery Range

375

93

Nevada
Test
Site
(56–60)

168
15 Virgin River
Mesquite **(68–69)**
Bunkerville **(65–67)**
Logandale **(61–62)**
Moapa River
Indian Reservation
Overton
(63–64)

Mercury

160
373
Toiyabe
National
Forest
156
95
157
• 32
N. Las Vegas **(30–31)**
34
Las Vegas **(1–29)**
Lake Mead
372
159
33 •
Henderson **(35–39)**
160
93 Hoover Dam
(51–52)
Goodsprings **(55)**
Boulder
City
(40–50)
Colorado
River
165
15
95

N

Miles
0   30

164
Lake
Mohave

163 Laughlin **(53–54)**

Fort Mojave
Indian
Reservation

Nevada, building the first casino resorts on the edges of Las Vegas. These glamorous complexes set the standard for the casinos of today.

Southern Nevada's seemingly barren landscape has produced some of the nation's strangest architecture. By most definitions, this part of the state had, and still has, little to offer in the way of regional or indigenous architecture. Although archaeologists excavated some of the extensive Anasazi pueblo ruins in the Muddy and Virgin river valleys in the 1920s and 1930s, these structures rarely influenced local architecture of the interwar period. By contrast, the federal government's numerous projects during the Great Depression, including Hoover Dam and the construction of many buildings by the Works Progress Administration (WPA), Public Works Administration (PWA), Civilian Conservation Corps (CCC), and National Youth Administration (NYA) in the Las Vegas area and in the agricultural communities to the northeast, shaped architecture somewhat by providing some of the best local examples of traditional and modern styles. Later government projects have left Nevada with an odd architectural legacy in the form of exploded or irradiated buildings, bridges, bunkers, and other structures on the Nevada Test Site, the location of atmospheric and underground testing from 1951 to 1992. In addition, Nevada may soon become home to the nation's only permanent high-level nuclear waste repository at Yucca Mountain.

Certainly the widest-known and greatest manifestations of Nevada's unusual architecture take form in the casinos on the Las Vegas Strip. In the open spaces of the desert, these buildings have grown to enormous proportions, with thousands of hotel rooms and thousands of square feet of casino space. The lack of a long regional tradition of architecture, combined with little regulation and an economy driven by tourism, has pushed casinos toward increasingly fanciful displays, taking on such forms as medieval castles, Roman forums, and even entire cities, competing with one another to attract ever more tourists. This architecture seems to have had little direct influence elsewhere in the state, except in towns where gambling supports the economy. Border towns, including Laughlin, Mesquite, Stateline (also known as Primm), and Jean, have mastered the Strip look, erecting large, shiny casinos with huge parking lots and garages to capitalize on their locations. Casino architecture has also influenced development in other places where gambling has been legalized, such as Atlantic City, riverfronts along the Mississippi, and some Native American reservations. More significant, Las Vegas and the Strip, focused on the automobile, have provided a model for strip development across the country, a trend that continues unabated.

Las Vegas

The Las Vegas of today has changed drastically since the early twentieth century. Once just a stop on an overland mail route in the middle of Las Vegas Valley, the city has become one of the world's most famous entertainment centers. With its huge casinos, growing suburbs, and automobile traffic, it is hard to believe that Las Vegas began as a railroad town. Little trace of this beginning remains, but a careful examination of the layout reveals the city's debt to the railroad.

Before European and American explorers entered the Las Vegas Valley, the Anasazi and later the Southern Paiute inhabited the land. An oasis, fed by a spring known as Big Springs

Las Vegas

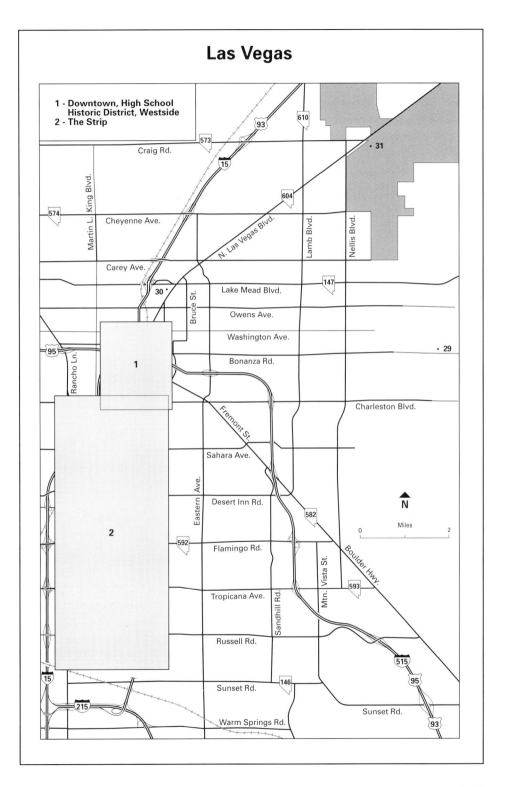

1 - Downtown, High School
Historic District, Westside
2 - The Strip

Craig Rd.

Martin L. King Blvd.

Cheyenne Ave.

N. Las Vegas Blvd.

Lamb Blvd.

Nellis Blvd.

• 31

Carey Ave.

30 •

Bruce St.

Lake Mead Blvd.

Owens Ave.

Washington Ave.

Rancho Ln.

Bonanza Rd.

• 29

1

Fremont St.

Charleston Blvd.

Sahara Ave.

Eastern Ave.

Desert Inn Rd.

N

Miles

0   2

2

Flamingo Rd.

Boulder Hwy.

Tropicana Ave.

Sandhill Rd.

Mtn. Vista St.

Russell Rd.

Sunset Rd.

Warm Springs Rd.

Sunset Rd.

or Las Vegas Springs, provided some sustenance in the harsh desert environment. Until the 1850s, only a few American explorers had passed through the valley, among them Jedediah Smith, John C. Frémont, and Kit Carson. Increased traffic began after April 1854, when Congress established a monthly mail route from Salt Lake City to San Diego and appropriated funds to construct a military road from Salt Lake to the California border. A year later, Brigham Young sent Mormon missionaries to settle the area; they constructed an adobe fort about four miles east of Big Springs, near the Las Vegas Creek. Part of this fort remains today. The Mormons managed to eke out an existence but left Nevada in 1857, when Brigham Young called back all western colonists to Utah. The natural springs provided enough water for a few families to ranch in the area, but not enough for a larger settlement.

The growth of Salt Lake City and Los Angeles was crucial to the development of Las Vegas. Salt Lake City was approximately 400 miles to the northeast, Los Angeles about 270 miles to the southwest. By 1902 Senator William Clark of Montana had acquired rights-of-way for his proposed San Pedro, Los Angeles, and Salt Lake City Railroad linking the main Union Pacific line in Utah to southern California. Its location roughly midway between the two cities made Las Vegas an ideal site for a railroad division point where crews and equipment could be changed. The railroad also exploited the available water sources by pumping water from underground aquifers, which supplied steam locomotives and a small townsite.

In 1905 Clark's railroad auctioned lots, and the town of Las Vegas was born. Its nucleus grew out of the grid of Clark's townsite, now bounded by the railroad, Stewart Avenue, Maryland Parkway, and Charleston Avenue. The railroad itself was aligned northeast to southwest, straight across the valley floor. Las Vegas Boulevard, completed in 1931—the major highway in the city until the construction of I-15 to the west—runs parallel to the railroad. Known alternately as Route 91, the Los Angeles Highway, and now the Strip, this road runs through downtown, then south to the airport.

The next boom occurred with the construction of Hoover (Boulder) Dam from 1931 to 1935. Although the federal government chose to build Boulder City to house workers near the dam site twenty-four miles away, Las Vegas prospered with the influx of funds and workers coming to the town for entertainment. In addition to the immediate economic benefits of construction, the dam ultimately permitted the widespread urbanization of the region by making substantial amounts of subsidized water available to Nevada and the neighboring states of California and Arizona.

Although Hoover Dam had a huge impact on the growth of the region, the legalization of gambling in 1931 had an even greater effect on Las Vegas itself during the rest of the twentieth century. Nevada and, more significantly, California entrepreneurs soon marketed gambling to tourists who came to see the dam. Downtown hotels quickly converted space into casinos, but the most important developments took place out of town, along the Los Angeles Highway. Here emerged a new form of architecture, following roadside motel and coffee shop prototypes. Over the years the land along the highway, which became known as the Strip in the 1940s, filled up with resorts that reached to ever greater architectural lengths to attract gamblers.

Beginning in the 1930s, the Los Angeles Highway brought traffic from California, encouraging increased development along the road south of downtown Las Vegas. This growth continued throughout the decade, accelerating after World War II to turn Las Vegas into a world-class tourist destination. Other factors encouraged this expansion. First, casino owners outside the city limits (Sahara Avenue on the south) could take advantage of more permissive county ordinances. Second, casinos along the highway could attract motorists from California before they reached downtown. Casino architecture played to the road very early in the development of Las Vegas. Although the railroad continued to bring many tourists and new residents to the city during World War II, the growing importance of the highway, rather than the railroad, shaped the look and layout of Las Vegas and the Strip. From the 1930s to the 1970s, casinos along the Strip had plenty of open desert land on which to build sprawling, motel-inspired complexes. Downtown casinos, on the other hand, developed in a more urbanized landscape within walking distance of the depot and thus followed the more traditional model of the hotel. The differences in development of the two areas are still apparent today; Strip casinos have continued to grow to enormous sizes and to adopt extraordinary appearances, whereas downtown casinos have grown taller but remained smaller overall.

Las Vegas continues to be the ultimate boom town. From only 945 inhabitants in 1910, the city has grown exponentially during most of the twentieth century. The population of the Las Vegas metropolitan area surpassed one million in 1995. The city continues to stretch toward the edges of the valley as more and more tract housing developments and planned communities such as Summerlin take up the remaining open space. Summerlin, encompassing nearly thirty-six square miles in Clark County, is expected to reach a population of about 160,000 residents in the early twenty-first century. Designed to be self-contained, it includes golf courses, shopping centers, community centers, and casinos. When completed, Summerlin will comprise thirty distinct villages. Intended to create a sense of community, they will be differentiated in terms of size, population, and housing type and price range, among other features. This form of development for meticulously planned growth has become typical in Las Vegas and surrounding cities.

Though limitations loom, such as lack of an adequate water supply and large blocks of undevelopable federal and tribal land, prospects for continued growth appear, for now, to be unrestricted. The federal government has continued to assist the city's growth through land exchanges, opening more public land to private development. The federal government, usually through the Bureau of Land Management, sells land to be developed in southern Nevada and buys private land elsewhere in the state, which then comes under the management of a federal agency, usually the Bureau of Land Management or the U.S. Forest Service. The newly privatized land provides new open space to be used for residential subdivisions and shopping centers. This form of development parallels that along Las Vegas Boulevard, where large empty lots have been filled by ever larger casinos. Thus the hunger for more open space continues to be fed, an outcome of the still pervasive myth of the frontier.

Nevertheless, the increased population density in the region has forced Las Vegas and surrounding Clark County to consider the social, economic, and cultural needs of residents. The construction of schools, libraries, museums, and government buildings has changed the character of this former desert outpost. These buildings have allowed architecture in Las

Vegas to take a different course—supplementing the architecture of entertainment with one of community that requires building a visible civic presence. Las Vegas's role as a city rather than just a resort destination now requires it to confront the problems of rapid growth and limited resources. It remains to be seen if the community will successfully manage growth and merge touristic interests with those of residents. Some positive developments on the cultural front include the construction of a new fine arts museum, as part of the Sahara West Library branch, and a neon museum downtown.

With the exception of the casinos and some recent public and private buildings, little of Las Vegas's architecture can be considered exceptional, let alone at the leading edge. Over the years, many of its most acclaimed structures have been designed by architects from outside Nevada. However, the current climate of growth and prosperity has given local architects the opportunity to design more appealing and innovative structures, so that the architectural community is now thriving.

Though growth is rapidly filling the valley, undeveloped areas can still be found only fifteen miles outside the city. Numerous state parks and national recreation areas offer opportunities for the public to enjoy southern Nevada's mountains and deserts. The vernacular buildings in these locations respond to the natural environment in a way that few structures in Las Vegas do.

Downtown

Downtown Las Vegas, the oldest developed section of the city, has the highest density of buildings of any place in Nevada, with the possible exception of downtown Reno. Laid out by the railroad on a grid in 1905, it was the obvious spot in which to build because of the proximity of the depot and water supply. After the legalization of gambling in 1931, entrepreneurs built larger hotels to meet the recently created demand for gambling. Although Las Vegas began as a railroad town, few structures associated with the railroad remain. Amtrak now stops at a platform without a depot, behind the Union Plaza Hotel. Buildings in the nearby Union Pacific yards have burned down or been demolished. Only a few early twentieth-century hotels and the remnants of railroad cottages along South Main Street remind us why Las Vegas was founded.

Today downtown Las Vegas compactly balances casinos with government buildings, small businesses, a historic district, and a few residences. Gambling is the dominant industry, however, giving the area the atmosphere of a round-the-clock carnival. Fremont Street, the main thoroughfare, has seen a marked evolution, as casino and business owners downtown have sought ways to compete effectively with the larger, showier Strip casinos to the south. It retains many vintage neon signs, including "Vegas Vic," the 60-foot-tall image of a smiling cowboy. However, the closure of the street to car traffic and construction of the Fremont Street Experience—a large space frame on which elaborate light shows are projected at night—have transformed the street into a pedestrian mall, destroying much of its former random mix of road traffic and raffishness.

SO01 Las Vegas Mormon Fort

1855. 900 Las Vegas Blvd. N.

The Las Vegas Mormon Fort is one of Nevada's oldest extant buildings. In 1855 the first Euro-American settlers in the area, leaders of the Church of Jesus Christ of Latter-day Saints, built this mission on the Spanish-Mormon Trail between Salt Lake City and San Bernardino, California, to assert Mormon interests in this part of the West and to serve as a base for converting Native Americans to the Mormon faith and as a way station for travelers on the trail.

They also selected this site because it was adjacent to the Las Vegas Springs, one of the few good sources of water in the Las Vegas Valley. The mission was fortified against attack by Native Americans or hostile non-Mormon emigrants. After two years of difficult labor trying to establish crops and convert Native Americans with little success, the Mormons left in 1857. The fort site subsequently served as a ranch and, in the 1920s, as a concrete laboratory for the Bureau of Reclamation when it was conducting tests prior to construction of Hoover Dam.

Only a 10-foot-by-30-foot building survives of what once was a 150-foot-square walled settlement. The walls of adobe brick are 2 feet thick at the bottom and 1 foot thick at the top (the base of the walls had to be thick enough to support the weight of the walls above it). Though its caretakers have made alterations to replace adobe, which is vulnerable to erosion, the basic simple, functional design of the building remains.

SO02 Las Vegas Library and Lied Discovery Museum

1986–1990, Antoine Predock. 833 Las Vegas Blvd. N.

Rising above Las Vegas Boulevard in a mass of geometric shapes, Predock's library and children's museum strikes a balance between whimsy and function. This building was the first in Clark County's effort to expand its library system by constructing a decentralized network of branches. These have been paired with cultural facilities such as theaters or museums, the better to serve Clark County's sprawling population.

Seeking to draw attention to the project and to give Las Vegas a preeminent cultural center, the Clark County Library District commissioned a major out-of-state architect. Predock was ideally suited for the job. Based in Albuquerque, he began his career designing houses in New Mexico that were inspired by regional vernacular forms and that responded to the local culture. Since then, he has received much larger commissions and has embraced a variety of architectural forms and materials that reach beyond the regional qualities of the Southwest. Nevertheless, he is known for designs that are appropriate to the environment of the arid Southwest. Predock views architecture as being able to create a surrogate landscape, tapping into the sense of place. Sensitive to how materials and colors appear in the bright light of the desert, he uses simple but bold forms devoid of ornamentation, which would be lost in the glare of sunlight. For this project, he also wanted to create a building that would respond to the unique nature of Las Vegas. The building stands near the Las Vegas Mormon Fort and the path of the old Spanish-Mormon Trail. Thus he designed a series of articulated spaces meant to indicate the place as a crossroads. Rather than build a "decorated shed," he designed a structure with substantial volumes that, according to Predock, is "more about space than surface."

SO01 Las Vegas Mormon Fort (left)

SO02 Las Vegas Library and Lied Discovery Museum (right)

Las Vegas — Downtown, High School Historic District, Westside

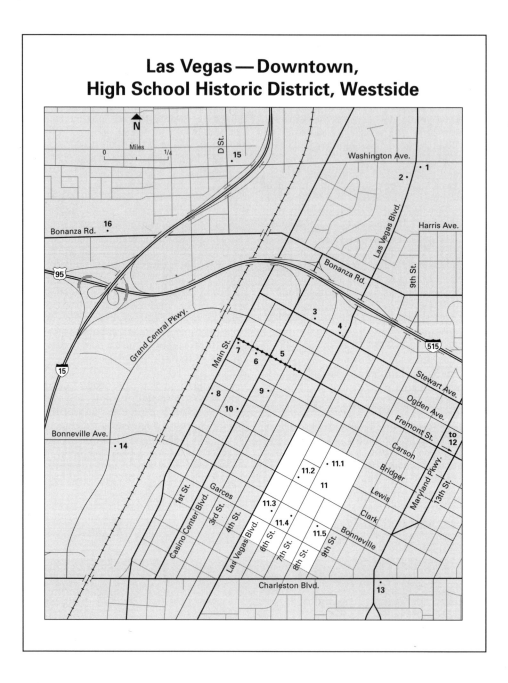

Geometric volumes define the various activities pursued in individual sections of the building. A central triangular administration block, clad in red sandstone from the nearby Spring Mountains, divides the library and the museum. Near the entrance is a white precast concrete cone that serves as a birthday-party room. Intended to resemble a birthday hat, the structure is also designed to educate; its apertures follow a Fibonacci series of numbers. A barrel-vaulted wing extending from the museum end to the library end of the building contains the children's reading room. A gray concrete 112-foot-tall science tower spirals above the complex, providing views of the city. Seemingly randomly placed windows take advantage of views. The building is designed for the harsh desert environment; native sandstone and concrete help deflect heat, as do small courtyards within the complex. Drought-resistant landscaping with desert species, such as palm trees, Joshua trees, and yucca plants, surrounds the building and the hill sloping toward Las Vegas Boulevard, creating the effect of an oasis. Displaying the diversity of desert vegetation, this type of landscaping has become increasingly popular in Las Vegas, at least for public buildings.

Since completion of the Las Vegas Library and Lied Discovery Museum, other library/cultural centers have been built or renovated, many designed by out-of-state architects. Among them are the Clark County Library and Theater (SO28), renovated by Michael Graves with JMA Architects of Las Vegas, and the twenty-third and last of the branches, the Flamingo Sahara West Library and Fine Arts Museum, by Meyer, Scherer, and Rockcastle of Minneapolis.

SO03 **Las Vegas Downtown Post Office** (U.S. Federal Courthouse and Post Office)

1931–1933, James A. Wetmore. 301 E. Stewart Ave.

The post office, on a strip of land called the Civic Center, seems out of place across the street from casino parking garages. When built, the three-story, steel-frame building in the Beaux-Arts classical style, designed by the Office of the Supervising Architect of the U.S. Treasury Department, was the most elaborate in Las Vegas, signifying its important role as the home of the main post office, federal courts, and other federal agencies. Central steps lead to the first story, containing a series of arched openings with doors and windows, flanked by massive end bays clad in brick on the two upper floors. A central bay projects slightly over the main entrance, covered entirely by creamy white terra-cotta tiles. Above the arches of the entranceway, eight Ionic pilasters separate vertical stacks of windows. Terra-cotta tiles also clad the first floor of the building on the sides and rear, as on the front.

The choice of Beaux-Arts classicism reflects the taste of the Treasury Department's supervising architects of the 1890s and early 1900s; in the 1930s this style would give way to the far simpler PWA Moderne. As in other small Nevada towns during the Great Depression, this building signified an increased federal presence, contrasting dramatically with the bars and hotels surrounding it.

SO04 **Las Vegas City Hall**

1973, Daniel, Mann, Johnson, and Mendenhall. 400 E. Stewart Ave.

The monumental city hall provides a strong contrast in style and form to the Beaux-Arts post office and other buildings on Stewart Avenue. The marble-and-glass-clad structure has two components: a wedge-shaped office tower and, behind it, a round, three-story office wing surrounding an open plaza. Set on a corner lot, the wedge presents a curving blank wall to downtown, enlivened only by a large abstract sculpture made up of colorful translucent plastic strips applied to the building's face in a rainbow pattern. The main entrance is located in the back of the tower in a wall of bronze-framed smoked glass.

By the early 1970s Las Vegas had become Nevada's largest city, and the new city hall reflected this preeminence. Unfortunately it was erected at a time when urban renewal wiped out entire city blocks to accommodate large civic structures or apartment houses. Though the city hall is eye-catching, it rejects the scale of the older downtown grid and can hardly be called welcoming.

SO05 Fremont Street Experience

1995, Jon Jerde Partnership. Fremont St. from S. Main to 4th sts.

This massive space frame, supported by 90-foot-tall columns, covers four blocks of Fremont Street. The frame forms a barrel-vaulted, semi-transparent ceiling connecting the buildings on opposite sides of the street. Bolted onto the underside of this frame is a steel lighting trellis with 2.1 million fixtures, designed by Young Electric Sign Company, maker of numerous signs along the Strip. By day the structure provides the street with some shade and a sense of enclosure. At night the bulbs light up hourly for a seven-minute sound-and-light show for which the structure is named.

In order to lure visitors from the Strip, the city and casinos along the street cooperated to build this project, banishing cars and converting Fremont into a pedestrian mall. However, the street has become de facto a private space; in return for paying most of the bill, casinos are permitted to close the street to the public periodically for their own use. Although the Experience appears to be a commercial success, its construction has certainly compromised this historic area of Las Vegas.

SO06 Golden Nugget

1945, 1976. 1983, Fred Doriot. 1984, Joel Bergman. 129 Fremont St.

Casino mogul Steve Wynn's acquisition and remodeling of the Golden Nugget in the 1980s marked a shift in the public's perception of downtown Las Vegas as the shabby sister of the Strip. Although Fremont Street had developed as the earliest center for gambling in the city, by the 1970s and 1980s many visitors rejected this area, which had grown rather rundown, for the more glamorous attractions of the Strip.

Although it had gained a hotel tower in 1976, by the early 1980s the Nugget retained much of its original appearance, based on what architectural critic Alan Hess calls the western vernacular of San Francisco during the Gold Rush—the Barbary Coast style. The casino's large corner sign, designed by Kermit Wayne of the Young Electric Sign Company in 1957, had become famous for its rococo forms, dominated by a large outward bulge at the bottom and scroll-work on top. The interior contained heavy draperies, glass globe chandeliers, ornately carved wood furniture, and paintings of nudes. The "Vegas Vic" sign added to the Pioneer Club in 1951 remains as an example of Fremont Street's former enthusiasm for the frontier look. Although this look had set the standard in the 1940s and 1950s, by the 1980s it was long out of date.

To effect the Nugget's transformation from a Barbary Coast–style club to a sleek, modern casino, Wynn's architect, Fred Doriot, removed the Golden Nugget's rococo sign and sheathed the exterior in white and gold. Doriot designed a tower for suite and spa accommodations in 1976; a third tower, designed by Joel Bergman, was erected in 1984. The main entrance corner still displays a Golden Nugget sign, but its letters curve in an arch against a gold background. Large arched windows covered with white awnings punctuate the exterior walls along Fremont Street and Casino Center Boulevard. The interior is similarly streamlined. The success of the Nugget's makeover in attracting new business has spurred the owners of neighboring casinos to remodel their buildings, giving Fremont Street a fresh appearance.

SO07 Golden Gate Hotel and Casino

1906, 1931. 1964, addition, Jack Miller and Associates (removed in 1990). 1 Fremont St.

The Golden Gate, a survivor from the railroad era, is Las Vegas's oldest extant hotel. The building stands at the corner of Fremont and Main streets, across the street from the site of the city's first two depots. The first two stories were constructed in 1906 as the Hotel Nevada. In 1931 the building acquired a third floor, buttresses, and multipane casement windows, as well as a new name, the Sal Sagev (Las Vegas spelled backward). Businessmen from San Francisco bought the hotel in 1955, changed its name to the Golden Gate, and opened a casino. They expanded the building in 1964, adding a bright, metal-screen facade to give the hotel a modern look. In 1990 the owners removed this last addition, one of the few examples of restoring a casino to its earlier appearance. The vertical Golden Gate sign and awning along Main Street remain from the makeover of the 1960s.

SO07 Golden Gate Hotel and Casino

SO09 Clark County Courthouse

SO08 **Victory Hotel**

1910, Moore and Rhoads. 307 S. Main St.

Known for years as the Lincoln Hotel, the Victory is one of the last remaining buildings from Las Vegas's railroad days. The Victory stood across the street from the railroad tracks, clearly visible to arriving passengers. The building, though extensively altered, typifies the downtown hotel of the early twentieth century. It retains a two-story arcaded facade, common in the city in the early twentieth century, as was its simplified Mission Revival style, also used for the first railroad depot in town (now demolished).

SO09 **Clark County Courthouse**

1958, Walter Zick and Harris Sharp Architects. 200 S. 3rd St.

The Clark County Courthouse replaced an older Spanish Colonial Revival structure designed by Frederick J. DeLongchamps. The newer, International Style structure soars to a height of seven stories in concrete, steel, and glass. Simple colonnades along the recessed first floor originally supported the rest of the building above. The concrete end walls, painted powder blue, are perforated, revealing the holes for the bolts that attach the concrete panels to the frame of the building. These walls contrast with the long sides of the structure, composed of bands of windows alternating with bands of steel, scored off by thin vertical steel strips. During the 1980s county officials autho-

rized an addition—a two-story Brutalist structure surrounding part of the older one—which detracts from it. Massive scored concrete walls run along the sidewalk, their lines continued by a colonnade of the same material.

SO10 **Clark County Detention Center**

1981–1984, JMA Architects with Hellmuth, Obata and Kassabaum. 330 Casino Center Blvd.

Because the Clark County Detention Center is situated near the county courthouse and only a few blocks away from Fremont Street's casinos, the architects had to design a jail that would not look like one. The 350,000-square-foot, twelve-story facility looks more like an office building, successfully blending with the high-rise casinos and parking garages nearby. Narrow horizontal bands of tinted recessed windows wrap around the vertical cores of the structure. Glazed brick cladding and rounded corners blend with the curved canopy marking the main entrance. Underground passageways connect the jail to the courthouse so that inmates can be moved securely from one to the other.

SO11 **Las Vegas High School Historic District**

Roughly bounded by E. Bridger, S. 9th, E. Gass, and Las Vegas Blvd.

The Las Vegas High School Historic District stands just a few blocks away from the downtown core in an area that developed soon after the high school opened in 1930. Despite the Depression, the early 1930s were prosperous years for Las Vegas, as money and people flooded the area during the construction of Hoover Dam. The district has a range of revival styles represented in mostly modest structures. The Spanish Colonial Revival style, popular in the early twentieth-century Southwest, is particularly common. Because of the neighborhood's proximity to downtown, many houses have been converted to offices over the years, while others have been demolished.

SO11.1 **Las Vegas Academy of International Studies and Performing Arts** (Las Vegas High School)

1930, George A. Ferris and Lehman A. Ferris. 315 S. 7th St.

Las Vegas's only high school until the 1950s, this building is certainly the best example of the Art Deco style in the city. Designed by the father-son firm of George A. and Lehman A. Ferris of Reno, the three-story concrete building has a five-part facade marked by a central pavilion and two corner pavilions flanking two recessed sections, all marked off by buttresses. The stucco-covered walls are smooth, embellished with an intricate cast concrete frieze of repetitive animal and vegetal forms. The central pavilion, containing the main entrance, is the most elaborate element. Four buttresses rise along the facade, decorated at the tops with cast concrete reliefs representing stylized grapevines and embellished with polychrome medallions. The recessed entrance has a surround depicting squirrels, snakes, and other animals among vines. A cast concrete frieze of interlocking wreaths above a repeating pattern of chevrons near the top of the wall extends around the rest of the building. Although the exterior is well preserved, the interior has been substantially altered.

SO11.2 **Offices** (House)

1938, Arthur Lacy Worswick. 431 S. 6th St.

This single-story frame and stucco house has an L-shaped plan, with a low octagonal cupola rising above the junction of the two wings. Wraparound metal casement windows at the main

SO11.1 Las Vegas Academy of International Studies and Performing Arts (Las Vegas High School) (top)

SO11.5 Duplex (bottom)

corners of the house nod to the Moderne style. Worswick designed a number of buildings in Las Vegas during the boom of the 1930s and 1940s.

SO11.3 **Offices** (Jay Dayton Smith House)

1931–1932, Warner and Nordstrom. 624 S. 6th St.

The Spanish Colonial Revival style of this one-story stuccoed house is common in this district. The building is modest in size and ornamentation but typifies the local interpretation of this style. The asymmetrical form incorporates a variety of masses, with two front-gabled roof sections at the ends flanking a round tower and a shed-roofed porch covering the entry. Large arched windows, one rounded and one pointed, pierce the gable ends. Simple ornamentation includes roof-beam ends jutting below the narrow eaves, decorative vents in the tower, and a wrought iron grill over the tower window.

SO11.4 House

1939, Hampton Brothers. 610 S. 7th St.

The Tudor Revival, here greatly simplified, was another popular style in the neighborhood. A steeply pitched, side-gabled section is embellished with two gabled projections facing the street. The lower, central gable contains the entrance, while the taller one rises to the left. The four Hampton brothers, trained as carpenters, designed and erected numerous buildings in the district and in Las Vegas.

SO11.5 Duplex

1931, Hampton Brothers. 802 E. Bonneville Ave.

Built for a doctor, this structure is unusual in the neighborhood—a duplex rather than a single-family home. The Spanish Colonial Revival building has typical features, such as a wing wall with an arched opening leading to stairs that wind around a two-story tower with a conical roof. Creamy stuccoed walls meet a red tile roof.

SO12 Green Shack

1932. 2504 E. Fremont St.

The Green Shack Restaurant has been a fixture in Las Vegas for over sixty years. Occupying a long, rectangular, one-story former barracks, it has a gable roof and a shed-roofed porch extending along the north side. The business, founded by Mettie Jones, originally operated out of town, along the road to the Colorado River. In 1932 Jones purchased a green-painted barracks from the Union Pacific Railroad and moved it alongside the recently completed Boulder Dam Highway (Fremont Street), just inside the city limits. Jones relocated her business, which has operated here ever since. Initially a destination for Boulder Dam workers coming into town, the restaurant is now surrounded by strip development. Additions to the barracks have obscured

the lines of the original structure, but the bright green paint is reminiscent of the Union Pacific's colors.

SO13 Huntridge Theater

1943–1944, S. Charles Lee. 1208 E. Charleston Blvd.

The Moderne theater stands at the busy intersection of Charleston Boulevard and Maryland Parkway at the edge of the Huntridge neighborhood, built during the 1940s. The one-story brick and concrete theater has a 75-foot-tall tower that catches the eyes of passersby. Atop the fluted tower is a neon sign that reads "Huntridge." A porthole punctuates the transition from fluting below to the sign above. A bank of glass doors, flanked by rectangular piers supporting the marquee, opens into the lobby. Both the exterior and interior are plain, in keeping with the streamlined aesthetic of the Moderne. The theater's construction during World War II, when materials for nonmilitary efforts were in short supply, also explains the lack of ornament.

S. Charles Lee of Los Angeles, one of the country's best-known theater architects in the first half of the twentieth century, designed more than 300 theaters throughout the United States during his long career. Many of his projects still stand; some of the best examples can be found on Broadway in downtown Los Angeles.

SO14 Clark County Government Center

1992–1995, C. W. Fentress, J. H. Bradburn and Associates. 500 S. Grand Central Pkwy.

The massive county government center rises out of the flat valley in geometric masses clad in native red stone. Located on a section of the old Union Pacific Railroad Yards, across the tracks from downtown, the complex reflects a new trend in Las Vegas—the belief that public architecture should be first class. Instead of looking to downtown or the Strip, the Denver-based architects drew inspiration from the expansive desert landscape. They also used classic forms—pyramid, tower, and amphitheater—to refer to the historic public function of architecture. Sections of the building curve around a large circular entrance plaza, bordered in part by a portico that evokes Native American brush shelters. The cafeteria is housed in a large pyramid suggesting

SO14 Clark County Government Center

those of Central American civilizations or North American mound architecture. In the center of the main building, between higher and lower office wings, is a lobby tower ending in a spiral parapet. The landscaping of palm trees and low-lying desert plants against a backdrop of reddish-pink gravel helps to soften the unadorned building.

Westside

The west side of Las Vegas, the area west of I-15 and north of West Bonanza Road, is a traditionally African American neighborhood once known as McWilliams's Township. It developed across the railroad tracks from downtown because of segregation; many African Americans arrived in the area in the 1930s, and their numbers increased dramatically after World War II. The city's laws and policies prohibited people of color from living in most parts of Las Vegas until the late 1960s. For much of its history, the Westside was chronically underserved; running water and paved streets arrived long after other parts of the city received these amenities. The city's decision to allow construction of I-15 through the district was a further detriment. Although the civil rights movement of the 1960s and its legacy have made Las Vegas a more integrated place, the Westside remains predominantly African American.

SO15 Westside School

1922, Allison and Allison. Northeast corner of Washington and D sts.

This small Mission Revival building served African Americans and children of the Paiute Indian tribe in Las Vegas. It remains the city's oldest surviving school building. The reinforced concrete and stucco structure originally had two rooms, one on each side of the gabled entrance. In 1928 two more rooms were added at the rear.

SO16 Moulin Rouge Hotel and Casino

1955, Walter Zick and Harris Sharp Architects. 900 W. Bonanza Rd.

The Moulin Rouge opened on 24 May 1955 as the first racially integrated hotel and casino in Nevada. Although it closed only five months later, the Moulin Rouge helped pave the way for integrated casinos and hotels. Before its opening, no casino in the state admitted African American patrons. Black entertainers performing at these casinos could not gamble or mingle with guests. Segregation forced them to find lodgings in rooming houses in the Westside.

Zick and Sharp of Las Vegas designed the one-story casino and theater attached to a two-story, V-shaped hotel to the west. The most striking features of the exterior are the four-story tower at the southeastern corner of the building and the giant "Moulin Rouge" sign mounted on the roof, in red neon script. The shingled mansard roofs on the casino and tower were added at a later date, most likely in the 1960s. The Moulin Rouge contains a large auditorium with a bar and murals depicting cancan dancers, fancy cars, and elegantly dressed people.

On the border between the black and white sections of town, the resort became famous for its "third show," a program starting at 2:15 a.m. that featured entertainers from the Strip. Black and white performers, including Frank Sinatra, Dean Martin, Harry Belafonte, Louis Armstrong, and Sammy Davis, Jr., appeared onstage together or attended shows at the Moulin Rouge.

Las Vegas Strip

The Strip—that four-mile stretch of road lined with casinos and lights—is what characterizes the city in the minds of most visitors. It is the ultimate example of both the desert oasis and the human capacity to exploit the environment. Once a dusty road leading to Los Angeles, the Strip has evolved into an entertainment extravaganza filled with crowds every day of the week. Guy McAfee, a gambler and former police captain from Los Angeles who purchased the Pair-O-Dice Club in Las Vegas in 1939, is credited with naming the Strip in the 1940s because it reminded him of the Sunset Strip in Los Angeles.

Lying outside the Las Vegas city limits and therefore subject to Clark County's lenient zoning laws, the Strip developed with few restrictions on height or density. This permissive zoning was no accident. In 1950 casino owners organized their own unincorporated township, called Paradise City, which fought Las Vegas's attempts to annex the Strip. To this day, the stretch of road and adjacent property remain in county hands.

The lack of regulations allowed casino owners to build resorts in almost any form they wished. The first era of casinos along the Strip, built in the 1930s and 1940s, followed the layout of motels—low buildings no more than four stories tall stretching back from the road and surrounded by parking lots. It is easy to see why large signs set along the road and placed on the buildings would become popular as a way for casinos to differentiate their low-slung complexes from one another. In 1955, with the construction of the nine-story Riviera, casinos began departing from the motel model, erecting high-rise structures to provide more hotel rooms and to increase their visibility along the Strip. In the 1960s Caesars Palace ushered in the era of the theme resort, a trend that continues to this day. Another trend, begun in the late 1960s with the erection of the International Hotel, now the Hilton, was the three-wing hotel tower. This form has continued to be popular because the three wings can accommodate more rooms with views without sprawling across the casino property. Also, the three-wing tower is more visible from a variety of viewpoints than less expansive forms. Examples of this type include the Mirage, Treasure Island, and Bellagio.

After decades of changing casino styles, the opening of the Mirage Hotel and Casino in 1989 ushered in the era of the mega-resort. With tens of thousands of square feet devoted to gambling and thousands of hotel rooms, these resorts seem to embody the current craze for gambling enveloped in entertainment. Sophisticated indoor environments have been created in these huge structures to enhance the experience of leaving the real world behind. Other mega-resorts such as Excalibur and Luxor use specific themes—King Arthur's court or ancient Egypt—to lure people inside and keep them there. These casinos have introduced to Las Vegas the concept of total entertainment, aimed at luring families away from Disneyland and other theme parks. Consequently a number of casinos have added roller

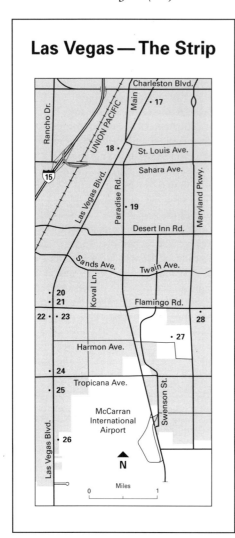

Las Vegas — The Strip

Charleston Blvd.

Rancho Dr.

UNION PACIFIC

Main

• 17

18 •

St. Louis Ave.

15

Las Vegas Blvd.

Paradise Rd.

Sahara Ave.

Maryland Pkwy.

• 19

Desert Inn Rd.

Sands Ave.

Twain Ave.

Koval Ln.

• 20
• 21

Flamingo Rd.

22 • • 23

28

• 27

Harmon Ave.

• 24

Tropicana Ave.

Swenson St.

• 25

McCarran
International
Airport

Las Vegas Blvd.

• 26

▲
N

Miles

0   1

This density has altered the Strip from a space built around cars to one that must also accommodate pedestrians. Aside from public buses, no mass transit exists except for private monorails connecting some of the casinos. The value of land has pushed parking lots to the rear of casinos or into multistory garages, freeing the street frontage. New casinos, such as the Mirage and New York New York, have attractions on or near the sidewalk, letting visitors watch a volcano erupt or a roller coaster zoom past the Manhattan skyline. But the goal remains the same as ever—to entice visitors inside. Though signs are still very much a part of the landscape, casino buildings have become their own signs—a pyramid, a castle, or a lion—to advertise their uniqueness in an environment jammed with attractions and distractions. But given the Strip's propensity to reinvent itself, a new streetscape of casinos will probably replace the present one in another five or ten years.

SO17 Little White Chapel

1955, many alterations. 1301 Las Vegas Blvd. S.

The wedding chapel, on the north Strip amid a clutter of motels and fast-food restaurants, is itself unprepossessing, but it boasts a drive-up window. "Wedding windows" have become popular in Las Vegas in recent years. Couples in a hurry to marry pull up and push a button to call the minister. Speakers around the window broadcast music as the ceremony is performed. The bride and groom never have to leave their vehicle. Roadside signs prominently advertise the window, on the north side of the chapel, to motorists. A large gable with an open metal peak encompasses a series of three receding gables above a row of windows with large dome-shaped awnings. Abundant plants embellish the windows and the otherwise plain stucco facade. On the front is a gable with scalloped trim surmounted by a steeple outlined in neon.

SO18 Stratosphere Tower

1991–1996, Ned Baldwin. 2000 Las Vegas Blvd. S.

Ned Baldwin, architect of the CN Tower in Toronto, designed the 1,149-foot concrete Stratosphere Tower, the tallest building west of

coasters and attractions such as a version of Times Square or a replica of King Tut's tomb. Despite these changes, the Strip and its casinos remain an adult's world where gambling is still the focus.

Today the Strip is more densely built and congested than it was ten, or even five, years ago. Most small hotels, businesses, and gas stations have been crowded out by enormous entertainment complexes. Casinos once had open lots between them, but now they stand side by side, creating odd juxtapositions as one moves from classical Rome to King Arthur's court to New York City.

SO17 Little White Chapel

SO18 Stratosphere Tower (at right, with the Sahara Hotel)

the Mississippi and perhaps the best example of excess in Las Vegas. The tower rises from a three-pronged base on a podium to a twelve-story pod at the top, which contains a revolving restaurant, two observation decks, three wedding chapels, and an outdoor roller coaster, among other attractions.

SO19 **Las Vegas Hilton**

1969, Martin J. Stern, Jr.. 1973. 3000 W. Paradise Rd.

Though the Hilton, originally the International, is now one of the more mundane-looking casinos near the Strip, in 1969 it marked a break with the casinos of the 1950s and early 1960s. Martin J. Stern, Jr., an architect based in Beverly Hills, designed numerous hotels and casinos in Nevada, most of them in Las Vegas. The building was the largest three-wing tower constructed in the city at that time; yet only four years later, in 1973, it gained a 1,500-room wing, doubling its capacity. The hotel's curved sides add some interest to the otherwise monotonous rows of windows. Built just off the Strip on Paradise Road, the Hilton, lacking the highway as a focus, stands as a self-contained monument, unrelated to the earlier buildings surrounding it. Though constructed for an independent entrepreneur, Kirk Kerkorian, the hotel represented the move toward a corporate style in Las Vegas that left its mark on all casinos built in the 1970s. This style, characterized by massive, boxy towers, looked more to office building architecture than to the unique resort environment of Las Vegas.

SO20 **The Mirage**

1989, Joel Bergman. 3400 Las Vegas Blvd. S.

The luxurious Mirage triggered a building boom in the early 1990s that continues unabated. The brainchild of casino owner Steve Wynn, the Mirage is geared toward high rollers but also entertains passersby on the sidewalk with a volcano that erupts every fifteen minutes in a blaze of red lights, water, steam, and gas-jet flames. The casino's three-wing, thirty-story tower, containing more than 3,000 rooms, rises monotonously in horizontal bands of white beams and gold-tinted windows, reaching to a simple frieze decorated only with the hotel's name. The complex has the requisite roadside sign, an electronic, rather than neon, signboard rising to a height of 160 feet. Set at the bend in Las Vegas Boulevard, the sign serves as a distance marker on the Strip.

The bulk of the casino stands far back from the street but beckons tourists with a large lake surrounding the volcano. A causeway over the lagoon leads visitors to the porte-cochere. Hotel guests register at a counter to the right of the entrance. Behind the clerks extends a long tropical fish tank containing specimens beautiful enough to distract guests while they wait. When they return to the hotel's main axis, immediately inside the entrance door, they see directly in front of them a tropical rain forest of palms, ferns, orchids, a waterfall, and Chinese-style statues in an atrium 90 feet tall, covered by a glass and metal dome. The casino games begin only beyond that point, as the Mirage—

unlike Treasure Island, the Rio, and others—caters to those who might find endless acres of gambling tables disappointing after the landscaping and amusements outdoors. The casino space is divided into areas for various games, identified by separate thatched roofs—part of a vaguely Asian/Polynesian overall theme. Some higher-stakes zones are higher and airier, with more widely spaced tables set under ceilings of plaster impressed with leaf designs.

Other attractions, located beyond the gambling areas, include Asian restaurants designed to look like garden pavilions in China and Japan, a dolphin pool, and a white-tiger habitat extending from an artificial white cave indoors to an outdoor garden. A spacious convention center, often a feature of casino hotels, is decorated with tasteful examples of modern Japanese art and craftsmanship. These continue the casino's exotic theme, emphasizing the tropical fantasy aspects of a place that actually rises from the desert.

SO21 Caesars Palace

1966, Melvin Grossman. 1970, 1974, 1979, 1986, 1989, additions. 1992, Marnell Corrao Associates. 1996–1997, David Rockwell. 3570 Las Vegas Blvd. S.

Caesars Palace broke with the roadside motel form common along the Strip and introduced something new: the theme casino. Entrepreneur Jay Sarno hired Miami architect Melvin Gross-

man to design something monumental, but not just high-rise. This was to be an entire complex, based loosely on the theme of classical Rome.

Initially the casino had a central curved tower set far back from the Strip. Flanking this convex form, symmetrical arcaded wings curved outward toward the Strip, a composition faintly but sufficiently like that of an ancient forum to justify the building's name. Cars, relegated to parking lots along the wings, did not intrude upon a long central access plaza adorned with fountains and Italian cypress trees. At the entrance stood symmetrically disposed statues, a mixture of late Greek, Roman, and Renaissance figures reduced by the copyists to the same height; the fact that the Winged Victory of Samothrace was not Roman did not disturb the suggestion of a stylized ancient theme. (A new plaza displaying an even more unrestrained classicism stands just to the north of the original plaza and now serves as the principal automobile entrance to the complex.)

Immediately inside the door a reception area curved along the building's perimeter. Dimly lit and imperfectly ventilated, it accommodated guests waiting for their rooms to be ready. A few steps away, however, a bright and airy rotunda beckoned, filled with gambling machines. (This design is common to many casinos: entries and service areas are uninviting, while the spaces for gambling tend to be easily accessible, large, and colorful, well or even ex-

SO21 Caesars Palace

cessively lit. Design and lighting may also differ in areas devoted to various types of games.)

Since 1969, Caesars has been owned by a series of corporations, the latest being ITT. Since 1970, a dizzying array of added canopies, pavilions, porches, and statues has made the resort seem always up to date, although the high-rise hotel towers built in 1970, 1974, 1979, and 1996–1997 are not all related to the classical Roman theme. The latest tower faces Flamingo Road rather than the Strip, taking advantage of Caesars' prominent corner location. Like the Bellagio and several other hotel towers of the late 1990s, it recalls skyscrapers of about 1910, with several floors grouped as a base, then a shaft of many identical stories, and finally a crowning set of identical floors adorned with classical details and perhaps capped by decorative roofs.

One of the city's most enjoyable urban experiences is to be had, ironically, inside the Forum Shops, not outdoors on the Strip. This shopping mall was designed by Dougall Design Associates and built at Caesars Palace in 1994. An inclined moving sidewalk rises from street level under a series of imitation triumphal arches to one end of the mall, where a short, broad street under a ceiling painted to simulate the sky is lined with one-story shops topped by balustrades. At the end of the street is the first of several plazas, connected by additional shopping streets, each with facades different in scale, height, and design. The plazas also have varied shapes, and while the decoration of some of them was inspired by palace courtyards of the Italian Renaissance or the interiors of famous church buildings, the largest one manages to resemble an outdoor civic square somewhere in modern Italy. Lavish but coarsely executed fountains and sculptures adorn the plazas. Although this is clearly an indoor mall, its design skillfully suggests the experience of a stroll along varied streets leading to differentiated plazas in a Mediterranean tourist town.

SO22 Bellagio

1996–1998, DeRuyter O. Butler with Jon Jerde Partnership. Southwest corner of Flamingo Rd. and Las Vegas Blvd. S.

The latest of Mirage Resorts' mega-resorts, Bellagio—very loosely based on the Italian village at Lake Como—makes an effort to bring a European ambience to the Strip. Built at a cost of $1.6 billion, the resort covers 122 acres, formerly the site of the Dunes Hotel, which was im-

ploded in 1993. Like the Mirage, Bellagio is surrounded by a contrived landscape, including tropical gardens and an eleven-acre man-made lake. The public attraction here is a water ballet of fountains, accompanied by lights and music. Beyond the lake is the hotel's thirty-six-story main building, with three wings spreading from a central curved shaft topped by a cupola. At the base of the tower is a cluster of buildings with red tile roofs emulating Italian villas and containing elegant, expensive shops and restaurants.

Bellagio's artificial nostalgia for a prosperous past and glamorous foreign resorts is characteristic of appeals to the newly rich since the 1990s. It is one of a number of new hotel-casinos reaching out to affluent customers by offering luxurious rooms, branches of expensive and well-known restaurants, and shopping malls featuring exclusive stores. Bellagio's first owner, Steve Wynn, opened a gallery here to display his French Impressionist and old master paintings—a first for a Strip resort. Also designed to attract visitors is the private monorail carrying guests from Bellagio to Monte Carlo, another Mirage Resorts casino on the Strip. The monorail not only enables patrons to avoid driving or walking on crowded roads or sidewalks but also encourages them to remain in casinos owned by the same company. In 2000 MGM Grand, Inc., purchased Mirage Resorts, including Bellagio. It is likely that MGM will sell off most of the art collection.

SO23 Paris Las Vegas

1998–1999, Leidenfrost, Horowitz and Associates, and Bergman, Walls & Youngblood Ltd. 3655 Las Vegas Blvd. S.

One of the Strip's newest hotel-casinos, Paris Las Vegas continues the trend of drawing on a well-known European city for its theme, following the success of Bellagio (SO22). Like New York New York (SO24), Paris confronts the visitor with landmarks of a great city, in this case dominated by a 50-story replica of the Eiffel Tower with glass elevators that carry guests to an observation deck at the top. Nearby are two-thirds-scale replicas of other icons of the City of Light: the Arc de Triomphe, the facade of the Louvre (incorporating a restaurant with outdoor seating), and the Paris Opera, all intended as accurate representations. As in other newer resorts, the desire for authenticity creates a hyperreal environment in which structures appear realistic but use faux materials, such as styrofoam and clay for stone and painted rivets for metal ones. The tri-wing hotel tower, rising thirty-four stories and containing 2,916 rooms, applies decorative details from the Hôtel de Ville to a formulaic shape, seen in a number of other Strip resorts, that reveals the influence of corporate hotel architecture. Despite its appeal to the new, Paris Las Vegas is yet another reworking of a now familiar paradigm.

The casino itself covers approximately 85,000 square feet. Though the space is crowded with slot machines and game tables, the Parisian theme continues inside. Three of the Eiffel Tower's four legs rise through the casino structure itself. Street scenes decorate the walls, and a painted twilight sky ornaments the 40-foot-high ceiling, helping to open up the rather claustrophobic, noisy space. Additional elements include cobblestone paths, ornate street signs, and a replica of the Pont Alexandre III. Connecting the hotel-casino to its neighbor, Bally's, is Le Boulevard, an enclosed mall with shops and restaurants that presents a Disney-esque version of the rue de la Paix, a Parisian shopping street.

SO24 New York New York

1995–1997, Gaskin and Bezanski; Yates-Silverman, interior. Las Vegas Blvd. S.

Continuing the trend of building ducks rather than decorated sheds, one of Las Vegas's newest casinos presents a compressed skyline of Manhattan. Modified versions of such famous landmarks as the Statue of Liberty, Ellis Island, the Empire State Building, and Lever House, at about one-third their actual size, rise from the base of a single building housing the casino. These towers contain hotel rooms and elevator shafts. Walking south on the Strip, visitors cross a scale model of the Brooklyn Bridge to enter the casino. Though these structures evoke their models, the garish colors, lights, and roller coaster racing around the exterior of the complex leave no doubt that this is Las Vegas. The dark interior, typical of many casinos, allows illuminated gambling machines to dominate the experience by shining brightly in the gloom. Yates-Silverman, a Las Vegas design firm responsible for many of the Strip's newest interiors, created echoes of Times Square and Little Italy as themes for various areas of the gambling floor; a large room called SoHo houses shops. The cage, where much of the casino's cash is stored, is hidden beyond a copy of the

New York Stock Exchange facade. Though New York is the theme, the casino's owners intended to re-create not contemporary Manhattan but rather the New York of a generation ago—a mythical and glamorous city. Only the crowds inside give New York New York the population density of the metropolis.

SO25 Luxor

1993, Veldon Simpson; Yates-Silverman, interior. 1996, hotel towers. 3900 Las Vegas Blvd. S.

Simpson designed this massive black glass pyramid to function as a sign directed less at motorists than at airline passengers. The Strip developed along the highway, but most visitors now arrive in Las Vegas by airplane. Only three blocks from the edge of McCarran International Airport, Luxor can be seen clearly from descending aircraft. The four-sided pyramid is unmistakable by day; laser lights shining from its tip display the building's edges by night. The ancient Egyptian theme is continued on the exterior by an enormous sphinx and, at roadside, an obelisk with the word "Luxor" running down its length.

Here, as in most of Simpson's recent casino designs, a low entry leads to a vast interior. Rooms are located on the perimeter of the pyramid, leaving an immense central space of 29 million cubic feet. The casino fills much of the space, but other attractions, including pylons, porticoes, and, upstairs, a reconstruction of King Tutankhamen's tomb, also provide entertainment. Always expanding, Luxor gained two stepped, pyramid-shaped hotel towers to the north of the main structure in 1996.

SO26 Little Church of the West

1942, Walter Zick and Harris Sharp Architects, and William J. Moore. 4617 Las Vegas Blvd. S.

The first known structure designed and built exclusively for use as a wedding chapel in Las Vegas, this modest Neo-Gothic wood-frame church stands at the south end of the Strip. The dark-stained cedar board-and-batten siding and minimal decoration were meant to make the chapel look like a church in a western frontier town. The steeply pitched gable roof covers a cathedral ceiling with exposed beams. California redwood clads the interior walls and is used for the altar. The chapel owes its remarkable survival from the early days of the Strip to its small size, which has enabled three moves from

SO24 New York New York (above)

SO25 Luxor (right)

SO26 Little Church of the West (below)

its original site. Initially built in 1942 by the Last Frontier Casino on the Strip, the building was moved first in 1954 to another part of the casino property, then in 1979 to the grounds of the Hacienda Hotel after the Last Frontier was demolished. Since 1979, independent owners have operated the chapel. In 1996 the building was moved again before Circus Circus Enterprises (now known as Mandalay Resort Group) imploded the Hacienda to make way for a new mega-resort. Like every other building on the Strip, the little church has a roadside sign supported by a dark brown column and surmounted by a steeply pitched gable roof.

SO27 University of Nevada, Las Vegas

1956, many additions. 4505 Maryland Pkwy. (roughly bounded by Tropicana Ave., Maryland Pkwy., and Flamingo and Paradise rds.)

The University of Nevada, Las Vegas (UNLV), has grown, like its city, at a tremendous rate. Opened in 1951 as an extension program of the University of Nevada, Reno, it soon became a junior college. In 1969 the school became a full-fledged member of the state's university system; today it is the largest.

The campus was established in 1956 with the groundbreaking for its first building, Maude Frazier Hall. Now covering 335 acres in southeastern Las Vegas, not far from the Strip and McCarran International Airport, the university has over 20,000 students. Though some residential neighborhoods are located nearby, most of the faculty and staff live all over the Las Vegas Valley.

The same is true of students; only a little over 1,000 live on campus. The buildings, many designed by local architects, date from the 1950s to the present and represent a variety of styles from modern to postmodern. The main entrance to the campus faces Maryland Parkway. In the local manner of siting, parking lots front the road, and buildings are set far back from the street.

The landscape design is perhaps the most impressive part of the complex, incorporating native desert plants and a drought-tolerant demonstration garden. Two quadrangles form a right angle at the northeast corner of the campus, creating large public spaces lined by buildings. One of Nevada's earliest examples of public art, *Flashlight* (1981), a 38-foot-tall sculpture by Claes Oldenburg and Coosje van Bruggen, stands in the plaza between the fine arts and performing arts buildings.

Despite the cohesiveness of the quads, UNLV's rapid growth has made overall planning difficult. The school has had three master plans over the years, none of which has been followed for long. In addition, UNLV has made some puzzling planning decisions, perhaps motivated by the need for money. Though the university had an opportunity to establish its presence at the busy intersection of Tropicana Avenue and Maryland Parkway, it sold the land; now a gas station, bank, and fast-food restaurants mirror the strip development of the other corners. Given its location in the middle of Las Vegas, UNLV can be considered an urban campus, yet it still looks inward, reflecting a more suburban approach to development. On campus, the only reminder that the university is near one of the world's greatest

SO27.3 James R. Dickinson Library

tourist centers is the constant noise of passenger airplanes approaching and leaving the airport.

SO27.1 Maude Frazier Hall

1956–1957, Walter Zick and Harris Sharp Architects

Named after Maude Frazier, an educator and legislator who helped found UNLV, this unassuming, one-story white-painted structure is historically significant as the first building on campus. The long, angular structure has a wide cornice of plain stuccoed panels above walls punctuated by doors and plate glass windows. It stands at the main entrance to the campus on Maryland Parkway, providing a transition between that busy street and the university's main north-south quadrangle.

SO27.2 William D. Carlson Education Building

1971–1972, Jack Miller and Associates

Many American universities have a legacy of Brutalist design, and UNLV is no exception. One of two buildings in this style on the campus is the three-story concrete education building, near the intersection of UNLV's two quadrangles. A curved fascia softens the building's chunky, rectangular shape, and its white-painted walls, in contrast to the bare gray concrete typical of Brutalism, subdue the visual effect of the rough surfaces and evenly spaced perforations left by the concrete molds. Despite its Brutalist style, the building exhibits features that reveal the architects' attention to the site and its location in the desert. Most of the large windows are recessed or shaded by slanting panels above to keep out the sun; this is especially important on the long south side of the structure.

SO27.3 James R. Dickinson Library

1965–1967, James McDaniel. 1981, JMA Architects

UNLV's library, designed by a local architect, won a design award from the American Institute of Architects in 1965, two years before its completion. Since then, the building has had few alterations apart from the closing of the original main entrance. White aggregate panels clad the walls around two bands of recessed windows. A low dome swells over the center of the building. Inside, on the top floor below the dome, recessed floodlights illuminate the ceil-

ing, evoking stars. The unsympathetic rectangular addition at the north by JMA Architects (1981) overwhelms the original structure. Narrow columns support its bulky red and white facade. A red skyway with round bubble windows connects the new building to the old one. Upon completion of the Lied Library, these two buildings will become administrative offices and the home of UNLV's William S. Boyd School of Law, established in 1997.

SO27.4 Paul B. Sogg Architecture Building

1996–1997, Swisher and Hall

Construction of the Sogg Building not only provided much-needed space for the UNLV School of Architecture but also enabled the school to satisfy accreditation requirements. When the school began as the Architectural Studies Program in the 1980s it was housed in a collection of construction trailers that did not meet the standards of the National Architecture Accrediting Board. It launched a design competition for its building in 1991. The process went awry, however, when a controversy developed over whether architects on the school's faculty could compete. Although the local partnership JMA Architects/Lucchesi-Galati initially received the commission, they eventually lost it to second-place Swisher and Hall of Las Vegas, with Barton Myers as design consultant. Professional disagreements leading to Myers's exit from the project, along with budget constraints and design changes, resulted in a large warehouse of a building, representing a missed opportunity to design a distinguished—or even functionally satisfactory—structure. The building does, however, respond in small ways to its environment. Drought-resistant plants surround the school and metal-screen fins shelter narrow windows from the southern sun.

The School of Architecture offers undergraduate degrees in four programs—architecture, interior architecture and design, landscape architecture, and urban planning—as well as a master of architecture degree. Though it is currently a small school, it is growing rapidly. All the programs focus on the unique environment of the Las Vegas area in order to address issues of designing for a desert climate and the needs of tourism and recreation.

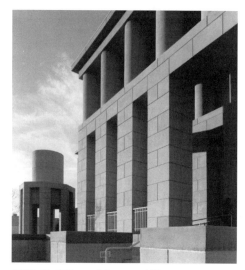

SO28   Clark County Library and Theater

SO27.5 Donald W. Reynolds Student Services Complex

1993–1994, Holmes Sabatini

One of the better-planned buildings at UNLV in terms of its siting and interaction with surrounding buildings, the student services complex reaches out toward campus with a two-story, barrel-vaulted entry. The warm tones of the stucco and stone walls are those of the desert environment. The cylindrical tower, rising over the central lobby and ending in a clerestory, opens up the interior space and serves as an anchor for two long wings that accommodate offices for student services and a center for advising, tutoring, and testing. The complex also contains the Jean Nidetch Women's Center.

SO28 Clark County Library and Theater

1971, Edwards and Daniels Associates. 1986, Fielden and Associates. 1991–1994, Michael Graves with JMA Architects. 1401 E. Flamingo Rd.

Following Antoine Predock's library and museum on Las Vegas Boulevard, Graves's library redesign and theater addition continued the county library district's efforts to create architecturally exceptional branch libraries that include cultural functions. The original structure, built in 1971, had already been remodeled once, but Graves's design completely altered and enlarged the library, introducing a theater and a new addition on the south side. The building's stucco walls are scored to resemble

stone and painted in warm tones of orange and pink. As one would expect in a work by Graves, the library exhibits a stripped classicism, which can be seen in its massive facades, unadorned wall planes, and simple cornice. In keeping with the automobile culture of Las Vegas, the main (south) entrance, through a central two-story portico with square piers on the first level and cylindrical ones above, is on the rear parking lot rather than facing Flamingo Road.

The entrance leads into the library's circulation area, which also functions as a gallery space for small exhibitions. Beyond are the reading area and other specialized sections of the library. The interior is brightly lit, with large windows along the east side. The theater lobby, down a short flight of steps from the main level of the library, is a simple space, long and narrow and lit by clerestory windows.

SO29 Las Vegas Mormon Temple

1989, Tate and Snyder, Architects. Northwest corner of Temple View Dr. and E. Bonanza Rd. Only temple grounds are open to the public.

Southern Nevada has long been home to a large community of Mormons, but it only recently acquired a temple. The temple is the most important building in the hierarchy of church structures, considered a physical representation of God's presence on earth, open only to church members for ordinances, such as sealing in marriage. Second to the temple is the tabernacle, also a sacred space but used for public worship. The meetinghouse, third in the hierarchy, is also a place of worship but accommodates other functions, including recreational activities, and is generally much smaller and simpler in design than the temple and the tabernacle.

Like Mormon temples around the country, this stunning example enjoys a prominent location in the city, in the foothills of Sunrise Mountain at the east edge of Las Vegas Valley. The walls are precast architectural concrete clad with white marble aggregate panels that contrast with the warm red tones of the rugged hills to the east. Thin vertical windows are set between steel posts, rising to a steeply angled copper roof ending in projecting points. Six gold-capped spires, perhaps a reference to the six spires of the Salt Lake City Temple (1853–1893), rise above the perimeter of the structure. A statue of the Angel Moroni covered with gold leaf tops the easternmost spire.

North Las Vegas

Today a booming city within the Las Vegas metropolitan area, North Las Vegas began in the 1910s as a sparsely populated, unregulated subdivision. During Prohibition it was known as an area of bootlegging, and in the 1930s it became a popular location for inexpensive housing. The establishment of the Las Vegas Army Air Corps Flexible Gunnery School (later Nellis Air Force Base) during World War II spurred growth in the 1940s and subsequent decades. In 1946 North Las Vegas incorporated and later was able to ward off annexation attempts by its larger neighbor to the south. Well into the 1960s, North Las Vegas was still known as a "slum," according to historian Eugene Moehring, but it has shaken the old image and is now a desirable bedroom community. The landscape is dominated by residential subdivisions popping up along the valley floor as fast as developers can build them.

SO30 Washington School

1932. 1901 N. White St.

Built shortly after the completion of Las Vegas High School, this one-story Moderne structure was one of many primary schools erected in the early 1930s to accommodate rapid population growth in Las Vegas. The building has a symmetrical cruciform plan formed by the main rectangle of the building with a projecting entry and a small rear rest-room wing. Concrete-block walls end in stepped parapets hiding a flat roof.

SO31 Nellis Air Force Base

1940, many additions. Craig Rd. Access by permission only

Founded in 1940 as the Las Vegas Army Air Corps Flexible Gunnery School, Nellis Air Force Base now covers over 2 million acres of land in southern Nevada—2.1 million acres for the bombing and gunnery range and 11,000 acres for the base. Its purpose is to train pilots. The original base included a rudimentary runway used by Western Air Express for commercial passenger and airmail flights. With the nation's entry into World War II, the base expanded to include barracks, aircraft hangars, and runways long enough to accommodate bombers. Since the 1950s, Nellis has continued to grow, eventually becoming a self-sufficient town of military, administrative, and domestic buildings. In the 1980s many of the wartime structures were stuccoed and given red tile roofs to create a Spanish Colonial Revival appearance, but overall the buildings are interesting because of the variety of types and forms they represent rather than for aesthetic reasons.

SO31.1 Base Operations Building
(McCarran Air Field Terminal)

1939, Wilson, Merrill, and Alexander. 1988, 1990s

This building is the only example on the base of the Pueblo Revival style dating from the

1930s and 1940s. The use of a regional architectural style reflects the building's originally planned function as a commercial Western Air Express depot serving as a gateway to Las Vegas and the Southwest. It was built jointly by the Army Air Force and the city of Las Vegas as part of a program to develop the terminal in conjunction with the army's need for a wartime gunnery school. After the war, the city agreed to construct a new commercial air terminal at the current site of McCarran International Airport, and the depot became part of the permanent military base. The Air Force has remodeled the building so many times that little of the original fabric remains. Stucco covers brick walls; windows have been replaced; and the interior has been virtually gutted and redone.

SO31.2 Thunderbird Hangar

1942, 1985–1986

Home of the Thunderbirds, the Air Force's aerobatic flight team, the 160-foot-by-200-foot hangar has a red, white, and blue exterior, distinguishing it from the other hangars on the base. A steel Warren truss system, clad in metal panels, supports the structure. The gable ends consist of ten sliding-door sections, each glazed with multipane metal sashes. The Thunderbirds have used the hangar since 1986.

SO31.3 Conference Center (Recreation Center, School)

1943, 1987

The conference center originally functioned as an Air Training Command school with twenty-five classrooms. In 1954 the Air Force converted the building into a recreation center, and in 1987 into a conference center. This one-story, H-plan building originally had wood siding but has been heavily remodeled to fit in with the new Spanish Colonial Revival look of many of the base's buildings.

SO31.4 Ammunition Magazine (Building 1045)

1943

The magazine is one of six enclosed in a fenced compound across Craig Road from the core of the base. Concrete and earth form the structure, which is composed of two separate, freestanding

sections, each with a flat-topped triangular retaining wall of reinforced concrete. Railroad tracks running between these sections allowed easy delivery and removal of explosives. A ventilation shaft protrudes above the structure. The magazines were built to store ammunition and explosives used in practice combat maneuvers by the Air Force. They now store other materials.

Las Vegas Vicinity

SO32 Tule Springs Ranch, Floyd Lamb State Park

1914–1948. 9200 Tule Springs Rd.

Though only fifteen miles northwest of downtown Las Vegas, the old ranch, set in a quiet spot in the valley, feels much farther away. Natural springs made the area a watering hole for prehistoric animals and humans, and, later, a Native American campsite. However, its poor grazing, hot climate, and distance from any urban center discouraged development until the early twentieth century. The first owners of this property eked out a living on a small ranch, but it was not until the 1940s that Tule Springs flourished as a dude ranch, whose guests consisted mostly of socialites waiting for their Nevada divorces. The ranch could accommodate ten to twelve guests. In the 1960s, as Nevada's divorce industry declined, the property became a cattle ranch and then, in 1977, a state park, with little change in its dude-ranch appearance.

Most of the twenty-one buildings in the complex are one-story structures with concrete-block walls and wood-frame gable roofs. The core of the ranch is a cluster of buildings around a low hill, with tall trees, lawns, and roaming peacocks. To the north, the animal buildings and caretaker's house stand in a row running east-west. Just to the north of these is a large barn. Many of the buildings are closed to the public, although the grounds are open.

SO32.1 Visitor Center (Foreman's House)

1940s

The largest domestic building on the ranch, this house has a small central entry section with a low porch flanked by lower, increasingly recessed room sections. A low ell extends from the rear. Gable ends are sheathed with horizontal wood boards, and the concrete block walls are covered with thick paint. Most windows are metal casement; some wrap around the building's corners in a manner derived from publications about the International Style.

SO32.2 **Guest House**

1940s

The long, rectangular house, built for guests establishing residency for Nevada divorces, stands at the north end of the ranch's domestic area. A full-length, shed-roofed porch resting on square columns shades doors and windows on the south facade, which faces the other domestic buildings. The building has a rustic quality that is entirely in keeping with the ranch setting.

SO32.3 **Water Tower**

1940s

This picturesque tower rises at the top of the hill around which the domestic buildings cluster. The wood-frame structure has a clapboarded base that tapers to a second story, with vertical wood siding and rectangular vents, which contains the tank. The tapered frame maximizes support for the water tank above. The change in siding differentiates the two sections of the structure, and the vertical siding emphasizes the tower's height. A narrow balcony with a plain wood railing extends around three sides of the tower at the juncture of the two sections and rests on beams with exposed ends. A low-pitched hipped roof with exposed rafters flares over the structure.

SO32.4 **Adobe Hut**

c. 1914–1918

Early settlers in the Las Vegas Valley frequently used adobe as a building material because it was more readily available than wood and because of its natural insulating characteristics. Few adobe buildings remain in good condition. This small hut, made of adobe blocks and mortar, shows extensive deterioration from the elements, but parts of its wood roof and wood window and door frames survive. A large open shed constructed over the hut after the site became a state park has offered some protection from further damage.

SO33 **Spring Mountain Ranch** (Sandstone Ranch)

1867, many additions. 5 miles west of the Blue Diamond turnoff, Red Rock Canyon National Conservation Area

The ranch is one of the oldest settled sites in the Las Vegas Valley. Its fifty-two springs made it an ancient watering hole that attracted Native Americans and, later, Euro-American settlers. By the 1830s it had become a campsite for explorers using the alternate route of the Spanish Trail between Santa Fe and Los Angeles. Continued habitation from the 1860s to the 1970s has left a variety of buildings and structures, ranging from late nineteenth-century stone cabins to a mid-nineteenth-century main house and outbuildings. Jim Wilson and his heirs ran the property as a cattle ranch through the 1920s. The ranch continued operation under several owners, including Howard Hughes, who used his wealth as an aviation mogul to buy up numerous properties in Las Vegas and the surrounding area in the late 1960s. In 1974 the state's acquisition of the ranch saved it from becoming a residential subdivision. The idyllic setting in Red Rock Canyon has abundant water and vegetation and is noticeably cooler than the desert site of Las Vegas, only fifteen miles to the east. The park is open to the public, and many of the buildings are open for either guided or self-guided tours.

SO33.1 **Visitor Center** (Main House)

1948–1955

Chester Lauck, a radio entertainer, built the house and ran a boys' camp on the ranch. Constructed of native stone, with a wood-shingle roof and redwood siding, the house stands on a hill with a commanding view of the ranch and the Wilson Cliffs. The stone living-room wing, facing north, contains the main entrance, sheltered by a shed-roofed porch. To the west is a two-story wing with a similar porch along its west side, built in 1955 when Vera Krupp, wife of the German munitions industrialist, purchased the property. To the east is a round tower with a conical roof. Another wing leads to a gambrel-roofed garage with stone walls and wood-clad gable ends. The rustic, sprawling style of the house is well suited to the ranch atmosphere and reflects earlier building materials and forms on the property.

SO33.1 Visitor Center (Main House)

SO33.2 Chinchilla Shed

1929–1935

Willard George, a Hollywood furrier who owned the ranch from 1929 to the mid-1940s, had this one-story, rectangular fieldstone shed built for raising chinchillas. These small South American rodents were introduced to the United States in 1923 and raised for their fine-textured fur. Stone was well suited as a building material for this shed because it provided insulation against the desert heat. Stone may also have been used to provide protection from predators such as coyotes.

SO33.3 Cabin

1867–1868

Jim Wilson and his adopted sons lived in this one-room, gable-roofed sandstone cabin, one of the oldest buildings remaining on the ranch. The early cabins constructed here are clustered on the northwestern part of the ranch, where large trees provide shade. A small wooden shed projects from the southeast end of the facade in line with a small shed-roofed porch covering the remainder of the facade. The thick stone walls of the cabin keep the interior cool even during the hottest time of day.

SO33.4 Blacksmith Shop

1867–1868

Like the cabin, the blacksmith shop is constructed of native sandstone. The low-pitched roof barely rises above the walls, giving the interior a low ceiling and a closed-in feeling. Various blacksmithing tools remain in the shop. A shed porch rests on a worn tree trunk in front. The structure, which had been deteriorating, underwent extensive restoration work in the 1980s. Both the blacksmith shop and Jim Wilson's cabin are believed to be the only structures of their type in the Las Vegas Valley and are certainly among the oldest buildings in the area.

SO34 Camp Lee Canyon

1937–1946, Works Progress Administration. NV 156, approximately 45 miles northwest of Las Vegas

Camp Lee Canyon is one of several federally funded projects built in the Las Vegas area during the Great Depression. The camp was built on seventeen acres of land on Mt. Charleston given to the U.S. Department of Agriculture in 1936. The U.S. Forest Service currently owns the property and leases it to Clark County as a summer campsite used mainly by area residents. The WPA, using local labor and materials, built most of the nineteen buildings in 1937. The structures are ranged along both sides of a dirt road running through a heavily wooded narrow canyon. The majority of the buildings are wood-frame with gable roofs and beveled siding of alternating wide and narrow boards. Their utilitarian design, typical of WPA architecture, has served the camp well over the decades.

SO34.1 **Cabin**

1937

This one-story, rectangular cabin has a steeply pitched gable roof with a central brick chimney. The symmetrical facade has a central door flanked by pairs of windows with plain surrounds. The interior consists of one large room with concrete floors, plaster walls, and tongue-and-groove wood walls. Wood floors once covered the concrete, and stoves were once connected to the chimney, but these have been removed. Nevertheless, all the cabins at the camp appear much as they did when they were constructed. The building is typical of the simple facilities provided at camps built by the federal government in the 1930s. The cabins at Camp Lee Canyon continue to serve the public today.

SO34.2 **Recreation Hall** (Administrative Building)

1937

One of the largest buildings at the camp, this one-story, L-shaped hall was built as the administrative building and included space for a small infirmary, recreation hall, and staff offices. One ell contains a large recreation room featuring a high ceiling open to the gable roof and a massive stone chimney. The other wing contains five small rooms, a lounge, a kitchen, and a bathroom. All of these rooms have wood floors and tongue-and-groove wood ceilings.

SO33.3 Cabin (top)

SO34.1 Cabin (bottom)

Henderson

Compared with Las Vegas, Henderson is a newcomer in southern Nevada. It began as Basic Townsite, a suburb for workers at the Basic Magnesium plant. Contractors for the federal government constructed the plant in 1941 to produce magnesium—the main ingredient of incendiary bombs—from magnesite and brucite, mined in Gabbs 300 miles to the north. The abundant water and energy supplied by Hoover Dam made the Las Vegas area an attractive location for wartime industries.

Workers were in such short supply during the war that African Americans from the South were brought to Henderson to work at Basic. Because of the company's segregation policies, in 1943 it established a separate townsite, Carver Park, to house African American workers; others lived in Las Vegas's Westside. One-story buildings of wood or concrete accommodated families in one-, two-, or three-bedroom apartments and single workers in dormitories. The complex, designed by Paul Revere Williams, an African American architect in Los Angeles, was demolished in 1974.

Until recently, Henderson, incorporated in 1953, retained its blue-collar industrial image because of its association with Basic and companies that subsequently used the complex. In the past two decades, however, Henderson, like many other Las Vegas–area communities, has grown rapidly, expanding its middle- and upper-class neighborhoods through the development and construction of planned districts, such as Green Valley and Lake Las Vegas. The small company town has evolved into a city of over 100,000 residents. From 1990 to 1996, Henderson was the nation's fastest-growing city, and is expected to surpass Reno as Nevada's second largest city in the next few years. Gaming corporations have also discovered Henderson as a place to build casinos aimed at a burgeoning local audience rather than the international clientele catered to by the larger, more opulent casinos along the Las Vegas Strip. In recent years Henderson has seen the construction of several casinos along the "Boulder Strip"—the nickname for Boulder Highway, connecting Las Vegas and Boulder City via Henderson.

SO35 Henderson Townsite

Thirteen thousand construction workers, living in a tent city, hastily erected a town and the adjacent Basic Magnesium plant in 1941–1942. One thousand wood-frame houses, in two- and three-bedroom models, lined the streets. Schools, stores, churches, a library, a theater, a hospital, and a bowling alley soon rounded out the burgeoning town.

Although designed as temporary dwellings, many Henderson houses survive. Their small size has encouraged owners to build additions, raise roofs, and install new windows, but a few examples with unaltered exteriors remain. One of these is a two-bedroom house (c. 1942) at 214 Gold Street. The one-story, wood-frame structure on a concrete slab is covered by drop siding of redwood. Though inexpensively built, the house was designed to suit the desert landscape. The flat roof has overhangs to shade the house, and a swamp cooler sits atop the roof. The cheap electricity provided by Hoover Dam made the operation of swamp coolers affordable, even for the owners of these low-cost buildings. Windows and doors are aligned to provide cross ventilation.

The original townsite, in the southwest quadrant of the intersection of Boulder Highway and Lake Mead Drive, is marked by short curved streets. Street names such as Gold, Zinc, Basic, and Tungsten recall the neighborhood's connection to the factory complex. Some of the original industrial buildings can still be seen nearby along Lake Mead Drive.

SO36 Heritage Street, Clark County Heritage Museum

1830 S. Boulder Hwy.

On its grounds the Clark County Heritage Museum has created a street where historic houses have found a permanent location. These buildings come from various parts of Clark County, including Las Vegas, Henderson, and Boulder City. This complex has examples of dwellings preserved in their original or near-original state that cannot be found elsewhere. However, historic house "graveyards" cannot re-create the buildings' original settings.

SO36.1 Townsite House

c. 1942

This one-story house with a classic flat roof, drop siding, and roof-mounted swamp cooler, characteristic of Townsite dwellings, is the only example with an intact interior that is open to the public. A flat-roofed porch supported on square wood posts shelters half of the facade, including the front entrance. The only decorative touches are the small curved brackets joining the porch beams to the house. The restored interior is compactly arranged, containing two small bedrooms, kitchen, living room, dining room, and bathroom. Interior walls and ceilings are sheathed in $1/4$-inch plywood with battens covering the seams.

SO36.2 Babcock and Wilcox House

1933, E. D. Wagner

This one-story, wood-frame dwelling is a rare surviving example of a worker's house erected by the Babcock and Wilcox Company, which built the steel penstocks for Hoover Dam as subcontractors. The L-shaped dwelling has a hipped roof stretching forward to cover an enclosed porch. Windows set in pairs pierce the clapboard-sided walls. This house and eleven identical ones stood at the center of Boulder City. In 1987 the buildings were auctioned and moved to make way for the construction of a new post office. At that time this house was donated to the Clark County Heritage Museum.

SO37 The Reserve

1995–1998, Conversano and Associates. 777 W. Lake Mead Dr.

Based on the theme of an African safari, the Reserve scarcely resembles any building one might see in Africa. Instead, it looks more like a mixture of the Pueblo Revival style, with its softly contoured buttresses and end towers, and a faintly German or Dutch expressionist style of the early twentieth century, seen in the flamelike forms atop the towers. Its design, inspired by a sense of drama and fantasy, is one of the more unusual among casinos in the Las Vegas area. The exterior walls are a dark reddish-brown color to suggest that the building was constructed of stone from the surrounding mountains. The walls display large applied arches, which frame murals of the sun setting on an African savanna, complete with silhouettes of elephants, giraffes, and other African wildlife. Towers at the building's northwest corner and at both ends of the hotel section terminate in large golden flaming urns. Perched atop slender attached columns ending below the level of the urns are golden monkeys holding torches. The casino's giant sign continues the safari theme with supports made to look like enormous elephant tusks. Both the sign and the building itself are oriented toward the intersection of I-515 and Lake Mead Drive in order to take advantage of traffic on these roads.

The entrance to the casino is covered by a large porte-cochere made to resemble a large canvas awning. The interior re-creates a jungle, with tall fake trees and carved wood statues of wildlife. The ceiling has moving cloud formations, with a "sky" that turns from day to night, opening up the interior space in a manner similar to that of the Forum Shops at Caesars Palace and of Sunset Station (see next entry). Overall, the Reserve is small by Las Vegas standards; the casino covers 37,000 square feet, and the hotel tower contains only 224 rooms. However, it stands on fifty-three acres of land, allowing its owners the option of future expansion.

SO38 Sunset Station

1996–1998, Morris-Brown. 1303 W. Sunset Rd.

Rising from the middle of a large parking lot, Sunset Station looks not unlike the Galleria Mall across the street, except that its Spanish/Mediterranean theme gives the exterior a more elaborate appearance than that of most malls. Like other casinos along the Boulder Strip, Sunset Station was intended to appeal to a largely local audience, but its size, well-defined theme, and ornate interior put it a step above most older casinos in the Henderson area. Domed towers, painted to look colorfully tiled, rise above the casino and its porte-cochere, vaguely suggesting a Mediterranean town. To the east stands the hotel tower, whose curved parapets vaguely evoke baroque missions.

The most interesting feature of the complex is inside. In the center of the 100,000-square-foot casino is the Gaudí Bar, a marvel of stained glass, tile, and curvilinear forms reminiscent of Antonio Gaudí's Casa Milá in Barcelona. Sunset Station also draws on elements of Las Vegas Strip casinos, most notably the Forum Shops at Caesars Palace. Part of the casino has varied building facades with a sky ceiling above, giving the interior the feel of narrow village streets. These features, as well as numerous restaurants, a twenty-four-screen cineplex, and a video arcade, are intended to attract a younger, more affluent audience currently populating Henderson.

SO39 Tate and Snyder Design Studio

1995, Tate and Snyder. 709 Valle Verde Ct.

A strong addition to southern Nevada's emerging regional architecture, this 9,000-square-foot studio has been designed in harmony with the desert landscape. The two-story structure, built into a steep hillside, has its main entrance on the second story. Tall glass windows on the south take advantage of natural light and spectacular views. Fins project inward between the windows, widening at the top to soften the effects of the intense desert light. The main space is the studio itself, with a two-story ceiling and clerestory windows. The architects used materials often found in rural Nevada, such as galvanized metal for the roof and corrugated metal for the ceilings. Ochre, used both inside and out, reflects the coloring of the desert.

Boulder City and Hoover Dam

Boulder City is an anomaly in Nevada. The small town seven miles southwest of Hoover Dam has a distinct center and architecture unified by the Spanish Colonial Revival style. The federal government and the Six Companies consortium of major western contracting firms (Utah Construction Co., Pacific Bridge Co., Henry J. Kaiser and W. A. Bechtel Co., MacDonald and Kahn Co., Morrison-Knudsen Co., and J. F. Shea Co.) designed and built the city to house construction workers near Boulder Dam (as Hoover Dam was originally named) be-

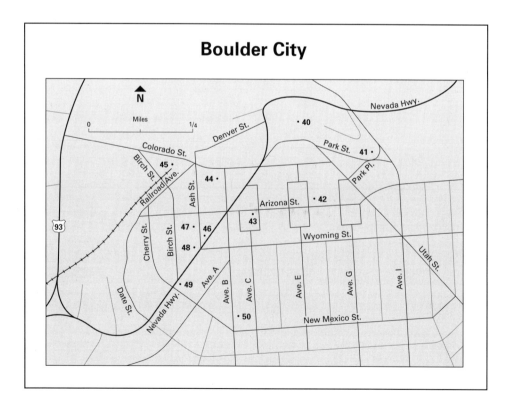

tween 1931 and 1935. Dutch-born city planner and landscape designer Saco R. DeBoer, known primarily for his design of parks and parkways in Denver, laid out Boulder City in civic, commercial, and residential zones, with a hilltop site for Bureau of Reclamation buildings. As a government town, Boulder City prohibited gambling and drinking, and remains today the only municipality in the state that prohibits gambling. Since it incorporated and received most of the townsite's property from the federal government in 1960, its residents have fought hard to retain a small-town character, partly by voting against proposed subdivisions.

Despite the loosening of the federal government's hold over the town, the Bureau of Reclamation maintains a strong presence through its supervision of Hoover Dam's operations. The bureau's offices are located in the old administration and dormitory buildings on the hill at the head of the city's central park. From there, the main roads radiate in a triangular shape filling the saddle between two hills. Along these roads are houses built for the managers and engineers of the dam project; downhill are more modest single-family houses, duplexes, apartments, and the commercial strip along the Nevada Highway. Many of the more than 400 structures erected by the federal government and the Six Companies consortium still stand, but about half of them have been altered over the years.

so40 **U.S. Bureau of Reclamation Administration Building**

1932, U.S. Bureau of Reclamation. North side of Park St. just east of Nevada Hwy.

The administration building, designed in a simplified Spanish Colonial Revival style, commands a spot on one of the two hills overlooking the city. Spreading below the building is a large park with mature trees. The two-story concrete building has an H-shaped plan with end sections projecting slightly forward and backward from the main mass. Cast concrete surrounds with quoins, a second-floor arcade, and a promi-

nent cornice mark the central entrance. The Bureau of Reclamation completed a major renovation of the building in 1994. At that time it also renovated the Administration Annex, originally Government Dormitory No. 1, next door.

so41 **House**

1932, U.S. Bureau of Reclamation. 700 Park St.

One of four houses that the Bureau of Reclamation built for its department heads, this two-story brick dwelling stands on a prominent curved hillside lot. The four-bedroom house—

SO40 U.S. Bureau of Reclamation Administration Building

SO41 House

one of the largest in town when it was built—has a cantilevered balcony and carved detailing of the porch eaves and exposed deck beams. Steel casement windows on the first floor have paneled wood shutters. The building displays an eclectic mix of styles, generally with Spanish references.

SO42 **Boulder City Hall** (Boulder City Elementary School)
1932, U.S. Bureau of Reclamation. 900 Arizona St.

Built for the elementary- and high-school-age children of dam workers, the Spanish Colonial Revival building has a dignified appearance and location at the center of town, which favored its adaptation as the city's administrative premises. The hall has concrete walls clad with brick and a hipped roof of red tiles. The main entry is surrounded by a two-story projecting arcade of three arches sheltering double doors leading into the central lobby. Decorative brickwork in a geometric pattern enlivens the end walls and the frieze running around the building under the roofline.

SO43 **Boulder Dam Hotel**
1933–1935, L. Henry Smith. 1305 Arizona St.

Boulder Dam Hotel, near the historic business district, provided elegant lodgings for visitors during the period of the dam's construction. Built in the Colonial Revival style, faintly echoing Mount Vernon, the hotel is unusual for Boulder City. It became a popular destina-

tion in the 1930s, when it offered the only lodgings in town. Originally U-shaped, the hotel underwent an expansion in 1935 that gave it an H-shaped plan. Exterior walls are concrete block rising to gable roofs. A two-story, full-length porch with paneled square columns covers the main facade. Pilasters and quoins flank the front entrance, topped by a pediment.

SO44 **House**
1932, U.S. Bureau of Reclamation. 412 Avenue B

Built as a temporary dwelling for a bureau employee and his family, this is one in a row of thirty identical houses erected when construction activity at the dam increased. More than sixty years later the cottages are still in use, though many have been altered. This one retains much of its original appearance. It follows a simple rectangular plan with clapboard-sided, wood-frame walls. A side-gabled roof has exposed rafter ends continued in the shed-roofed porch covering half of the facade and one gable end. The L-shaped porch was designed as a sleeping porch but has been converted into additional rooms.

SO45 **Water Filtration Plant**
1932, U.S. Bureau of Reclamation. 300 Railroad Ave.

Standing on a hill above the city, the plant, with its brick walls, square hip-roofed tower, and red tile roof, looks a bit like a Tuscan farmhouse. A two-story rectangular mass covered by a gable roof abuts the tower. Quoins decorate the cor-

SO43 Boulder Dam Hotel

SO48 Los Angeles Department of Water and Power Building (Los Angeles Bureau of Power and Light Administration and Maintenance Building)

ners of the main mass and tower. Smaller one-story sections surround the core of the plant, which provided Boulder City with its first potable water.

so46 **Coffee Cup Cafe**

c. 1940. 556 Nevada Hwy.

One of the best-preserved commercial structures from Boulder City's early years, the Coffee Cup is a concrete block structure with an irregular footprint following the oddly shaped corner lot on which it stands. The main facade has large windows and two entrances into the restaurant. A small hip-roofed tower sits atop the low-slung core of the building. Overhanging eaves have exposed rafters characteristic of the regional vernacular.

so47 **Duplexes**

1942, Los Angeles Bureau of Power and Light. 508–526 Ash St.

The Los Angeles Bureau of Power and Light (see next entry) built this complex of five duplexes around the corner from its Boulder City offices. Arranged in a U-shaped plan opening toward the street, the one-story buildings have brick walls rising from a concrete foundation. Though simple, the duplexes have well-designed features, including full-length front porches supported by pairs of square posts, bay windows on stone foundations, and pairs of porthole windows.

so48 **Los Angeles Department of Water and Power Building** (Los Angeles Bureau of Power and Light Administrative and Maintenance Building)

1940, Los Angeles Bureau of Power and Light. 600 Nevada Hwy.

The Los Angeles Department of Water and Power (LADWP), today the largest municipally owned utility in the nation, was one of two companies that operated power generators at Hoover Dam (the other was Southern California Edison). From 1936 to 1987, the Bureau of Reclamation contracted with the LADWP to run thirteen of Hoover Dam's generating units to supply power to southern California, Arizona, and Nevada. In the 1930s and early 1940s, the dam supplied nearly 75 percent of Los Angeles's power; by 1987 it supplied only 5 percent, as the city had turned to other sources of electricity. The LADWP's role in operating a part of the dam's power plant required a physical presence in Boulder City, represented by its administrative building.

The building, on a wedge-shaped corner lot along the main thoroughfare, is eclectic in its sources of design. An octagonal tower topped by a faceted sphere anchors the building at the corner; two one-story wings radiate along the street sides of the lot. Concrete blocks held together with thick, dripping mortar give the walls a rustic appearance. A paneled door leads into a lobby with a colorful tiled floor. Behind the lobby stands a large auditorium with exposed wood beams.

When the LADWP's contract ended in 1987, the Lower Colorado Regional Office of the Bureau of Reclamation took over all aspects of operation at Hoover Dam's power plant, and the LADWP vacated the building. In 1995, the city of Los Angeles turned over ownership of the building to Boulder City, which uses it for community functions.

so49 **Apartments**

1942, U.S. Bureau of Reclamation. 641 Nevada Hwy.

This plain, two-story building reflects the simplified forms favored by the federal government at the beginning of World War II. Built by the Defense Housing Corporation, it was one of seven identical structures that made up the Cherry Lynn Apartments, which housed employees working at the Basic Magnesium plant in Henderson. The buildings form a courtyard, with entrances facing the street or the court.

SO50 House

1931, George DeColmesnil. 651 Avenue B

One of the few remaining unaltered cottages built by the Six Companies, this house represents the early vernacular structures erected for married blue-collar dam workers. This housing type spread over much of the original town, along the base of the triangular plan. The one-story, wood-frame building has stuccoed walls, a front-gabled roof with a gabled vent, and plain door and window surrounds. A small shed-roofed porch stands off center along the facade.

SO51 Hoover Dam (Boulder Dam)

1931–1935, Gordon B. Kaufmann, U.S. Bureau of Reclamation. Approximately 7 miles east of Boulder City on U.S. 93

The first dam to hold back the waters of the mighty Colorado River, Hoover Dam can be regarded as a symbol either of human ingenuity or of human arrogance. Its construction drastically changed southern Nevada's landscape by filling in a dramatically beautiful canyon and creating Lake Mead, a 115-mile-long lake that flooded prehistoric and historic settlements. Built as Boulder Dam, it was renamed in 1947 for President Herbert Hoover.

The enormous resources marshaled to construct what was at the time the largest dam in the world signified the nation's determination to accomplish monumental engineering feats during the Great Depression. At the peak of construction, over 5,000 people worked on the project. The dam stands 726.4 feet high, and its crest length is 1,244 feet. The top width measures 45 feet; the bottom width 660 feet. The power plant at the base of the dam has two wings both roughly parallel with the river. Each is 650 feet long by 55 feet wide by 75 feet high. The Bureau of Reclamation uses the dam to control flooding and sediment deposits, to provide electric power, and to supply water for agricultural, domestic, and industrial use.

Even before the dam comes into view, the multitude of towers and power lines streaming across the landscape lead the way to it. As architecture, the concrete arch-gravity dam elegantly combines industrial design and a spare modern

style. Engineers chose this type of dam because the arch, with its convex side toward the lake, puts the concrete in compression, enabling the dam to carry the water load by both gravity action and horizontal arch action. A total of 6.6 million tons of concrete were used to build the dam. The concrete, made of a combination of coarse and fine aggregate for greater strength, was poured in blocks, then cooled by ice water run through pipes in the cement. Without this system the concrete would have taken more than a century to set. In addition to the practical uses of reinforced concrete, the material, used extensively beginning in the early twentieth century, was strongly associated with modernity and incorporated in a variety of buildings—industrial, commercial, and residential.

At the top of the dam, on the lakeside, rise the tops of four intake towers. By using the force of gravity, these channel water downward to penstocks—steel tubes 30 feet in diameter through which the water flows to set the turbines in motion. Sleek and metal-clad, the circular turbines punctuate long, austere chambers that flank the walls of the canyon near the base of the dam; rectangular windows mark these chambers on the exterior. Once released from the turbines, the water flows downstream, leaving the power plant complex through the Stoney Gate. Additional water enters the river from the Arizona Spillway tunnel that connects Lake Mead and the riverbed beyond the Stoney Gate.

Four square towers interspersed with small observation niches project above the top of the dam. Together these elements cast shadows along the crest of the dam, emphasizing the texture of the concrete. The outer towers house utilities and public rest rooms. The two inner towers—one in Nevada, one in Arizona—contain elevators that carry workers and visitors into the dam. As the public entrances to the dam, these towers display the only decorative treatment on the structure's exterior. Each has five concrete bas-reliefs executed by the sculptor Oskar J. W. Hansen; Nevada's tower depicts the benefits of Hoover Dam—flood control, navigation, irrigation, water storage, and power. Hansen also designed *Winged Figures of the Republic*, two 30-foot-tall bronze winged figures on a polished black diorite base, installed in a plaza of Hansen's design on the Nevada side of the river to commemorate the dam's construction. The U-shaped power plant, on the downstream side of the dam, nestled near the bot-

SO51 Hoover Dam (Boulder Dam)

tom of the canyon, has thick concrete walls, unadorned except for pilaster strips facing the water and flanking rows of windows. Four intake towers—two on the Nevada side, two on the Arizona side—rise on the upstream side of the dam. The towers, with their smooth piers and roofs topped by light globes, continue the dam's formal style.

SO52 Hoover Dam Visitor Center

1989–1995, Spencer Associates. West of Hoover Dam

SO51 Hoover Dam, urbine room

The Visitor Center, built into the canyon wall just downstream from the dam, appears as a blemish on the landscape because it consists primarily of a windowless cylinder of apricot-colored concrete. The idea may have been to imitate the dam's massive forms, but a design using the colors and textures of the dam or the landscape might have produced a more sensitive result. On one side is a glass tower, perhaps meant to recall the form of the dam's intake towers but more vividly recalling angular mannerisms in the late work of Frank Lloyd Wright. This is the main entrance to the center, but only while in this transitional element can visitors enjoy framed views of the scenery. Across U.S. 93 stands a six-story parking garage made of precast concrete components; it is equally insensitive to the dam's design but, having been blasted into the rock, is nearly hidden from several vantage points.

The center was constructed to help accommodate the more than one million annual visitors to the dam, thus taking pressure off the dam itself. The interior contains displays on the dam's construction and function, as well as a theater and a staging area for tours of the dam. Before its completion, the center became the focus of controversy when the public learned that it would cost nearly four times the originally estimated amount. Shocking, too, was the fact that it took twice as long to construct the center as it had to build the entire dam.

Laughlin

Laughlin is one of Nevada's newest boom towns, but unlike the mining towns that are often associated with this term, Laughlin's development rests entirely on gambling. In 1966 Don Laughlin bought a small beach along the Colorado River in the southern tip of Nevada wedged between Arizona and California. All that stood there at the time were a bait shop and a tiny motel. Laughlin already had a gambling license and was able to use that to build a small gambling empire, starting with the Riverside Hotel. By 1985 the town had only ninety-eight residents but was home to six large casinos that attracted tourists from neighboring states who preferred the low-key atmosphere to the glitter of Las Vegas. Today several high-rise hotel-casinos line the Nevada bank of the Colorado, a desert mirage including a riverboat, railroad, and frontier town. Laughlin's thriving economy has encouraged the construction of larger casinos, but the resorts here are still modest in design compared with their counterparts in Las Vegas.

As a border town, Laughlin has benefited from its proximity to large populations in Arizona and California. Extensive residential development did not occur until the mid-1980s, when

Clark County began providing services for the area and the federal government released land for private development. Though Laughlin faces stiff competition from the mega-resorts on the Las Vegas Strip, its rate of growth in the past ten years has often surpassed that of Las Vegas.

As a boom town, Laughlin is not without its problems. The focus on tourism and the scarcity of developable land have made the town's few residential areas extremely expensive. For workers in the gambling and tourism sector—the bulk of Laughlin's labor force—affordable housing has become a major problem. At various times, some workers have been forced to live in squatters' camps by the river. As in Nevada's other border towns, many employees live in the adjacent state and travel long distances to work. In recent years the county has constructed a library and public schools, and many new subdivisions now stand southwest of the casino center.

SO53 Riverside Hotel

1960s, 1970s, Rissman and Rissman. 1981, Frederick J. Perazzo. 1982, Martin J. Stern, Jr. 1994, Richard Youngblood. 1650 S. Casino Dr.

Like large casinos throughout Nevada, the Riverside has evolved almost continually since it began as a small motel in the 1960s. A separate casino building stood by the river until the 1970s, when major expansions began at a rapid pace. Today the Riverside has a large three-story casino serving as the base for two towers set perpendicular to one another. Martin J. Stern designed the north tower (1982) and Richard Youngblood the south tower (1994), which generally follows Stern's design. Both towers are slabs with columns of windows and gold metal cornices. Despite the increased competition from large casino chains such as the Flamingo Hilton and Harrah's, the Riverside remains a favorite destination of devoted regulars.

SO54 Colorado Belle

1986–1987, Marnell-Corrao. 2100 S. Casino Dr.

Unlike casinos in Las Vegas and Jean, which also take the form of a great riverboat, the Colorado Belle is actually located on a riverbank. Though the core of the building is a long rectangular block, decks, black smokestacks, and a large side paddlewheel give the building its distinctive appearance. As in other casinos, the Colorado Belle's interior shuts out any sense of the outdoors. It is inspired by a generic interpretation of late Victorian style, with dark red carpets and flocked wallpaper. A hotel tower stands to the north.

SO54 Colorado Belle

Goodsprings

Modest stone and wood-frame buildings, as well as a few water towers, remain from Goodsprings' early twentieth-century mining days. When the mines closed, the town managed to survive, though most of its downtown buildings are gone, and abandoned structures can be seen throughout the town. Today Goodsprings' location, about eight miles west of I-15 and the casinos of Jean, makes it a convenient place for casino workers' housing, though most commute from Las Vegas.

SO55 Goodsprings School

1913, C. W. Price. 1916, classrooms, Dodds and Williams. 1934, library. San Pedro Ave. approximately 100 feet east of Esmeralda St.

The Goodsprings School's additive plan reflects the changes the building has undergone to meet the town's needs. The one-story, T-shaped structure originally measured 21 by 40 feet and contained one classroom. Within three years, the school-age population had grown enough to need two more classrooms at the rear. In 1934 a small library room was built at the school's northwest corner. The building's wood frame and walls coated with cement plaster around 1934 rise to a hipped roof topped by a bell tower.

Nevada Test Site (Access by permission only)

Carved out of the Las Vegas (Nellis Air Force) Bombing and Gunnery Range in 1950, the Nevada Test Site covers 1,350 square miles of desert in southern Nevada, approximately eighty miles from Las Vegas. The Nevada congressional delegation fought hard for the test site, hoping that it would bring a much-needed economic boost to Las Vegas. The Atomic Energy Commission selected the site because it was already under government control and offered the advantages of dry, clear weather, fairly predictable winds, and vast unpopulated space. It designated areas where specific activities could take place, among them Mercury, Yucca Flat, and Frenchman Flat.

Mercury first accommodated a temporary camp to house workers. As the testing program geared up, the firm of Homes and Narver designed the town as the administrative and residential center of the test site. Quonset huts initially sheltered most functions. Now the buildings include wood-frame structures, concrete block dormitories and offices, and a trailer park.

Frenchman Flat was selected because its dry lake bed was well suited to testing and analyzing the results of explosions and effects of radiation on structures. Between 1951 and 1968, fourteen atmospheric and five underground tests occurred here. The military tested various building materials and forms to see which could withstand nuclear blasts. Today the site has an eerie quality, with scattered remnants of various tests bathed in the brilliant white sun.

Yucca Flat also became the site of many atmospheric and underground tests as well as radiation tests. Training exercises involving army troops at Camp Desert Rock took place here, in addition to tests used to analyze the results of bombing civilian areas. Parts of a town, built to replicate a suburban neighborhood, remain.

Between 1951 and 1963, when the signing of the Limited Nuclear Test Ban Treaty halted atmospheric testing, an average of twelve bombs per year exploded on the site. Underground testing continued until 1992. Since the 1992 moratorium on all nuclear testing, much of the test site has become something of a ghost town, though nonnuclear tests take place. Most scientific research now centers on the federal government's nuclear waste repository at Yucca Mountain. This site, 100 miles northwest of Las Vegas, could become the final resting place for all of the nation's highly radioactive nuclear waste.

The landscape of the test site appears remarkably untouched in areas that experienced atmospheric testing. Though dangerous areas are marked by signs warning visitors of high radiation levels, vegetation and animals have returned to these once-ruined areas. Underground testing has caused the most obvious physical damage. Subsidence craters, caused by the collapse of earth during the explosion of over 700 underground tests, form pockmarks across Yucca Flat. In the northwestern corner of the test site, rocky Pahute Mesa, the site of considerable underground testing, has shattered under the duress of numerous explosions.

The buildings at Mercury, like those at most other military installations, include Quonset huts, butler buildings, and concrete-block structures. Ordinary in appearance, the buildings and structures on the flats differ only in having been designed and built specifically for nuclear testing. Buildings of different materials and shapes, for example, aluminum domes of various thicknesses, were tested for resistance to physical damage during the detonation of bombs.

SO56 **Theater**

1954. Mercury

Quonset huts are among the most common building types at Mercury. This type of prefabricated, portable structure, developed for the U.S. military in 1941, was used extensively after the war because of its practicality and versatility. On the test site Quonsets provided storage space for autos and equipment and were also used for recreational purposes. This Quonset, which housed Mercury's theater, has no windows, only doors at the arched ends.

SO57 **Bailey Bridge**

c. 1955. Frenchman Flat

Built to test the effects on transportation systems of the 37-kiloton "Priscilla" detonation of 24 June 1957, this bridge embodied various types of bridge structures erected atop concrete bases. Four pairs of reinforced concrete walls support separate steel superstructures. The concrete weathered the blasts fairly well and still stands, though sections of reinforcing

bars are clearly visible. The steel fared worse; the superstructure is gone except for one section at the end.

SO58 **Domed Bunkers**

c. 1955. Frenchman Flat

This aluminum dome is one of a series made of aluminum or reinforced concrete and of various thicknesses for the "Priscilla" detonation. The explosion tore this dome's aluminum roof from its base, crushing and twisting it. Aluminum sustained more damage than concrete in this test.

SO59 **House**

1955. Yucca Flat

This two-story house is one of two left from the so-called Apple II test of the effects of nuclear blasts on civilian targets, including a complex of buildings, cars, communications equipment, and food supplies. The wood-frame house has a side-facing gable roof with clapboard siding over diagonal sheathing. The interior has ply-

SO59 House (left)

SO60 Japanese Village House (above)

wood walls and wood floors. A brick chimney stands at one end. The 29-kiloton Apple II test occurred on 5 May 1955; the house stood within 8,000 feet of ground zero. Although the building appears to be in relatively good condition, damage from the blast is clearly visible. The windows were blown out and the upper portion of the brick chimney has shifted slightly. A metal bracket now holds the chimney in place. Nearby is another house built for Apple II, identical in form except for its brick veneer.

SO60 Japanese Village Houses

1962. Yucca Flat

This village of three structures was designed to test the effects of radiation on wood-frame, Japanese-style houses. The houses were built as part of Operation BREN (Bare Reactor Experiment, Nevada), which was part of Project Ichiban. Ichiban was established to investigate

radiation fields from the Hiroshima and Nagasaki bombings by recording the location of survivors at the precise moment of the explosions and determining patterns of exposure to airborne radiation. Surveys showed that a significant percentage of bombing survivors were in their houses at the instant the bombs fell. Because of the structural similarity of these houses, further tests were conducted to determine what radiation-shielding qualities these buildings possessed. The site also included the BREN tower, from which radiation was released. This tower now stands at Area 25.

The most intact structure is a large (22-foot-by-37 1/2-foot) wood-frame house that originally stood two stories tall and had cement-asbestos board panels covering the exterior and a gable roof. The panels were used as a substitute for the mud and oyster-shell stucco used in traditional Japanese construction. The building stands on skids, ready to be moved to another part of the test site, although it was used only for this test and has never been moved. The frame is made of four-by-sixes, four-by-fours, and two-by-fours. Diagonal members brace the walls from sill to plate, and nails hold the posts together. Time has weathered the wood, and many nails have popped out, causing the top of the structure to collapse into the first floor. In its skeletal form the house seems eerie, standing on the flat with other frame remnants from Operation BREN.

Logandale

Logandale is located in the Moapa Valley near the Muddy River on the old site of St. Joseph, established in 1865 by Mormon settlers from Utah. Brigham Young had sent these settlers to establish orderly communities and produce cotton and other agricultural commodities to increase the self-sufficiency of the church. Though these missionaries set to work building adobe structures and planting fields, the difficulty of creating a sustainable agricultural community led them to abandon St. Joseph in 1870. In the 1880s Mormons returned to the site and established a viable community that was less strongly tied to the church. Today Logandale is a small farming community, though its proximity to Las Vegas, fifty-eight miles away, has drawn some new subdivisions.

SO61 Logandale Community Center (Logandale School)

SO61 **Logandale Community Center**
(Logandale School)

1935, 1938, Miles Miller. Northwest corner of NV 169 and Gann Ave.

This building consists of two parts. The first, a hip-roofed sandstone edifice in the Mission Revival style, was erected in 1935 as a school. Only a few years later, under the PWA, the community added a rectangular section on the east side facing Nevada 169, creating a new main facade that resembles the PWA-constructed gymnasiums in Bunkerville and Mesquite. Miles Miller, a Salt Lake City architect, designed all three. The building in Logandale is simpler in appearance, with Mediterranean Revival features, including a red tile roof and decorative brickwork.

SO62 **House** (Experimental Farmhouse)

1909. 1305 Gubler Ave.

Built as part of a state experimental farm, this two-story, concrete-block house is the only remaining structure of the complex. The farm was located near the Muddy River and ideally situated for pursuing innovations in irrigation.

Overton

Farther southeast along the Muddy River toward Lake Mead, Overton, like Logandale, was established by Mormons and survives as an agricultural community. Though still a small town, Overton is also experiencing growth as subdivisions develop on its edges. The town grid, consisting of a few blocks, lies between the Union Pacific Railroad tracks and Nevada 169, also known as Main Street. Modest houses, most dating from the early twentieth century, dot the streets. The Lost City Museum, the town's main attraction, stands on a hill at the south end of town.

SO63 **Overton Gymnasium**

1938, Miles Miller. Southwest corner of W. Thomas Ave. and S. Anderson St.

Unlike the three other PWA projects Miles Miller designed in the Muddy and Virgin river valleys, the brick gymnasium in Overton has a simple, straightforward Classical Revival design. The symmetrical main facade on Thomas Avenue contains an arched entry embellished with four attached fluted Doric columns rising to a simplified classical entablature.

SO64 **Lost City Museum**

1934–1935, many additions and alterations. 721 S. Moapa Valley Blvd.

The Lost City Museum, originally known as the Boulder Dam Park Museum, consists of an adobe brick building and two reconstructions—a pit house and a seven-room Puebloan house—all erected by the National Park Service (NPS) and the Civilian Conservation Corps (CCC) in 1934–1935. The museum occupies a hilltop one-quarter mile south of Overton. The CCC erected the building as part of the effort to recover and store artifacts excavated from Pueblo Grande de Nevada (known as the Lost City), Nevada's most significant Anasazi site, discovered in 1924. Excavations began the following year. Work continued into the 1930s until Lake Mead flooded the site. The two reconstructions are 1930s interpretations of Anasazi sites and culture. At this time, reconstructing prehistoric and historic sites was a common and accepted means of interpreting the past. The National Park Service attempted to recreate prehistoric structures faithfully rather than leave the ruins as they were found.

SO64.1 Museum (top)   SO64.2 Pueblo (bottom)

SO64.1 **Museum**

1934–1935, Dan Hall and Ed Sweeting, National Park Service. 1973, Wells-Kennedy. 1980–1981, Harry Campbell and Associates

The CCC built the one-story museum of handmade, sun-dried adobe brick in the Pueblo Revival style—rarely seen in Nevada but used here to complement the two reconstructions. The flat stepped roof is enclosed by a sandstone-capped parapet 18 inches high. Wooden and ceramic canales extend from the roof through the parapet. Exposed vigas are supported by vertical posts along the recessed wall at the southeast end of the building, forming a small porch. The roof located over the southwest entrance to the original rest rooms also has vigas supported in this way, creating another small porch. The original museum measured 1,990 square feet and contained two exhibit rooms as well as work space. Three additions since 1973 have quadrupled the size, adding more exhibit space and offices, a laboratory, and rest rooms.

The museum building itself reflects the early twentieth-century interest in Native American art and culture and the popularity of the Pueblo Revival style, whose rounded edges and rough surfaces emphasized the architectural craftsmanship favored in earlier movements such as the Arts and Crafts. The museum is significant not only as an attempt to capture the feeling of the pueblos at the Lost City but also as an excellent example of the style. Unfortunately the museum recently stuccoed over the original adobe brick, drastically altering the building's appearance.

SO64.2 Pueblo

1935

The reconstructed pueblo represents the prominent building type of the second Anasazi period, that of the Puebloans (A.D. 600–1150). The pueblo contains attached one-story houses and storage rooms of varying heights arranged in a semicircle. The CCC constructed it on Anasazi foundations dating from A.D. c. 1000, which were uncovered during excavations east of the museum building. Layers of adobe mud plaster over a wood and brush understructure, with irregularly shaped boulders inserted into the masses of adobe at random, make up the walls, which are 12 to 24 inches thick. Flat slabs of sandstone top the parapets. Vigas project through the walls, revealing the roof structure of the building. Rough-hewn logs form the vertical supports and lintels of the openings. Steps lead down from the entrances into the rooms. The earthen floors of the rooms are sunk below the ground at depths of 1 to 2 feet. The interior finish of the walls is rough stucco, like that of the exterior walls. Narrow latías laid close together on the vigas form the interior ceilings.

SO64.3 Pit House

1935

The reconstructed pit house demonstrates the major building type erected during the first Anasazi period, whose people are called the Basketmakers (300 B.C.–A.D.600). Measuring approximately 20 feet in diameter, the house was sunk into the ground. A dome-shaped wood frame, covered with hard-packed dirt, was built outside and over the pit, forming the roof. The frame is not visible from the exterior. A wood pole with notches served as a ladder used to enter the house through a hole in the center of the domical roof. The interior is a single round room with a domed ceiling and stuccoed walls; latías form the ceiling.

Bunkerville

Located a few miles off I-15, Bunkerville has escaped the traffic and tourists that its neighbor, Mesquite, has attracted as a border town. Bunkerville, with a population of about 1,000, retains the atmosphere of its early agricultural days when it was settled in 1877 by members of the Church of Jesus Christ of Latter-day Saints from St. George, Utah. Typical of Mormon settlers, the founders of Bunkerville, under the leadership of Edward Bunker, Sr., carefully planned their community. The location on Mesquite Flats along the Virgin River ensured a ready water supply.

Initially land was held in common under the "United Order." This Mormon system obligated settlers to work together to cultivate the land and construct irrigation ditches from the

Virgin River to the fields. The church sent people with a variety of skills to facilitate the settlement process, including farmers, builders, blacksmiths, and teachers. The town was laid out on a grid, with large blocks and large lots and farmland surrounding the town. After three years, the United Order was dissolved, but it had ensured the early success of the community. Some early buildings remain, but trailers and mobile homes appear to be the most popular housing in Bunkerville today.

SO65 **House** (Thomas Leavitt House)

c. 1895. 160 S. 1st West St.

The Thomas Leavitt House is one of the older and most substantial houses in Bunkerville. From a rubble stone foundation, walls made of local brick rise to a side-facing gable roof. An ell extends from the back of the house. Two-story framed additions at the rear fill in the corners of the T. The main facade has a symmetrical arrangement of windows and doors. The original interior consisted of three rooms on each floor, with no hallways. A stair in the rear room led upstairs.

The two front entrances of the house indicate that it was the home of a polygamous family. Leavitt erected the dwelling after marrying his second wife in 1887. He had a total of twenty-two children with his two spouses. The family soon outgrew the brick house, and Leavitt's second wife moved into a house constructed for her next door. Although the church officially abolished polygamy in 1890, Leavitt continued to live with both wives until his death in 1933. The numerous exterior doors were an additional means of circulation for a large family in a house with no corridors and only one interior stairway.

The large house reflects the unadorned style favored in Mormon communities at this time. Brick was commonly used, in part because lumber was scarce in the Virgin River Valley. Brigham Young exhorted his followers to build in brick and stone, which he considered more permanent than wood. This approach to building, particularly the emphasis on permanence, differs from much of Nevada's architecture, past and present.

SO66 **Community Center** (Bunkerville High School Gymnasium)

1939, Miles Miller. 1988, renovation, Salzner Thompson. Northwest corner of Virgin and 1st West sts.

Miles Miller designed this restrained one-story building as a PWA project for Bunkerville. Walls made of locally fired brick terminate in a parapet that partially hides a hipped roof over the taller gymnasium portion of the building, located toward the rear. The symmetrical facade has a long projecting mass containing a central entrance surrounded by a terra-cotta frontispiece of paired fluted pilasters. In addition to serving as the community center and justice court, the building contains a small library. In 1988 the Clark County Parks and Recreation Department renovated the building, lowering ceilings and replacing the original windows with aluminum ones.

SO67 **House** (Parley Hunt House)

1907. Canal St. near Virgin St.

Sited adjacent to fields and the Virgin River floodplain at the eastern end of Bunkerville, this one-and-one-half-story, L-shaped house has rough, random-laid stone walls and a cross-gable roof. Shingles line the gable ends, which flare at the base to meet the overhanging eaves. The house has two rooms in the front divided by a central chimney and one room in the rear for the kitchen. As in the Leavitt House, there are no hallways; rooms open directly into one another. Though altered over the years, the building retains much of its original shape and appearance.

Mesquite

Mormons from St. George founded Mesquite on the Spanish-Mormon Trail in 1880, abandoned it in 1892, then resettled it in 1895. As did those in Bunkerville, early settlers here laid out an orderly grid for streets and lots. Though established as an agricultural community, Mesquite has since capitalized on its border location by building large, flashy casinos to attract travelers as they enter Nevada. For much of the twentieth century, descendants of the town's settlers made up the majority of inhabitants, but recent growth has attracted many outsiders to work in the casinos and other service sectors of the local economy.

Few buildings remain from Mesquite's early years. The most architecturally significant ones, dating from the 1930s and 1940s, are federally funded but locally built structures. Mesquite's transformation into a tourist town in the 1980s has brought it high-rise hotel-casinos, new suburban subdivisions, and numerous trailer and RV parks.

SO68 Desert Valley Museum

1941, Walter Warren Hughes. 31 W. Mesquite Blvd.

The Pueblo Revival museum building is on Mesquite's main street, surrounded by a variety of residential and commercial structures. The L-shaped structure is compact, with an asymmetrical facade. One-story-tall rubble stone walls, 1 1/2 feet thick, rise from a concrete foundation and terminate in a flat parapet capped by concrete. Pine poles support the roof, their ends projecting about 6 inches beyond the exterior walls. Window and door openings have concrete lintels and sills.

SO68 Desert Valley Museum (below, left)

SO69 Senior Center (Mesquite High School Gymnasium, below) (right)

The building is one of only two known National Youth Administration structures in Nevada (the other is the Pershing County School District Building, the former Vocational-Agriculture Building, in Lovelock; see NO09). Originally planned as a museum and library, the building was used as a clinic and hospital from 1942 to 1977, then by the Boy Scouts, becoming a museum once again in 1985.

SO69 Senior Center (Mesquite High School Gymnasium)

1939, Miles Miller. 144 E. N. 1st St.

Miller designed this building, another PWA project, as a near twin to the Bunkerville Community Center (SO66), with the same red brick, terra-cotta ornamentation and massing of small rooms around three sides of the taller gymnasium. The Mesquite building, however, retains most of its original multilight, steel-frame sash windows and therefore more of its original appearance than the other example.

Caliente

In the late nineteenth century, railroads had not yet reached the southeastern corner of Nevada. By the turn of the century, however, the Union Pacific Railroad and the San Pedro, Los Angeles and Salt Lake line eyed the region, looking for ways to connect Salt Lake City to Los Angeles. Virtually the only possible route was through the narrow Meadow Valley Wash to Moapa and then across the Las Vegas Valley toward southern California. The two railroads each acquired title to part of the right-of-way and began laying track. When they met in Clover Valley, 150 miles northeast of Las Vegas and the site of present-day Caliente, fights ensued between workers of the rival companies, but the railroads finally reached a compromise. Caliente, given its name because of its hot springs, became a division point and maintenance center for the San Pedro, Los Angeles, and Salt Lake line. (Union Pacific later acquired the railroad.)

Like other railroad towns, Caliente gained a broad right-of-way, with commercial streets parallel to the track on both sides. The commercial district on Clover Street, located across the tracks from the main part of town, is a classic railroad row. Beginning with the Richard Railroad Hotel (c. 1925) at the east end and extending all the way to the depot, the buildings here reflect the boom of the 1920s, when Caliente flourished as an active division point, helper station, and passenger hub. Although new metal siding covers many of the historic facades, stone-faced concrete-block buildings and even an Art Deco theater are visible. Like other railroad rows, this one housed a diverse collection of services, including hotels, a market, and the local Odd Fellows Hall. Across the tracks, a row of railroad workers' housing lines one side of Spring Street (U.S. 93), the other main road in town.

Following World War II, Caliente declined in importance as a railroad center. The diesel locomotives that replaced steam engines in the late 1940s and early 1950s could run in multiples with one crew, eliminating the need for helpers. Nor did they require fuel, water, and servicing as frequently. As a result, the railroad gradually reduced forces and facilities. Union Pacific moved its shop facilities from Caliente to Las Vegas in 1948. Later the railroad removed the roundhouse, water tank, and excess yard tracks. Caliente has survived thanks to the establishment of three state parks nearby and traffic on U.S. 93.

SO70 Caliente Depot

1922–1923, John and Donald Parkinson

Many railroads in the West favored the Mission Revival style for stations because it drew inspiration from the region's Hispanic past and evoked images of the old West to travelers. Caliente's Mission Revival depot is the largest building in town. Because Caliente served as a division point, the building had to be large enough to accommodate a hotel and restaurant, waiting rooms, offices, and storage areas. The plan is asymmetrical, with two projecting wings topped by scrolled parapets characteristic of the Mission Revival style. Two arcades, one connecting the wings and the other running along the front of the waiting room, also add visual interest. The walls are stuccoed; red tile covers the gable roofs.

Los Angeles architects John and Donald Parkinson designed more than 100 structures in southern California, including, in Los Angeles, the city hall (1926), Bullocks Wilshire Department Store (1929), and the Union Passenger Terminal (1939), the last great metropolitan train station constructed in the country.

In 1970 Union Pacific turned over the depot to the city of Caliente on a long-term lease. The depot now houses city offices, the public library, the waiting room for Amtrak, and other tenants. Upstairs rooms accommodate classes offered through the Clark County Community College system.

Next to the depot stands a radiation monitoring station, part of a network surrounding the

Nevada Test Site, installed by the U.S. Department of Energy to measure background radiation in the environment as well as to increase public awareness of the results of such testing. The complex array of instruments is a reminder of the continuing legacy of atmospheric testing.

SO71 Houses (Union Pacific Railroad Workers' Houses)

1905 (1–16 Spring St.), 1924 (17–24 Spring St.)

This row of wood-frame houses is the best collection of railroad workers' housing remaining in the state. The dwellings are ranged in an orderly sequence along the east side of Spring Street running north from the railroad, their regularity expressing the order that the railroad imposed on the town. The railroad owned the houses and rented them to workers until the 1950s, when it sold them. The dwellings follow either of two plans, both with

SO70 Caliente Depot (below)

SO71 Houses (Union Pacific Railroad Workers' Houses) (right))

front-facing gables, which alternate along the street. The first is a one-story house with a shed-roofed porch on square posts covering the facade. The second has two stories with a similar porch and a single double-hung window centered in the gable end. In their use of standardized plans, the railroad rows anticipated some of the design conventions of mass-produced postwar subdivisions such as Levittown.

Panaca

Panaca, named after the Southern Paiute word for metal, *panaka*, has survived since its founding by Mormons in 1864—a longevity not shared by the Mormon towns to the south. Settling in a flat plain between two mountain ranges, Panaca's farmers irrigated their fields in the summer with water from the Meadow Valley Wash. The establishment in 1869 of Pioche, a mining town eleven miles to the north, provided a ready market for the Mormons' agricultural products.

Like other Mormon towns, Panaca is set on a grid, with wide streets and a large town square in the middle. The Mormon church, or meetinghouse, is on one side of the square, facing Main Street, with school buildings opposite. Panaca retains some historic adobe structures dating from the mid-nineteenth century, as well as brick and stone dwellings dating from the more prosperous years later in the century when the town had become established. Unfortunately many of these historic buildings have been demolished or irretrievably altered in the past ten years. Panaca remains a quiet, close-knit agricultural community populated by many descendants of the town's first settlers. Because of its distance from Las Vegas (over 160 miles), its proximity to the Nevada-Utah border, and its Mormon heritage, Panaca has more cultural and business ties to Utah's Cedar City and St. George than to southern Nevada.

SO72 **Panaca Historical Center**
(Wadsworth General Store)

c. 1880, James A. Wadsworth. Southwest corner of Main and 4th sts.

A general store built by one of the town's early settlers has been converted to Panaca's local museum. The adobe brick walls are in remarkably good condition, saved by Nevada's dry climate and diligent maintenance over the years. Like many other early settlers in Nevada, the Mormons frequently used adobe as a building material in the more arid parts of the state, where lumber was scarce. The front porch is a replica of the original. The interior is one large room with a ceiling covered by narrow tongue-and-groove wood boards. The store's central location made it a popular place for residents to share news when they came to purchase goods. After Wadsworth's death, his half-brother, Nephi J. Wadsworth, took over the business. In the early twentieth century he sold the building to the school district for use as an annex to the town's grammar school, but he bought back the structure in 1909 and reopened the general store. The store eventually closed again, and the building stood vacant until its conversion to a museum in the late 1990s.

SO73 **House** (Nephi J. Wadsworth House)

1895, Nephi J. Wadsworth. Northeast corner of Main and 5th sts.

The largest and most elaborate dwelling in Panaca, this two-story brick structure shows the influence of the Queen Anne style in a cross-gabled plan, gable-end stickwork, and shingles in the gable facing Main Street. The ingenuity of the builder is most evident in the unusual three-sided porch nestled between the two wings of the house and sheltering the front entry. Square columns of carved stone rise to a heavy stone balustrade enclosing a second-story balcony. A dormer wedged between the juncture of the two gables contains a door opening

SO73 House (Nephi J. Wadsworth House, left)

SO72 Panaca Historical Center (Wadsworth General Store) (right)

on the balcony. This porch faces the corner of Main and 5th streets, commanding attention from passersby. The Wadsworths, one of the more affluent families in Panaca, proudly displayed their prosperity by erecting this substantial house.

SO74 Frank R. Wilcox Auditorium and Panaca High School Gymnasium

1930. Edwards St. between 3rd and 4th sts.

The auditorium and gymnasium are identical structures with rectangular plans, brick walls, and bow-shaped roof trusses. On the stripped-classical facades pilasters divide each side into five bays, with a central entry marked by a cast concrete arch with tympanum and keystone. A new, T-shaped high school stands between the auditorium and gymnasium. These twin structures are the only extant historic example of such a pair of support buildings erected for a public school district in southern Nevada.

Pioche

Founded in 1869, Pioche rode the wave of mining discoveries beginning with the Comstock Lode strike in 1859 on the other side of the state. Though the Mormon community of Panaca stood nearby and might have had a moderating influence, Pioche's remoteness and lawlessness gave it a reputation for being one of the most dangerous towns in the West. Unlike some other mining towns, however, Pioche survived long enough to become more civilized. By the mid-1870s it had gained approximately 12,000 residents and, as the seat of enormous Lincoln County, oversaw a huge area that contained the entire southeastern corner of Nevada. But Pioche was not immune to the mining boom-and-bust cycle. Then, with the establishment of Las Vegas in 1905 as a railroad town, residents of that community fought to have their own county government with a seat closer than Pioche, 175 miles away. In 1909 the state legislature established Clark County with Las Vegas as its seat. Pioche remained the Lincoln County seat but lost its chance to oversee the growth of a new twentieth-century metropolitan area. Though it revived occasionally in the early twentieth century, since the end of World War II, Pioche has had to rely on tourism, with a little mining, ranching, and county government business, to support its economy. Today it looks and feels as if time has passed it by; its main street is still lined with small businesses and buildings dating from the late nineteenth to the mid-twentieth century. Mining has left its legacy in the tailings, headframe, and tramway high above the town. Roads wind through the narrow canyon with little order to them.

so75 Old Lincoln County Courthouse

1872, T. Dimmock and Thomas Keefe. Lacour St.

Known as the "million dollar courthouse," this Italianate structure is reputed to be the most expensive building erected by a county in nineteenth-century Nevada and stands as an example of government corruption. Construction costs totaled $75,000, equivalent to $1,084426 today—an amount far above the agreed-upon price. The debts incurred and the county's subsequent mismanagement resulted in a final cost of at least $800,000, equivalent to $11,567,213 today. The local government retired the debt in 1938, at the same time it was constructing a new Moderne courthouse.

Local designers T. Dimmock and Thomas Keefe provided the county with plans for the simple, two-story brick edifice with rubble stone side walls. The brick front elevation has three bays, separated by unadorned pilasters. An elegant fanlight and narrow side lights with arched caps surround the double wooden doors of the primary entrance. The second-story door, with arched transom and narrow side lights, leads to a wooden balcony. A simple brick cornice with dentils supports a parapet wall. The former courthouse now serves as a local history museum.

SO76 Thompson's Opera House (Brown's Opera House) and Gem Theater

c. 1873, Aleck Brown. 1937, movie theater. Main St.

Pioche's opera house is less fancy than those in Eureka and Virginia City, but it is one of the oldest surviving examples of the type in the state. Its simple wood-frame walls stand two stories tall, with a pedimented front-facing gable lending a classical touch. Originally a full-length porch with upper balustrade embellished this structure, but it disappeared long ago. Above three double doors and a single door at street level, four pairs of doors once opened onto the top of the porch. The dilapidated building has stood vacant for a number of years. In 1937 the Gem Theater was built next door, with a wood structure connecting the roofs of the two buildings. The solid brick walls of the Gem contrast with the wood-sided walls of the opera house, emphasizing the poor condition of the latter structure. The Gem still shows movies using the original 1930s projection equipment.

In recent years members of the local community have worked to save the old opera house and use it as a cultural center. In 1996 a nonprofit group won a grant from the state's Commission for Cultural Affairs to undertake foundation work and structural stabilization to prepare for its transformation.

so77 Lincoln County Elementary School

1909, Liljenberg Maeser. 1930s, 1940s. Northeast corner of Field and Main sts.

This one-story structure is the only Mission Revival building in Lincoln County besides the Caliente Depot. In the early twentieth century larger Nevada school districts in Reno and Las Vegas favored the style, but Lincoln County tended toward vernacular buildings. This school, designed by an architect in a fashionable style, displays the school district's desire for something that would stand out, not just in the community but also in southern

SO76 Thompson's Opera House (Brown's Opera House) and Gem Theater (left)

SO77 Lincoln County Elementary School (below)

Nevada. Built at a time when Lincoln County had lost nearly half of its territory to Clark County, the school may also have been a way to assert Pioche's progressiveness and educational standards as compared with those of Las Vegas, its burgeoning neighbor to the south. The building, one story on a raised basement, has reinforced concrete walls and a hipped roof that rises to a squat, hip-roofed cupola. Two identical scrolled parapets cap the roofline of the main facade above groups of three windows. The building originally contained four classrooms, but additions were made in the 1930s and 1940s. It is the oldest continually operating school in southern Nevada.

Bibliography

Publications on Nevada architecture have tended to discuss specific places, such as Las Vegas, or building types, such as ranches, county courthouses, mining towns, and casinos. Most of those in the latter category have focused on casinos, so much work remains to be done on the rest of the state's architecture. Architectural magazines report on recently constructed buildings, and journals of Nevada historical societies provide information on town development and historic structures. No publication treats the architecture of the state as a single topic or places it in the context of the Great Basin.

In Nevada, more than in states for which abundant publications exist, the architectural historian must rely on unpublished materials— archival sources and historic surveys—as well as knowledgeable individuals and fieldwork. Much of the work for this book is based on the files of the Nevada State Historic Preservation Office in Carson City, which contain extensive cultural resources surveys, architectural surveys, historic structures reports, and nominations for the State Register of Historic Places and the National Register of Historic Places. All of these documents were invaluable in identifying and researching buildings. In addition, the files and photograph collections of the Nevada Historical Society; the University of Nevada, Reno, Special Collections; the Nevada State Archives; the Nevada State Museum; the Special Collections and Architecture Studies Library of the University of Nevada, Las Vegas; and the Las Vegas News Bureau were resources on extant and destroyed examples of Nevada architecture. Files of the Historic American Buildings Survey at the Library of Congress

include historical texts, photographs, and measured drawings of historic buildings. The National Archives provided information on some of Nevada's structures erected by the Bureau of Indian Affairs. Finally, local newspaper articles and Sanborn Fire Insurance Maps of the late nineteenth and early twentieth centuries helped to establish building dates and identify architects.

The bibliography is divided into general and regional sources. Regional sections list sources for individual property entries followed by headings for towns or locales in alphabetical order.

GENERAL SOURCES

Adkins, Richard. "Steel Rails, Desert Vistas: Nevada Railroad Resources." Carson City: Division of Historic Preservation and Archeology, 1992. Photocopy.

Attebery, Jennifer E. *Building Idaho: An Architectural History*. Moscow, Idaho: University of Idaho Press, 1991.

Bancroft, Hubert Howe. *History of Nevada, Colorado and Wyoming, 1540–1888*. San Francisco: The History Company, 1890.

Basso, Dave. *The Architecture of Necessity and Opportunity in Nevada Ghost Towns*. Sparks, Nev.: Falcon Hill Press, 1988.

Bowers, Michael W. *The Sagebrush State: Nevada's History, Government, and Politics*. Reno: University of Nevada Press, 1996.

Bruns, James H. *Great American Post Offices*. New York: John Wiley and Sons, 1998.

Burton, Richard F. *The City of Saints and Across the*

Rocky Mountains to California. Edited with an introduction and notes by Fawn M. Brodie. New York: Alfred A. Knopf, 1963.

Carlson, Helen S. *Nevada Place Names: A Geographical Dictionary.* Reno: University of Nevada Press, 1974.

Carpenter, Charles H., Jr., with Mary Grace Carpenter. *Tiffany Silver.* New York: Dodd, Mead and Company, 1978.

Carter, Thomas, and Peter Goss. *Utah's Historic Architecture, 1847–1940: A Guide.* Salt Lake City: University of Utah Press, 1988.

Castleman, Deke. *Nevada Handbook.* 4th ed. Chico, Cailf.: Moon Publications, 1995.

Delehanty, Randolph. *Preserving the West: California, Arizona, Nevada, Utah, Idaho, Oregon, and Washington.* New York: Pantheon Books, 1985.

Douglas, William A. "Basque-American Identity: Past Perspectives and Future Prospects." In *Change in the American West: Exploring the Human Dimension,* edited by Stephen Tchudi. Reno: University of Nevada Press, 1996.

———. "Basques in Nevada." In *Towns and Tales,* vol. 1, *North.* Las Vegas: Nevada Publications, 1981.

Elliott, Russell R. *History of Nevada.* 2nd ed. Lincoln: University of Nebraska Press, 1987.

———. *Nevada's Twentieth-Century Mining Boom: Tonopah, Goldfield, Ely.* Reno: University of Nevada Press, 1966.

Findlay, John M. *People of Chance: Gambling in American Society from Jamestown to Las Vegas.* New York: Oxford University Press, 1986.

Fusco, Elmer R. *"Good Time Coming?" Black Nevadans in the Nineteenth Century.* Westport, Conn.: Greenwood Press, 1975.

Grant, H. Roger, and Charles W. Bohi. *The Country Railroad Station in America.* Boulder, Colo.: Pruett Publishing Company, 1978.

Grayson, Donald K. *The Desert Past: A Natural Prehistory of the Great Basin.* Washington, D.C.: Smithsonian Institution Press, 1993.

Hamilton, C. Mark. *Nineteenth-Century Mormon Architecture and City Planning.* New York: Oxford University Press, 1995.

Heath, Kingston. "False-Front Architecture on Montana's Urban Frontier." In *Images of an American Land,* edited by Thomas Carter. Albuquerque: University of New Mexico Press, 1997.

Hess, Alan. *Googie: Fifties Coffee Shop Architecture.* San Francisco: Chronicle Books, 1985.

History of Nevada. Oakland, Calif.: Thompson and West, 1881. Reprint. Edited by Myron Angel. New York: Arno Press, 1973.

Hopkins, Sarah Winnemucca. *Life Among the Piutes; Their Wrongs and Claims.* New York: G. P. Putnam's Sons, 1883.

Hudson, Karen E. *Paul R. Williams, Architect: A Legacy of Style.* New York: Rizzoli International Publications, 1993.

Hulse, James W. *The Silver State: Nevada's History Reinterpreted.* Reno: University of Nevada, 1991.

James, Ronald M. *Nevada Comprehensive Preserva-*

tion Plan. 2nd ed. Carson City: Division of Historic Preservation and Archaeology, 1991.

James, Ronald M. "Nevada's Historic Architect." *Nevada Magazine* 54:4 (July/August 1994), 20–23.

———. *Temples of Justice: County Courthouses of Nevada.* Reno: University of Nevada Press, 1994.

Jester, Thomas C., ed. *Twentieth-century Building Materials: History and Conservation.* New York: McGraw-Hill, 1995.

Jordan, Terry G. *North American Cattle-Ranching Frontiers: Origins, Diffusion, and Differentiation.* Albuquerque: University of New Mexico Press, 1993.

Kohl, Edith E. *Denver's Historic Mansions: Citadels to the Empire Builders.* Denver: Sage Books, 1957.

Krinsky, Carol Herselle. *Contemporary Native American Architecture: Cultural Regeneration and Creativity.* New York: Oxford University Press, 1996.

Lamm, Michael. "The Instant Building." *Invention and Technology* 13:3 (winter 1998): 68–70.

Loomis, David. *Combat Zoning: Military Land Use Planning in Nevada.* Reno: University of Nevada Press, 1993.

McCusker, John J. *How Much Is That in Real Money? A Historical Price Index for Use as a Deflator of Money Values in the Economy of the United States.* Worcester, Mass.: American Antiquarian Society, 1992.

McPhee, John. *Basin and Range.* New York: Farrar, Straus & Giroux, 1980.

Myrick, David. *Railroads of Nevada and California.* Berkeley: Howell-North Books, 1963.

Nabokov, Peter, and Robert Easton. *Native American Architecture.* New York: Oxford University Press, 1989.

Nespor, Maurice J., and Hyde L. Flippo. "Architects in Nevada: A Brief History." Photocopy furnished by the authors. 1977.

Nevada Atlas and Gazetteer. Freeport, Maine: DeLorme, 1996.

Nevada Division of Mines. *Major Mines of Nevada 1996.* Carson City: Nevada Division of Mines, 1997.

Noble, Allen G. *Wood, Brick, and Stone: The North American Settlement Landscape,* vol. 2, *Barns and Farm Structures.* Amherst: University of Massachusetts Press, 1984.

Paher, Stanley W. *Nevada Ghost Towns and Mining Camps.* Berkeley: Howell-North Books, 1970.

Persinos, John F., et al. "Boom Towns on the Border." *Nevada Magazine* 48:1 (January/February 1988): 10–23.

Potter, Janet Greenstein. *Great American Railroad Stations.* New York: John Wiley and Sons, 1996.

Radzilowski, John. "Same Town, Different Name." *Invention and Technology* 10:3 (winter 1995): 20–21.

Reisner, Marc. *Cadillac Desert: The American West and Its Disappearing Water.* Rev. ed. New York: Penguin Books, 1993.

Roth, Leland M. "Company Towns in the Western

United States." In *The Company Town: Architecture and Society in the Early Industrial Age*, edited by John S. Garner. New York: Oxford University Press, 1992.

———. *McKim, Mead and White, Architects*. New York: Harper & Row, 1983.

Rowley, William D. *Reclaiming the Arid West*. Bloomington: Indiana University Press, 1996.

Schlereth, Thomas J. *U.S. 40: A Roadscape of the American Experience*. Indianapolis: Indiana Historical Society, 1985.

Schwartz, J. R. *The Travellers Guide to the Best Cat Houses in Nevada*. Boise: J. R. Schwartz, 1995.

Shepperson, Wilbur S., ed. *East of Eden, West of Zion: Essays on Nevada*. Reno: University of Nevada Press, 1989.

Shepperson, Wilbur S. *Restless Strangers: Nevada's Immigrants and Their Interpreters*. Reno: University of Nevada Press, 1970.

Simpson, Pamela H. *Cheap, Quick, and Easy: Imitative Architectural Materials, 1870–1930*. Knoxville: University of Tennessee Press, 1999.

Stilgoe, John R. *Metropolitan Corridor: Railroads and the American Scene*. New Haven: Yale University Press, 1983.

Stoehr, C. Eric. *Bonanza Victorian: Architecture and Society in Colorado Mining Towns*. Albuquerque: University of New Mexico Press, 1975.

Stover, John F. *The Life and Decline of the American Railroad*. New York: Oxford University Press, 1970.

Swan, Sheila, and Peter Laufer. *Neon Nevada*. Reno: University of Nevada Press, 1994.

Twain, Mark. *Roughing It*. 1872. Reprint. New York: Penguin Classics, 1985.

Ulph, Owen. *The Fiddleback: Lore of the Linecamp*. Salt Lake City: Dream Garden Press, 1981.

Wheat, Margaret M. *Survival Arts of the Primitive Paiutes*. Reno: University of Nevada Press, 1967.

White, John H., Jr. *The American Railroad Passenger Car*. Baltimore: Johns Hopkins University Press, 1978.

Worster, Donald. *Rivers of Empire: Water, Aridity, and the Growth of the American West*. New York: Oxford University Press, 1992.

The WPA Guide to 1930s Nevada. With a new foreword by Russell J. Elliott. Reno: University of Nevada Press, 1991.

REGIONAL SOURCES

Northwestern Region

Cranston, Vanita Renee. "Vernacular Ranch Architecture: An Ethnohistorical Study." M.A. thesis, University of Nevada, Reno, 1991.

Dangberg, Grace. *Carson Valley: Historical Sketches of Nevada's First Settlement*. Douglas County, Nev.: Carson Valley Historical Society, 1972.

Douglas County Planning Department. *The Architectural Heritage of Carson Valley: A Survey of Genoa, Minden, and Gardnerville*. Minden, Nev.: Douglas County, 1981.

James, Ronald M. *Bonanza of the Mining West: Virginia City and the Famed Comstock Lode*. Reno: University of Nevada Press, 1998.

James, Ronald M., and C. Elizabeth Raymond, eds. *Comstock Women: the Making of a Mining Community*. Reno: University of Nevada Press, 1998.

Nicoletta, Julie. "Redefining Domesticity: Women and Lodging Houses on the Comstock." In *Comstock Women: The Making of a Mining Community*, edited by Elizabeth Raymond and Ronald M. James. Reno: University of Nevada Press, 1997.

Smith, Grant H. *The History of the Comstock Lode, 1850–1997*. With new material by Joseph V. Tingley. Reno: Nevada Bureau of Mines and Geology, 1998.

Carson City

Chambers, S. Allen, Jr. *The Architecture of Carson City, Nevada*. Selections from the Historic American Buildings Survey. No. 14. Washington, D.C.: National Park Service, n.d.

Gale, Frederick C. *The History of the Capitol Building and Governor's Mansion*. Carson City: Office of the Secretary of State, n.d.

Hickson, Howard. *Mint Mark: "CC" The Story of the Unites States Mint at Carson City, Nevada*. Carson City: Nevada State Museum, 1972.

Nylen, Robert A. *The Architecture of the Nevada State Capitol*. Carson City: Nevada State Museum, 1991.

Minden

Maule, Wynne M. *Minden, Nevada: The Story of a Unique Town, 1906–1992*. Minden: Wynne M. Maule, 1993.

Reno

Fey, Christine, et al. *City of Reno Historic Structures Handbook*. Reno: City of Reno, 1995.

Harmon, Mella Rothwell. "Divorce and Economic Opportunity in Reno, Nevada, during the Great Depression." M.A. thesis, University of Nevada, Reno, 1998.

Hulse, James R. *The University of Nevada: A Centennial History*. Reno: University of Nevada Press, 1974.

"Newlands Offers Restored Rooms with a View." *Preservation News* 28:1 (January 1985): 10.

Palmer, Christine Savage. "Art Moderne and Christian Science: The History of Reno's Loomis Manor." *Nevada Historical Society Quarterly* 36:4 (winter 1993): 263–273.

Pearson, Clifford A. "Showing Off Art in the High Sierras." *Architectural Record* 184:4 (April 1996): 72–79.

Rowley, William D. *Reno: Hub of the Washoe County*. Woodland Hills, Calif.: Windsor Publications, 1984.

Stremmel House: Mark Mack. Introduction by Mark Mack. New York: Monacelli Press, 1998.

Townley, John M. *Tough Little Town on the Truckee: Reno, 1868–1900*. Reno: Great Basin Studies Center, 1983.

Webb, Michael. "Architecture: Mark Mack: Contemporary Volumes Etched into the Nevada Landscape." *Architectural Digest* 52:12 (December 1995): 114–121, 196.

Virginia City

Browne, J. Ross. *A Peep at Washoe and Washoe Revisited*. 1863. Reprint. Balboa, Calif.: Paisano Press, 1959.

Lord, Eliot. *Comstock Mining and Miners*. 1883. Reprint. San Diego: Howell-North, 1959.

NORTHERN REGION

Carter, Thomas, and Blanton Owen, eds. *Designed for Work: The San Jacinto Ranch of Elko County, Nevada*. Salt Lake City: Graduate School of Architecture, University of Utah, 1993.

Graham, Andrea. "Railroad-Tie Architecture in Elko County, Nevada." In *Perspectives in Vernacular Architecture, III*, edited by Thomas Carter and Bernard L. Herman. Columbia: University of Missouri Press, 1989.

MacGregor, Greg. *Overland: The California Emigrant Trail of 1841–1870*. Albuquerque: University of New Mexico Press, 1996.

Patterson, Edna B., Louise A. Ulph, and Victor Goodwin. *Nevada's Northeast Frontier*. Sparks, Nev.: Western Printing and Publishing, 1969.

Elko

Aquirre, Angela. "It Began in Elko: Big Name Entertainment in Nevada." *Northeastern Nevada Historical Society Quarterly* 82:2 (fall 1982): 43–61.

Hall, Shawn. "A History of Elko, Nevada." *Northeastern Nevada Historical Society Quarterly* 95:3 (fall 1995): 127–157.

Hickson, Howard, comp. "Elko, Nevada: 1868–1968: A Pictorial History." *Northeastern Nevada Historical Society Quarterly* 84:3 (fall 1983): 118–149.

Jarbidge

Hickson, Howard. "Last Horsedrawn Stage Robbery, Jarbidge, Nevada: December 5, 1916." *Northeastern Nevada Historical Society Quarterly* 81:1 (winter 1981): 3–30.

———. "Letters from Jarbidge." *Northeastern Nevada Historical Society Quarterly* 78:2 (spring 1978): 47–80.

McDermitt Vicinity

National Archives. Fort McDermitt. Record Group 393, Part 5. Letters Sent. Vol. 1. May 1865, August 1865–January 1868, July 1868.

National Archives. Office of the Quartermaster General. Record Group 92. Consolidated Correspondence File, 1794–1915.

Owyhee

Hanley, Mike. *Owyhee Trails: The West's Forgotten Corner*. Caldwell, Idaho: Caxton Printers, 1973.

Harris, Jack S. "The White Knife Shoshoni of Nevada." In *Acculturation in Seven American Indian Tribes*, edited by Ralph Linton. 1940. Reprint. Gloucester, Mass.: Peter Smith, 1963.

McKinney, Whitney. *A History of the Shoshone-Paiutes of the Duck Valley Indian Reservation*. Salt Lake City: Institute of the American West and Howe Brothers, 1983.

National Archives. Records of the Bureau of Indian Affairs. Record Group 75. Records of the Construction Division, Files for PWA Projects, 1931–1943.

Paradise Valley

Marshall, Howard Wight, and Richard E. Ahlborn. *Buckaroos in Paradise: Cowboy Life in Northern Nevada*. Exh. cat. Lincoln: University of Nebraska Press, 1981.

Marshall, Howard Wight. "A Good Gridiron: The Vernacular Design of a Western Cow Town." In *Perspectives in Vernacular Architecture, II*, edited by Camille Wells. Columbia: University of Missouri Press, 1986.

———. *Paradise Valley, Nevada: The People and Buildings of an American Place*. Tucson: University of Arizona Press, 1995.

Purser, Margaret. "All Roads Lead to Winnemucca: Local Road Systems and Community Material Culture in Nineteenth-century Nevada." In *Perspectives in Vernacular Architecture, III*, edited by Thomas Carter and Bernard L. Herman. Columbia: University of Missouri Press, 1989.

CENTRAL REGION

Graham, Andrea, and Blanton Owen. *Lander County Line: Folklife in Central Nevada*. Reno: Nevada State Council on the Arts, 1988.

Hardesty, D. L. *The Pony Express in Central Nevada: Archaeological and Documentary Perspectives*. Cultural Resource Series, 1. Reno: Nevada State Office, Bureau of Land Management, 1979.

Austin

Abbe, Donald R. *Austin and the Reese River Mining District: Nevada's Forgotten Frontier.* Reno: University of Nevada Press, 1985.

Eureka

Eureka's Yesterdays: A Guide to a Historic Central Nevada Town. Reno: Nevada Historical Society, 1988.

Fallon

Misrach, Richard. *Bravo Twenty: The Bombing of the American West.* Baltimore: Johns Hopkins University Press, 1990.

McGill

Elliott, Russell R. *Growing Up in a Company Town: A Family in the Copper Camp of McGill, Nevada.* Reno: University of Nevada Press, 1990.

SOUTH-CENTRAL REGION

Hall, Shawn. *A Guide to the Ghost Towns and Mining Camps of Nye County, Nevada.* New York: Dodd, Mead and Company, 1981.

Goldfield

Paher, Stanley. *Goldfield, Boomtown of Nevada.* Las Vegas: Nevada Publications, 1977.
Shamberger, Hugh. *Goldfield: Its Early History, Development, and Water Supply.* Sparks, NV: Western Printing and Publishing Co., 1982.
Zanjani, Sally. *Goldfield: The Last Goldrush of the Western Frontier.* Athens, Ohio: Swallow Press/Ohio University Press, 1992.

Tonopah

McCracken, Robert D. *A History of Tonopah, Nevada.* Tonopah: Nye County Press, 1990.

SOUTHERN REGOIN

Brooks, Juanita. *Quicksand and Cactus: A Memoir of the Southern Mormon Frontier.* Logan: Utah State University Press, 1992.
Hulse, James W. *Lincoln County, Nevada: 1864–1909, History of a Mining Region.* Reno: University of Nevada Press, 1971.

Luster, Michael, and Blanton Owen. *In a High and Glorious Place: Folklife in Lincoln County, Nevada.* Reno: Nevada State Council on the Arts, Folk Arts Program, 1987.
McCracken, Robert D. *A History of Beatty, Nevada.* Tonopah, Nev.: Nye County Press, 1996.
Ritenour, Dorothy. "Education on the Frontier: The Country Schools of Southern Nevada." *Nevada Historical Society Quarterly* 27:1 (spring 1984): 34–41.
Titus, A. Costandina. *Bombs in the Backyard: Atomic Testing and American Politics.* Reno: University of Nevada Press, 1986.

Boulder City and Hoover Dam

Bureau of Reclamation. *Hoover Dam.* Washington, D.C.: U.S. Government Printing Office, 1985.
Kroloff, Reed. "Hoover Dam Shamed by New Visitors' Center." *Architecture* 85:1 (January 1996): 47.
Wilson, Richard Guy. "American Modernism in the West: Hoover Dam." In *Images of an American Land,* edited by Thomas Carter. Albuquerque: University of New Mexico Press, 1997.
———. "Massive Deco Monument: The Enduring Strength of Boulder (Hoover) Dam." *Architecture: The AIA Journal* 72:12 (December 1983): 45–47.

Caliente

Flacke, Christopher. "An Immense Inheritance." *Historic Preservation News* 34:5 (October/November 1994): 32–33, 42–43.

Las Vegas

Baker, Geoffrey. *Antoine Predock.* Architectural Monographs No. 49. Chichester, England: Academy Editions, 1997.
Balboni, Alan. *Beyond the Mafia: Italian Americans and the Development of Las Vegas.* Reno: University of Nevada Press, 1996.
Banham, Reyner. *Los Angeles: The Architecture of Four Ecologies.* London: Penguin Books, 1971.
Davenport, Robert W. "Early Years, Early Workers: The Genesis of the University of Nevada." *Nevada Historical Society Quarterly* 35:1 (spring 1992): 1–20.
Davis, Mike. "House of Cards." *Sierra* 80:6 (November/December 1995): 36–41, 76.
———. "Las Vegas Versus Nature." In *Reopening the American West,* edited by Hal K. Rothman. Tucson: University of Arizona Press, 1998.
Hess, Alan. "Vegas's NY-NY Casino-Hotel Shows How to Keep the Crowds Coming." *Architectural Record* 185:3 (March 1997): 76–79.
———. *Viva Las Vegas: After Hours Architecture.* San Francisco: Chronicle Books, 1993.

"Jails Within a Jail." *Architectural Record* 175:4 (April 1987): 88–91.

Kroloff, Reed. "The Other Las Vegas." *Architecture* 85:4 (April 1996): 78–89.

"Las Vegas Takes a Bite of the Big Apple." *World Architecture*, no. 3 (February 1997): 17.

McCracken, Robert D. *Las Vegas: The Great American Playground.* Fort Collins, Colo.: Marion Street Publishing, 1996.

Moehring, Eugene P. "Public Works and the New Deal in Las Vegas, 1933–1940." *Nevada Historical Society Quarterly* 24:2 (summer 1981): 107–129.

———. *Resort City in the Sunbelt: Las Vegas, 1930–1970.* Reno: University of Nevada Press, 1989.

Newman, Morris. "What Happens to a Street When it Becomes an Experience?" *Metropolis* 15:8 (April 1996): 23, 26.

Olson, Christopher. "Justice Facilities Challenge Designers and Contractors." *Building Design and Construction* 27:3 (March 1986): 80–84.

Spanier, David. *Welcome to the Pleasuredome: Inside Las Vegas.* Reprint. Reno: University of Nevada Press, 1993.

Stein, Karen D. "Down the Strip: Las Vegas Library/Discovery Museum." *Architectural Record* 178:11 (October 1990): 68–75.

Venturi, Robert, Denise Scott Brown, and Steven Izenour. *Learning from Las Vegas.* Rev. ed. Cambridge: MIT Press, 1977.

Wolfe, Tom. *The Kandy-Kolored Tangerine-Flake Streamline Baby.* New York: Farrar, Straus & Giroux, 1965.

Wright, Dorothy. *Wildcat Country: Las Vegas High School and Its Neighborhood, 1930–1945.* Las Vegas: Nevada State Museum and Historical Society, 1989.

Logandale

Hafner, Arabell Lee. *One Hundred Years on the Muddy.* Springville, Utah: Art City, 1967.

Nevada Test Site

Del Tredici, Robert. *At Work in the Fields of the Bomb.* New York: Harper & Row, 1987.

Freeman, Allen. "Echoes of the Cold War." *Historic Preservation* 46:1 (January/February 1994): 28–35.

Goin, Peter. *Nuclear Landscapes.* Baltimore: Johns Hopkins University Press, 1991.

Johnson, William Gray, Nancy G. Goldenberg, and Susan R. Edwards. "The Japanese Village at the Nevada Test Site: A Relic of Nuclear War." *CRM* 20:14 (1997): 21–22.

Overton

Lyneis, Margaret M. "A Spatial Analysis of Anasazi Architecture, A.D. 950–1150: Moapa Valley, Nevada." *Kiva* 52:1 (fall 1986): 53–74.

Glossary

AIA See AMERICAN INSTITUTE OF ARCHITECTS.

abacus The top member of a column capital. In the Doric order, it is a flat block, square in plan, between the echinus of the capital and the architrave of the entablature above.

Academic Gothic See COLLEGIATE GOTHIC.

acroterium, acroterion (plural: acroteria) **1** A pedestal for a statue or similar decorative feature at the apex or at the lower corners of a pediment. **2** Any ornamental feature at these locations.

Adamesque A mode of architectural design, with emphasis on interiors, reminiscent of the work of the Scottish architects Robert Adam (1728–1792) and his brother James (1732–1794). It is characterized by attenuated proportions, bright color, and elegant linear detailing. Adamesque interiors, as one aspect of the broader Neoclassical movement, became popular in the late eighteenth century in Britain, Russia, and elsewhere in northern Europe. Simplified versions of these interiors began to be seen in the United States around the year 1800 in the work of Charles Bulfinch (1763–1844) and Samuel McIntire (1757–1811). Adamesque interiors, often emulating original Adam designs, were again popular in the 1920s. See also the related term FEDERAL.

adobe Sun-dried brick made of clay mixed with vegetable matter. It is believed to be African in origin, the word being derived from the Arabic for brick. Adobe dwellings are common in the southwestern United States and in Mexico, and the ruins of early pueblos evidence such construction. Before contact with Spanish explorers, indigenous peoples in the American Southwest used clumps of adobe mud for their buildings. The Spanish introduced the concept of forming adobe into bricks for construction purposes; this method was adopted by Native Americans.

aedicule, aedicular An exterior niche, door, or window, framed by columns or pilasters and topped by an entablature and pediment. Meaning has been extended to a smaller-scale representation of a temple front on an interior wall. Distinguished from a tabernacle (definition 1), which usually occurs on an interior wall. See also the related term NICHE.

Aesthetic movement A late nineteenth-century movement in interior design and the decorative arts, emphasizing the application of artistic principles in the production of objects and the creation of interior ensembles. Aesthetic movement works are characterized by a broad eclecticism of materials and styles (especially the exotic) and by a preference for "conventionalized" (i.e., stylized) ornament, rather than naturalistic. The movement flourished in Britain from the 1850s through the 1870s and in the United States from the 1870s through the 1880s. Designers associated with the movement include William Morris (1834–1896) in England and Herter Brothers (1865–1905) in America. The Aesthetic movement evolved into and overlapped with the Art Nouveau and the Arts and Crafts movement. See also the related term QUEEN ANNE (definition 4).

ambulatory A passageway around the apse of a church, allowing for circulation behind the sanctuary.

American Adam Style See FEDERAL.

American bond See COMMON BOND.

American Foursquare See FOURSQUARE HOUSE.

263

American Institute of Architects (AIA) The national professional organization of architects, established in New York in 1857. The first national convention was held in New York in 1867, and at that meeting, provision was made for the creation of local chapters. In 1889, the American Institute of Architects absorbed the independent Chicago-based Western Association of Architects (established 1884). The headquarters of the national organization moved from New York to Washington in 1898.

American Renaissance Ambiguous term. See instead BEAUX-ARTS CLASSICISM, COLONIAL REVIVAL, FEDERAL REVIVAL.

Anglo-Palladianism, Anglo-Palladian An architectural movement in England motivated by a reaction against the English Baroque and by a rediscovery of the work of the English Renaissance architect Inigo Jones (1573–1652) and the Italian Renaissance architect Andrea Palladio (1508–1580). Anglo-Palladianism flourished in England (c. 1710s–1760s) and in the British North American colonies (c. 1740s–1790s). Key figures in the Anglo-Palladian movement were Colen Campbell (1676–1729) and Richard Boyle, Lord Burlington (1694–1753). Sometimes called Burlingtonian, Palladian Revival. See also the more general term Palladianism and the related terms GEORGIAN PERIOD, JEFFERSONIAN.

antefix. In classical architecture, a small upright decoration at the eaves of a roof, originally devised to hide the ends of the roof tiles. A similar ornament along the ridge of the roof.

anthemion (plural: anthemions) A Greek ornamental motif based upon the honeysuckle or palmette. It may appear as a single element on an antefix or as a running ornament on a frieze or other banded feature.

antiquity The broad epoch of Western history preceding the Middle Ages and including such ancient civilizations as Egyptian, Greek, and Roman.

apse, apsidal A semicircular or polygonal feature projecting as a major element from an important interior space, especially at the chancel end of a church. Distinguished from an exedra, which is a semicircular or polygonal space, usually containing a bench, in the wall of a garden or nonreligious building. A substantial apse in a church, containing an ambulatory and radiating chapels, is called a chevet. The terms apse and chevet are used to describe the *form* of the end of the church containing the altar, while the terms chancel, choir, and sanctuary are used to describe the liturgical *function* of this end of the church and the spaces within it. Less substantial projections in nonreligious buildings are called bays if polygonal or bowfronts if curved.

arbor 1 An openwork structure covered with climbing plants. Distinguished from a trellis, which is generally a simpler, more two-dimensional structure, often attached to a wall. Distin-

guished from a pergola, which is an openwork structure supported by a colonnade, creating a shaded walk. **2** A grouping of closely planted trees or shrubs, trained together and self-supporting.

arcade 1 A series of arches, carried on columns or piers or other supports. **2** A covered walkway, one side of which is part of a building, while the other is open, as a series of arches, to the exterior. **3** In the nineteenth and early twentieth centuries, an interior street or other extensive space lined with shops and stores.

arch A curved construction that spans an opening. (Some arches may be flat or triangular, and many have a complex or compound curvature.) A masonry arch consists of a series of wedge-shaped parts (voussoirs) that press together toward the center while being restrained from spreading outward by the surrounding wall or the adjacent arch.

architrave 1 The lowest member of a classical entablature. **2** The moldings on the face of a wall around a doorway or other opening. Sometimes called the casing. Distinguished from the jambs, which are the vertical linings perpendicular to the wall planes at the sides of an opening. Distinguished from surround, a term usually applied to the entire door or window frame considered as a unit.

archivolt The group of moldings following the shape of an arched opening.

arcuation, arcuated Construction using arches.

Art Deco A decorative style stimulated by the 1925 Exposition Internationale des Arts Décoratifs et Industriels Modernes, held in Paris. As the first phase of the Moderne, Art Deco is characterized by sharp angular and curvilinear forms, by a richness of materials (including polished metal, stone, and exotic woods), and by an overall sleekness of design. The style was often used in the commercial and residential architecture of the 1930s (e.g., skyscrapers, hotels, apartment buildings). Sometimes called Art Deco Moderne, Deco, Jazz Moderne, Zigzag Moderne, Zigzag Modernistic. See also the more general term MODERNE and the related terms MAYAN REVIVAL, PWA MODERNE, STREAMLINE MODERNE.

Art Moderne See MODERNE.

Art Nouveau A style in architecture, interior design, and the decorative arts that flourished principally in France and Belgium in the 1890s. The Art Nouveau is characterized by undulating and whiplash lines and by sensuous organic forms. The Art Nouveau in Britain and the United States evolved from and overlapped with the Aesthetic movement.

Arts and Crafts A late nineteenth- and early twentieth-century movement in interior design and the decorative arts, emphasizing the importance of hand crafting for everyday objects. Arts and Crafts works are characterized by rectilinear geometries and high contrasts between figure and ground, and the furniture often features expressed construction. The term originated with the Arts and Crafts Exhibition Society, founded in England in 1888. Designers associated with the movement include C. F. A. Voysey (1857–1941) in England and the brothers Charles S. Greene (1868–1957) and Henry M. Greene (1870–1954) in America. The Arts and Crafts movement evolved from and overlapped with the Aesthetic movement. For a more specific term, used in the United States after 1900, see also CRAFTSMAN.

ashlar Squared blocks of stone that fit tightly against one another.

atelier 1 A studio where the fine arts, including architecture, are taught. Applied particularly to the offices of prominent architects in Paris who provided design training to students enrolled in or informally attached to the Ecole des Beaux-Arts. By extension, any working office where some organized teaching is done. **2** A place where artworks or handicrafts are produced by skilled workers. **3** An artist's studio or workshop.

attic 1 The area beneath the roof and above the main stories (or story) of a building. Sometimes called a garret. **2** A low story above the entablature, often a blocklike mass that caps the building.

axis An imaginary center line to which are referred the parts of a building or the relations of a number of buildings to one another.

axonometric drawing A pictorial drawing using axonometric projection, in which horizontal lines that are perpendicular in an object, building, or space are drawn as perpendicular (usually at two 45-degree angles from the vertical, or at complementary angles of 30 and 60 degrees). Consequently, all angular and dimensional relationships in plan remain the same in the drawing as in the thing depicted. Sometimes called an axon or an axonometric. See also the related terms ISOMETRIC DRAWING, PERSPECTIVE DRAWING.

balloon frame construction A system of light frame construction in which single studs extend the full height of the frame (commonly two stories), from the foundation to the roof. Floor joists are fastened to the sides of the studs. Structural members are usually sawn lumber, ranging from two-by-fours to two-by-tens, and are fastened with nails. Sometimes called balloon framing. The technique, developed in Chicago and other boomtowns of the 1830s, has been largely replaced in the twentieth century by platform frame construction.

baluster One of a series of short vertical members, often vase-shaped in profile, used to support a handrail for a stair or a railing. Balusters that are thinner and simpler in profile are sometimes called banisters.

balustrade A series of balusters or posts supporting a rail or coping across the top (and sometimes resting on a lower rail). Balustrades are often found on stairs, balconies, parapets, and terraces.

band course Ambiguous term. See instead BAND MOLDING or STRINGCOURSE.

band molding In masonry or frame construction, any horizontal flat member or molding or group of moldings projecting slightly from a wall and marking a division in the wall. Not properly a synonym for band course. Simpler horizontal bands in masonry are generally called stringcourses.

bandstand A small pavilion, usually polygonal or circular in plan, designed to shelter bands during public concerts in a garden, park, green, or square. See also the related terms GAZEBO, KIOSK.

banister 1 Corrupted spelling of baluster, in use since about the seventeenth century. Now occasionally used for balusters that are thinner and simpler in profile than classical vase-shaped balusters. **2** Improperly used to mean the handrail of a stair.

bargeboard An ornate fascia board that is attached to the sloping edges (verges) of a roof, covering the ends of the horizontal roof timbers (purlins). Bargeboards are usually ornamented with carved, turned, or jigsawn forms. Sometimes called gableboards, vergeboards. Less ornate boards along the verges of a roof are simply called fascia boards.

Baroque A style of art and architecture that flourished in Europe and colonial North America during the seventeenth and eighteenth centuries. Although based on the architecture of the Renaissance, Baroque architecture was more dynamic, with circles frequently giving way to ovals, flat walls to curved or undulating ones, and separate elements to interlocking forms. It was a monumental and richly three-dimensional style with elaborate systems of ornamental and figural sculpture. See also the related terms RENAISSANCE, ROCOCO.

Baroque Revival See NEO-BAROQUE.

barrel vault A vaulted roof or ceiling of semicircular or semielliptical cross section, forming a tunnel-like enclosure over an apartment, corridor, or similar space.

Barryesque Term applied to Italianate buildings showing the influence of the English architect Sir Charles Barry (1795–1860), who introduced a derivative form of the Italian High Renaissance palazzo in his Travelers Club in London, 1829–1832. The style was brought to the United States by the Scottish-trained architect John Notman (1810–1865) and was popular from the late 1840s through the 1860s, especially for institutional and government buildings. Distinguished from the Italian Villa Style, which has the northern Italian rural vernacular villa as its prototype. See also the more general term ITALIANATE.

basement 1 The lowest story of a building, either partly or entirely below grade. **2** The lower part of the walls of any building, usually articulated distinctly from the upper part of the walls.

batten 1 A narrow strip of wood applied to cover a joint along the edges of two parallel boards in the same plane. **2** A strip of wood fastened across two or more parallel boards to hold them together. Sometimes called a cross batten. See also the related term BOARD-AND-BATTEN SIDING.

battered (adjective). Inclined from the vertical. A wall is said to be battered or to have a batter when it recedes as it rises.

battlement, battlemented See CRENELLATION.

Bauhaus 1 Work in any of the visual arts by the faculty and students of the Bauhaus, the innovative design school founded by Walter Gropius (1883–1969) and an active force in German modernism from 1919 until 1933. **2** Work in any of the visual arts by the former faculty and students of the Bauhaus, or by individuals influenced by them. See also the related terms INTERNATIONAL STYLE, MIESIAN.

bay 1 The interval between two recurring members. A facade is frequently measured by window bays, a skeletal frame by structural bays. **2** A polygonal or curved unit of one or more stories, projecting from the wall and usually containing grouped windows (bay windows) on each story. See also the more specific term BOWFRONT.

bay window The horizontally grouped windows in a projecting bay (definition 2), or the projecting bay itself, if it is not more than one story. Distinguished from an oriel, which does not rise from the foundation and has a suspended rather than rooted appearance. A semicircular or semielliptical bay window is called a bow window. A bay window with a central section of plate glass in a late nineteenth-century commercial building is called a Chicago window.

beam A structural spanning member of stone, wood, iron, steel, or reinforced concrete. See also the more specific terms GIRDER, I-BEAM, JOIST.

bearing wall A wall that is fully structural, carrying the load of the floors and roof all the way to the foundation. Sometimes called a supporting wall. Distinguished from curtain wall. See also the related term LOAD-BEARING.

Beaux-Arts Historicist design on a monumental scale, as taught at the Ecole des Beaux-Arts in Paris throughout the nineteenth century and early twentieth century. The term Beaux-Arts is generally applied to an eclectic Roman-Renaissance-Baroque architecture of the 1850s through the 1920s, disseminated internationally by students and followers of the Ecole des Beaux-Arts. As a general style term Beaux-Arts connotes an academically grounded discipline for historical eclecticism, rather than one single style, as well as the disciplined development of a *parti* into a fully visualized design. More specific style terms include Néo-Grec (1840s–1870s) and Beaux-Arts classicism (1870s–1930s). See also the related terms NEOCLASSICISM, for describing Ecole-related work from the 1790s to the 1840s, and SECOND EMPIRE, for describing the work from the 1850s to the 1880s.

Beaux-Arts classicism, Beaux-Arts classical Term applied to eclectic Roman-Renaissance-Baroque architecture and urbanism after the Néo-Grec and Second Empire phases, i.e., from the 1870s through the 1930s. Sometimes called Classic Revival, Classical Revival, McKim classicism, Neoclassical Revival. See also the more general term BEAUX-ARTS and the related terms CITY BEAUTIFUL MOVEMENT, PWA MODERNE.

belfry A cupola, turret, or room in a tower where a bell is housed.

bell cote A small gabled structure astride the ridge of a roof, which shelters a bell. It is usually close to the front wall plane of the building.

belt course See STRINGCOURSE.

belvedere 1 Any building, especially a pavilion or shelter, that is located to take advantage of a view. See also the related term GAZEBO. **2** See CUPOLA (definition 2).

beveled siding Horizontal wood covering of boards with slanted top and bottom edges, which, when laid together, create recessed V-joints or grooves.

blind (adjective) Term applied to the surface use of elements that would otherwise articulate an opening but where no opening exists. Used in such combinations as blind arcade, blind arch, blind door, blind window.

board-and-batten siding A type of siding for wood frame buildings, consisting of wide vertical boards with narrow strips of wood (battens) covering the joints. (In rare instances, the battens may be fastened behind the joints. If the gaps between boards are wide and the back battens approach the width of the outer boards, the siding is called board-on-board.) See also the related term BATTEN.

board-on-board siding A type of siding for wood frame buildings, consisting of two layers of vertical boards, with the outer layer of boards covering the wide gaps between the boards of the inner layer.

bowfront A semicircular or semielliptical bay (definition 2).

bow window A semicircular or semielliptical bay window.

brace A single wooden or metal member placed diagonally within a framework or truss or beneath an overhang. Distinguished from a bracket, which is a more substantial triangular feature, and from a strut, which is essentially a post set in a diagonal position.

braced frame construction A combination of heavy and light timber frame construction, in which the principal vertical and horizontal framing members (posts and girts) are fastened by mortise and tenon joints, while the one-story-high studs are nailed to the heavy timber frame. The overall frame is made more rigid by diagonal braces. Sometimes called braced framing.

bracket Any solid, pierced, or built-up triangular feature projecting from the face of a wall to support a projecting element, like the top member of a cornice or the verges or eaves of a roof. Brackets are frequently used for ornamental as well as structural purposes. Distinguished from a brace, which is a simple barlike structural member. Distinguished from the more specific term console, which has a height greater than its projection from the wall. See also the related term CORBEL.

Bracketed Style A nineteenth-century term for Italianate.

brick bonds, brickwork See the more specific terms COMMON BOND, ENGLISH BOND, FLEMISH BOND, RUNNING BOND.

British colonial A term applied to buildings, towns, landscapes, and other artifacts from the period of actual British colonial occupation of large parts of eastern North America (c. 1607–1781 for the United States; c. 1750s–1867 for much of Canada). The British colonial period saw the introduction into the New World of various regional strains of English and Scotch-Irish folk culture, as well as high-style Anglo-European Renaissance, Baroque, and Neoclassical design. Sometimes called English colonial. Loosely called colonial or Early American. See also the related term GEORGIAN PERIOD.

Brutalism An architectural style of the 1950s through 1970s, characterized by complex massing and by a frank expression of structural members, elements of building systems, and materials (especially concrete). Some of the work of Paul Rudolph (born 1918) is associated with this style. Sometimes called New Brutalism.

bungalow A low one- or one-and-one-half-story house of modest pretensions with a low-pitched gable or hipped roof, a conspicuous porch, and projecting eaves. This house type was a popular builders' type from around 1900 to 1930. The term bungalow was also loosely applied to any vernacular building of a semirustic nature, including vacation cottages and lodges.

Burlingtonian See ANGLO-PALLADIANISM.

butler building Generic term for any utilitarian, prefabricated building made with a metal frame and metal sheathing. The building type took its name from the Butler Manufacturing Company of the United States, which introduced an all-metal, prefabricated building in 1910.

buttress An exterior mass of masonry bonded into a wall that it strengthens or supports. Buttresses often absorb lateral thrusts from roofs or vaults.

Byzantine Term applied to the art and architecture of the Eastern Roman Empire centered at Byzantium (i.e., Constantinople, Istanbul) from the early 500s to the mid–1400s. Byzantine architecture is characterized by massive domes, round arches, richly carved capitals, and the extensive use of mosaic.

Byzantine Revival See NEO-BYZANTINE.

campanile In Italian, a bell tower. While usually freestanding in medieval and Renaissance architecture, it was often incorporated as a prominent unit in the massing of picturesque nineteenth-century buildings.

canale A clay rainwater gutter projecting horizontally from a parapet, usually seen in Pueblo Revival or Spanish Colonial Revival buildings.

cantilever A beam, girder, slab, truss, or other structural member that projects beyond its supporting wall or column.

cap A canopy, ledge, molding, or pediment over a window. Sometimes called a window cap. Distinguished from a hood, which is a similar feature over a door. See also the related term HEAD MOLDING.

capital The moldings and carved enrichment at the top of a column, pilaster, pier, or pedestal.

Carpenter's Gothic Term applied to a version of the Gothic Revival (c. 1840s–1870s), in which Gothic motifs are adapted to the kind of wooden details that can be produced by lathes, jigsaws, and molding machines. Sometimes called Carpenter Gothic, Gingerbread Style, Steamboat Gothic. See also the more general term GOTHIC REVIVAL.

carriage porch SEE PORTE-COCHERE.

casement window A window that opens from the side on hinges, like a door, out from the plane of the wall. Distinguished from a double-hung window.

casing See ARCHITRAVE (definition 2).

cast iron Iron shaped by a molding process, generally strong in compression but brittle in tension. Distinguished from wrought iron, which has been forged to increase its tensile properties.

cast iron front An architectural facade made of prefabricated molded iron parts, often markedly skeletal in appearance with extensive glass infilling. Prevalent from the late 1840s to the early 1870s.

castellated Having the elements of a medieval castle, such as crenellation and turrets.

cavetto cornice See COVED CORNICE.

cement A mixture of burnt lime and clay with water, which hardens permanently when dry. When a fine aggregate of sand is added, the cement may be used as a mortar for masonry construction or as a plaster or stucco coating. When a coarser aggregate of gravel or crushed stone is added, along with sand, the mixture is called concrete.

chamfer The oblique surface formed by cutting off a square edge at an equal angle to each face.

chancel 1 The end of a Roman Catholic or High Episcopal church containing the altar and set apart for the clergy and choir by a screen, rail, or steps. Usually the entire east end of a church beyond the crossing. In churches that have a long chancel space, the part of the chancel between the crossing and the apse, where the singers participate in the service, is called the choir. The innermost part of the chancel, containing the principal altar, is called the sanctuary. **2** In less extensive Catholic and Episcopal churches, the terms chancel and choir are often used interchangeably to mean the entire eastern arm of the church.

Chateauesque A term applied to masonry buildings from the 1870s through the 1920s in which stylistic references are derived from early French Renaissance chateaux, from the reign of Francis I (1515–1547) or even earlier. Sometimes called Chateau Style, Chateauesque Revival, Francis I Style, François Premier.

chevet In large churches, particularly those based upon French Gothic precedents, a substantial apse surrounded by an ambulatory and often containing radiating chapels.

Chicago School A diverse group of architects associated with the development of the tall (i.e., six- to twenty-story), usually metal frame commercial building in Chicago during the 1880s and 1890s. William Le Baron Jenney, Burnham and Root, and Adler and Sullivan are identified with this group. Sometimes called Chicago Commercial Style, Commercial Style. See also the related term PRAIRIE SCHOOL.

Chicago window A tripartite oblong window in which a large fixed center pane is placed between two narrow sash windows. Popularized in Chicago commercial buildings of the 1880s–1890s. See also BAY WINDOW.

chimney girt In timber frame construction, a major wooden beam that passes across the breast of the central chimney. It is supported at its ends by the longitudinal girts of the building and sometimes carries one end of the summer beam.

chinking A mortar of plaster or adobe, usually mixed with straw, used to fill the gaps between logs in a log cabin.

choir 1 The part of a Roman Catholic or High Episcopal church where the singers participate in the service. Usually the space within the chancel arm of the church, situated between the crossing to the west and the sanctuary to the east. **2** In less extensive Catholic and Episcopal churches, the terms choir and chancel are often used interchangeably to mean the entire eastern arm of the church.

Churrigueresque Term applied to Spanish and Spanish colonial Baroque architecture resembling the work of the Spanish architect José Benito de Churriguera (1665–1725) and his brothers. The style is characterized by a freely interpreted assemblage of such elements as twisted columns, broken pediments, and scroll brackets. See also the related term SPANISH COLONIAL.

cinquefoil A type of Gothic tracery having five parts (lobes or foils) separated by pointed elements (cusps).

City Beautiful movement A movement in architecture, landscape architecture, and planning in the United States from the 1890s through the 1920s, advocating the beautification of cities in the image of some of the most urbane places of the time: the world's fairs. City Beautiful schemes emphasized civic centers, boulevards, and waterfront improvements, and sometimes included comprehensive metropolitan plans for parks, parkways, and transportation facilities. See also the related term BEAUX-ARTS CLASSICISM.

clapboard A tapered board that is thinner along the top edge and thicker along the bottom edge, applied horizontally with edges overlapping to provide weathertight siding on a building of wood construction. Early clapboards were split (rived, riven) and were used for barrel staves and for wainscoting. The term now applies to any beveled siding board, whether split or sawn, rabbeted or not, regardless of length or width. (The term is sometimes applied only to a form of bevel siding used in New England, about four feet long and quarter-sawn.) Sometimes called weatherboards.

classical orders See ORDER.

classical rectangle See GOLDEN SECTION.

Classical Revival Ambiguous term, suggesting (1) Neoclassical design of the late eighteenth and early nineteenth centuries, including the Greek Revival; or (2) Beaux-Arts classical design of the late nineteenth and early twentieth centuries. Sometimes called Classic Revival. See instead BEAUX-ARTS CLASSICISM, GREEK REVIVAL, NEOCLASSICISM.

classicism, classical, classicizing Terms describing the application of principles or elements derived from the visual arts of the Greco-Roman era (seventh century B.C. through fourth century A.D.) at any subsequent period of Western civilization, but particularly since the Renaissance. More a descriptive term for an approach to design and for a general cultural sensibility than for any particular style. See also the related term NEOCLASSICISM.

clerestory A part of a building that rises above the roof of another part and has windows in its walls.

clipped gable roof See JERKINHEAD ROOF.

coffer A recessed panel, usually square or octagonal, in a ceiling. Such panels are also found on the inner surfaces of domes and vaults.

collar beam A horizontal tension member in a pitched roof connecting opposite rafters, generally halfway up or higher. Its function is to tie the angular members together and prevent them from spreading.

Collegiate Gothic 1 Originally, a secular version of English Gothic architecture, characteristic of the older colleges of Oxford and Cambridge. 2 A secular version of Late Gothic Revival architecture, which became a popular style for North American colleges and universities from the 1890s through the 1920s. Sometimes called Academic Gothic.

colonial 1 Not strictly a style term, but a term for the entire period during which a particular European country held political dominion over a part of the Western Hemisphere, Africa, Asia, Australia, or Oceania. See also the more specific terms BRITISH COLONIAL, DUTCH COLONIAL, FRENCH COLONIAL, SPANISH COLONIAL. 2 Loosely used to mean the British colonial period in North America (c. 1607–1781 for the United States; c. 1750s–1867 for much of Canada).

Colonial Revival Generally understood to mean the revival of forms from British colonial design. The Colonial Revival began in New England in the 1860s and continues nationwide into the present. Sometimes called Neo-Colonial. See also the more specific term GEORGIAN REVIVAL and the related terms FEDERAL REVIVAL, SHINGLE STYLE.

colonnade A series of freestanding or engaged columns supporting an entablature or simple beam.

colonnette A diminutive, often attenuated, column.

colossal order See GIANT ORDER.

column 1 A vertical supporting element, usually cylindrical and slightly tapering, consisting of a base (except in the Greek Doric order), shaft, and capital. See also the related terms ENTABLATURE, ENTASIS, ORDER. 2 Any vertical supporting element in a skeletal frame.

Commercial Style See CHICAGO SCHOOL.

common bond A pattern of brickwork in which every fifth or sixth course consists of all headers, the other courses being all stretchers. Sometimes called American bond. Distinguished from running bond, in which no headers appear.

Composite order An ensemble of classical column and entablature elements, particularly characterized by large Ionic volutes and Corinthian acanthus leaves in the capital of the column. See also the more general term ORDER.

concrete An artificial stone made by mixing cement, water, sand, and a coarse aggregate (such as gravel or crushed stone) in specified proportions. The mix is shaped in molds called forms. Distinguished from cement, which is the binder without the aggregate.

console A type of bracket with a scroll-shaped or S-curve profile and a height greater than its projection from the wall. Distinguished from the more general term bracket, which is usually applied to supports whose projection and height are nearly equal. Distinguished from a modillion, which usually is smaller, has a projection greater than its height (or thickness), and appears in a series, as in a classical cornice.

coping The cap or top course of a wall, parapet, balustrade, or chimney, usually designed to shed water.

corbel A projecting stone that supports a superincumbent weight. In medieval architecture and its derivatives, a support for such major features as vaulting shafts, vaulting ribs, or oriels. See also the related term BRACKET.

corbeled construction Masonry that is built outward beyond the vertical by letting successive courses project beyond those below. Sometimes called corbeling.

corbeled cornice A cornice made up of courses of projecting masonry, each of which extends farther outward than the one below.

Corinthian order An ensemble of classical column and entablature elements, particularly characterized by acanthus leaves and small volutes in the capital of the column. See also the more general term ORDER.

cornice The crowning member of a wall or entablature.

Corporate International Style A term, not widely used, for curtain wall commercial, institutional, and governmental buildings since the Second World War, which represent a widespread adoption of selected International Style ideas from the 1920s. See also the more general term INTERNATIONAL STYLE.

Corporate Style An architectural style developed in the early industrial communities of New England during the first half of the nineteenth century. This austere but graceful mode of construction was derived from the red-brick Federal architecture of the early nineteenth century and is characterized by the same elegant proportions, cleanly cut openings, and simple refined detailing. The term was coined by William Pierson in the 1970s. Not to be confused with Corporate International Style.

cottage 1 A relatively modest rural or suburban dwelling. Distinguished from a villa, which is a more substantial and often more elaborate dwelling. 2 A seasonal dwelling, regardless of size, especially one located in a resort community.

cottage orné A rustic building in the romantic, picturesque tradition, noted for such features as bay windows, oriels, ornamented gables, and clustered chimneys.

course A layer of building blocks, such as bricks or stones, extending the full length and thickness of a wall.

coved ceiling A ceiling in which the transition between wall and ceiling is formed by a large concave panel or molding. Sometimes called a cove ceiling.

coved cornice A cornice with a concave profile. Sometimes called a cavetto cornice.

Craftsman A style of furniture and interior design belonging to the Arts and Crafts movement in the United States, and specifically related to *The Craftsman* magazine (1901–1916), published by Gustav Stickley (1858–1942). Some entire houses known to be derived from this publication can be called Craftsman houses. See also the more general term ARTS AND CRAFTS.

crenellation, crenellated A form of embellishment on a parapet consisting of indentations (crenels or embrasures) alternating with solid blocks of wall (merlons). Virtually synonymous with battlement, battlemented; embattlement, embattled.

cresting An ornamental strip or fencelike feature, usually of metal or tile, along the ridgeline or summit of a roof.

crocket In Gothic architecture, a small ornament resembling bunched foliage, placed at intervals on the sloping edges of gables, pinnacles, or spires.

crossing In a church with a cruciform plan, the area where the arms of the cross intersect; specifically, the space where the transept crosses the nave and chancel.

cross rib See LIERNE.

cross section See SECTION.

crown The central, or highest, part of an arch or vault.

crown molding The highest in a series of moldings.

crowstep Any one of the progressions in a gable that ascends in steps rather than in a continuous slope.

cruciform In the shape of a cross. Usually used to describe the ground plans of buildings. See also the more specific terms GREEK CROSS, LATIN CROSS.

cupola 1 A small domed structure on top of a belfry, steeple, or tower. **2** A lantern, square or polygonal in plan, with windows or vents, which is located at the summit of a roof. Sometimes called a belvedere. Distinguished from a skylight, which is a lesser feature located on the slope of a roof. **3** In historic English usage, synonymous with dome. A dome is now understood to be a more substantial feature.

curtain wall In skeleton frame or reinforced concrete construction, a thin nonstructural cladding of stone, brick, terra cotta, glass, or metal veneer. Distinguished from bearing wall. See also the related term LOAD-BEARING.

cusp The pointed, roughly triangular intersection of the arcs of lobes or foils in the tracery of windows, screens, or panels.

dado A broad decorative band around the lower portion of an interior wall, between the baseboard and dado rail or cap molding. (The term is often applied to this entire zone, including baseboard and dado rail.) The dado may be painted, papered, or covered with some other material, so as to have a different treatment from the upper zone of the wall. Dado connotes any continuous lower zone in a room, equivalent to a pedestal. A wood-paneled dado is called a wainscot.

Deco. See ART DECO.

dentil, denticulated A small ornamental block forming one of a series set in a row. A dentil molding is composed of such a series.

dependency A building, wing, or room, subordinate to or serving as an adjunct to a main building. A dependency may be attached to or detached from a main building. Distinguished from an outbuilding, which is always detached.

diaper An overall repetitive pattern on a flat surface, especially a pattern of geometric or representational forms arranged in a diamond-shaped or checkerboard grid. Sometimes called diaper work.

discharging arch See RELIEVING ARCH.

dome A major hemispherical or curved roof feature rising from a circular, polygonal, or square base. Distinguished from a cupola, which is a smaller, usually subordinate, domical element.

Doric order An ensemble of classical column and entablature elements, particularly characterized by the use of triglyphs and metopes in the frieze of the entablature. See also the more general term ORDER.

dormer A roof-sheltered window (or vent), usually with vertical sides and front, set into a sloping roof. Sometimes called a dormer window.

dosseret See IMPOST BLOCK.

double-hung window A window consisting of a pair of frames, or sashes, one above the other, arranged to slide up and down. Their movement is sometimes stabilized by a system of cords and counterbalancing weights contained in narrow boxing at each side of the window frame. Sometimes called guillotine sash.

double-pen In vernacular architecture, particularly houses, a term applied to a plan consisting of two rooms side by side or separated by a hallway.

double-pile In vernacular architecture, particularly houses, a term applied to a plan that is two rooms deep and any number of rooms wide.

drip molding See HEAD MOLDING.

drop siding Wood siding made of horizontal boards joined by rabbets, leaving a decorative channel.

drum 1 A cylindrical or polygonal wall zone upon which a dome rests. **2** One of the cylinders of stone that form the shaft of a column.

dugout A dwelling formed by an excavation in the ground, usually in a slope or bank, roofed with turf, canvas, or other material.

Dutch colonial A term applied to buildings, towns, landscapes, and other artifacts from the period of actual Dutch colonial occupation of the Hudson River valley and adjacent areas (c.

1614–1664). Meaning has been extended to apply to the artifacts of Dutch ethnic groups and their descendants, even into the early nineteenth century.

Dutch Colonial Revival The revival of forms from design in the Dutch tradition.

ear A slight projection just below the upper corners of a door or window architrave or casing. Sometimes called a shouldered architrave.

Early American See BRITISH COLONIAL.

Early Christian A style of art and architecture in the Mediterranean world that was developed by the early Christians before the fall of the Western Roman Empire, derived from late Roman art and architecture and leading to the Romanesque (early fourth to early sixth century).

Early Georgian period Not strictly a style term, but a term for a period in British and British colonial history approximately coinciding with the reigns of George I (1714–1727) and George II (1727–1760). See also the related term LATE GEORGIAN PERIOD.

Early Gothic Revival A term for the Gothic Revival work of the late eighteenth to the midnineteenth century. See also the related term LATE GOTHIC REVIVAL.

Eastlake A decorative arts and interior design term of the 1860s and 1880s sometimes applied to architecture. Named after Charles Locke Eastlake (1836–1906), an English advocate of the application of Gothic principles of construction and design, rather than mere Gothic elements. Characterized by simplicity and solidity of forms, which are sometimes embellished with chamfered, turned, or incised details. Sometimes called Eastlake Gothic, Modern Gothic. See also the related term QUEEN ANNE.

eaves The horizontal lower edges of a roof plane, usually projecting beyond the wall below. Distinguished from verges, which are the sloping edges of a roof plane.

echinus A heavy molding with a curved profile placed immediately below the abacus, or top member, of a classical capital. Particularly prominent in the Doric and Tuscan orders.

eclecticism, eclectic A sensibility in design, prevalent since the eighteenth century, involving the selection of elements from a variety of sources, including historical periods of high-style design (Western and non-Western), vernacular design (Western and non-Western), and (in the twentieth century) contemporary industrial design. Distinguished from historicism and revivalism by drawing upon a wider range of sources than the historical periods of high-style design.

Ecole, Ecole des Beaux-Arts See BEAUX-ARTS.

Egyptian Revival Term applied to eclectic works or elements of those works that emulate forms in the visual arts of ancient Egyptian civilization.

elevation A drawing (in orthographic projection) of an upright, planar aspect of an object or building. The vertical complement of a plan.

Sometimes loosely used in the sense of a facade view or any frontal representation of a wall, whether photograph or drawing, whether measured to scale or not.

Elizabethan Manor Style See NEO-TUDOR.

Elizabethan period A term for a period in English history coinciding with the reign of Elizabeth I (1558–1603). See also the more general term TUDOR PERIOD and the related term JACOBEAN PERIOD for the succeeding period.

embattlement, embattled See CRENELLATION.

encaustic tile A tile decorated by a polychrome glazed or ceramic inlay pattern.

engaged column A half-round column attached to a wall. Distinguished from a free-standing column by seeming to be built into the wall. Distinguished from a pilaster, which is a flattened column. Distinguished from a recessed column, which is a fully round column set into a niche-like space.

English bond A pattern of brickwork in which the bricks are set in alternating courses of stretchers and headers.

English colonial See BRITISH COLONIAL.

English Half-timber Style See NEO-TUDOR.

entablature In a classical order, a richly detailed horizontal member resting on columns or pilasters. It is divided horizontally into three main parts. The lowest is the architrave (definition 1), the structural part, and is generally an unornamented continuous beam or series of beams. The middle part is the frieze (definition 1), which is generally the most freely ornamented part. The uppermost is the cornice. Composed of a sequence of moldings, the cornice overhangs the frieze and architrave and serves as a crown to the whole. Each part has the moldings and decorative treatment that are characteristic of the particular order, but modern adaptations often alter canonical details. See also the related terms COLUMN, ORDER.

entablature block A block bearing the canonical elements of a classical entablature on three or all four sides, placed between a column capital and a feature above, such as a balcony or ceiling. Distinguished from an impost block, which has the form of an inverted truncated pyramid and detailing typical of medieval architecture.

entasis The slight convex curving of the vertical profile of a tapered column.

exedra A semicircular or polygonal space usually containing a bench, in the wall of a garden or a building other than a church. Distinguished from a niche, which is usually a smaller feature higher in a wall, and from an apse, which is usually identified with churches.

exotic revivals A term occasionally used to suggest a distinction between revivals of European styles (e.g., Greek, Gothic Revivals) and non-European styles (e.g., Egyptian, Moorish Revivals). See also the more specific terms EGYPTIAN REVIVAL, MAYAN REVIVAL, MOORISH REVIVAL.

extrados The outer curve or outside surface of an arch. See also the related term INTRADOS.

eyebrow dormer A low dormer with a small segmental window or vent but no sides. The roofing warps or bows over the window or vent in a wavy line.

facade An exterior face of a building, especially the principal or entrance front. Distinguished from an elevation, which is an orthographic drawing of a building face.

false half-timbering A surface treatment that simulates half-timber construction, consisting of a lattice of broad boards and stucco applied as an exterior veneer on a building of masonry or wood frame construction. Most commonly seen in domestic architecture from the late nineteenth century onward.

fanlight A semicircular or semielliptical window over a door, with radiating mullions in the form of an open fan. Sometimes called a sunburst light. See also the more general term TRANSOM (definition 1) and the related term SIDE LIGHT.

fan vault A type of Gothic vault in which the primary ribs all have the same curvature and radiate in a half circle around the springing point.

fascia 1 A plain, molded, or ornamented board that covers the horizontal edges (eaves) or sloping edges (verges) of a roof. Distinguished from the more specific term bargeboards, which are ornate fascia boards attached to the sloping edges of a roof. Distinguished from a frieze (definition 2), which is located at the top of a wall. **2** One of the broad continuous bands that make up the architrave of the Ionic, Corinthian, or Composite order.

Federal A version of Neoclassical architecture in the United States popular from New England to Virginia, and in other regions influenced by the Northeast. It flourished from the 1790s through the 1820s and is found in some regions as late as the 1840s. Sometimes called American Adam Style. Not to be confused with Federalist. See also the related terms JEFFERSONIAN, ROMAN REVIVAL.

Federal Revival Term applied to eclectic works (c. 1890s–1930s) or elements of those works that emulate forms in the visual arts of the Federal period. Sometimes called Neo-Federal. See also the related terms COLONIAL REVIVAL, GEORGIAN REVIVAL.

Federalist Name of an American political party and the era it dominated (c. 1787–1820). Not to be confused with Federal.

fenestration Window treatment: arrangement and proportioning.

festoon A motif representing entwined leaves, flowers, or fruits, hung in a catenary curve from two points. Distinguished from a swag, which is a motif representing a fold of drapery hung in a similar curve. See also the more general term GARLAND.

fillet 1 A relatively narrow flat molding. **2** Any thin band.

finial A vertical ornament placed upon the apex of an architectural feature, such as a gable, turret, or canopy. Distinguished from a pinnacle, which is a larger feature, usually associated with Gothic architecture.

fireproofing In metal skeletal framing, the wrapping of structural members in terra-cotta tile or other fire-resistant material.

flashing A strip of metal, plastic, or various flexible compositional materials used at roof valleys and ridges and at chimney corners to keep water out. Any similar material used to protect door and window heads and sills.

Flemish bond A pattern of brickwork in which the stretchers and headers alternate in the same row and are staggered from one row to the next. Because this creates a more animated texture than English bond, Flemish bond was favored for front facades and more elegant buildings.

Flemish gable A gable whose upper slopes ascend in steps rather than in a straight line. These steps may be rectilinear or curved, or a combination of both.

fluting, fluted A series of parallel grooves or channels (flutes), usually semicircular or semielliptical in plan, that accentuate the verticality of the shaft of a column or pilaster.

flying buttress In Gothic architecture a spanning member, usually in the form of an arch, that reaches across the open space from an exterior buttress pier to that point on the wall of the building where the thrusts of the interior vaults are concentrated. Because of its arched construction, a flying buttress exerts a counterthrust against the pressure of the vaults contained by the vertical strength of the buttress pier.

foliated (adjective). In the form of leaves or leaflike shapes.

folk Not a style term in itself, but a descriptive term, applicable to all the visual arts and all styles and periods. Applied to (1) a regional, often ethnic, tradition in which continuities through the years in the overall appearance of artifacts (including buildings) are more important than changes in stylistic embellishment; (2) the work of individual artists and artisans unexposed to or uninterested in prevailing or avant-garde ideals of form and technique. Approximate synonyms include anonymous, naive, primitive, traditional. For architecture, see also the more general term VERNACULAR and the related term POPULAR.

four-part vault See QUADRIPARTITE VAULT.

foursquare house A hip-roofed, two-story house with four principal rooms on each floor and a symmetrical facade. It usually has a front porch across the full width of the house and one or more large dormers on the roof. A common suburban house type from the 1890s to the 1920s. Sometimes called American Foursquare, Prairie Box.

frame construction, frame See BRACED FRAME CONSTRUCTION, LIGHT FRAME CONSTRUCTION (BALLOON FRAME CONSTRUCTION, PLATFORM FRAME CONSTRUCTION), SKELETON CONSTRUCTION, TIMBER FRAME CONSTRUCTION.

Francis I Style See CHATEAUESQUE.

François Premier See CHATEAUESQUE.

French colonial A term applied to buildings, towns, landscapes, and other artifacts from the period of actual French colonial occupation of large parts of eastern North America (c. 1605–1763). The term is extended to apply to the artifacts of French ethnic groups and their descendants well into the nineteenth century.

French Norman A style associated since the 1920s with residential architecture based on rural houses of the French provinces of Normandy and Brittany. While not a major revival style, it is characterized by asymmetrical plans, round stair towers with conical roofs, stucco walls, and steep hipped roofs. Sometimes called Norman French.

fret An ornament, usually in series, as a band or field, consisting of a latticelike interlocking of right-angled linear elements.

frieze 1 The broad horizontal band that forms the central part of a classical entablature. **2** Any long horizontal band or zone, especially one that has a chiefly decorative purpose, located at the top of a wall. Distinguished from a fascia, which is attached to the horizontal edge of a roof.

front gabled Term applied to a building whose principal gable end faces the front of the lot or some feature like a street or open space. Sometimes called gable front. Distinguished from side gabled.

gable The wall area immediately below the end of a gable, gambrel, or jerkinhead roof.

gableboard See BARGEBOARD.

gable front See FRONT GABLED.

gable roof A roof in which the two planes slope equally toward each other to a common ridge. Sometimes called a pitched roof.

gambrel roof A roof that has a single ridgepole but a double pitch. The lower plane, which rises from the eaves, is rather steep. The upper plane, which extends from the lower plane to the ridgeline, has a flatter pitch.

garland A motif representing a rope of entwined leaves, flowers, ribbons, or drapery, regardless of its shape or position. It may be formed into a wreath, festoon, or swag, or follow the outline of a rectilinear architectural element.

garret See ATTIC (definition 1).

gauged brick A brick that has been cut or rubbed to a uniform size and shape.

gazebo A small pavilion, usually polygonal or circular in plan and serving as a garden or park shelter. Distinguished from a kiosk, which generally has some commercial or public function. See also the related terms BANDSTAND, BELVEDERE (definition 1).

General Grant Style See SECOND EMPIRE.

geodesic dome A domed or vaulted structure of lightweight straight elements that form interlocking polygons, developed by R. Buckminster Fuller after World War II as a low-cost and efficient method of modular space-frame construction.

Georgian period A term for a period in British and British colonial history, and not, in architecture or the other visual arts, a sufficiently specific style term. The Georgian period begins with the coronation of George I in 1714 and extends until about 1781 in the area that became the United States (and in Britain, until the death of George IV in 1830). See also the related terms ANGLO-PALLADIANISM, BRITISH COLONIAL.

Georgian plan See DOUBLE-PILE plus DOUBLE-PEN(i.e., a four-room plan with central hallway).

Georgian Revival A revival of Georgian period forms—in England, from the 1860s to the present, and in the United States, from the 1880s to the present. Sometimes called Neo-Georgian. See also the more general term COLONIAL REVIVAL and the related term FEDERAL REVIVAL.

giant order A composition involving any one of the five principal classical orders, in which the columns or pilasters are nearly as tall as the height of the entire building. Sometimes called a colossal order. See also the more general term ORDER.

Gingerbread Style See CARPENTER'S GOTHIC.

girder A major horizontal spanning member, comparable in function to a beam, but larger and often built up of a number of parts. It usually runs at right angles to the beams and serves as their principal means of support.

girt In timber frame construction, a horizontal beam at intermediate (e.g., second-floor) level, spanning between posts.

glazing bar See MUNTIN.

golden section Any line divided into two parts so that the ratio of the longer part to the shorter part equals the ratio of the length of the whole line to the longer part: $a/b = (a+b)/a$. This ratio is approximately 1.618:1. A golden rectangle, or classical rectangle, is a rectangle whose long side is related to the short side in the same ratio as the golden section. It is proportioned so that neither the long nor the short side seems to dominate. In a Fibonacci series (i.e., 1, 2, 3, 5, 8, 13, . . .), the sum of the two preceding terms gives the next. The higher one goes in such a series, the closer the ratio of two sequential terms approaches the golden section.

Googie 1 A term, not widely used, to refer to roadside architecture of the 1950s characterized by curvilinear forms such as flying saucers, boomerangs, starbursts, and kidney beans. **2** Coined by architectural historian Douglas Haskell in 1952 after the Los Angeles coffee shop, Googie's, considered an exemplar of the style. Sometimes called Populuxe.

Gothic An architectural style prevalent in Europe from the twelfth century into the fifteenth in Italy (and into the sixteenth century in the rest of Europe). It is characterized by pointed arches and ribbed vaults and by the dominance of openings over masonry mass in the wall. The Gothic was preceded by the Romanesque and followed by the Renaissance.

Gothic Revival A movement in Europe and North America devoted to reviving the forms and the spirit of Gothic architecture and the allied arts. It originated in the mid-eighteenth century. Sometimes called the Pointed Style in the nineteenth century, and sometimes called Neo-Gothic. See also the more specific terms CARPENTER'S GOTHIC, EARLY GOTHIC REVIVAL, HIGH VICTORIAN GOTHIC, LATE GOTHIC REVIVAL.

Grecian A nineteenth-century term for Greek Revival.

Greek cross A cross with four equal arms. Usually used to describe the ground plan of a building. See also the more general term CRUCIFORM.

Greek Revival A movement in Europe and North America devoted to reviving the forms and the spirit of Classical Greek architecture, sculpture, and decorative arts. It originated in the mid-eighteenth century, culminated in the 1830s, and continued into the 1850s. Sometimes called Grecian in the nineteenth century. See also the more general term NEOCLASSICAL.

groin The curved edge formed by the intersection of two vaults.

guillotine sash See DOUBLE-HUNG WINDOW.

HABS See HISTORIC AMERICAN BUILDINGS SURVEY.

HAER See HISTORIC AMERICAN ENGINEERING RECORD.

half-timber construction A variety of timber frame construction in which the framing members are exposed on the exterior of the wall, with the spaces between timbers being filled with wattle-and-daub (i.e., woven lath and plaster) or masonry materials, such as brick or stone. These masonry materials may also be covered with stucco. Sometimes called half-timbered construction.

hall-and-parlor house, hall-and-parlor plan A double-pen house (i.e., a house that is one room deep and two rooms wide). Usually applied to houses without a central through-passage, to distinguish from hall-passage-parlor houses.

hall-passage-parlor house, hall-passage-parlor plan A two-room house with a central through-passage or hallway.

hammerbeam A short horizontal beam projecting inward from the foot of the principal rafter and supported below by a diagonal brace tied into a vertical wall post. The hammer beams carry much of the load of the roof trussing above. Hammer beam trusses, which could be assembled using a series of smaller timbers, were often used in late medieval England instead of conventional trusses, which required long horizontal tie beams extending across an entire interior space.

haunch The part of the arch between the crown or keystone and the springing.

header A brick laid across the thickness of a wall, so that the short end of the brick shows on the exterior.

head molding A molding or set of moldings designed to shelter and embellish the top of a door or window. Sometimes called a drip molding. See also the related terms CAP(for windows) and HOOD(for doors).

heavy timber construction See TIMBER-FRAME CONSTRUCTION.

high style or high-style (adjective) Not a style term in itself, but a descriptive term, applicable to all the visual arts and all styles and periods. Applied to the works of the masters and their schools and disciples, usually reflecting a cosmopolitan awareness of traditions beyond a particular place or time. Usually contrasted with vernacular (including the folk and popular traditions).

high tech Term applied to architecture in which building materials and elements of building systems are used to celebrate contemporary technology. Elemental geometric forms, primary colors, and metallic finishes are used to heighten the technological imagery.

High Victorian Gothic A version of the Gothic Revival that originated in England in the 1850s and spread to North America in the 1860s. Characterized by polychromatic exteriors inspired by the medieval Gothic architecture of northern Italy. Sometimes called Ruskin Gothic, Ruskinian Gothic, Venetian Gothic, Victorian Gothic. See also the more general term GOTHIC REVIVAL.

hipped gable roof See JERKINHEAD ROOF.

hipped roof A roof that pitches inward from all four sides. The edge where any two planes meet is called the hip.

Historic American Buildings Survey (HABS) A branch of the National Park Service of the United States Department of the Interior, established in 1933 to produce detailed documentation of American architecture. HABS documentation typically includes historical and architectural data, photographs, and measured drawings, and is deposited in the Prints and Photographs Division of the Library of Congres. See also the related term HISTORIC AMERICAN ENGINEERING RECORD.

Historic American Engineering Record (HAER) A branch of the National Park Service of the United States Department of the Interior, established in 1969 to produce detailed documentation of sites and structures associated with industry, transportation, and other areas of technology. See also the related term HISTORIC AMERICAN BUILDINGS SURVEY.

historicism, historicist, historicizing A type of eclecticism prevalent since the eighteenth century, involving the use of forms from historical periods of high-style design (usually in the Western tradition) and, occasionally, from favored traditions of vernacular design (such as the various colonial traditions in the United States). Historicist influences are designated by the use of the prefix Neo- with a previous historical style (e.g., Neo-Baroque). Distinguished from the more general term eclecticism, which draws upon a wider range of sources in addition to the historical. See also the more specific term REVIVALISM.

hollow building tile A hollow terracotta building block used for constructing exterior bearing walls of buildings up to about three stories, as well as interior walls and partitions.

hood A canopy, ledge, molding, or pediment over a door. Distinguished from a cap, which is a similar feature over a window. Sometimes called a hood molding. See also the related term HEAD MOLDING.

horizontal plank frame construction A system of wood construction in which horizontal planks are set or nailed into the corner posts of a timber frame building. There are, however, no studs or intermediate posts connecting the sill and the plate. See also the related term VERTICAL PLANK FRAME CONSTRUCTION.

hung ceiling See SUSPENDED CEILING.

hyphen A subsidiary building unit, often one story, connecting the central block and the wings or dependencies.

I-beam The most common profile in steel structural shapes (although it also appears in cast iron and in reinforced concrete). Used especially for spanning elements, it is shaped like the capital letter *I* to make the most efficient use of the material consistent with a shape that permits easy assemblage. The vertical face of the *I* is the web. The horizontal faces are the flanges. Other standard shapes for steel framing elements are *H*s, *T*s, *Z*s, *L*s (known as angles), and square-cornered *U*s (channels).

I-house A two-story house, one room deep and two rooms wide, usually with a central hallway. The I-house is a nineteenth-century descendant of the hall-and-parlor houses of the colonial period. The term is commonly applied to the end-chimney houses of the southern and mid-Atlantic traditions. The term most likely derives from the resemblance between the tall, narrow end walls of these houses and the capital letter *I*.

impost The top part of a pier or wall, upon which rests the springer or lowest voussoir of an arch.

impost block A block, often in the form of an inverted truncated pyramid, placed between a column capital and the lowest voussoirs of an arch above. Distinguished from an entablature block, which has the details found in a classical entablature. Sometimes called a dosseret or supercapital.

in antis Columns in antis are placed between two projecting sections of wall, in an imaginary plane connecting the ends of the two wall elements.

intermediate rib See TIERCERON.

International Style A style that originated in the 1920s and flourished into the 1970s, characterized by the expression of volume and surface and by the suppression of historicist ornament and axial symmetry. The term was originally applied by Henry-Russell Hitchcock and Philip Johnson to the new, nontraditional, mostly European architecture of the 1920s in their 1932 exhibition at the Museum of Modern Art and in their accompanying book, *The International Style.* Also called International, International Modern. See also the more specific term CORPORATE INTERNATIONAL STYLE and the related terms BAUHAUS, MIESIAN, SECOND CHICAGO SCHOOL.

intrados The inner curve or underside (soffit) of an arch. See also the related term EXTRADOS.

Ionic order An ensemble of classical column and entablature elements, particularly characterized by the use of large volutes in the capital of the column. See also the more general term ORDER.

isometric drawing A pictorial drawing using isometric projection, in which all horizontal lines that are perpendicular in an object, building, or space are drawn at 60-degree angles from the vertical. Consequently, a single scale can be used for all three dimensions. Sometimes called an isometric. See also the related terms AXONOMETRIC DRAWING, PERSPECTIVE DRAWING.

Italianate 1 A general term for an eclectic Neo-Renaissance and Neo-Romanesque style, originating in England and Germany in the early nineteenth century and prevalent in the United States between the 1840s and 1880s, not only in houses but also in Main Street commercial buildings. The Italianate is characterized by prominent window heads and bracketed cornices. Called the Bracketed Style in the nineteenth century. See also the more specific terms BARRYESQUE and ITALIAN VILLA STYLE, and the related terms RENAISSANCE REVIVAL, ROUND ARCH MODE, SECOND EMPIRE. **2** A specific term for Italianate buildings that are predominantly symmetrical in plan and elevation. Distinguished from Barryesque, which is applied to more formal institutional and governmental buildings.

Italian Villa Style A subtype of the Italianate style (definition 1), originating in England and Germany in the early nineteenth century and prevalent in the United States between the 1840s and 1870s, mostly in houses, but also churches and other public buildings. The style is characterized by asymmetrical plans and elevations, irregular blocklike massing, round arch arcades and openings, and northern Italian Romanesque detailing. Larger Italian Villa buildings often had a campanile-like tower. Distinguished from the more symmetrical Italianate style (definition 2) by having the northern Italian rural vernacular villa as prototype.

jacal (plural: jacales) A small hut with walls consisting of vertical poles, often plastered with mud.

Jacobean period A term for a period in British history coinciding with the rule of James I (1603–1625). See also the related term ELIZABETHAN for the immediately preceding period, which itself is part of the Tudor period.

Jacobethan Revival See NEO-TUDOR.

jamb The vertical side face of a door or window opening, amounting to the full thickness of the wall, and usually enriched with paneling, moldings, or jamb shafts (which are engaged columns set into a splayed, or angled, jamb). In an opening containing a door or window, the jamb is distinguished from the reveal, which is the portion of wall thickness between the door or window frame and the outer surface of the wall. (In an opening without a door or window, the terms jamb and reveal are used interchangeably.) Also distinguished from an architrave (definition 2), which consists of the moldings on the face of a wall around the opening.

Jazz Moderne See ART DECO.

Jeffersonian A personal style of Neoclassicism identified with the architecture of Thomas Jefferson (1743–1826), derived in part from Palladian ideas and in part from Imperial Roman prototypes. The style had a limited influence in the Piedmont of Virginia and across the Appalachians into the Ohio River valley. Sometimes called Jeffersonian Classicism. See also the related terms ANGLO-PALLADIANISM, FEDERAL, ROMAN REVIVAL.

jerkinhead roof A gable roof in which the upper portion of the gable end is hipped, or inclined inward along the ridgeline, forming a small triangle of roof surface. Sometimes called a clipped gable roof or hipped gable roof.

jigsawn trim Ornate wood trim, usually with curved cutout designs.

joist One of a series of small horizontal beams that support a floor or ceiling.

keystone The central wedge-shaped stone at the crown of an arch.

king post In a truss, the vertical suspension member that connects the tie beam with the apex of opposing principal rafters.

kiosk Originally, a Turkish summer palace. Since the nineteenth century, the term has been applied to any small pavilion or stand, usually found in public gardens, parks, streets, and malls, where it serves some commercial or public function. Distinguished from a gazebo, which may be found in public or private gardens or parks, but which usually serves as a sheltered resting place. See also the related term BANDSTAND.

label 1 A drip molding, over a square-headed door or window, which extends for a short distance down each side of the opening. **2** A similar vertical downward extension of a drip molding over an arch of any form. Sometimes called a label molding.

label stop 1 An L-shaped termination at the lower ends of a label. **2** Any decorative boss or other termination of a label.

lancet arch An arch generally tall and sharply pointed, whose centers are farther apart than the width or span of the arch.

lantern 1 The uppermost stage of a dome, containing windows or arcaded openings. **2** Any feature, square or polygonal in plan and usually containing windows, rising above the roof of a building. The square structures that serve as skylights on the roofs of nineteenth-century buildings—particularly houses—were also called lantern lights, and, in Italianate and Second Empire buildings, came to be called cupolas.

Late Georgian period Not strictly a style term, but a term for a period in British and British colonial history approximately coinciding with the reigns of George III (1760–1820) and George IV (1820–1830). In the United States, the Late Georgian period is now understood to end sometime during the Revolutionary War (1775–1781) and to be followed by the Federal period (c. 1787–1820). In Britain, the Late Georgian period includes the Regency period (1811–1820s). See also the related term EARLY GEORGIAN PERIOD.

Late Gothic Revival A term for the Gothic Revival work of the late nineteenth and early twentieth centuries. See also the more specific term COLLEGIATE GOTHIC (definition 2) and the related term EARLY GOTHIC REVIVAL.

lath A latticelike, continuous surface of small wooden strips or metal mesh nailed to walls or partitions to hold plaster.

latía Also *latilla* (Spanish for little log). Small peeled poles used as a lath in beamed ceilings, often laid in a herringbone fashion across roof beams.

Latin cross A cross with one long and three short arms. Usually used to describe the ground plans of Roman Catholic and Protestant churches. See also the more general term CRUCIFORM.

leaded glass Panes of glass held in place by lead strips, or cames. The panes, clear or stained, may be of any shape.

lean-to roof See SHED ROOF.

lierne In a Gothic vault, a short ornamental rib connecting the major transverse ribs and the secondary tiercerons. Sometimes called a cross rib or tertiary rib.

light frame construction A type of wood frame construction in which relatively light structural members (usually sawn lumber, ranging from two-by-fours to two-by-tens) are fastened with nails. Distinguished from timber frame construction, in which relatively heavy structural members (hewn or sawn timbers, measuring six by six and larger) are fastened with mortise-and-tenon joints. See the more specific terms BALLOON FRAME CONSTRUCTION, PLATFORM FRAME CONSTRUCTION.

lintel A horizontal structural member that supports the wall over an opening or spans between two adjacent piers or columns.

living hall In Queen Anne, Shingle Style, and Colonial Revival houses, an extensive room, often containing the entry, the main staircase, a fireplace, and an inglenook.

load-bearing Term applied to a wall, column, pier, or any vertical supporting member, constructed so that all loads are carried to the ground through the wall, column, or pier. See also the related terms BEARING WALL, CURTAIN WALL.

loggia **1** A porch or open-air room, particularly one set within the body of a building. **2** An arcaded or colonnaded structure, open on one or more sides, sometimes with an upper story. **3** An eighteenth- and nineteenth-century term for a porch or veranda.

Lombard A style term applied in the United States in the mid-nineteenth century to buildings derived from the Romanesque architecture of northern Italy (especially Lombardy) and the earlier nineteenth-century architecture of southern Germany. Characterized by the use of brick for both structural and ornamental purposes. Also called Lombardic. See also the related term ROUND ARCH MODE.

lunette **1** A semicircular area, especially one that contains some decorative treatment or a mural painting. **2** A semicircular window in such an area.

Mannerism, Mannerist **1** A phase of Renaissance art and architecture in the mid-sixteenth century, characterized by distortions, contortions, inversions, odd juxtapositions, and other departures from High Renaissance canons of design. **2** (Not capitalized) A sensibility in design, regardless of style or period, characterized by a knowledgeable violation of rules and intended as a comment on the very nature of convention.

mansard roof A hipped roof with double pitch. The upper slope may approach flatness, while the lower slope has a very steep pitch, sometimes flaring in a concave curve (or swelling in a convex curve) as it comes to the eaves. This lower slope usually has windows, and the area under the roof often amounts to a full story. The name is a corruption of that of François Mansart (1598–1666), who designed roofs of this type, which was revived in Paris during the Second Empire period.

Mansard Style, Mansardic See SECOND EMPIRE.

masonry Construction using stone, brick, block, or some other hard and durable material laid up in units and usually bonded by mortar.

massing The grouping or arrangement of the primary volumetric components of a building.

Mayan Revival Term applied to eclectic works or elements of those works that emulate forms in the visual arts of the Maya civilization of Central America. See also the related term ART DECO.

McKim classicism, McKim classical Architecture of, or in the manner of, the firm of McKim, Mead and White, 1890s–1920s. See BEAUX-ARTS CLASSICISM.

medieval Term applied to the Middle Ages in European civilization between the age of antiquity and the age of the Renaissance (i.e., mid-400s to mid-1400s in Italy; mid-400s to late 1500s in England). In architecture and the other visual arts, the medieval period included the end of the Early Christian period, then the Byzantine, the Romanesque, and the Gothic styles or periods.

Mediterranean Revival A style generally associated since the early twentieth century with residential architecture based on Italian villas of the sixteenth century. While not a major revival style, it is characterized by symmetrical arrangements, stucco walls, and low-pitch tile roofs. Sometimes called Mediterranean Villa, Neo-Mediterranean. See also the related term SPANISH COLONIAL REVIVAL.

metope In a Doric entablature, that part of the frieze which falls between two triglyphs. In the Greek Doric order the metopes often contain small sculptural reliefs.

Middle Ages See MEDIEVAL.

Miesian Term applied to work showing the influence of the German-American architect Ludwig Mies van der Rohe (1886–1969). See also the related terms BAUHAUS, INTERNATIONAL STYLE, SECOND CHICAGO SCHOOL.

Mission Revival A style originating in the 1890s, and making use of forms and materials from the Spanish and Mexican mission architecture of the eighteenth and early nineteenth centuries. Not to be confused with Mission furniture of the Arts and Crafts movement. See also the more general term SPANISH COLONIAL REVIVAL.

modern Ambiguous term, applied in various ways during the past century to the history of the visual arts and world history generally: (1) from the 1910s to the present (see also the more specific terms BAUHAUS, INTERNATIONAL STYLE; (2) from the 1860s, 1870s, 1880s, or 1890s to the present; (3) from the Enlightenment or the advent of Neoclassicism or the industrial revolution, c. 1750, to the present; (4) from the Renaissance in Italy, c. 1450, to the present.

Modern Gothic See EASTLAKE.

Moderne A term applied to a wide range of design work from the 1920s through the 1940s, in which aspects of traditionalism and modernism coexist and in which eclecticism (from a historical, exotic, or machine aesthetic) is inseparable from the urge for stylization. Sometimes called Art Moderne, Modernistic. See also the more specific terms ART DECO, PWA MODERNE, STREAMLINE MODERNE.

modillion One of a series of small, thin scroll brackets under the projecting crown molding of a classical cornice. It is found in the Corinthian and Composite orders. Distinguished from a console, which usually is larger and has a height greater than its projection from the wall.

molding A running surface composed of parallel and continuous sections of simple or compound curves and flat areas.

monitor An extensive shed-roofed feature on a roof, containing a band of windows or vents. It may be located along one of the roof slopes (a trap-door monitor) or along the ridgeline (a clerestory monitor), and it usually runs the entire length of the roof. Distinguished from a skylight, which is a low-profile or flush-mounted feature in the plane of the roof.

Moorish Revival Term applied to eclectic works or elements of those works that emulate forms in the visual arts of those parts of North Africa and Spain under Muslim domination from the seventh through the fifteenth century. See also the related term ORIENTAL REVIVAL.

mortar A mixture of cement or lime with water and a fine aggregate of sand used to secure bricks or stones in masonry construction.

mortise-and-tenon joint A timber framing joint that is made by one member having its end shaped into a projecting piece (tenon) that fits exactly into a hole (mortise) in the other member. Once joined, the pieces are held together by a peg that passes through the tenon.

mullion 1 A post or similiar vertical member dividing a window into two or more units, or lights, each of which may be further subdivided (by muntins) into panes. **2** A post or similar vertical member dividing a wall opening into two or more contiguous windows.

muntin One of the small vertical or horizontal members that hold panes of glass within a window or glazed door. Distinguished from a mullion, which is a heavier vertical member separating paired or grouped windows. Sometimes called a glazing bar, sash bar, or window bar.

mushroom column A reinforced concrete column that flares at the top in order to counteract shear stresses in the vicinity of the column.

National Register of Historic Places A branch of the National Park Service of the United States Department of the Interior, established by the National Historic Preservation Act of 1966, to maintain files of documentation on districts, sites, buildings, structures, and objects of national, state, or local significance. Properties listed on the National Register are afforded administrative—and, ultimately, judicial—review in instances where projects funded or assisted by federal agencies might have an impact on the historic property. Properties listed on the register may also be eligible for certain tax benefits.

nave 1 The entire body of a church between the entrance and the crossing. **2** The central space of a church, between the side aisles, extending from the entrance end to the crossing.

Neo-Baroque Term applied to eclectic works or elements of those works that emulate forms in the visual arts of the Baroque style or period. Sometimes called Baroque Revival.

Neo-Byzantine Term applied to eclectic works or elements of those works that emulate forms in the visual arts of the Byzantine style or period. Sometimes called Byzantine Revival.

Neoclassical Revival See BEAUX-ARTS CLASSICISM.

Neoclassicism, Neoclassical A broad movement in the visual arts which drew its inspiration from ancient Greece and Rome. It began in the mid-eighteenth century with the advent of the science of archeology and extended into the mid-nineteenth century (in some Beaux-Arts work, into the 1930s; in some postmodern work, even into the present). See also the related terms BEAUX-ARTS, BEAUX-ARTS CLASSICISM, CLASSICISM, and the more specific terms GREEK REVIVAL, ROMAN REVIVAL.

Neo-Colonial See COLONIAL REVIVAL.

Neo-Federal See FEDERAL REVIVAL.

Neo-Georgian See GEORGIAN REVIVAL.

Neo-Gothic Term applied to eclectic works or elements of those works that emulate forms in the visual arts of the Gothic style or period. The cultural movement that produced so many such works in the eighteenth, nineteenth, and twentieth centuries is called the Gothic Revival, though that term covers a wide range of work.

Néo-Grec An architectural style developed in connection with the Ecole des Beaux-Arts in Paris during the 1840s and characterized by the use of stylized Greek elements, often in conjunction with cast iron or brick construction. See also the more general term BEAUX-ARTS.

Neo-Hispanic See SPANISH COLONIAL REVIVAL.

Neo-Mediterranean See MEDITERRANEAN REVIVAL.

Neo-Norman Term applied to eclectic works or elements of those works that emulate forms in the visual arts of the eleventh- and twelfth-century Romanesque of Norman France and Britain.

Neo-Palladian See PALLADIANISM.

Neo-Renaissance Term applied to eclectic works or elements of those works that emulate forms in the visual arts of the Renaissance style or period. The mid- to late nineteenth-century cultural movement that produced so many such works is called the Renaissance Revival, though that term covers a wide range of work.

Neo-Romanesque Term applied to eclectic works or elements of those works that emulate forms in the visual arts of the Romanesque style or period. The mid-nineteenth-century cultural movement that produced so many such works is called the Romanesque Revival, though that term covers a wide range of work.

Neo-Tudor Term applied to eclectic works or elements of those works that emulate forms in the visual arts of the Tudor period. Sometimes loosely called Elizabethan Manor Style, English Half-timber Style, Jacobethan Revival, Tudor Revival.

New Brutalism See BRUTALISM.

New Formalism A style prevalent since the 1960s, characterized by symmetrical arrangements, rich materials (marble cladding, metal grille-work), and stylized classical (even Gothic) detailing. Architects associated with this style include Philip Johnson (born 1906), Edward Durell Stone (1902–1978), and Minoru Yamasaki (born 1912).

newel post A post at the head or foot of a flight of stairs, to which the handrail is fastened. Newel posts occur in a variety of shapes, in profile and cross section, and are generally more substantial elements than the individual balusters that support the handrail.

niche A recess in a wall, usually designed to contain sculpture or an urn. A niche is often semicircular in plan and surmounted by a half dome or shell form. See also the related terms AEDICULE, TABERNACLE(definition 1).

nogging Brickwork that fills the spaces between members of a timber frame wall or partition.

Norman French See FRENCH NORMAN.

octagon house A rare house type of the 1850s, based on the ideas of Orson Squire Fowler (1809–1887), who argued for the efficiencies of an octagonal floor plan. Sometimes called octagon mode.

oculus A circular opening in a ceiling or wall or at the top of a dome.

ogee arch A pointed arch formed by a pair of opposing S-shaped curves.

order The most important constituents of classical architecture are the orders, first developed as a structural-aesthetic system by the ancient Greeks. An order has two major components. A column with its capital is the main vertical supporting member. The principal horizontal member is the entablature. The Greeks developed three different types of order, the Doric, Ionic, and Corinthian, each distinguishable by its own decorative system and proportions. All three were taken over and modified by the Romans, who added two orders of their own, the Tuscan, which is a simplified form of the Doric, and the Composite, which is made up of elements of both the Ionic and the Corinthian. The Romans often used the orders as a structural system in the same manner as the Greeks. Unlike the Greeks, however, they also applied them as decoration to the surfaces of walls that were supported by other means. Sometimes called classical orders. See also the related terms COLUMN, ENTABLATURE, GIANT ORDER, SUPERPOSITION(definition 1).

oriel A projecting polygonal or curved window unit of one or more stories, supported on brack-

ets or corbels. Sometimes called an oriel window. Distinguished from a bay window, which rises from the foundation and has a rooted rather than a suspended appearance. However, a multi-story projection in a tall building, whether cantilevered out or built from the foundation, is called a projecting bay or a unit of bay windows.

Oriental Revival Ambiguous term, suggesting eclectic influences from any period in any culture in the "Orient," or Asia, including Turkish, Persian, Indian, Chinese, and Japanese, as well as Arabic (even the Moorish of North Africa and Spain). Sometimes called Oriental style. See also the related term MOORISH REVIVAL.

orthographic projection A system of visual representation in which all details on or near some principal plane, object, building, or space are projected, to scale, onto the parallel plane of the drawing. Orthographic projection thus flattens all forms into a single two-dimensional picture plane and allows for an exact scaling of every feature in that plane. Distinguished from pictorial projection, which creates the illusion of three-dimensional depth. See also the more specific terms ELEVATION, PLAN, SECTION.

outbuilding A building subsidiary to and completely detached from another building. Distinguished from a dependency, which may be attached or detached.

overhang The projection of part of a structure beyond the portion below.

PWA Moderne A synthesis of the Moderne (i.e., Art Deco or Streamline Moderne) with an austere late type of Beaux-Arts classicism, often associated with federal government buildings of the 1930s and 1940s during the Public Works Administration. See also the more general term MODERNE and the related terms ART DECO, BEAUX-ARTS CLASSICISM, STREAMLINE MODERNE.

Palladianism, Palladian Work influenced by the Italian Renaissance architect Andrea Palladio (1508–1580), particularly by means of his treatise, *I Quattro Libri dell'Architettura* (*The Four Books of Architecture*, originally published in 1570 and disseminated throughout Europe in numerous translations and editions until the mid-eighteenth century). The most significant flourishing of Palladianism was in England, from the 1710s to the 1760s, and in the British North American colonies, from the 1740s to the 1790s. Sometimes called Neo-Palladian, Palladian classical. See also the more specific term ANGLO-PALLADIANISM.

Palladian motif A three-part composition for a door or window, in which a round-headed opening is flanked by lower flat-headed openings and separated from them by columns, pilasters, or mullions. The flanking sections, and sometimes the entire unit, may be blind (i.e., not open).

Palladian Revival See ANGLO-PALLADIANISM.

Palladian window A window subdivided as in the Palladian motif.

parapet A low wall at the edge of a roof, balcony, or terrace, sometimes formed by the upward extension of the wall below.

pargeting Elaborate stucco or plasterwork, especially an ornammental finish for exterior plaster walls, sometimes decorated with figures in low relief or indented. Found in late medieval, Queen Anne, and period revival buildings. Sometimes called parging, pargework. See also the more general term STUCCO.

parquet Inlaid wood flooring, usually set in simple geometric patterns.

parti The essential solution to an architectural program or problem; the basic concept for the arrangement of spaces, before the development and elaboration of the design.

patera (plural: paterae) A circular or oval panel or plaque decorated with stylized flower petals or radiating linear motifs. Distinguished from a roundel, which is always circular.

pavilion 1 A central or corner unit that projects from a larger architectural mass and is usually accented by a special treatment of the wall or roof. 2 A detached or semidetached structure used for specialized activities, as at a hospital. 3 In a garden or fairground, a temporary structure or tent, usually ornamented.

pediment 1 In classical architecture, the low triangular gable end of the roof, framed by raking cornices along the inclined edges of the roof and by a horizontal cornice below. 2 In Renaissance and Baroque and later classically derived architecture, the triangular or curvilinear culmination of a prominent part of a facade. 3 A similar but smaller-scale feature over a door or window. It may be triangular or curvilinear.

pendentive A concave surface in the form of a spherical triangle that forms the structural transition from the square plan of a crossing to the circular plan of a dome.

pergola A structure with an open wood framed roof, often latticed, and supported by a colonnade. It is usually covered by climbing plants, such as vines or roses, and provides shade for a garden walk or a passageway to a building. Distinguished from arbors or trellises, which are less extensive accessory structures lacking the colonnade.

period house Term applied to suburban and country houses in which period revival styles are dominant.

period revival Term applied to eclectic works—particularly suburban and country houses—of the first three decades of the twentieth century, in which a particular historical or regional style is dominant. See also the more specific terms COLONIAL REVIVAL, DUTCH COLONIAL REVIVAL, GEORGIAN REVIVAL, NEO-TUDOR, SPANISH COLONIAL REVIVAL.

peripteral (adjective) Surrounded by a single row of columns.

peristyle A range of columns surrounding a building or an open court.

perspective drawing A pictorial drawing representing an object, building, or space, as if seen from a single vantage point. The illusion of three dimensions is created by using a system based on the optical laws of converging lines and vanishing points. See also the related terms AXONOMETRIC DRAWING, ISOMETRIC DRAWING.

piano nobile (plural: piani nobili) In Renaissance and later architecture, a floor with formal reception, living, and dining rooms. The principal and often tallest story in a building, usually one level above the ground level.

piazza 1 A plaza or square. 2 An eighteenth- and nineteenth-century term for a porch or veranda.

pictorial projection A system of visual representation in which an object, building, or space is projected onto the picture plane in such a way that the illusion of three-dimensional depth is created. Distinguished from orthographic projection, in which the dimension of depth is excluded. See also the more specific terms AXONOMETRIC DRAWING, ISOMETRIC DRAWING, PERSPECTIVE DRAWING.

picturesque An aesthetic category in architecture and landscape architecture in the late eighteenth and early nineteenth centuries. It is characterized by relationships among buildings and landscape features that evoke the qualities of landscape paintings, in which the eye is led past a variety of forms and spaces into the distance and the mind is led to contemplate a sense of age (by means of ruins, fallen trees, weathered rocks, and mossy surfaces on all of these). In actual settings, asymmetrical and eclectic buildings, indirect approaches, and contrasting clusters of plantings heighten the experience of the picturesque.

pier 1 A freestanding mass, supporting a concentrated load from an arch, a beam, a truss, or a girder. While generally rectilinear in plan, piers in buildings based upon medieval precedents are often curvilinear in plan. 2 An upright portion of a wall that performs a columnar function. The pier may be continuous with the plane of the wall, or it may be distinguished from the plane of the wall to give it a column-like independence.

pier and spandrel A type of skeletal wall organization in which the vertical metal columns (and their square-cornered cladding) project in front of the plane of windows and their spandrel panels. The spandrel panels may be exposed structural spanning members. More often they provide decorative covering for the structure.

pilaster 1 A flattened column, with or without fluting, that is attached to a wall. It is usually finished with the same capital and base as a freestanding column. 2 Any narrow, vertical strip attached to a wall. Distinguished from an engaged column, which has a convex curvature.

pillar Ambiguous term, often used interchangeably with column, pier, or post. See instead one of those terms. (Although the term pillar is sometimes applied to columns that are square in plan, the term pier is preferable.)

pinnacle In Gothic architecture, a small spirelike element providing an ornamental finish to the highest part of a buttress or roof. It has a slender pyramidal or conical form and is often articulated with crockets or ribs and is topped by a finial. Distinguished from a finial, which is a smaller feature appearing by itself.

pitched roof See GABLE ROOF.

plan A drawing (in orthographic projection) representing all or part of an object, building, or space, as if viewed from directly above. A floor plan is a drawing of a horizontal cut through a building, usually at the level of the windows, showing the configuration of walls and openings. Other types of plans may illustrate ceilings, roofs, structural elements, and mechanical systems.

plank construction General term. See instead the more specific terms HORIZONTAL PLANK FRAME CONSTRUCTION, VERTICAL PLANK CONSTRUCTION.

plate 1 In timber frame construction, the topmost horizontal structural member of a wall, to which the roof rafters are fastened.   **2** In platform and balloon frame construction, the horizontal members to which the tops and bottoms of studs are nailed. The bottom plate is sometimes called the sill plate or sole plate.

Plateresque Term applied to Spanish and Spanish colonial Renaissance architecture from the early sixteenth century onward, in which the delicate, finely sculptured detail resembles the work of a silversmith (*platero*). See also the related term SPANISH COLONIAL.

platform frame construction A system of light frame construction in which each story is built as an independent unit and the studs are only one story high. The floor joists of each story rest on the top plates of the story below, and the bearing walls or partitions rest on the subfloor of each floor unit or platform. Platform framing is easier to construct and more rigid than balloon framing and has become the common framing method in the twentieth century. Structural members are usually sawn lumber, ranging from two-by-fours to two-by-tens, and are fastened with nails. Sometimes called platform framing, western frame, western framing.

plinth The base block of a column, pilaster, pedestal, dado, or door architrave.

Pointed Style A nineteenth-century term for Gothic Revival.

polychromy, polychromatic, polychrome A many-colored treatments, especially the combination of materials in various colors or the application of surface color, to articulate wall and roof planes and to highlight structure.

popular A term applied to vernacular architecture influenced by such publications as books of the orders, builders' guides, style books, pattern books, mail-order catalogs, architectural periodicals, and household magazines. Architecture in the popular tradition may be built according to commercially available plans or from widely distributed components; or it may be built by local practitioners (architects, builders, contractors) emulating buildings that are represented in publications. The distinction between popular architecture and high-style architecture by lesser-known architects depends on one's point of view with regard to the division between vernacular and high-style. See also the more general term VERNACULAR and the related term FOLK.

Populuxe See GOOGIE.

porch A structure attached to a building to shelter an entrance or to serve as a semienclosed sitting, working, or sleeping space. Distinguished from a portico, which is either a pedimented feature at least one story in height supported by classical columns or a more extensive colonnaded feature.

porte-cochere A porch projecting over a driveway and providing shelter to people leaving a vehicle and entering a building or vice versa. Also called a carriage porch.

portico 1 A porch at least one story in height consisting of a low-pitched roof supported on classical columns and finished in front with an entablature and pediment.   **2** An extensive porch supported by a colonnade.

post A vertical supporting element, either square or circular in plan. Posts are the integral vertical members of a frame or truss, whether of wood or metal. Posts may also carry fences or gates, or may serve as freestanding markers (e.g., mileposts).

post-and-beam construction A structural system in which the main support is provided by vertical members (posts) carrying horizontal members (beams or lintels). Sometimes called post and girt construction, post and lintel construction, trabeation, trabeated construction.

post-and-pier foundation A type of foundation made of short wood posts resting on short piers, usually of brick or stone, that allows a small crawl space beneath the structure.

postmodernism, postmodern A term applied to work that involves a reaction against the ideas and works of various twentieth-century modern movements, particularly the Bauhaus and the International Style. Postmodern work makes use of historicism, yet the traditional elements are often merely applied to buildings that, in every other respect, are products of modern movement design. The term is also applied to works that are attempting to demonstrate an extension of the principles of various modern movements.

Prairie Box See FOURSQUARE HOUSE.

Prairie School, Prairie Style A diverse group of architects working in Chicago and throughout the Midwest from the 1890s to the 1920s, strongly influenced by Frank Lloyd Wright and to a lesser degree by Louis Sullivan. The term is applied mainly to domestic architecture. An architect is said to belong to the Prairie School; a work of architecture is said to be in the Prairie Style. Sometimes called Prairie, for short. See also the related terms CHICAGO SCHOOL, WRIGHTIAN.

pre-Columbian Term applied to the major cultures of Latin American (e.g., Aztec, Maya, Inca) that flourished prior to the discovery of the New World by Columbus in 1492 and the Spanish conquests of the sixteenth century. Distinguished from North American Indian, which is generally applied to indigenous cultures within the area that would become the United States and Canada.

pressed metal Thin sheets of metal (usually galvanized or tin-plated iron) stamped into patterned panels for covering ceilings and exterior and interior walls or into molding profiles and other details for assembly into exterior and interior cornices. Loosely called pressed tin or stamped metal. Prevalent from the 1870s through the 1920s.

program The list of functional, spatial, and other requirements that guides an architect in developing a design.

proscenium In a recessed stage, the area between the orchestra and the curtain.

proscenium arch In a recessed stage, the enframement of the opening.

prostyle Having a columnar portico in front, but not on the sides and rear.

provincialism, provincial Term applied to work in an isolated area (such as a province of a cosmopolitan center or a colony of a mother country), where traditional practices persist, with some awareness of what is being done in the cosmopolitan center or the homeland.

Pueblo Revival Twentieth-century style influenced by Native American (Pueblo and Anasazi) architecture. Characteristics include stepped, irregular massing, blunt or rounded shapes, flat roofs, and protruding roof beams, or vigas. The style sometimes incorporates Mission Revival features such as rounded parapets, tile, and wrought iron.

purlin In roof construction, a structural member laid across the principal rafters and parallel to the wall plate and the ridge beam. The light common rafters to which the roofing surface is attached are fastened across the purlins. See also the related term RAFTER.

pylon 1 Originally, the gateway facade of an Egyptian temple complex, consisting of a truncated broad pyramidal form with battered (inclined) wall surfaces on all four sides, or two truncated pyramidal towers flanking an entrance portal. **2** Any towerlike structure from which bridge cables or utility lines are suspended.

quadripartite vault A vault divided into four triangular sections by a pair of diagonal ribs. Sometimes called a four-part vault.

quarry-faced See ROCK-FACED.

quatrefoil A type of Gothic tracery having four parts (lobes or foils) separated by pointed elements (cusps).

Queen Anne Ambiguous but widely used term. **1** In architecture, the Queen Anne Style is an eclectic style of the 1860s through 1910s in England and the United States, characterized by the incorporation of forms from postmedieval vernacular architecture and the architecture of the Georgian period. Sometimes called Queen Anne Revival. See also the more specific term SHINGLE STYLE and the related terms EASTLAKE, STICK STYLE. **2** In architecture, the original Queen Anne period extends from the late seventeenth into the early eighteenth century. **3** In the decorative arts, the Queen Anne Style and period properly refer to work of the early eighteenth century during the reign of Queen Anne (1702–1714, i.e., after William and Mary and before Georgian). **4** In the decorative arts, eclectic work of the 1860s to 1880s is properly referred to as Queen Anne Revival. See also the related term AESTHETIC MOVEMENT.

quoin One of the bricks or stones laid in alternating directions, which bond and form the exterior corner of a building. Sometimes simulated in wood or stucco.

rabbet A channel or recess cut out of the edge or face of a surface.

rafter One of the inclined structural members of a roof. Principal rafters are primary supporting elements spanning between the walls and the apex of the roof and carrying the longitudinal purlins. Common rafters are secondary supporting elements fastened onto purlins to carry the roof surfacing. See also the related term PURLIN.

raking cornice A cornice that finishes the sloping edges of a gable roof, such as the inclined sides of a triangular pediment.

random ashlar A type of masonry in which squared and dressed blocks are laid in a random pattern rather than in straight horizontal courses.

recessed column A fully round column set into a nichelike space only slightly larger than the column. Distinguished from an engaged column, which appears to be built into the wall.

reentrant angle An acute angle created by the juncture of two planes, such as walls.

refectory A dining hall, especially in medieval architecture.

regionalism 1 The sum of cultural characteristics (including material culture, language) that define a geographic region, usually extending beyond a single state or province, and coinciding with one or more large physiographic areas. **2** The conscious use, within a region, of forms and materials identified with that region, creating an architecture that is in keeping with the historical architecture of the region, and even a distinctive new regional style.

register A horizontal zone of a wall, altarpiece, or other vertical feature. Usually synonymous with story, but more inclusive, allowing for the description of zones with no corresponding interior spaces.

relieving arch An arch, usually of masonry, built over the lintel of an opening to carry the load of the wall above and relieve the lintel of carrying such load. Sometimes called a discharging arch or safety arch.

Renaissance The period in European civilzation identified with a rediscovery or rebirth (*rinascimento*) of classical Roman (and to a lesser extent, Greek) learning, art, and architecture. Renaissance architecture began in Italy in the mid–1400s (Early Renaissance) and reached a peak in the early to mid–1500s (High Renaissance). In England, Renaissance architecture did not begin until the late 1500s or early 1600s. The Renaissance in art and architecture was preceded by the Gothic and followed by the Baroque.

Renaissance Revival 1 In architecture, applied to *(a)* Italianate work of the 1840s through 1880s and *(b)* Beaux-Arts classical work of the 1880s through 1920s. **2** In the decorative arts, an eclectic furniture style incorporating a variety of Renaissance, Baroque, and Néo-Grec architectural motifs and utilizing wood marquetry, incised lines (often gilded), and ormolu and porcelain ornaments. Sometimes called Neo-Renaissance.

rendering Any drawing, whether orthographic (plan, elevation, section) or pictorial (perspective), in which shades and shadows are represented.

reredos A screen or wall at the back of an altar, usually with architectural and figural decoration.

return The continuation of a molding, cornice, or other projecting member, in a different direction, as in the horizontal cornice returns at the base of the raking cornices of a triangular pediment.

reveal 1 The portion of wall thickness between a door or window frame and the outer face of the wall. **2** Same as jamb, but only in an opening without a door or window.

revival, revivalism A type of historicism prevalent since the eighteenth century, involving the adaptation of historical forms to contemporary functions. Distinguished from a more pervasive historicism by an ideological conviction that sought to rationalize the choice of a historical style according to the values of the historical period that produced it. (The Gothic Revival, for instance, was associated with the Christianity of the Middle Ages.) Revival works, therefore, tend to invoke a single historical style. More hybrid works are manifestations of a less dogmatic historicism or eclecticism. See also the general terms HISTORICISM, ECLECTICISM.

rib The projecting linear element that separates the curved planar cells (or webs) of vaulting. Originally these were the supporting members for the vaulting, but they may also be purely decorative.

Richardsonian Term applied to any work showing the influence of the American architect Henry Hobson Richardson (1838–1886). See the note under the more limiting term RICHARDSONIAN ROMANESQUE.

Richardsonian Romanesque Term applied to Neo-Romanesque work showing the influence of the American architect Henry Hobson Richardson (1838–1886). While many of Richardson's works make eclectic use of round arches and Romanesque details, many of his works show a creative eclecticism that transcends any particular historical style. The term Richardsonian, therefore, is a more inclusive term for the work of his followers than Richardsonian Romanesque—a term that continues to be widely used. Sometimes called Richardson Romanesque, Richardsonian Romanesque Revival.

ridgepole The horizontal beam or board at the apex of a roof, to which the upper ends of the rafters are fastened. Sometimes called a ridge beam, ridgeboard, ridge piece.

rinceau An ornamental device consisting of a sinuous and branching scroll elaborated with leaves and other natural forms.

rock-faced Term applied to the rough, unfinished face of a stone used in building. Sometimes called quarry-faced, rough-faced.

Rococo A late phase of the Baroque, marked by elegant reverse-curve ornament, light scale, and delicate color. See also the related term BAROQUE.

Romanesque A medieval architectural style which reached its height in the eleventh and twelfth centuries. It is characterized by round arched construction and massive masonry walls. The Romanesque was preceded by the Early Christian and Byzantine periods in the eastern Mediterranean world and by a variety of localized styles and periods in northern and western Europe; it was followed throughout Europe by the Gothic.

Romanesque Revival Applied to (1) Rundbogenstil and Round Arch work in the United States as early as the 1840s and (2) Richardsonian Romanesque work into the 1890s (later in some areas). Sometimes called Neo-Romanesque.

Roman Revival A term, not widely accepted, for a version of Neoclassicism involving the use of forms from the visual arts of the Imperial Roman period. Applied to various works in Italy, England, and the United States, where it is most clearly visible in the architecture of Thomas Jefferson. See also the related terms FEDERAL, JEFFERSONIAN, NEOCLASSICISM.

rood screen An ornamental screen that serves as a partition between the crossing and the chancel or choir of a church.

rosette A circular floral ornament similar to an open rose.

rotunda 1 A circular hall in a large building, especially an area beneath a dome or cupola. **2** A building round both inside and outside, usually domed.

Round Arch mode The American counterpart of the German Rundbogenstil, characterized by the predominance of round arches, whether these are accentuated by Romanesque or Renaissance detailing or left as simple unadorned openings. See also the related terms ITALIANATE, LOMBARD, RUNDBOGENSTIL.

roundel A circular panel or plaque. Distinguished from a patera, which is oval shaped.

rough-faced See ROCK-FACED.

rubble masonry A type of masonry utilizing uncut or roughly shaped stone, such as fieldstone or boulders.

Rundbogenstil Literally, "round arch style," a historicist style originating in Germany in the 1820s and spreading to Britain and the United States from the 1840s through the 1860s. It is characterized by an eclectic combination of Romanesque and Renaissance elements. See also the related term ROUND ARCH MODE.

running bond A pattern of brickwork in which only stretchers appear, with the vertical joints of one course falling halfway between the vertical joints of adjacent courses. Sometimes called stretcher bond. Distinguished from common bond, in which every fifth or sixth course consists of all headers.

Ruskin Gothic, Ruskinian Gothic See HIGH VICTORIAN GOTHIC.

rustication, rusticated Masonry in which the joints are emphasized by narrow recessed channels or grooves outlining each block. Sometimes simulated in wood or stucco.

sacristy A room in a church where liturgical vessels and vestments are kept.

safety arch See RELIEVING ARCH.

sanctuary 1 The part of a church that contains the principal altar. Usually the innermost space within the chancel arm of the church, situated to the east of the choir. **2** Loosely used to mean a place of worship, a sacred place.

sash Any framework of a window. It may be movable or fixed. It may slide in a vertical plane (as in a double-hung window) or may be pivoted (as in a casement window).

sash bar See MUNTIN.

Secession movement The refined classicist Austrian (Viennese) version of the Art Nouveau style, so named beause the artists and architects involved seceded from the official Academy in 1897. Josef Hoffmann (1870–1956) is the architect most frequently mentioned in association with this movement.

Second Chicago School A term sometimes applied to the International Style in Chicago from the 1940s to the 1970s, particularly the work of Mies van der Rohe. See also the related terms INTERNATIONAL STYLE, MIESIAN.

Second Empire Not strictly a style term but a term for a period in French history coinciding with the rule of Napoleon III (1852–1870). Generally applied in the United States, however, to a phase of Beaux-Arts governmental and institutional architecture (1850s–1880s) as well as to countless hybrids of Beaux-Arts and Italianate forms in residential, commercial, and industrial architecture (1850s–1880s). Sometimes called General Grant Style, Mansard Style, Mansardic. See also the related terms BEAUX-ARTS, ITALIANATE (definition 1).

section A drawing (in orthographic projection) representing a vertical cut through an object, building, or space. An architectural section shows interior relationships of space and structure, and may also include mechanical systems. Sometimes called a cross section.

segmental arch An arch formed on a segmental curve. Its center lies below the springing line.

segmental curve A curve that is a segment (i.e., less than half the circumference) of a circle or an ellipse. The baseline of the curve is a chord measuring less than the diameter of the larger circle from which the segment is taken.

segmental pediment A pediment whose top is a segmental curve.

segmental vault A vault whose cross section is a segmental curve. A dome built on segmental curves is called a saucer dome.

setback 1 In architecture, particularly in the design of tall buildings, a series of upper stories that are stepped back to allow more sunlight to reach the streets. **2** In planning, the amount of space between the lot line and the perimeter of a building.

shaft The tall part of a column between the base and the capital.

shed roof A roof having only one sloping plane. Sometimes called a lean-to roof.

Shingle Style A term applied primarily to American domestic architecture of the 1870s through the 1890s, in which broad expanses of wood shingles dominate the exterior roof and wall planes. Rooms open widely into one another and to the outdoors, and the ample living hall or stair hall is often the dominant feature of the interior. The term was coined in the 1940s by Vincent Scully for a series of seaside and suburban houses of the northeastern United States. The Shingle Style is a version of the Anglo-American Queen Anne Style. See also the related terms COLONIAL REVIVAL, STICK STYLE.

shouldered architrave See EAR.

side gabled Term applied to a building whose gable ends face the sides of a lot. Distinguished from front gabled.

side light A framed area of fixed glass alongside a door or window. See also the related term FANLIGHT.

sill course In masonry, a stringcourse set at windowsill level, usually differentiated from the wall by its greater projection, its finish, or its thickness. Not applicable to frame construction.

sill plate See PLATE (definition 2).

skeleton construction, skeleton frame A system of construction in which all loads are carried to the ground through a rigid framework of iron, steel, or reinforced concrete. The exterior walls are curtain walls (i.e., not load-bearing).

skylight A window in a roof, specifically one that is flush with the roof plane or only slightly protruding. Distinguished from a cupola (definition 2), which is a major centralized feature at the summit of a roof. Distinguished from a monitor, which is an extensive roof feature containing a band of windows or vents.

skyway An enclosed aerial walkway or larger space connecting two buildings, usually built over a street.

soffit The exposed underside of any overhead component, such as an arch, beam, cornice, or lintel. See also the related term INTRADOS.

sole plate See PLATE (definition 2).

space frame A series of trusses placed side by side and joined to one another by triangulated rods, tubes, or beams, so that the individual planar trusses are united into a three-dimensional structural framework. Often used in roof structures requiring long spans.

spandrel 1 The quasi-triangular space between two adjoining arches and a line connecting their crowns, or between an arch and the columns and entablature that frame it. **2** In skeletal construction, the wall area between the top of a window and the sill of the window in the story above. Sometimes called a spandrel panel.

Spanish colonial A term applied to buildings, towns, landscapes, and other artifacts from the various periods of actual Spanish colonial occupation in North America (c. 1565–1821 in Florida; c. 1763–1800 in Louisiana and the Lower Mississippi valley; c. 1590s–1821 in Texas and the southwestern United States; c. 1769–1821 in California). The term is extended to apply to the artifacts of Hispanic ethnic groups (e.g., Mexicans, Puerto Ricans, Cubans) and their descendants, even into the early twentieth century. See also the related terms CHURRIGUERESQUE, PLATERESQUE.

Spanish Colonial Revival The revival of forms from Spanish colonial and provincial Mexican design. The Spanish Colonial Revival began in Florida and California in the 1880s and continues nationwide into the present. Sometimes called Neo-Hispanic, Spanish Eclectic, Spanish Revival. See also the more specific term MISSION REVIVAL and the related term MEDITERRANEAN REVIVAL.

Spanish Eclectic A style using forms and decorative details from the entire history of Spanish architecture, including Moorish, Romanesque, Byzantine, Gothic, and Renaissance derivations. A broader term than Spanish Colonial Revival.

spindle A turned wooden element, thicker toward the middle and thinner at either end, found in arch screens, porch trim, and other ornamental assemblages. Banisters (i.e., thin, simple balusters) may be spindle-shaped, but the term spindle, when used alone, usually connotes shorter elements.

spire A slender pointed element surmounting a building. A tall, attenuated pyramidal form with any number of thin triangular faces that are unbroken or articulated only with crockets, pinnacles, or small dormers. Distinguished from a steeple, which is divided into stages and which may be topped with a spire.

splay The slanting surface formed by cutting off a right-angle corner at an oblique angle to one face. A reveal at an oblique angle to the exterior face of the wall.

springing, springing line, springing point The line or point where an arch or vault rises from its supports and begins to curve. Usually the juncture between the impost of the support below and the springer, or first voussoir, of the arch above.

squinch An arch, lintel, or corbeling, built across the interior corner of two walls to form one side of an octagonal base for a dome. This octagonal base serves as the structural transition from a square interior crossing space to an octagonal or round dome.

stair A series of steps, or flights of steps connected by landings, which connects two or more levels or floors.

staircase The ensemble of a stair and its enclosing walls. Sometimes called a stairway.

stair tower A projecting tower or other building block that contains a stair.

stamped metal See PRESSED METAL.

Steamboat Gothic See CARPENTER'S GOTHIC.

steeple 1 A tall structure rising from a tower, consisting of a series of superimposed stages diminishing in plan, and usually topped by a spire or small cupola. Distinguished from a spire, which is not divided into stages. **2** Less commonly used to mean the whole of the tower, from the ground to the top of the spire or cupola.

stepped gable A gable in which the wall rises in a series of steps above the planes of the roof.

stereotomy The science of cutting three-dimensional shapes from stone, such as the units that make up a carefully fitted masonry vault.

Stick Style A term applied primarily to American domestic architecture of the 1850s through the 1870s, in which exterior wall planes are subdivided into bays and stories outlined by narrow boards called "stickwork." The term was coined by Vincent Scully in the 1940s for a series of houses with clearly articulated wall panels and sticklike porch supports and eaves brackets. Sources include the English and German picturesque traditions, as well as the French rationalist tradition. See also the related terms QUEEN ANNE, SHINGLE STYLE.

story (plural: stories). The space in a building between floor levels. British spelling is storey, storeys. Sometimes called a register, a more inclusive term applied to horizontal on a vertical plane zones that do not correspond to actual floor levels.

Streamline Moderne A later phase of the Moderne, popular in the 1930s and 1940s and characterized by stucco surfaces with rounded corners, by horizontal banding, overhangs, and window groupings, and by other details suggestive of modern Machine Age aerodynamic forms. Sometimes called Streamline Modern, Streamline Modernistic. See also the more general term MODERNE and the related terms ART DECO and PWA MODERNE.

stretcher A brick laid the length of a wall, so that the long side of the brick shows on the exterior.

stretcher bond See running bond.

string In a stair, an inclined board that supports the ends of the steps. Sometimes called a stringer.

stringcourse In masonry, a horizontal band, generally narrower than other courses, extending across the facade of a building and in some instances encircling such features as pillars or columns. It may be flush or projecting; of identical or contrasting material; flat, molded, or richly carved. Not applicable to frame construction. Sometimes called a band course or belt course. More elaborate horizontal bands in masonry or frame construction are generally called band moldings.

strut A column, post, or pole that is set in a diagonal position and thus serves as a stiffener by triangulation. Distinguished from a brace, which is usually a shorter bracketlike member.

stucco 1 An exterior plaster finish, usually textured, composed of portland cement, lime, and sand, which are mixed with water. **2** A fine plaster used for decorative work or moldings. See also the more specific term PARGETING.

stud One of the vertical supporting elements in a wall, especially in balloon and platform frame construction. Studs are relatively lightweight members (usually two-by-fours).

Sullivanesque Term applied to work showing the influence of the American architect Louis Henry Sullivan (1856–1924).

sunburst light See FANLIGHT.

supercapital See IMPOST BLOCK.

supercolumniation See SUPERPOSITION (definition 1).

superimposition, superimposed See SUPERPOSITION.

superposition, superposed 1 The use of an ensemble of the classical orders, one above the other, as the major elements articulating a facade. When this is done, the Doric, considered the simplest order, is used on or near the ground story. The Ionic, considered more complex, comes next; and the Corinthian, considered the most complex, is used at the top. Sometimes the Tuscan order or rusticated masonry may be used for the ground story beneath the Doric order, and the Composite order may be used above the Corinthian order. Sometimes called supercolumniation, superimposition. See also the related term ORDER. **2** Less commonly, any vertical relationship of architectural elements (e.g., windows, piers, colonnettes) in any style or period.

superstructure A structure raised upon another structure, as a building upon a foundation, basement, or substructure.

Supervising Architect The Supervising Architect of the United States Treasury Department, whose office was responsible for the design and construction of all major federal government buildings (such as courthouses, customhouses, and post offices) from the 1850s through the 1930s. The Office of the Supervising Architect was formally established by Congress in 1864 and lasted until 1939, when its functions were absorbed into the Public Buildings Administration (and in 1949, into the General Services Administration).

supporting wall See BEARING WALL.

surround An encircling border or decorative frame around a door or window. Distinguished from architrave (definition 2), a term usually applied to the frame around an opening when considered as a series of relatively flat face moldings.

suspended ceiling A ceiling suspended from rodlike hangers below the level of the floor above. The interval between the floor slab above and the suspended ceiling often serves as a space for ducts, utilities, and air circulation. Sometimes called a hung ceiling.

swag A motif representing a suspended fold of drapery hanging in a catenary curve from two points. Distinguished from a festoon, which is a motif representing entwined leaves, flowers, or fruits, hung in a similar curve. See also the more general term GARLAND.

tabernacle **1** A niche or recess, usually on an interior wall, framed by columns or pilasters and topped by an entablature and pediment. Distinguished from an aedicule, which more often occurs on an exterior wall. See also the related term NICHE. **2** In the Jewish religion, a portable sanctuary. **3** In Protestant denominations, a large auditorium church.

terra cotta A hard ceramic material used for (1) fireproofing, especially as a fitted cladding around metal skeletal construction; or (2) an exterior or interior wall cladding, which is often glazed and multicolored.

Territorial Style An early to mid-nineteenth-century vernacular style typical of the territorial period in the southwestern United States, i.e., the years between U.S. acquisition from Mexico and statehood. The style combines traditional Spanish colonial adobe construction with superimposed Anglo-influenced elements and materials (pitched roofs, columned porches, shingles, milled lumber, fired brick) and Greek Revival wood details, including door and window pediments.

tertiary rib See LIERNE.

thermal window A large lunette window similar to those found in ancient Roman baths (*thermae*). The window is subdivided into three to five parts by vertical mullions. Sometimes called a *thermae* window.

three-hinged arch An arch in two major segments anchored with cylindrical "hinge" pins at either end and at the crown. Movement within the arch, caused by temperature changes, the torsion of wind movements, or other forces, can be absorbed by the movement of the arch around the pins, thereby avoiding stresses that would occur in the structural frame if the arches were fixed.

tie beam A horizontal tension member that ties together the opposing angular members of a truss and prevents them from spreading.

tier A group of stories or any zone of architectural elements arranged horizontally.

tierceron In a Gothic vault, a secondary rib that rises from the springing to an intermediate position on either side of the diagonal ribs. Sometimes called an intermediate rib.

tie rod A metal rod that spans the distance between two structural members and, by its tensile strength, restrains them against tendencies to collapse outward.

timber-frame construction, timber framing A type of wood frame construction in which heavy timber posts and beams (six-by-sixes and larger) are fastened using mortise and tenon joints. Sometimes called heavy timber construction. Distinguished from light frame construction, in which

relatively light structural members (two-by-fours to two-by-tens) are fastened with nails.

trabeation, trabeated construction See POST-AND-BEAM CONSTRUCTION.

tongue and groove A joint made by fitting a projection on the edge of a board into a matching depression on another board.

tracery Decoration within an arch or other opening, made up of narrow curvilinear bands or more elaborately molded strips. In Gothic architecture, the curved interlocking stone bars that contain the leaded stained glass.

transept The lateral arm of a cross-shaped church, usually between the nave (the area for the congregation) and the chancel (the area for the altar, clergy, and choir).

transom **1** A narrow horizontal window unit, either fixed or movable, over a door. Sometimes called a transom light. See also the more specific term fanlight. **2** A horizontal bar, as distinguished from a vertical mullion, especially one crossing a door or window opening near the top.

transverse rib In a Gothic vault, a rib at right angles to the ridge rib.

trefoil A type of Gothic tracery having three parts (lobes or foils) separated by pointed elements (cusps).

trellis Any open latticework made of strips of wood or metal crossing one another, usually supporting climbing plants. Distinguished from an arbor, which is generally a more substantial yet compact three-dimensional structure, and from a pergola, which is a more extensive colonnaded structure.

triforium In a Gothic church, an arcade in the wall above the arches of the nave, choir, or transept and below the clerestory window.

triglyph One of the slightly raised blocks in a Doric frieze. It consists of three narrow vertical bands separated by two V-shaped grooves.

triumphal arch **1** A freestanding arch erected for a victory procession. It usually consists of a broad central arched opening, flanked by two smaller bays (usually with open or blind arches). The bays are usually articulated by classical columns supporting an entablature and a high attic. **2** A similar configuration applied to a facade to denote a monumental entryway.

truss A rigid triangular framework made up of beams, posts, braces, struts, and ties and used for the spanning of large spaces. The major horizontal or inclined members are called chords. The connecting vertical and diagonal elements are called the web members.

Tudor arch A low-profile arch characterized by two pairs of arcs, one pair of tight arcs at the springing, another pair of broad (nearly flat) arcs at the apex or crown.

Tudor period A term for a period in English history coinciding with the rule of monarchs of the house of Tudor (1485–1603). Tudor period architecture is Late Gothic, with only hints of the Renaissance. See also the more specific term ELIZABETHAN PERIOD for the end of this period, and the related term JACOBEAN PERIOD for the succeeding period.

Tudor Revival See NEO-TUDOR.

turret A small towerlike structure, often circular in plan, built against the side or at an exterior or interior corner of a building.

Tuscan order An ensemble of classical column and entablature elements, similar to the Roman Doric order, but without triglyphs in the frieze and without mutules (domino-like blocks) in the cornice of the entablature. See also the more general term ORDER.

tympanum (plural: tympana) **1** The triangular or segmental area enclosed by the cornice moldings of a pediment, frequently ornamented with sculpture. **2** Any space similarly delineated or bounded, as between the lintel of a door or window and the arch above.

umbrage A term used by Alexander Jackson Davis (1803–1892) as a synonym for veranda, the implication being a shadowed area.

vault An arched roof or ceiling, usually constructed in brick or stone, but also in tile, metal or concrete. A nonstructural plaster ceiling that simulates a masonry vault.

Venetian Gothic See HIGH VICTORIAN GOTHIC.

veranda A nineteenth-century term for porch. Sometimes spelled verandah.

vergeboard See BARGEBOARD.

verges The sloping edges of a gable, gambrel, or lean-to roof, usually projecting beyond the wall below. Distinguished from eaves, which are the horizontal lower edges of a roof plane.

vernacular Not a style in itself, but a descriptive term, applicable primarily to architecture, covering the vast range of ordinary buildings that are produced outside the high-style tradition of well-known architects. The vernacular tradition includes the folk tradition of regional and ethnic buildings whose forms (plan and massing) remain relatively constant through the years, in spite of stylistic embellishments. The term vernacular architecture is often used as if it meant only folk architecture. However, the vernacular tradition in architecture also includes the popular tradition of buildings whose design was influenced by such publications as books of the orders, builders' guides, style books, pattern books, mail-order catalogs, architectural periodicals, and household magazines. Usually contrasted with high-style. See also the more specific terms FOLK, POPULAR.

vertical plank construction A system of wood construction in which vertical planks are set or nailed into heavy timber horizontal sills and plates. A building so constructed has no corner posts and no studs. Two-story vertical plank buildings have planks extending the full height

of the building, with no girt between the two stories. Second-floor joists are merely mortised into the planks. Distinguished from the more specific term vertical plank frame construction, in which there are corner posts.

vertical plank frame construction A type of vertical plank construction, in which heavy timber corner posts are introduced to provide support for the plate, to which the tops of the planks are fastened. See also the related term HORIZONTAL PLANK FRAME CONSTRUCTION.

vestibule A small entry hall between the outer door and the main hallway of a building.

Victorian Gothic See HIGH VICTORIAN GOTHIC.

Victorian period A term for a period in British, British colonial, and Anglo-American history, and not, in architecture or the other visual arts, a sufficiently specific style term. The Victorian period extended across eight decades, from the coronation of Queen Victoria in 1837 to her death in 1901. See instead EASTLAKE, GOTHIC REVIVAL, GREEK REVIVAL, QUEEN ANNE, SHINGLE STYLE, STICK STYLE and other specific style terms.

Victorian Romanesque Ambiguous term. See instead RICHARDSONIAN ROMANESQUE, ROMANESQUE REVIVAL, ROUND ARCH MODE.

viga Spanish for a log or beam supporting the roof and projecting beyond the wall surface.

villa 1 In the Roman and Renaissance periods, a suburban or rural residential complex, often quite elaborate, consisting of a house, dependencies, and gardens. **2** Since the eighteenth century, any detached suburban or rural house of picturesque character and some pretension. Distinguished from the more modest house form known as a cottage.

volute 1 A spiral scroll, especially the one that is a distinctive feature of the Ionic capital. **2** A large scroll-shaped buttress on a facade or dome.

voussoir A wedge-shaped stone or brick used in the construction of an arch. Its tapering sides coincide with radii of the arch.

wainscot A decorative or protective facing, usually of wood paneling, applied to the lower portion of an interior partition or wall. Distinguished from a dado, which is the zone at the base of a wall, regardless of the material used to cover it. Wainscot properly connotes woodwork. Sometimes called wainscoting.

water table 1 In masonry, a course of molded bricks or stones set forward several inches near the base of a wall and serving as the cap of the basement courses. **2** In frame construction, a ledge or projecting molding just above the foundation to protect it from rainwater. **3** In masonry or frame construction, any horizontal exterior ledge on a wall, pier, or buttress. Often sloped and provided with a drip molding to prevent water from running down the face of the wall below.

weatherboard See CLAPBOARD.

weathering The inclination given to the upper surface of any element so that it will shed water.

web 1 The relatively thin shell of masonry between the ribs of a ribbed vault. **2** The portion of a truss between the chords, or the portion of a girder or I-beam between the flanges.

western frame, western framing See PLATFORM FRAME CONSTRUCTION.

wickiup A circular or oval structure of slender, arched poles covered with brush or mats of reeds. The term is usually applied to traditional Apache dwellings but is also used for shelters of this type constructed by other Native American peoples.

winder A step, more or less wedge-shaped, with its tread wider at one end than the other.

window bar See MUNTIN.

window cap See CAP.

window head A head molding or pedimented feature over a window.

Wrightian Term applied to work showing the influence of the American architect Frank Lloyd Wright (1867–1959). See also the related term PRAIRIE SCHOOL.

wrought iron Iron shaped by a hammering process to improve the tensile properties of the metal. Distinguished from cast iron, a brittle material, which is formed in molds.

Zigzag Moderne, Zigzag Modernistic See ART DECO.

Illustration Credits

All photos not otherwise credited are © Bret Morgan.

Introduction

Pages 9, 14, 15, 17 (top), Special Collections Department, University of Nevada, Reno, Library; **p. 17 (bottom),** Central Nevada Historical Society Collection, University of Nevada, Las Vegas, Library; **p. 18,** Nevada Historical Society, Reno; **p. 19,** Nevada State Highway Department Photograph, Special Collections Department, University of Nevada, Reno, Library; **p. 20,** Special Collections Department, University of Nevada, Reno, Library; **p. 21,** Nevada Historical Society, Reno; **p. 23,** Special Collections Department, University of Nevada, Reno, Library; **pp. 25, 26, 30, 31,** Nevada Historical Society, Reno; **p. 33,** Las Vegas News Bureau; **p. 36 (top),** Special Collections Department, University of Nevada, Reno, Library; **p. 36 (bottom),** Nevada Historical Society, Reno; **p. 39,** Las Vegas News Bureau Collection, University of Nevada, Las Vegas, Library; **p. 40,** Las Vegas News Bureau; **p. 47,** Nevada State Museum, Carson City; **p. 50,** Las Vegas News Bureau; **p. 51,** Las Vegas News Bureau Collection, University of Nevada, Las Vegas, Library

Northwestern Region

NW003.1, NW003.4 Julie Nicoletta; **NW055** Library of Congress; **NW068.1** Carleton Watkins photo, 1876 (Nevada State Library and Archives); **NW068.3** Nevada State Library and Archives; **NW080.3** Nevada State Historic Preservation Office

Northern Region

NO71 Julie Nicoletta

South-Central Region

SC22 (left) Nevada Historical Society

Index